S0-BQW-296

PSYCHOLINGUISTIC MODELS OF PRODUCTION

PSYCHOLINGUISTIC MODELS OF PRODUCTION

Edited by
Hans W. Dechert
and
Manfred Raupach

Gesamthochschule Kassel
Kassel, West Germany

Ablex Publishing Corporation
Norwood, N.J. 07648

Copyright © 1987 by Ablex Publishing Corporation.

All rights reserved. No part of this publication may be reproduced, stored in a retrieval system, or transmitted, in any form or by any means, electronic, mechanical, photocopying, microfilming, recording, or other wise, without permission of the publisher.

Printed in the United States of America.

Library of Congress Cataloging-in-Publication Data

Psycholinguistic models of production.

Papers presented at an international Workshop on ''Psycholinguistic Models on Production'', held in Kassel, Federal Republic of Germany, from July 13–17, 1980.
Bibliography: p.
Includes indexes.
1. Psycholinguistics—Congresses.   I. Dechert, Hans W. (Hans-Wilhelm)   II. Raupach, Manfred.   III. Workshop on Psycholinguistic Models of Production (1980 : Kassel, Germany)
P37.P7546 1987   401'.9   87-17575
ISBN 0-89391-211-5

Ablex Publishing Corporation
355 Chestnut Street
Norwood, New Jersey 07648

Contents

v

Preface

Twenty-four researchers from various academic disciplines dealing with the production of language, such as theoretical and applied linguistics, sociolinguistics, social psychology, psycholinguistics, and psychology of language met for an international Workshop on ''Psycholinguistic Models of Production'' in Kassel, Federal Republic of Germany, from July 13 to 17, 1980. Scholars from other German universities as well as guests from abroad participated in the Workshop.

A first call for papers and thematic suggestions about a year in advance of the Workshop was followed by correspondence with those who accepted the invitation. Only the topics which aroused the greatest interest among the majority of the future participants were chosen. Some topics we suggested as being closely related to the psycholinguistics of production, such as speech pathology, were dropped. Other topics, originally not included in our proposals, such as written production or understanding and producing were added. All participants thus took active part in the thematic organization of the Workshop, a procedure which may have added to the homogeneity of the program in spite of its interdisciplinary make up. It is only natural that many other important areas, such as psychology of memory, artificial intelligence, neurolinguistics, and speech production in the narrower, physiological, sense of the term were neglected.

The Workshop ultimately consisted of five Sessions:

- Psycholinguistic Models of Production
- Second Language Speech Production
- Cognition and Production
- Narrative Understanding and Production
- Verbal Interaction

Each Session was presided over by a chairperson who was to lead the discussion following the presentations and to summarize the main points of argument and disagreement at the beginning of the Final Discussion at the end of the Workshop. Each Session was opened by one or two main addresses from scholars who are experts in the field. They were followed by the presentation of discussion papers which sought to raise questions and offer additional comments or criticism. The main addresses and discussion papers had been distributed among the participants of each Session in advance. After the reading of papers, discussions among the participants of the Session as well as the audience followed. We would very much have liked to publish at least the highlights of these discussions; because of obvious restrictions of space, only the Final Discussion at the closing of the Workshop has been included in this volume. After the

Workshop all contributors were given the opportunity to revise the original drafts of their papers. Many of them did. The articles in this volume are presented in the order they were read.

The Workshop's main topic ''Psycholinguistic Models of Production'' was intended to initiate a theoretical and metatheoretical discussion of the processes preceding and accompanying the mental planning and execution of language. This discussion, it was felt, has long been avoided, and hardly begun. Several reasons have been claimed for this neglect: historical, methodological, theoretical, organisational; above all it is the enormous complexity and hence difficulty that seem to be responsible for the fact that we know so little about production, in contrast to perception and comprehension. To avoid any misunderstanding: it is self-evident that, in the face of this state of the art, none of us would have expected ''models of production'' to be presented during the Workshop. It was, rather, our intention to come to a general picture of the range of questions and methods of investigation dealing with language production, not to answer any of them. The label ''psycholinguistic'' in our topic was meant to imply that discussion should not be restricted to one linguistic theory only or one academic discipline such as linguistics or psychology. Corresponding to our intention to have the participants of the Workshop take active part in its conceptual and thematic planning and framing, the central term ''production'' was purposely left somewhat vague. Was comprehension to be totally excluded from the Workshop? Was oral or written production aimed at? Was it production of speech, of language, or of discourse? Was production of words, of utterances, of sentences, of texts to be discussed? Now, after the Workshop, one can easily answer these questions. Independently, the participants came to the almost unanimous conclusion that the oral and written production of texts in a communicative setting was the most challenging issue to be talked about! While preparing their papers they must have already had a rather multidimensional notion of production.

There seems to be little doubt, especially in connection with the long and lively discussion in the Fourth Session, that the ''information processing revolution'' (Herbert Simon) has had and in the near future will continue to have a deep influence on the modeling and assessment of language production. Future models to be developed, however, will have to include more variables than the computation model at present suggests in order to be ecologically valid; they surely will have to be preoccupied with system architecture, but at the same time they will have to take into account human interaction with reality, from which world knowledge is continuously derived. Models of production will have to be approximate and opportunistic in accord with the particular level of processing and area of production under treatment in order to include the necessary degrees of freedom.

If Charles Osgood's remarks on the future of psycholinguistics approaching the year 2000, in his 1975 New York Academy of Sciences lecture, do in fact anticipate the true development of the art away from the fate of the start, the Kassel Workshop may reflect one or two steps in this direction:

- In spite of the rather controversial discussions on generative grammar there has been a strong emphasis on performance.
- In almost all presentations, striking examples of the contextual embedding of language production have been given.
- Very little, indeed, has been said about syntax; meaning has been the focus of attention.
- There have been a number of indications of a new type of process-oriented dynamic *psycho*linguistics.
- Throughout the Workshop there was a cross-linguistic frame of reference, not only because native and non-native speakers of English conversed with each other in a non-English environment, but also because a number of papers and data presented, especially in the Second Session, were evidence of "Contrastive Psycholinguistics."

The 1980 Kassel Workshop certainly cannot claim to stand for a re-marriage of the various disciplines represented; but perhaps it does announce an engagement!

Our very special thanks go to Dan O'Connell, S.J., now at Loyola University in Chicago, who at the time of the Workshop was spending a year with us as a Fulbright-Hayes scholar, and to Richard Wiese, now at the Technische Universität Berlin, who used to work with us in the Kassel Psycho- and Pragmalinguistic Research Group (KAPPA). In the conceptual planning and practical organization of the Workshop we benefited considerably from their support and friendly cooperation.

We are also indebted to Gabriela Appel, now at the University of Delaware, Manfred Goldberg, and our graduate students Dietmar Fütterer, Christa Meuser, Ursula Sandrock, and Rolf Schreiner, who have done invaluable jobs assisting us in organizing the Workshop and this volume.

The Workshop was financially supported by the Volkswagen Foundation and by the Gesamthochschule Kassel, Universität des Landes Hessen. The City of Kassel also contributed to its organization. In line with the policy of the Volkswagen Foundation a high percentage of young scholars were invited to the Workshop. We feel that all of us have profited from this arrangement.

We are grateful to our sponsors and to all of our colleagues who have contributed to the Workshop and to this volume.

Kassel, Federal Republic of Germany
January 1981
HWD and MR

First Session: Psycholinguistic Models of Production

Chair: W. Kintsch

CHAPTER 1

The State of the Art: The Fate of the Start

DANIEL C. O'CONNELL
RICHARD WIESE
Gesamthochschule Kassel

We begin with something of an overview of the state of the art. But two arts are intended in our title. Primarily intended is the scientific discipline which has as its object a better understanding of speech production, where by speech production we mean the production of spoken language in the broadest sense, from the earliest phase of its initiation to the final phase of production. The second art is the art of speaking itself; call it an overlearned habit if you will. We hope that the sense of awe and wonder at what Osgood (1963) has referred to as humanity's highest achievement will not be diminished by any technical sophistication we might attain.

The play on words goes still further. We have taken the liberty of assigning a subtitle to our paper: The fate of the start. It is not entirely facetious in intent. Our first question is, how are we to present an overview? In this year of the Leipzig International Congress, one could well be tempted to go back all the way to Wilhelm Wundt, or to present a complete review of the literature. Our purpose, however, is to establish a conceptual framework, to spark lively discussion, and to catalyze creative and integrative thought among conference participants. We intend, therefore, to consider the middle of the present century as our starting point and trace its fate, not in detail, nor in every respect, but rather in a few broadly conceptualized paradigms.

PSYCHOLOGY AND LINGUISTICS

One more preliminary to this paper is necessary. We are, respectively, a psychologist and a linguist. As such, we symbolize and embody many of the problems of identity, role, and cooperation which have characterized psycholinguistics in general, and more specifically, approaches to speech production. It has never been clear what the relationship of psychology and linguistics should properly be in this venture. At one extreme we have the now famous position of Chomsky (1968) that linguistics should be considered a branch of cognitive psychology.

On the other hand, as Pawley and Syder (1976) put it:

> With a few exceptions linguists have been content to leave the systematic study of questions about speech formulation to other disciplines—experimental psychology, experimental phonetics, neurology, speech pathology, clinical psychology, and psychiatry. (p. 11)

Paul Ricoeur (1971) puts the same division of labor in more systematic terms:

> The language-speech distinction is the basic distinction which furnishes linguistics with a homogeneous object; whereas speech belongs to physiology, psychology, sociology, language, as the system of rules of which speech is the exception, belongs only to linguistics. . . . linguistics considers only systems of entities which possess no absolute meaning and which are defined only by their difference from all the other unities. (p. 140)

Nonetheless, it would surely be a vast oversimplification on our part were we to content ourselves with saying that the linguist must be concerned with the system of language, and the psychologist with the user of language. The linguistic categories and units of research tend to become more and more those of the linguist; the observational and experimental methodologies those of the psychologist; the inferential and theoretical domains a no man's land battled over by both. We do not see these altercations as necessarily detrimental to scientific progress. Indeed, the situation in which the formalities of discourse remain peacefully unacknowledged on either side is far worse; unaligned psycholinguistics is usually a synonym for chaos.

Since both the de facto and de jure relationships between psychology and linguistics are of such fundamental importance, we think it worthwhile to dwell on the matter somewhat further. It is quite evident from the archival literature that psychological studies of speech production depend to a considerable degree on linguistic concepts and insights. In addition, a large number of the units and measures used in such research are taken over from linguistics. Concrete evidence for our assertions is to be found in constructs like surface and deep structure, units of varying length from phoneme to discourse, and classifications such as content and function words. It is important to note, however, that none of these can be adequately understood, much less properly applied in research, without recourse to the linguistic theories that have evoked them and in which they are conceptually imbedded.

On the other hand, there are approaches to research on speech production in which the very opposite is true, namely the use of units of production that are themselves either very much de-emphasized in linguistic theory or poorly integrated with it. A number of the theories of speech production have relied, for example, on the syllable, the phonemic clause, or the tone group as basic linguistic units of production, although all of these have failed, at least until quite recently, to find a proper place in general linguistic theory. Correspondingly, the units important in linguistic theory—the phoneme, the morpheme, the word, and the clause at a deep or surface structure level—have played only a minor role in consideration of speech production. As Whitaker (1970) put it a decade ago, "syllables have remarkably little usefulness in linguistic models but apparently a great deal of usefulness in speech production models."

In view of the preceding discussion, we feel it is fair to characterize the study of speech production from a linguistic point of view as a concentration on the organization of various levels of linguistic structure. There has been minimal concern for the actual psychological procedures involved. Such psychological concepts as have been made use of have played a minor role, typically a role not well-integrated with the origin of a given concept in psychological theory. An excellent example of such inadequate integration is to be found in Lounsbury (1954):

> Encoding and decoding processes being as complex as they are, it is always difficult to discover easy checks on the type of model described above. The fact that *habit strength is inversely correlated with the latency between S and R* seems to offer one avenue of approach, however. At any level of the model just described, the stronger the transitional habits, and hence the lower the transitional entropy or uncertainty, the shorter should be the pausal durations separating sequential events. (p. 98)

Since the occurrence of pauses cannot be traced back to a unitary psychological process, the logical connection between S-R theory on the one hand, and measurable behavioral phenomena such as pauses on the other hand, is not as straightforward as Lounsbury claims. His strong hypotheses about speech processing were inevitably wrong, given the state of the art at that time. Nonetheless, Lounsbury's effort to combine psychological, structural, and statistical aspects of language into a theory of speech production is historically important.

TRADITIONAL PSYCHOLINGUISTICS

Let us return now to our theme: the fate of the start. What has transpired since the modern beginnings of psycholinguistics at the middle of this century? What can we say by way of diagnosis and prognosis?

One of the most influential researchers during these past thirty years has been George Miller. He expressed an interpretation of the history of psycholinguistics during this period in a chapter called "Toward a Third Metaphor for Psycholinguistics" (1974). There are really only two metaphors, since the first of the three characterizes only the time before 1950. Up until then, however, the "association" metaphor made the psychology of language a section within the psychology of learning. Analogously, then, speech production should have been considered a learned skill. Miller feels that during this period linguists pursued the psychological implications of their work quite minimally. But in the end, it was the weakness in the "association" metaphor itself which brought about a change; it could not provide the needed combinatorial theory—a grammar to account for sentences.

The Chomskyan revolution is for Miller a shift to the second, so-called "communication" metaphor. What Miller intends in this metaphor is both an emphasis on information theory and a characterization of all possible signals in a communication system; for natural language it was hoped that generative grammar would provide this characterization. From the beginning this shift proved quite inadequate to cope with semantics. He therefore calls for "a third metaphor which should characterize what a person *is doing* when he produces or understands linguistic signals."

This new emphasis on performance leads Miller to his third, or "computation" metaphor, from which he hopes to obtain "a coherent, explicit, formal statement" of psycholinguistic theory: "If such a theory were achieved in full generality, it might give cognitive psychologists a formal language in which to describe the procedures that a language user must be able to carry out." It should be noted that the procedures Miller has in mind include both linguistic and nonlinguistic components. In spite of his enthusiasm for the computational metaphor, Miller himself suggests the likelihood "that how people understand sentences has nothing to do with how computers compile programs." Further, Miller acknowledges that the computation metaphor "has little place for the affective components of language" and "is obviously weakest in its characterization of a speaker." In spite of its attractiveness for some cognitive and artificial intelligence theorists, we find this third metaphor largely unpalatable precisely in view of our preoccupation with speech production.

One further notion of Miller's is rather dramatically diagnostic of a very limited view of psycholinguistics. He insists that the use of nonlinguistic information, the organization of lexical concepts into semantic domains, the setting of goals and the construction of plans, and the use of imagery and metaphor are all "matters that outrun even a broad definition of the scope of psycholinguistics." But in fact, precisely these aspects of language use are being emphasized in recent research in psycholinguistics (Marková, 1978; Rommetveit, 1974).

We feel no particular inclination to accept without considerable reservations either Miller's interpretation of history or his prognostications for the future of psycholinguistics. An alternative view of the situation is provided by Charles Osgood, himself a veteran of the same Thirty Years' War. He, too, traces the history of the period of growth in modern psycholinguistics, under the title "*A Dinosaur Caper: Psycholinguistics Past, Present and Future*" (1975). His metaphor does not lay claim to being at the same time a paradigm. It is instead an extended chronology of the on-again off-again love affair between psychology and linguistics. As early as 1963 Osgood had rejected the computer paradigm later endorsed by Miller:

For sentence *encoding* we would need SELECTORS, DICTIONARIES, SYN-TACTIC GENERATORS, COMPARATORS, UNITIZERS, and EXPRESSORS. Computer models of this kind are exercises in problem setting rather than problem solving. Terms like DICTIONARY, UNITIZER, COMPARATOR, and SYN-

TACTIC GENERATOR merely point to processes that must be accounted for in any psychological theory, rather than providing explanations in and of themselves . . . (Osgood, quoted in Jakobovits & Miron, 1967, p. 110)

Osgood's predictions for psycholinguistics "as we approach the year 2000" could, in reality, have been observations on what was already going on in 1974:

> There will be a complete shift from emphasis upon Competence to emphasis upon Performance. . . . there will be an increasing avoidance of dealing with sentences-in-isolation. . . . Semantics will be moving into the foreground as syntax moves, reciprocally, into the background. . . . logical, rationalist models of language will be shown to be inappropriate for ordinary speakers and will be superceded by more gutsy, dynamic psycho-logical models. . . . There will be a shift from ethno-lingo-centrism toward what might appropriately be called anthropo-linguo-centrism. (1975, pp. 23–24)

For the rest, Osgood's own theorizing has not shifted extensively over the years.

Both Osgood and Miller reflect mainstream psycholinguistic research over the past thirty years fairly well, though of course from different points of view. Osgood & Bock's (1977) statement describes quite accurately the neglect of speech production in that research tradition:

> apart from studies of language acquisition, there seems to have been little concern with "where do sentences *come from?*", as one of the authors put it (Osgood, 1971)—the production problem. Rather, the focus of research interest has been on "where do sentences *go to?*"—the comprehension problem. (p. 89)

In a similar vein, Danks (1977) suggests the reasons for the neglect of research on sentence production:

> Why has the study of production processes in adult speakers lagged? The problems of experimental control in production are the reverse of those in comprehension. If the experimenter attempts to control the input to the speaker, any stimulus— picture, word, sentence, or symbol—presented to the subject for him to respond to verbally must first be comprehended by the subject before responding. Since the investigator is interested in production and not comprehension, this comprehension phase represents contamination, just as response production is contamination in comprehension studies. (p. 234)

Note the emphasis on sentence production, that is so characteristic of previous mainstream research. Emphasis on message structure, discourse, or communicative finality is almost entirely missing.

Valian (1977) faults Lounsbury, Osgood, McNeill, and Schlesinger all alike "for a similar underlying reason: an unwillingness to accord sufficient importance to a specifically linguistic component in the speech production process." She also suggests what the aims of a speech production theory ought to be:

> To trace the course of production from the initiating idea to the speech expressing the idea. . . . To isolate the determinants of production. . . . To relate production to perception. . . . To explain child acquisition of language. (pp. 107–109)

In addition, she makes it quite clear that for purposes of speech production theory the speaker can be characterized as a language machine. Cognition (as well as perception, personality, etc.) is external to this machine and therefore not an intrinsic component of a theory of speech production. Accordingly, she considers the concepts of actor, action, and object to be linguistic concepts rather than primarily perceptuo-cognitive concepts.

Valian's theme of emphasis of linguistic or nonlinguistic aspects of speech production is engaged quite differently by Schlesinger (1967) and Ingram (1971), respectively, in "A Note on the Relationship between Psychological and Linguistic Theories" and "A Further Note on the Relationship between Psychological and Linguistic Theories." They both make the point that linguistic descriptions in the form of abstract, atemporal algorithms must be fundamentally disparate from the real-time, strategic processes speakers utilize. The corollary is that an adequate model of speech production cannot be sought in a linguistic theory alone, particularly a linguistic theory of the kind proposed in a generative grammar. Ingram herself particularly emphasizes the matter of available processing time:

> The stubborn problems which face any attempt to account for language acquisition and language behavior are: (a) the vast number of choices that have to be made; and (b) the short time that is available for them to be made in. (p. 345)

For the moment we will only comment in passing that the major problems of theory formation are not in the domain of the nanosecond; the nature, rather than the duration, of the psychological processes required for speech production is the critical problem.

What lies behind all purely linguistic models of speaking, however, is the linguist's claim that the language we use is an extraordinarily complex structure and that psychological principles could hardly account for the fact that every human speaker is quite able to use these complex, multilevel linguistic structures. Even if we do not assume that people go through one of the derivational chains proposed by generative grammarians, a theory of speech production would have to explain how people are able to produce utterances which, among other things, show a remarkable degree of linguistic structure, partly universal and partly language specific.

In any event, reviews of the literature on speech production are in general agreement that the available evidence is still too limited to support a particular model (Fodor, Bever, & Garrett, 1974; Rosenberg, 1977). A quite general problem in the study of speech production, which has been noted many times before now, is how one develops a theory for a process of which only the output can be observed. Both input and process have to be inferred with the help of theoretical considerations and empirical data. Given the insufficiency of evidence, some, like Fodor, Bever, and Garrett, would like to use the subsystems of the linguistic rule apparatus as theoretical components, whereas others, like

Kintsch and van Dijk (1978), would prefer cognitive schemata as theoretical components. What components are eventually going to be crucial for an adequate model of speech production remains a matter of serious disagreement. It does seem clear, however, that for the sake of simplicity current theoreticians are neglecting some components in order to concentrate on others.

SOME PHILOSOPHERS

We would like to turn our attention now to some of the philosophers of language, and in particular some of the speech act philosophers. These would appear to be leading us in a non-traditional direction, particularly with regard to the sentence as an isolated unit and with regard to the separation of linguistic from cognitive and other components of the speech act.

Already in 1955, Austin (1975) had emphasized in his William James Lectures, "the more we consider a statement not as a sentence (or proposition) but as an act of speech . . . the more we are studying the whole thing as an act" (p. 20). But what does he mean by "the whole thing"? He makes that clear when he adds, further on in his lectures: "We must consider the total situation in which the utterance is issued." And again he adds: "There is no shortcut to expounding simply the full complexity of the situation." Uhlenbeck (1963) echoes the same conviction:

> Every sentence needs to be interpreted in the light of various extra-linguistic data. These data are (1) the situation in which the sentence is spoken, (2) the preceding sentences, if any, (3) the hearer's knowledge of the speaker and the topics which might be discussed with him. (p. 11)

Apel (1966) also expresses a convergent view:

> A sentence is initially endowed with meaning because it is placed in the context of a wider meaning which is composed of language and the practice of living. (p. 72)

It should not be forgotten that the philosopher of language is free to engage the comprehensive speech act only as long as he remains in the philosophical domain. The empirical study of speech acts always necessitates concrete constraints upon the scope of investigation.

BACK TO PSYCHOLOGY

Rommetveit (1974), after a long critique of what he prefers to call "the perspective of the expanded Harvard-M.I.T. approach" and of the Platonic heritage of spatializing and detemporalizing, insists that "the fallacy of assigning propositional content to semantic potentialities can only be avoided by a radical change of approach."

What he means by "radical change of approach" is specified further as follows:

> What is needed at the present stage is thus neither additional formal devices nor more subdisciplines, but a more comprehensive and thorough analysis of basic premises for intersubjectivity and contractual aspects of verbal communication. (p. 125)

Rommetveit is in essential agreement with Birdwhistell (1971), whose argument, he quotes to the effect that:

> what is preserved in typed transcripts of face-to-face dialogues is in fact only "the cadaver of speech." And an essential part of what is lost in the transcription has to do with what Roman Jakobson refers to as meta-linguistic operations, i.e., with shifting premises of communication conveyed by, for example, body movement, gesture, facial expression and tone of voice. What is made known by speech when it is "alive" can hence, according to Birdwhistell, only be assessed by a joint exploration of the "integrational" and the "new information" aspects of the entire, multifaceted process of interaction. (pp. 62–63)

If it is the case, as Uhlenbeck (1963) says, that "every single sentence, also a seemingly trivial sentence, has to be interpreted by the hearer with the help of extralinguistic data," then it is hard for us to understand how a theory of speech production that takes into account only linguistic components can be anything but wide of the mark. Perhaps the very opposite to Valian's argument could be defended, namely that the social-behavioral components of speech production have been neglected in theorizing about it. Bransford, Barclay, and Franks (1972), too, argue

> against the tacit assumption that sentences "carry meaning." People carry meanings, and linguistic inputs merely act as cues which people can use to recreate and modify their previous knowledge of the world. (p. 207)

Hörmann (1981) voices pretty much the same sentiment:

> Thus the utterance in itself does not convey any information to the hearer; it only guides the hearer in creating the information for himself. That the hearer knows how to do this, and that he is able to follow the instructions built into the utterance, is the outcome of his incessant striving to *make* the world and all events around him fully intelligible. (p. 308)

A more recent statement in the same vein is from Lachman, Lachman, and Butterfield (1979). Not only does it provide a succinct formulation, it also exemplifies in printed format the eternal tension between competence and performance: "The effects of linguistic variables on performance depends [sic] largely on extralinguistic factors." Hörmann's view is also quite contrary to the position of Norman & Rumelhart (1975) that "people use language to convey information about their ideas or feelings." Speaking is more for Hörmann than simply information transfer.

We can be grateful to the cognitive theorists for drawing linguists' attention to the importance of cognitive content and processes which are antecedent to and concomitant with speech production. However, cognitive models such as those of Kintsch and van Dijk (1978) or Norman and Rumelhart (1975) tend to stop at exactly the point where conceptual components are "translated" into language. Their models are, almost by definition, meant to account for the general processes of human cognition, and hence have more to say about the cognitive processes entailed in perception and thinking than about language–specific processes themselves.

To recapitulate somewhat, we have noted that serious deficiencies arise in psycholinguistic theory and research when either behavioral or linguistic considerations are neglected. There are, to be sure, areas of research in which such a balance may, indeed, be less crucial. Neurophysiological and phonetic research on speech production seem, by and large, to deal successfully with their own concerns without the discipline–related tensions so generally characteristic of psycholinguistics. The same may be said of the largely applied research on speech production in the domain of pathologies such as asphasia, stuttering, delayed speech onset, etc.

For a general psycholinguistic approach to speech production, however, most particularly at the level of theories or models, we find it difficult to imagine that linguists would feel free to disregard important behavioral or psychological factors, or that psychologists would feel free, correspondingly, to disregard important linguistic factors. Undoubtedly, the lack of such balance accounts for much of the confusion and dissension of the past and will continue to be the occasion of confusion and dissension in the future. But perhaps we can still learn some things from the past: All theories are reformable or discardable; yet we cannot but operate within some theoretical framework. We would all be well advised to consider even our most cherished theorizings to be, by their very nature as scientific formulations, thoroughly tentative. Whether they originate from linguistic or behavioral considerations is then of minor import. Both are to be accepted formally as calculated risks.

But some of us claim to be in direct contact with pure, unadulterated empirical reality, unbesmirched by the follies of theory. In some respects this is the most dangerous stance of all, for the epistemology, empirical assumptions, and methodological limitations of such research are completely latent and unacknowledged. Here, let it suffice to say that modern science cannot proceed with such underpinnings.

ORPHANED ASPECTS OF SPEAKING

We have called for a balance of psychological and linguistic considerations in theorizing about speech production. Let us now discuss some psychological aspects of speech production which we feel have been neglected or distorted up until now.

In beginning our discourse about orphaned considerations from the point of view of psychology, we must acknowledge our debt to two European psychologists who have themselves dared to step back from the mainstream of psycholinguistics—and have even distanced themselves from the term psycholinguistics—in order to analyze the epistemological and theoretical underpinnings of a psychology of language use. They are Hans Hörmann (1981) and Ragnar Rommetveit (1974).

In a striking reversal of orthodox thinking about speech production, Rommetveit makes ellipsis the prototype of verbal communication:

> In accordance with Wittgenstein's suggestive metaphors about utterances as moves within different language games, embedded in streams of social life (Wittgenstein 1968)—and with some confidence in Tolstoy's intuitive insight into conditions of human communication—we may thus reverse the traditional linguistic approach to ellipsis: *ellipsis, we may claim, appears to be the prototype of verbal communication under ideal conditions of complete complementarity in an intersubjectively established, temporarily shared social world.* Full sentences—and even sequences of sentences—may be required in order to make something known, however, under conditions of deficient complementarity and less than perfect synchronization of intentions and thoughts. (p. 29)

It was Henry Miller (not George Miller; the latter [1974, p. 404] as a matter of fact, suggests that Wittgenstein's "language game" may be proper to economics rather than linguistics or psychology) who suggested that "speaking begins only at the point where communication is endangered" (1965).

Rommetveit is preoccupied with what he calls *message structure;* with a speaker's reasons for speaking and what he wants to communicate. It is in the sense of message structure that Hörmann characterized language as "a means of directing the consciousness of the hearer" (1981). And it is within such a conceptual framework that we would like to call attention to a number of specific characteristics of speech production which we feel have been neglected.

The central concept among these is *intentionality*. Speaking is intentional insofar as it involves two or more conscious participants, speaker(s) and hearer(s). It is precisely here that the "computation" metaphor breaks down. Speaking simply cannot be adequately described as information exchange between two or more central nervous systems. It entails a finality which completely transcends information transfer in its intended effectiveness in changing consciousness. Speaking is purposefully conscious, not at every moment and in every respect, but in its essence.

Speaking is communicative. Not only does it transcend information exchange; it transcends cognitive exchange. Affective, attitudinal, emotional, volitional communication cannot be reduced to strictly cognitive components. As Neisser (1967) commented somewhat ironically about his own *Cognitive Psychology*, cognition cannot be adequately treated without incorporating the affective. Since speaking does convey affective nuances, the neglect of affective variables has been one of the factors responsible for the sterility of speech production theorizing to date. Zajonc (1980), in his thorough analysis of the importance of affect, asserts quite bluntly that "contemporary cognitive psychology simply ignores affect." In acknowledging a few notable exceptions he includes Miller and Johnson-Laird (1976), but goes on to regard with dismay their decision to "have little to say about *Feel*" since they admit that "*Feel* is an indispensable predicate for any complete psychology and that it probably lies much closer than *Perceive, Remember,* and *Intend* to the basic sources of energy that keep the whole system running." (p. 112)

Speaking is contractual. It is simpleminded to think that speech is something that just happens when sounds come out of a mouth directed at an ear. People *agree* upon the terms—momentarily, habitually, conventionally, exceptionally, explicitly, or implicitly. There is always a structure of mutual purposes and understandings and strivings, even if they are often comprised of cross-purposes, misunderstandings, and conflictual strivings. All of these agreements constitute part of the subjective context of speaking. They are codeterminants of meaning and of message structure.

Speaking is cultural. Indeed, language is itself a cultural phenomenon. But the arbitrary conventions surrounding and involving speaking are by no means limited to language. Many of them are extra- or non-linguistic. Many of them are paralinguistic—which means, of course, that they are linguistic phenomena which linguists have not yet learned to cope with.

Speaking is social. It is always intended to be heard by an other, even if only at some remove in distance or time. And it would be unheard of for the speaker not to monitor what he or she says for its effect on the hearer—not without error, but consistently. Speakers who do not commune with themselves through their speaking are probably communing with nobody.

Speaking is creative in the sense that what the spaker wants to talk about does not completely determine how the speaker talks about it (see Chafe, 1977). The options open to a speaker are content- and context-relative, but all production experiments show variation between and within speakers in expressing the "same" thing. Such creativity clearly adds to the methodological difficulties already mentioned with regard to studies of speech production. But do we want to exclude, either from our theory or from subjects' responses, this fundamental aspect of speaking?

All these characteristics are compatible with the Hörmann and Rommetveit discussions. By its very communicative force speaking transcends the intersubjectivity established here and now of time and place. But all these characteristics could be disregarded with impunity, were it not for one further characteristic of speaking. Speaking is also a behavior; not a loosely knit or chaotic behavior, but a closely organized, complex, subjective Gestalt. Multitudinous components of the ambient, nonlinguistic world determine this behavior as much as any or all linguistic variables; message structure can be thereby altered, canceled, reversed, nuanced. This throws additional light on Rommetveit's refusal to speak of meaning as inherent in propositions and his insistence on assessing "the entire range of semantic potentialities inherent in some segment of speech." "Indeed to examine what is conveyed by that segment under conditions of different reciprocally endorsed meta–contracts," we must invoke the characteristics of speaking described above.

A psycholinguistic theory of speech production that significantly incorporated these characteristics would not be traditional, mainstream psycholinguistics. Rommetveit is not exaggerating at all when he speaks of "a radical change of approach." His "architecture of intersubjectivity" is a salient social and psychological conceptualization of message structure.

In light of the preceding discussion, the comments of Leontjev (1972) are meaningful:

> It is quite indicative that the Soviet Union was almost the only country in which psycholinguistics though quite developed did not succumb to the Generative Grammar epidemic. . . . The explanation is to be found in the specific scientific tradition which Soviet Psycholinguistics from its very origination has been based on. . . . Unlike American Psycholinguistics which is consistently antipsychological, theories prevalent in Soviet Psycholinguistics in the 20–50ies were not in the least alien to the analysis of a man's speech activity, on the contrary, they were aimed at closing with psychology. (p. 2)

In placing such a strong emphasis on a number of neglected psychological variables, however, we must not lose sight of other aspects of performance such as the unconscious, automatic, neurophysiological, informational, and temporal. These too must enter into any genuinely empirical conceptualization of speech production, and without them the pursuit of a comprehensive model of speech production is in principle impossible. Recent investigations into a variety of spontaneous and more formalized speaking situations (Dechert & Raupach, 1980; Goldman-Eisler, 1968; Siegman & Feldstein, 1979) give promise of precisely such a balance in psycholinguistic research on speaking.

In our considerations we must never lose sight of the central role played by the speaker. All speakers seek to optimize communication of their subjective message structure; no one in their right mind seeks to be the ideal speaker according to the prescriptions of Clark and Clark (1977). In particular, speakers do not stop only to select words. In fact, there is no such thing as "the ideal delivery," but rather an appropriately different, unique delivery each time the semantic potentialities of an utterance are actualized in a discourse context. Ideal speaking— indeed the very concept of fluency—can no longer be conceptualized simply in terms of sequential and temporal integrity.

CONCLUSION

Whatever model or models emerge from the present ferment of enthusiasm about speech production, it is our hope that they be fully adequate. But to be fully adequate a model dare not disregard any determinative component of speaking. Mainstream psychology has traditionally done so, as have mainstream linguistics and even psycholinguistics. It is clearly time for a change of stream.

REFERENCES

Apel, K.O. (1966). Wittgenstein und das Problem des hermeneutischen Verstehens. *Zeitschrift für Theologie und Kirche, 63,* 49–87.

Austin, J.L. (1962). *How to do things with words.* Oxford: Oxford University Press.

Birdwhistell, R.L. (1971). *Kinesics and Context.* London: Allan Lane.

Bransford, J.D., Barclay, J.R., & Franks, J.J. (1972). Sentence memory: A constructive versus interpretive approach. *Cognitive Psychology, 3,* 193–209.

Chafe, W.L. (1977). Creativity in verbalization and its implications for the nature of stored knowledge. In R.O. Freedle (Ed.), *Discourse production and comprehension* (pp. 41–55). Norwood, N.J.: Ablex.

Chomsky, N. (1968). *Language and mind.* New York: Harcourt, Brace & World.

Clark, H.H., & Clark, E.V. (1977). *Psychology and language: An introduction to psycholinguistics.* New York: Harcourt Brace Jovanovich.

Danks, J.H. (1977). Producing ideas and sentences. In S. Rosenberg (Ed.), *Sentence production: Developments in research and theory* (pp. 229–258). Hillsdale, N.J.: Lawrence Erlbaum.

Dechert, H.W., & Raupach, M. (Eds.). (1980). *Temporal variables of speech: Studies in honour of Frieda Goldman-Eisler.* The Hague: Mouton.

Fodor, J.A., Bever, T.G., & Garrett, M.F. (1974). *The psychology of language: An introduction to psycholinguistics and generative grammar.* New York: McGraw-Hill.

Goldman-Eisler, F. (1968). *Psycholinguistics: Experiments in spontaneous speech.* London, New York: Academic Press.

Hörmann, H. (1981). *To mean—to understand.* Berlin: Springer.

Ingram, E. (1971). A further note on the relationship between psychological and linguistic theories. *International Review of Applied Linguistics, 9,* 335–346.

Jakobovits, L.A., & Miron, M.S. (Eds.). (1967). *Readings in the psychology of language.* Englewood Cliffs, N.J.: Prentice–Hall.

Kintsch, W., & van Dijk, T. (1978). Toward a model of text comprehension and production. *Psychological Review, 85,* 363–394.

Lachman, R., Lachman, J.L., & Butterfield, E.L. (1979). *Cognitive psychology and information processing.* Hillsdale, N.J.: Lawrence Erlbaum.

Leontjev, A. A. (1972). *Soviet psycholinguistics—new trends.* Paper presented at the 10th International Congress of Psychology, Tokyo.

Lounsbury, F.G. (1954). Transitional probability, linguistic structure, and systems of habit-family hierarchies. In C.E. Osgood & T.A. Sebeok (Eds.), *Psycholinguistics: A survey of theory and research problems* (pp. 93–101). Baltimore, Md.: Waverley Press.

Marková, I. (Ed.). (1978). *The social context of language.* Chichester: Wiley.

Miller, G.A. (1974). Toward a third metaphor for psycholinguistics. In W. Weimer & D. Palermo (Eds.), *Cognition and the symbolic processes* (pp. 397–413). Hillsdale, N.J.: Lawrence Erlbaum.

Miller, G.A., & Johnson-Laird, P.N. (1976). *Language and perception.* Cambridge, Mass.: The Belknap Press of Harvard University Press.

Miller, H. (1965). *Sexus.* New York: Grove Press.

Neisser, U. (1967). *Cognitive psychology.* New York: Appleton-Century-Crofts.

Norman, D.A., & Rumelhart, D.E. (1975). *Explorations in cognition.* San Francisco: Freeman.

Osgood, C.E. (1963). On understanding and creating sentences. *American Psychologist, 18,* 735–

751. (Reprinted in L.A. Jakobovits & M.S. Miron (Eds.), *Readings in the psychology of language* (pp. 104–127). Englewood Cliffs, N.J.: Prentice-Hall, 1967.)

Osgood, C.E. (1971). Where do sentences come from? In D.D. Steinberg & L.A. Jakobovits (Eds.), *Semantics: An interdisciplinary reader in philosophy* (pp. 497–529). London: Cambridge University Press.

Osgood, C.E. (1975). A dinosaur caper: Psycholinguistics past, present, and future. In D. Aaronson & R.W. Rieber (Eds.), *Developmental psycholinguistics and communication disorders* (pp. 16–26). (Annals of the New York Academy of Sciences, *263*.) New York: New York Academy of Sciences.

Osgood, C.E., & Bock, J.K. (1977). Salience and sentencing: Some production principles. In S. Rosenberg (Ed.), *Sentence production: Developments in research and theory* (pp. 89–140). Hillsdale, N.J.: Lawrence Erlbaum.

Pawley, A., & Syder, F. (1976, August). *Sentence formulation in spontaneous speech: The one-clause-at-a-time hypothesis.* Paper presented at the New Zealand Linguistic Society Congress.

Ricoeur, P. (1971). What is a text? Explanation and interpretation. In D. Rasmussen (Ed.), *Mythic-symbolic language and philosophical anthropology: A constructive interpretation of the thought of Paul Ricoeur* (Appendix, pp. 135–150). The Hague: Nijhoff.

Rommetveit, R. (1974). *On message structure.* London, New York: Wiley.

Rosenberg, S. (Ed.). (1977). *Sentence production: Developments in research and theory.* Hillsdale, N.J.: Lawrence Erlbaum.

Schlesinger, I.M. (1967). A note on the relationship between psychological and linguistic theories. *Foundations of Language, 3,* 397–402.

Siegman, A.W., & Feldstein, S. (Eds.). (1979). *Of speech and time.* Hillsdale, N.J.: Lawrence Erlbaum.

Uhlenbeck, E.M. (1963). An appraisal of transformational theory. *Lingua, 12,* 1–18.

Valian, V. (1977). Talk, talk, talk: A selective critical review of theories of speech production. In R.O. Freedle (Ed.), *Discourse production and comprehension* (pp. 107–139). Norwood, N.J.: Ablex.

Whitaker, H.A. (1970). Some constraints on speech production models. (Language Centre Occasional Paper No. 9, pp. 1–13). Essex: University of Essex.

Wittgenstein, L. (1968). *Philosophische Untersuchungen—Philosophical investigations.* Oxford: Blackwell.

Zajonc, R.B. (1980). Feeling and thinking: Preferences need no inferences. *American Psychologist, 35,* 151–175.

CHAPTER 2

A Psycholinguistic Model of Speech Emission[1] in Concrete Communication Situations (The "Dynamic-Contextual Model")

TATIANA SLAMA-CAZACU

University of Bucarest

Many years ago, I elaborated (both theoretically and by way of experiments) the model of communication on which the present paper is based.[2] In this model, one cannot isolate the production of speech from the act of reception. The validity of this claim becomes obvious if one considers emission part of an act of communication, rather than simply the verbal production of an isolated speaker, or of a speaker who speaks somehow for himself. In this model, therefore, emission and reception are complementary parts of a whole which is *communication.*

From one point of view, the act of speech production becomes a thing of the *past* at the precise moment expression is achieved. The *present,* for a message, on the other hand, is always to be found in its reception, which constitutes the very reason that messages exist. Even in face-to-face dialogue,[3] emission precedes and is, therefore, past tense with respect to reception. This is even more clearly the case with a written text (e.g., a literary one). I will not discuss here the act of reception itself, but we must always keep it in mind when referring to

[1]In this paper, quite consistently with my previous work, I prefer to use what I feel to be the more comprehensive term "emission" instead of the more restricted term "speech production"; speech production hardly ever occurs without additional extralinguistic and even nonverbal components.

[2]This model, which was based on earlier research and a study carried out in 1949, was first presented in Slama-Cazacu 1956, 1961; (from previous research and a study elaborated in 1949); theory and model were modified in some details and completed in subsequent publications (see 1963, 1964, 1973a, 1973b, etc.). I present it in the form it has here not only to make a point about historical scientific reality, but also—and primarily—because many aspects dealt with here are representative of modern trends. More precisely: what today appears to some scientists and authors of surveys to be a "radical change" is, in fact, fully continuous with my own previous approach.

[3]Though this is the expression now in fashion, I prefer the Latin notion of communication "partibus praesentibus," because such a dialogue can also occur between partners who are present in the same situation (a room for instance), though sitting back to back.

the act of production or emission. We must also keep in mind the fact that emission always occurs in a context (the context of communication itself, in which the emitter encounters the receiver, as well as the situational context, the historical context, etc. [see Figure 3]).

COMMUNICATIVE INTENTION

An act of communication entails entering into mutual contact through *emission* and *reception* (see Figure 1).[4] The emitter expresses some psychological content with the *intention* of communicating it, sharing it, or giving information about it, while the other, to whom the interlocutor is speaking, adopts the requisite receptive attitude. (Without such an intention, there can only be some sort of involuntary expression—of emotion, for example.)

Thus, both emission and reception are intentional. In the actual communicative act these two attitudes, as represented by different individuals, are almost simultaneous. But they also alternate in a single individual, who can be an emitter as well as a receiver (see Figure 2). (At times, the same individual can play both roles at almost the same time, as in simultaneous translation.)

The two acts influence one another reciprocally in the same individual as well as from one individual to another: an individual presents himself or herself in a particular way in order to communicate a specific content, and thereby influence the other. Consequently, the emitter has a precise intention in mind: to achieve a specific goal with respect to a receiver. But because this purpose presupposes understanding, the initiator has to make use of semiotic means that have meaning for the receiver. Communicative intention is therefore correlated to the intention to signify, that is, to endow communicative acts with meaning by employing a system of signs familiar to a partner, thus enabling the partner to decode the message. In most cases the system is one of verbal or linguistic signs, and it is this system with which we will be concerned here. At the same time, it is important not to disregard the fact that the emitter also makes frequent use of nonverbal signs associated with the sender's "language repertoire." Gestures, facial expressions, and so on, are directly related to the verbal signs in a message, and may replace verbal signs in a sequence of discourse (which I have investigated, and call "mixed syntax"—see Slama-Cazacu 1970, 1976, 1977).

The intention to signify operates by means of specific strategies (which I have

---

[4]This model of communication appears, at first, to follow the well-known model proposed by Shannon (1948), and, indeed, it had that as its starting point. It is however, completely different, by virtue, on the one hand, of the semantic implications of the terms used—Shannon's model represents mechanical communication; mine refers to human communication—and, on the other, of the difference in the terms used: "source/transmitter" (Shannon) becomes "emitter," "receiver/destination" becomes "receiver"; "context" is added, and is a basic component. A further difference is that in my model the reversibility of the relationship between sender and receiver is stressed. These differences are underlined in Slama-Cazacu, 1961.

Figure 1.   The act of communication (Slama-Cazacu, 1973a, p. 52)

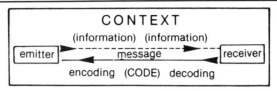

referred to as "techniques of *langage*"[5]—see Slama-Cazacu, 1961). These strategies rely on the *repertoires* of signs which have already been acquired by the speaker (constantly modified, however, and supplemented). In the case of verbal signs, the repertoires form a system and various subsystems, registers, etc., which I refer to as the "individual linguistic system" (ILS), that is realized in the specific context (see Figure 3) and in the messages or "individual linguistic events" (ILE) of every communicative act (Slama-Cazacu, 1973a). The same strategies mediate selection of words and grammatical forms from the repertoire, and provide meanings and semantic nuances that are suited to each new situation, thus allowing an appropriate alternation of signs, while consistency is also preserved (the "basic signifying nuclei," see Slama-Cazacu, 1961).[6] This constitutes a Strategy of *message organization*.

In a model of speech production that at the same time takes into account the receiver, every strategy of the emitter is reasonable precisely insofar as it is related to its target: the receiver.

The emitter keeps the addressee in mind, and adapts to both addressee and common setting, including those elements of the situation presumed to be mutual (one of the determinants of "presupposition," of the "implicit" in a message). Thus, Dante presumed a familiar setting shared by his readers. His contemporaries could interpret all that was implicit in the *Divina Commedia*—nuance, irony, names of characters, plots—whereas we must have recourse to textual commentaries. What is implicit becomes operational in the communicative act precisely because the strategy of presupposition and implicitness is accepted by the receiver. Hence, though not taking on a concrete form of expression, the implicit becomes a part of message production.

In the following, I will analyze the internal planning of strategies for message production, which is initiated in the intention to communicate and signify, and which in turn transforms global psychological content into concrete spatiotemporal sequences by very rapid inner activity or even "internal acts"; and the strategies of organizing the message itself, governed by the same intentions, namely a correct and complete decoding by the receiver.

[5]Because there is no term in English exactly corresponding to French *langage* (the set of psychological processes making it possible to create and use a system of signs, i.e., *language,* French *langue*), I use the French term *langage* in order to avoid ambiguity.

[6]See also the experimental evidence on this matter in Slama-Cazacu 1961.

Figure 2.   Reversibility of the relation E-R (Slama-Cazacu, 1961, p. 195)

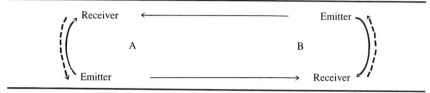

THE INTERNAL PLANNING OF STRATEGY

Even if we limit our considerations to the emitter, we find that *langage* transcends the moment of emissions, and emission in turn transcends the locution itself. Emission is not only the external component—the articulation that produces the message as it reaches the receiver—but includes in addition an array of internal activities that precede articulation. During the period preceding externalization, the material to be expressed is organized internally; this pre-locutionary activity remains by and large imperceptible to the receiver.

I will say very little about emission as articulation or externalization. Nonetheless, it is important to mention one point: With the exception of involuntary paralinguistic features and emotional expressions, which may simply co-occur with a communication, every articulatory motion in the act of communication represents a specific intention to signify on the part of the emitter and is encoded by means of a definite system of signs.

Figure 3.   Contextual levels of communication (Slama-Cazacu, 1973a, p. 82)

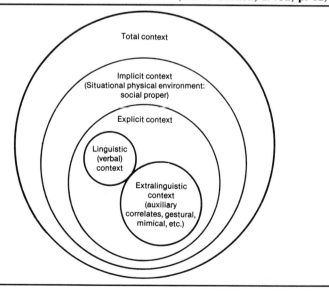

The message does not consist solely of physical forms (e.g., sounds) directly perceivable by the receiver, nor merely of articulatory motions that the emitter might seem to produce automatically and without any intermediate level. A succession of sounds is not *eo ipso* a message, but rather becomes a vehicle of information for a receiver only insofar as it involves a meaning accessible to the receiver, and hence only if the receiver can decode it. Moreover, I am convinced that an appropriate concept of message and of message transmission must view meaning not as something added by the receiver, but at most as something completed by the interpreter. The message is so constituted physically as to bear meaning, and the receiver is in turn the recipient of this meaning engendering seed. Herein lies the reason that the process of emission is far more complex than simple articulation, and that reception goes beyond the simple perception of different stimuli.

The intention to signify, with all of its implications, is included in the process of articulation. The emitter's problem is not just to articulate, no matter how or what, but to select from an interiorized array of phonematic habits the components needed to build a specific meaningful sequence. To accomplish this, not only continuous perceptual feedback (i.e., self-regulatory systems operating by means of perception of one's own articulatory movements and acoustic production) is needed, but also far more complex processes of selection and control operating at a higher level. On the one hand, the oppositional distribution of phonemes and of corresponding sounds, or even of certain sequences, belongs, due to frequent repetition, to the individual's repertoire of automatic habits; but on the other hand, there are many components of articulation which cannot become completely automatic since they necessitate flexible adaptation from moment to moment. Thus, the construction of a chain of discourse with an appropriate intonational contour and the correct distribution of accents—beginning with the articulation of the first elements of any segment—implies the involvement, even in the articulation of each sound or sound sequence, of a higher level of organization. The involvement of higher integrative processes becomes even clearer if one adverts to the organization of sounds as such, to the production of sequences of meaningful segments, to their arrangements according to definite rules, and so on.

Using language contributes to the organization of thought; nonetheless, without thought *langage* could not exist. *Langage* puts order into thought, and thought in turn makes the requisite organization of *langage* possible. This reciprocity is also evident in the preparation of expression, at the point where one must choose lexical and grammatical forms most suitable for expression.

In fact, preparatory operations take place throughout the process of expression and are often manifested overtly by pauses and hesitations (see, for example, Goldman-Eisler, 1968). These are nothing but concrete markers of intersections of alternatives which require particular deliberation in order to discriminate or select the more appropriate elements. These processes directly influence discourse, not only through the introduction of pauses corresponding to moments of deliberation, but also through the anticipatory nature of preparatory operations. The operations just mentioned make possible continuous control over expression so that it unfolds not as a purely mechanical or random improvization, but represents the implementation of a plan, of an internal program.

At the moment of emission speech is the result of three phases, during which "internal materials" (psychological content) are prepared, elaborated, and adapted so as to make possible a spatiotemporal result.

Let us take as a starting point the perception, by an individual who will become an emitter, of a mountain with a snow-covered peak below which it is covered with green trees. In the first phase the mountain elicits within the speaker some psychological experience—objective realizations, scientific interest, or perhaps aesthetic appreciation—and inspires the intention to communicate this experience, to transform it into information for an interlocutor. The individual then endeavors to express the experience by recourse to some "technique" or strategy. In the second phase the material to be expressed (the psychological state or experience) is processed, elaborated, and adapted in keeping with the intention to communicate. In this way message content is worked out according to a general plan guided by communicative intent. In the third phase the emitter systematically sets out to construct the expression by means of special "tools." He or she selects appropriate signs and arranges them in a definite order to give the message a codified form. At this point, in order for the *langage* event to be complete, production of the expression itself is required. But before accomplishing this goal the intent to communicate and the selection of a form of expression appropriate to the psychological content have been absolutely essential.

Let us examine the phases more closely, especially the third preliminary internal phase. First of all, in the preliminary, internal phase of organization, expression presupposes analysis of some ensemble—the psychological content. This continuum, or better this "global syncretic datum"—the components of which are simultaneous, often inextricably intertwined each other and intermingled with affective drives—must somehow be dissected, analyzed, and finally recomposed. It is then organized and arranged in a definite order, so as to form an expression characterized by discontinuity insofar as it is composed of distinct elements: a sequential expression.

Analysis of the internal material is accomplished by making use of language components which provide socially understandable, more or less uniform parsings; then a synthesis must be made by choosing all the requisite components and grouping them in an organized whole to form the message (see below "The Organization of Messages").

Thought, caught in inner speech proceeds rapidly and elliptically, is discontinuous and does not use words at every stop. Expression (the external, sequential utterance) requires the choice of suitable signs to translate into intelligible forms the same inner content in its entirety.

The phenomenon of word choice is far from simple and elementary; it is in reality a most complex process. The process of relating a word to the object it is to represent in a given situation is not just mechanical and direct, not simply the association of word and object or concept (as in the behaviorist model). Rather, it is above all the revealing of the relationship between an object and the entire context in which it appears. Hence, even the basis of word selection is far more than a simple act of memory, as is assumed in S-R models in which the elicitation of words is due to previously established, mechanical connections. Word selection is preeminently a high level, intellectual, mental activity, even if intermingled with affective components, some of which escape conscious control.

This process is also a selection among different alternatives, and therefore a process of detailed differentiation. Words are chosen not only because of their relationships to one another within the language, but also in view of their own nuances of meaning. This is obvious in the stylistic variants of literary production, but ordinary communication of any kind requires similarly discriminating word selection. Every choice is first and foremost the actualization of some core of meaning (what I have called a "semantic nucleus," Slama-Cazacu, 1961). The meaning of a sign in a specified context is creatively realized by the filling out of such cores by the emitter—and subsequently by the receiver (see below "The Organization of Messages").

Expressing oneself is, of course, not the ultimate goal of communication. Since we express ourselves with the intention of influencing (or, at least, of "reaching") our listener through what is communicated, expression has also to be intelligible. Therefore, expression must, first, be based on a consideration of the receiver's capacity to decode. Secondly, expression must be organized in such a way that the linking of individual words endows them with the ability to express reality in all its richness from moment to moment, without sacrificing what is general in them as valid points of universal reference within the same language. (The principle of the relationship between constant and variable explains the possibility of conveying novel information without the use of new tools.)

The process of choosing linguistic tools is certainly not limited to memorizing requisite signs and selecting them as such from stored repertoires. It can be characterized as a structural operation, a systematic differentiation among signs. Their potential roles and the actual functions they have to play dictate the specific forms and locations they will take in the sequence to be produced. In other words, form and place ("contextual position") are determined not only by the role each sign has in the ILS, but also by the role it is given by the actual whole, by its function according to its importance in just that context.

An expression itself sequentially externalizes the components of the finished synthesis that immediately precedes it. However, the components of the internal synthesis can only appear, on the external level, in a sequential chain that is preprogrammed. An expression is organized on the internal level, that is, in the phase immediately preceding the actual expression, as a general plan, signs

Figure 4.   Reciprocal adaptation to communicative context (Slama-Cazacu, 1961, p. 193)

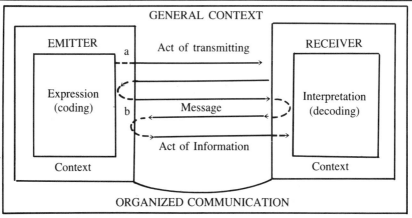

generally assuming the form and role they are to have externally. (Evidence to this effect is to be found in corpora of slips of the tongue, in which a word appearing early in a phrase is altered by another which is to occur later; see Slama-Cazacu, 1961.)

Our knowledge, primarily based on evidence from experimental psychology, of how internal materials are processed to become the spatiotemporal sequences that form an expression seems to be quite limited. Nonetheless, today I can assert with a great deal more assurance than when I first began to work out the present model of message production, that the preparatory (properly called "pre–locutionary") stage plays a very important role, and that there are indeed intermediate intellectual and logical processes.[7] These take place, for the most part, at a conscious level rather than being mechanical or purely affective, even though the subject may not experience them as conscious. Mental processes are extremely rapid: what is to be expressed (and therefore to be externalized as spatiotemporal forms) is worked out as an entire program, though quite compressed and codified in abbreviations. These processes are for investigation by the experimental psychology of the future, when more accurate and more sensitive technologies will make available, for instance, devices with low inertia which are capable of recording psychological measurements of very short durations, and hence of adequately decoding, or interpreting, them.

THE ORGANIZATION OF MESSAGES

A communicative act, and particularly emission, can hardly be understood if we do not adopt, at least in this matter, a pragmatic approach. Both emitters and

---

[7]Production itself and not only comprehension, include such intellectual, and logical, processes.

receivers are motivated to achieve mutual understanding (see Figure 4). The emitter deals with the intention of being understood by implementing a variety of strategies. The emitter adapts to the receiver's level of knowledge, both linguistic and contextually implicit (see Figure 3), to the receiver's temperament, mood, and to the situation in which the two find themselves. This adaptation is also reflected by the basic strategy of the act of emission, that of organizing the message, in such a way as to afford the receiver optimal opportunity to decode the information, that is, to take it in with minimal loss. The receiver's part entails a strategy of interpretation of the same message organization by whatever explicit or implicit means are available.

I have already discussed the internal activity that precedes expression and is as important as its external product. The latter consists of signs which divide the emission into segments, in keeping with the requirements of the spatiotemporal sequencing of the components of the communicative act.

The emitter provides an expression with an organization quite different in nature from that of the general language system: first of all because it belongs to the emitter's ILS, secondly because it appears at a completely different level— that of the concrete moment of communication (see the ILE). This organization endows signs with valences appropriate to the situation and representative of the intentions of the emitter. These valences are momentary relationships: oppositions (rhythmic, phonological, semantic, etc.); signs of hierarchization (stress and accentuation, deletion and ellipses of what is considered superfluous); and different contextual positions according to the role of each component in the whole. They contribute to the construction of a coherent or organized expression with segments of varying import. Thus, meanings are specified and sometimes even created by the overall sense of an entire whole discourse.

As has been mentioned already, signs are chosen on the basis of a specific invariant or constant core (the conventional, semantic, meaningful nucleus), which must be maintained in order to provide a base of reference for the interlocutor. But this basic semantic nucleus is enriched by the context in which each word is included. At the same time, the emitter has recourse (simultaneously, or successively; see "mixed syntax," Slama-Cazacu, 1970, 1976, 1977) to nonverbal supplements in order to optimally clarify the communicative intention, as well as to deliver the message as rapidly and economically as possible. (Some examples of nonverbal supplements are gestures, facial expressions, nonlinguistic vocalizations, and signs created with external materials or props.) Also available are deliberate and quite meaningful paralinguistic devices such as meaningful coughing or vocally marked hesitation. The emitter can also take advantage of the particular situation, or what I have long referred to as "the (situational) correlates" (Slama-Cazacu, 1961; see Figure 3). The emitter can say "here," for example, without further specification if the receiver already knows where the emitter is. This fact became abundantly clear as soon as I endeavoured to encompass the domain of *langage* events relevant for expression (Slama-Cazacu, 1961), and therefore included all the means intentionally used to promote communication and emphasized that their hierarchical importance is relative. Although in most cases in our complex modern society, verbal forms are predominant, both in importance and frequency, and other forms play the role of auxiliaries, however indispensable, there are times when one or another of these latter forms, such as gesture, can assume a dominant role; as became evident to me when doing research on the relations between communication and work (Slama-Cazacu, 1963, 1964, 1973a).

Every expression involves an abundance of signs. These include the internal connections by which words are related to one another; the oppositions between words; hierarchical values that give a word a particular intonation or accent within the rhythm of the sentence, or sometimes a special location in the text, which orients the receiver toward a desired meaning; and finally, gestures, facial expressions, situational correlates, and directly emotional reactions, all of which are, to a certain degree, voluntary. All these signs are part and parcel of the same intentional communicative design. Thus, many components work together within the same span of time to give an expression a characteristically multidimensional totality rather than just the simplicity of a temporal sequence.

Throughout the entire process of organizing expression, the emitter is guided by the intention of adapting to the receiver. Simultaneous with the act of expression, the emitter makes rapid "inquiries" concerning the state, the reactions, the decoding capacity of an interlocutor (see Figure 4.) The emitter chooses from among the signs in the linguistic system known by the receiver, selects meanings presumably known by the receiver, and makes use of situational correlates which they share. At every moment, the emitter makes use of the situation common to both—the fact that both are taking part in the same historical moment or perhaps have the same training, or are engaged in the same profession. On the other hand, the emitter may also take into account the fact that the two each participate in different collectivities.

In order to understand the emitter's expression, the receiver must in turn engage the specifics of the expression's organization (see Figure 4). Reception is a rapid act (based, inter alia, on short-term memory), by which signs, along with their semantic nuclei, are interlinked and related to systems of reference, to contexts, and to what is implicit, after which a new step in the process of reception occurs: apprehension of the total message. The trend toward full decoding, or "integral communication," is essential to the act of communication for both emitter and receiver, even if it is rarely achieved in its ideal form; loss of information often occurs because expression is not adequately organized and/or the receiver does not interpret the message with the use of all the organizational cues deliberately provided by the emitter. Whether the message is emitted in an ideal form or not, understanding it must be an interpretation of the organization of the expression.

In most cases reception entails a certain amplification of the data provided by the explicit expression and assumes reference first to an implicit context and then finally to a total context (see Scheme 3, and other schemes in Slama-Cazacu, 1973a, 1973b).[8]

ADAPTATION TO CONTEXT

Speech production is presented in the present model, as a highly complex act, occurring, both physiologically and psychologically, in an extraordinarily short period of time.

This act can never be properly understood as an act which takes place in a real communicative setting without referring it to reception, which is the intentional goal of the emitter in organizing his expression.

A fundamental role is played in this organization by what I have referred to for many years as the law or principle of adaptation to context (Slama-Cazacu, 1956, 1961). "Context" is to be taken here in both its most restricted acceptations and its broadest sense, which includes both emitter and receiver (see Figures 1 and 3).

Message cohesion, or coherence, (important analytic components of current "text linguistics" [*Textlinguistik*]) are, in fact, nothing other than the organization of expression, which I have spoken about for a long time (as the subtitle of my book *Langage et contexte*, 1961, indicates: "The problem of *langage* in theory of expression and interpretation by contextual organization").

It remains impossible for any linguistic theory, such as text linguistics, or for any model developed within the framework of current approaches, including "pragmalinguistics" and "discourse analysis," or for the theories inappropriately labelled "speech act theory" (Searle, 1969, and more recent works), to account for the organization of a text or of the message in communicative discourse, without keeping in mind *the prerequisites* we have been discussing here.

In brief, the above would have to include at least the following: (a) The receiver must be incorporated in a model of production or of emission. (b) The internal processes which precede the expression itself and are guided by the intention of adapting the expression to the addressee and the addressee's situation must be considered. (c) Nonverbal signs, which become a constitutive and integral part of speech production, must be included in the model of speech production. (d) Every phase, beginning with the internal act and ending with the expression itself, is to be integrated into more inclusive wholes, which I have long preferred to call "contexts." Because it is a vague concept when isolated from broader contextual levels, the term "text," taken in itself, is inadequate for solving the problems of linguistics and, of course, of psycholinguistics, in this

---

[8]This model of reception has also been applied to stylistic analysis in Slama-Cazacu, 1967, and 1973a. The "dynamic–contextual method" has been used in analyses of literary works.

respect.[9] (e) A dynamic view is necessary in order to study adequately the events occurring in the reality of communication (including production), which is a dynamic event itself. And, in fact, in Slama-Cazacu, 1973a, and other places, I call the present theory and methodology a "dynamic contextual theory."

REFERENCES

Goldman-Eisler, F. (1968). *Psycholinguistics: Experiments in spontaneous speech.* London, New York: Academic Press.

Searle, J. (1969). *Speech acts.* London, New York: Cambridge University Press.

Shannon, C.E. (1948). A mathematical theory of communication. *Bell System Technical Journal, 3,* 379–424.

Slama-Cazacu, T. (1956). Principe de l'adaptation au contexte. *Revue Roumaine de Linguistique, 1,* 79.-118.

Slama-Cazacu, T. (1961). *Langage et contexte: Le problème du langage dans la conception de l'expression et de l'interprétation par des organisations contextuelles.* The Hague: Mouton.

Slama-Cazacu, T. (1963). Remarques sur quelques particularités du message verbal déterminées par le travail. *Linguistics, 1,* 60–84.

Slama-Cazacu, T. (1964). *Communicarea în procesul muncii.* Bucureşti: Ed. Stiintifică.

Slama-Cazacu, T. (1967). Sur les rapports entre la stylistique et la psycholinguistique. *Revue Roumaine de Linguistique, 12,* 309–330.

Slama-Cazacu, T. (1970). L'étude du roumain parlé: Un aspect négligé—L'indicatio ad oculos. *Actele Congresului XII International de Lingvistică şi Filologie Romanică,* vol. 2, pp. 591–599. Bucureşti: Ed. Academiei.

Slama-Cazacu, T. (1972). Sur le concept "socio-psycholinguistique". *Bulletin de Psychologie, 26,* 246–251.

Slama-Cazacu, T. (1973a). *Introduction to psycholinguistics.* The Hague, Paris, and New York: Mouton.

Slama-Cazacu, T. (1973b). Is a socio-psycholinguistics necessary? *International Journal of Psycholinguistics, 1,* 93–104.

Slama-Cazacu, T. (1976). Nonverbal components in message sequence: "Mixed syntax". In W.C. McCormack & S.A. Wurm (Eds.), *Language and man: Anthropological issues* (pp. 217–227). (Proceedings of the IXth International Congress of Anthropological and Ethnological Sciences, Chicago, 1973). The Hague, Paris: Mouton.

Slama-Cazacu, T. (1977). Le concept de "syntaxe mixte": Recherches autour d'une hypothèse. *Etudes de Linguistique Appliquée, 27,* 114–123.

---

[9]Were adjustments to be made so that "text" were included in "context" in its fullest sense (an absolute prerequisite in this case) then the whole theory would become a "contextual theory". It could then cope with problems and considerations more precisely and systematically and take into account more recent developments, especially interdisciplinary developments, that have expanded our knowledge.

CHAPTER 3

Psycholinguistic Models of Production: Some Linguistic Remarks

PETER HARTMANN*

Universität Konstanz

The present paper is intended to serve as a basis for discussion. It presents a point of view which may be useful in evaluating the current state of linguistics, and suggests some conceivable perspectives and appropriate methodologies for the future.

The linguistic viewpoint represented here is that of general linguistics, or more specifically, that sector of linguistics which concentrates on an analysis of the foundations of linguistic endeavor. By "foundations" I mean: the level which has as its general goal the evaluation of scientific methods of procedure in order to judge their legitimacy, their aims, and their effectiveness. This approach is sometimes referred to—sometimes ironically—as metalinguistic.

THE CURRENT SITUATION

If we look at the entire spectrum of linguistic teaching and research, we find over the years an increasing involvement with disciplines and questions which, in any narrow understanding of linguistics, would have to be categorized as either extralinguistic or at least as belonging to so-called bordering areas. For linguistic research has increasingly come to include areas intuitively and obviously closely connected with language as it occurs in actual communication between individuals, and the factors that influence the realization of communication and are necessary conditions for much of what is linguistically observable. At the linguistic level these areas constitute a complex which, at the level of actual language use, can be characterized as follows:

- Human language always and only occurs embedded in human activities of some other kind, and can only thus be effective.

I am indebted to Mr. Peter R. Williams from the Sprachlehrinstitut of the University of Konstanz, who has translated this paper into English.

* Deceased.

- No matter what role one assigns to the organizing power of language, it is these qualitatively different "contexts" which determine success or failure, usefulness or uselessness, etc. and which determine, in fact, even the origin of language and even whether language and linguistic functions and effects arise at all.

It is perhaps surprising that it is precisely a linguistic approach to the overall picture that leads directly to an interpretation that could well be characterized as subversive of the autonomy of linguistics (or in Slama-Cazacu's terms, a "contextualization" of language).[1] However, the situation outlined above indicates a development toward a more realistic view of language problems. Linguistics should gradually reorient itself in the direction of a more realistic science of language. This does not imply a naive position of "pure contact" with reality, rightly rejected by O'Connell and Wiese (p. 11). Instead, the question is that of incorporating a number of areas which until now have often been quite consciously considered outside the domain of linguistic research.

SOME PERSPECTIVES

If we now consider what can be succinctly referred to as the border areas of linguistics, among which are the so-called hyphenated linguistic disciplines, an additional characteristic becomes clear: Occupants of the linguistic side of these areas are not always well-informed about the viewpoints, basic concepts, and achievements of occupants on the other side of the border. O'Conell and Wiese have pointed out that this situation is, in the case of linguistics and psychology, a mutual deficiency. The same deficiency is valid with respect to sociology, education, theology, and other related disciplines, whose practitioners often have inexact notions of linguistics. Two of these disciplines, in particular, should be taken more seriously by linguists than hitherto with respect to both their achievements and their prospective contributions. They are philosophy and sociology.

PHILOSOPHY

There can be no question of attempting to review the entire contribution of philosophy to the study of language. If one considers, however, the broad range of philosophical positions relevant to language, whatever their origins and aims, that has characterized the history of philosophy—quite often outside the philosophy of language itself—one might well expect that in the course of time some of these positions have been mutually negating. But one can also expect to find positions that still cannot be thought of as abandoned, it would be worthwhile for open–minded linguists to directly take into account—if for no other reason than

---

[1]All subsequent citations of O'Connell and Wiese, and Slama-Cazacu, will refer to their work in the current volume.

that it is quite unlikely that linguists will discover on their own, much less improve on, what these philosophers have already found.

One position deserving of mention, despite the orientation out of which it developed, is that of Hegel. For example, it is important to notice (and informative for the "non–autonomist" or "realistic" linguist) that in the Hegelian system multidimensional as it is, language, the principal and favorite concern of all linguists and philosophers, is not allocated a place among the philosophically central themes. In Hegel's system, only those themes appear in which "mind has found itself and become conscious." These themes have consequently been elevated or can in principle be elevated, via conceptualization, from so-called immediacy (naturalness) to the status of knowledge (science). Although language is granted an important constitutive function at the level of immediate mental expression, nonetheless language is not identical with mind having become conscious of itself, but is instead "only" the prerequisite for its existence.

These observations might seem trivial to someone sceptical about Hegel, since even a sceptic would not be likely to consider language synonymous with consciousness and knowledge. Nonetheless, even a sceptic should find Hegel's view of language to be of interest and pursue it further. This leads to questions such as the following: What is the nature of a philosophy of language which considers language an all–important philosophical theme rather than a background phenomenon to intellectual endeavor? What is to be made of advocates of analytic philosophy who so emphatically and directly concern themselves with language, whereas for Hegel language is to be considered a pre-historical topic?

But enough of these abstract basic questions, especially since more concrete issues confront us. Both the "orphaned aspects" mentioned by O'Connell and Wiese and the stages of interior ("preparatory operations") prerequisites for speech production ("emission") included in Slama-Cazacu's model have as their goal much broader and more comprehensive access to speech production behavior than do previous psycholinguistic approaches. It would be of some heuristic value to investigate how many and which of these "aspects" were, in fact, actually present in Hegel or other philosophers—and this without demanding of language more than it can deliver. Moreover, it might be worthwhile to investigate the exact extent to which the concept of "intellectual activity"— foreign to Hegel's view of language—opens up to us an understanding of the nature of intelligence, as mentioned at significant points by O'Connell and Wiese, and Slama–Cazacu. Both the "orphaned aspects" and the "internal premises" deal with the necessity of consciousness and/or control in respect to the operations required to produce utterances.

SOCIO-ECONOMIC CONDITIONS

There is a generally strong trend in linguistics toward questions that go beyond the purely linguistic. This trend is clearly recognizable in Slama-Cazacu and O'Connell and Wiese. In general, one can speak of an increasingly anthropological orientation. Further, and perhaps more interesting, there is also a clearly increasing acknowledgment and consideration of socio-economic approaches, the theoretical and research aspects of which extend far into social institutions and structures. Precursors and examples of these approaches are to be found particularly in the domain of scientific materialism.

The advantage of such approaches is that they neither begin nor end in the extreme of the ideally isolated individual or in the extreme of anthropologically general universals, both of which can be regarded as the result of a systematic tendency to think in terms of the particular or the general. There is nothing negative about including particulars regarding professional and class membership in the "broader contexts" of Slama-Cazacu or "orphaned aspects" such as the "cultural" and "social" from O'Connel and Wiese. Such inclusions, however, should include details of their origins and the forms of the respective bodies of views, or ideologies, adhered to by particular groups. The real question is the following: How concrete a concept of language or language use, or even "langage," do (linguistic) scientists want, or how concretely do they wish to view the world of language they seek to understand? Depending on the answers they give to this question, researchers can establish their epistemology or their brand of systematic truth at a greater or lesser distance from the concrete reality of language.

METHODOLOGY

If we now consider the current research situation in the various disciplines, such as linguistics and psychology, as discussed by O'Connell and Wiese, the following important tasks emerge:

- A conscious self-restraint in the presentation of results characteristic of current research must be exercised.
- We must first seek to make a modest determination of whatever might play a role in this multidimensional and complex domain, so that, should it prove necessary to isolate the "practicable," we remain aware of what cannot be tackled and why not, and what this might imply for the resultant scientific findings.
- An adequate heuristic method must be developed. This is the principal task to be faced, given a constellation of problems of both animate and material nature, in which a number of dimensions such as intellectuality, sociality, habituality, institutions, conventions, language, and language use functionally interact, and for which a comprehensive (differentiating/generalizing) scientific understanding is sought.

The term "heuristic" does not refer here to a stage which occurs before the actual research and then dissolves into a sort of self-evident background knowledge. Rather, it refers to developing a research orientation that is in keeping with its goals and dependent on context, and which results from adequate experience and a reflective attitude. Since we are dealing with a heuristic for scientific purposes, it is evident that existing methodologies will be applied, in partial analyses, for example, in order to advance a particular area of research. Nevertheless, it is important that unfamiliarity, and resistance to as yet thoroughly unexplored matters not be concealed by one's own statement of issues; this would be tantamount simply to seeking the confirmation of a hypothesis derived from one's own thoughts (cf. Bodammer, 1969).

In reality, an adequate heuristic requires consideration and evaluation not only of positions already mentioned here, but also of current developments related to aspects of the communicative reality, in which case one cannot arrive at plausible conclusions without taking production into account. Aspects of communication that require consideration include text production, translation, and spoken discourse; in short, all areas in which language use is the central factor and in which language occurs only as the realization of an attempt to produce effective utterances in the context of social or interindividual cooperation in the broadest sense.

During the initial consciously heuristic stage the primary goals must be the determination of the functions and roles mentioned previously. As O'Connell and Wiese and Slama-Cazacu have noted, adequate experimental strategies must be developed appropriate to specific hypotheses. Accordingly, it might prove advantageous, in place of the unitary concept of "process," as it is often used, to distinguish between "operations" and "processes" according to their role in language production. The term "operations" could then be used to refer to the decision and control functions involved in the preparatory formulation of utterances; the term "processes" could be restricted to the externalized utterance, which can be described in terms of causal sequences. This teminology would take into account the distinction to be expected between decision structures and sequential structures. O'Connell and Wiese have rightly noted that cognitively oriented production models have hitherto terminated exactly where the "translation of conceptual components" into language should follow. This means, then, that the most important methodological step to be taken is the clarification of the translation of operations into processes.

PROSPECTS

If we consider the interpersonal communicative event, it is both intuitively clear and in accord with experience that such communication functions to a large extent, although by no means uniquely, through meanings or sense constituents. Whenever a communicative event takes place it is triggered by some intentional component (see Slama-Cazacu) and therefore always entails, as a goal-directed act, an internal, and fundamental "politicality." Hence, its reality is not simply that of language, although it contains, among other things, a language component, which is used in an operative framework of what Slama-Cazacu calls *langage*.

Accordingly, we might ask whether the frequently investigated logic inherent in a communicative linguistic event might not be only one of many other means made use of. In keeping with the recommended heuristic, it is crucial to ascertain whether and to what extent the logical element in communicative and productive speech has to be "de-autonomized," as has already been suggested for language with respect to linguistics. Perhaps scientific experience in neighboring areas can contribute to a shift away from the questions of cognition so often (and for what reason?) emphasized, to those concerned with actual communicative behavior—particularly with regard to its function and role in real life. This could be accomplished by distinguishing and analyzing where, under what circumstances, for what reason and with what inducement, to what purpose, and for how long specific factors (cognitive, affective, etc.) are introduced and contribute to success in a given situation.

A further but far–reaching and difficult question concerns the type of theory construction that should be employed if we engage fields of communication in which the productive use of language in itself is both the reality and the goal; that is to say, in certain forms of artistic expression. Here we come up against clear and plausible counterpositions to familiar and commonly accepted, scientific contentions. This suggests that such positions might eventually make further dialectical development of (linguistic) science possible—given linguists sensitized to the issues involved. A similar effect could come about from positions which derive from the scientific sector, but which are consciously antisystematic and directly criticize important fundamental concepts such as intention and meaning. What makes adequate accounts of the two aspects previously mentioned difficult, is that the first step, mere understanding of the "products" or assertions, requires something more and other than simple rational reconstruction.

REFERENCES

Bodammer, T. (1969). *Hegels Deutung der Sprache.* Hamburg: Meiner.

CHAPTER 4

Communicative Approaches to Speech, Language, and the Study of Grammar

JAAKKO LEHTONEN

University of Jyväskylä

This paper comments on the preceding papers by Tatiana Slama-Cazacu ("A psycholinguistic model of speech emission in concrete communication situations") and Daniel O'Connell and Richard Wiese ("Psycholinguistic models of production"). In the standard commentary the arguments of the papers under discussion are refuted by counterarguments and alternative models and theories. If that is expected here, this commentary will be a disappointment. There are no theoretical or other substantial issues in either of the two papers which I could, or would like to, contradict. As a result, the following observations have only a loose connection with the papers under consideration.

To begin with, I wish to repeat with emphasis the first lines of Professor Slama-Cazacu's paper: "In a model of speech communication, one cannot isolate the production of speech from the act of reception." Indeed, language is used by individuals for communication, and the speaker creates his message to be understood. It is, therefore, not possible to construct a model for speech production without considering the process of speech perception. The interrelationship between production and perception is not only a philosophical theme; it is actually one of the fundamental problems in the models of language processing. The questions which are involved here include, for instance, the following: Are the processes of word-recall from the mental lexicon identical in speech production and speech perception? Are the basic units—if there are, in fact, any such "basic units"—for speech production and perception similar or different? Accordingly, it is not just unintentional confusion if concepts of production and reception are not systematically kept apart in a discussion of speech processing. My discussion may focus slightly more on perception than on production, a phenomenon which can also be seen in psycholinguistic literature and research activity in general. This is, in part, explained by the fact that the mental processes of perception are more easily made accessible through a variety of testing procedures. But the importance attached to processes taking place beyond production may also be motivated by the importance of receptive skills in the acquisition of foreign languages: just as with the native language, a foreign language (FL) is acquired via perception, and the reason for many errors and problems lies in the student's FL perception. From the point of view of contrastive psycholinguistics, which aims at explaining the FL student's learning difficulties, perception assumes priority to production because of the communicative situation in which FL students find themselves: a native listener can rely on an entire arsenal of L1 linguistic knowledge and has a good chance of understanding a learner's message, even if it is marked by a heavy foreign accent, but a student has to learn to understand the normal accent of an interlocutor. Without perception, there cannot be any further FL intake or acquisition.

My second point concerns the status of grammars in theories of message production and perception. In a recent discussion in Finland concerning interlanguage and language acquisition, the adequacy of existing grammars and linguistic theories (distributional grammar, generative transformational grammar, dependency grammar, etc.) was also taken up. The conclusion reached was that all existing grammars share one common feature: none of them is able to describe or explain how linguistic knowledge is represented in the brain, or how this knowledge interacts with the processes of understanding and producing speech or writing. This, even though grammar, which includes the dichotomy between distinctive and meaningful structures ("double articulation"), as well as the structures of syntax and the network of lexicon and semantics—that is, the entire "system of voluntarily produced symbols"—is the system of signification which is operative in every event of human speech communication. It is important to keep in mind here that the sentence "The study of grammar is useless for psycholinguistics" is *not* a paraphrase of "Grammar or a rule of a grammar does not describe the processes of production and perception of language." In the present state of the art, the latter statement is true, but the former is definitely false.

The goal of a grammar is to describe the regularities in the linguistic behavior of speakers of a given language. Accordingly, grammatical rules are formulations of the structural regularities, or of the speaker's knowledge of the regularities, of the sentences of the language. They are not theories about mental processes involved in speech processing. But an adequate descriptive grammar is important for psycholinguistics because in order to approach the mechanism of production, we must learn, first of all, about the structure of its products (cf. Clark & Clark, 1977, p. 191). In the terminology of general semiotics, the study of the "system of signification" equals the study of grammar, in contrast to the study of the "process of communication" (or "sign production"), which is, in the linguistic sciences, the goal of psycholinguistic studies. In semiotics the concept of "system" is a construct which has an abstract mode of existence independent of any potential communicative acts it makes possible. As with any semiotic system, including linguistic communication, "every act of communication . . . presupposes a signification system as its necessary condition" (Eco,

1976, p. 9). Analysis and description of sign systems are integral parts of the analysis of the entire structure of linguistic communication. But it is important to be aware that the hierarchies of levels of grammar, and the hierarchies in derivational rules that have been posited to describe variations in "surface structure," may have nothing to do with the actual processes that take place in the brain of the speaker or listener.

Unfortunately, with regard to the objectives of psycholinguistics, we are today in a situation in which the most prominent feature of a typical presentation in psycholinguistics is the lack of any discussion of grammar (especially of morphology). If grammar is discussed, the link between it and what we call psycholinguistics is loose. This gives the impression that for a psycholinguist grammar is a nasty word which must be avoided by using paraphrases such as "language," "linguistic system," "linguistic factors," etc. It may be only a matter of chance that the word "grammar" occurs in the paper by O'Connell and Wiese only in the context of "generative," and then, it seems, in a pejorative sense. The word "grammar" could, however, and should be used within the framework of psycholinguistics, too. But this requires a reorientation toward the notion of grammar. When reference is made to grammar in a communicative approach, it should imply no particular grammatical model, only such characteristics of the communicative mechanism as make it possible for a native speaker to produce a grammatically acceptable text or an utterance and make it possible for a native speaker to interpret the information embedded in a text in a reliable way.

The point about grammar and the choice of an appropriate theory of grammar for psycholinguistics can be summarized as follows: Structural grammar (including transformational grammar and other "generative" approaches) aims at a description of regularities in a text or linguistic product, or stated differently, at a description of the speaker's competence, or the speaker's intuitions about the speech delivery of an ideal speaker. The object of a dynamic, psycholinguistic, or communicative grammar, on the other hand, should be to describe how linguistic knowledge participates in the processes of message production and perception. Psycholinguistic and linguistic grammars are not alternative approaches; both are necessary. They both have their internal criteria for adequacy, and therefore it is not self-evident that a "good" linguistic grammar will be the best description of structural regularities for use in a psycholinguistic theory of linguistic processes (cf. Sajavaara & Lehtonen, 1980). Extrication from the chains of structural linguistics should not imply negligence of all grammar in psycholinguistic studies. After all, the ultimate goal of psycholinguistic studies should be a better understanding of human speech and language. Crucial steps toward that goal will be taken through information about the way grammar interacts with the processes of speech production and perception.

A good example of a recent theory in which the magic surrounding the notion of grammatical hierarchy has been broken is the on-line interactive language processing theory developed by Marslen–Wilson and his colleagues (e.g., Marslen-Wilson & Tyler, 1980). According to this theory, lexical, syntactic, and interpretative knowledge sources interact during the process of language understanding. There does not seem to be any reason why a similar interaction of grammar and other kinds of ''knowledge'' would not be possible in the process of speech production, within, for example, the tentative model of the sequence of communicative events outlined by the Jyväskylä research group illustrated in Figure 1. In this model, the speaker's communicative goal, which is influenced by affective and emotional factors, and which also determines the speakers' interpretation of events in the external world, assigns to the ''message parlor'' the task of planning the optimal communicative act for achieving the goal. An activated motive for communication starts the process of message planning, which includes, among other things, the recall and evaluation of relevant knowledge, the review of available vocabulary and idioms (especially important in the case of a foreign language), and the planning of a skeletal message. The latter may include preselection of the syntactic structures to be actualized, but it is possible that for the most part the planning and execution of the linguistic product resembles the operation of a finite state automaton. The selection of the actual linguistic elements can be described as a Markov process in which the choice of each subsequent element is made among alternatives that have been activated in memory as having the highest transitional probabilities at a given moment. The resulting message consists of both verbal and nonverbal components, or of nonverbal behavior only, which merge with nonintentional features of the speaker's behavior. It is worth noting that the model in Figure 1 is hierarchical, but not in the way a generative or structural grammar is, since it does not specify the order in which the rules or constraints operate in message processing (cf. Sajavaara, this volume, Figure 2, p. 51).

The final goal of a dynamic, or communicative model is not a comprehensive description of language as a system of rules for structures in which actual messages only have the value of raw material. The objective is to describe the entire realm of human communication, both from the perspective of the speaker and the listener and from that of society. The fact that the description does not focus on language alone, but also on messages, affects the meaning of several basic concepts. One such concept is the *''proposition.''* When speaking of propositions, the linguist has an autonomous sentence in mind. In actual communication, however, the proper meaning, or the intended, logical, basic content of a message, may be conveyed through other channels, such as gesture, body movement, and paralanguage (cf. Knapp, 1978, pp. 20–26; Lehtonen & Hurme, 1980). There may or may not be a concomitant linguistic utterance, either in accord with or in contradiction to the meaning of the nonverbal message. As is well known, the listener normally resorts, in the latter case, to the nonverbal information for the intended meaning of the message.

I would like to mention one more noticeable difference between the linguistic and communicative approaches in this connection: the attitude adopted toward

Figure 1. A Model of the Sequence of Communicative Events

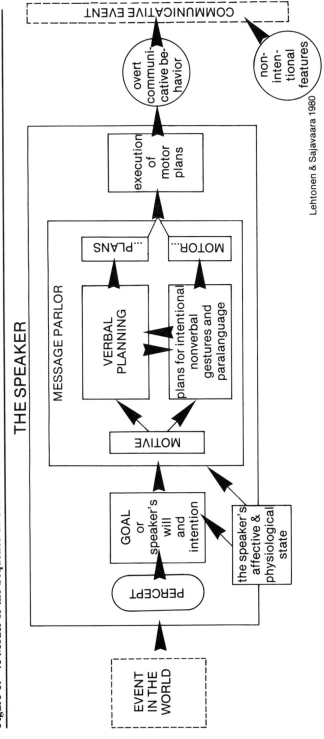

THE SPEAKER

MESSAGE PARLOR

VERBAL PLANNING

...PLANS

plans for intentional nonverbal gestures and paralanguage

MOTOR...

MOTIVE

execution of motor plans

GOAL or speaker's will and intention

PERCEPT

the speaker's affective & physiological state

EVENT IN THE WORLD

overt communi-cative be-havior

non-inten-tional features

COMMUNICATIVE EVENT

Lehtonen & Sajavaara 1980

the individual speaker/listener. While linguistics is traditionally interested in structures, rules, and texts, the interest in a psycholinguistic approach is on the individual and his or her communicative activity; going beyond the speaker's purely linguistic production, the communicative approach takes into consideration the speaker's motivations, communicative needs, and intentions, as well as the use of paralanguage, kinesics, and the socio–cultural setting. I believe that these are also among the essential features in the psycholinguistic model of communication presented by Professor Slama-Cazacu in her paper.

At the beginning of his book *Psychological Reality in Phonology* (1979), the Swedish linguist Per Linell lists four possible attitudes that a linguist may have toward the "psychological reality" of grammar: (a) radical physicalism, which implies that language is described solely in terms of overt physical or physiological events; (b) pessimism, which says that although speakers do possess knowledge of their language, that is, they know its grammar, discovering the properties of these psychological structures is an unattainable goal; (c) moderate realism, which takes into account biological, psychological, and social realities, but still makes plausible, and even metaphysic, assumptions about the nature of language; and (d) naive optimism, belief in "God's truth" and linguistic mysticism, which Linell—maybe more strongly than would have been necessary—considers equal to Chomsky's position and transformational generative grammar. Though it may be doubtful whether theoretical linguists and more psychologically oriented researchers of communication and human interaction will ever attach the same meaning to the concept of psychological reality, similar research attitudes can also be found in psycholinguistics. My own choice from among the alternatives that Linell has proposed is the third: moderate realism. I do not think any "truly adequate" final truth will emerge from present enthusiasm, as O'Connell and Wiese predict in the conclusion of their paper, and I do not think a search for such an integrated model is useful, either. There is always the danger that such a model means nothing but replacing one black box with another black box which is just as obscure as the earlier one (cf. Frumkina, 1976, p. 13). Integrated models are necessary for testing hypotheses and for the illustration of the entity in which various individual problems lie. But until the model has been tested by experimentally verifying and falsifying hypotheses derived from the model, it remains hypothetical—as right or as wrong as any one of the competing psycholinguistic models for message production and perception. Such models inevitably also include black boxes, or decision demons—blocks in the hypothetical flow of events which are deliberately left unspecified to be replaced by various alternative partial models in the course of the testing procedure.

It is also vital to define the concept of model itself whenever models are discussed in psycholinguistics: Is it used in the rigid sense of model theory in mathematical logic, as an exact isomorphic *analogon* of reality, or is it used as an illustration of the theoretical framework and of the complex of variables to which the problems under investigation belong? In the latter case, the model serves as a kind of auxiliary construct based on existing data. Its purpose becomes the generation of hypotheses in the form of predictions, to be verified or falsified experimentally. Computer simulations of theories are often regarded as models in the narrow sense, as replicas of reality. Yet, a successful computer simulation only proves that the algorithms written for the computer are correct; it does not prove that the model is isomorphic with the actual processes in the human central nervous system. The great number and variety of solutions available in computer-based speech synthesizers, speech recognizers, and speech understanding systems (see e.g., Flanagan, 1972; Lea, 1980) provide us with good examples of artificial systems which arrive at similar results through entirely different procedures, none of which are necessarily identical with the human information processing system.

The second alternative, a less exact definition of the concept of model, uses a model as a theoretical framework to specify research hypotheses, list relevant factors to be taken into consideration in experimental testing, and also incorporate existing knowledge on various branches of relevant disciplines. Figure 1 of this paper, and Figure 2 in the paper by Kari Sajavaara in this volume, are graphic illustrations of typical models belonging to the latter category.

One more reservation is needed for the discussion of the concept of model. Both types of model discussed above may either aim at the description of the linguistic or communicative capacity of the idealized speaker/listener, or they may present hypotheses concerning the actual mental or neurolinguistic processes in the speaker and/or listener. In the present state of our knowledge about psycholinguistics, the latter type of model necessarily also contains black boxes, highly hypothetical structures and processes.

Linell (1979, p. 268) concludes his study by saying that our knowledge of the psychological and behavioral aspects of phonology is still very sketchy. This holds true also for the whole area of psycholinguistics: what we have really learned of the cognitive and neurological processes that take place in producing and understanding speech is the fact that we now know much more about what we do not know, or we know that what we believed some 20 years ago about language processing no longer seems as simple—or as complicated.

REFERENCES

Clark, H., & Clark, E. (1977). *Psychology and language*. New York: Harcourt Brace Jovanovich.

Eco, U. (1976). *A theory of semiotics*. Bloomington, London: Indiana University Press.

Flanagan, J.L. (1972). *Speech analysis, synthesis and perception*. New York: Springer.

Frumkina, R.M. (1976). The relationship between theory, model, and experiment in psycholinguistic studies. *Soviet Psychology, 15*, 8–14.

Knapp, M. (1978). *Non-verbal communication in human interaction* (2nd ed.). New York: Holt, Rinehart & Winston.

Lea, W.A. (Ed.). (1980). *Trends in speech recognition*. Englewood Cliffs, N.J.: Prentice-Hall.

Lehtonen, J., & Hurme, P. (1980). The speech chain and the theory of speech. In P. Hurme (Ed.),

Voice, speech and language: Reports and reviews (Papers in Speech Research 2, 1–27). Jyväskylä, Finland: University of Jyväskylä. Institute of Finnish Language and Communication.

Linell, P. (1979). *Psychological reality in phonology: A theoretical study.* Cambridge: Cambridge University Press.

Marslen-Wilson, W., & Tyler, L. K. (1980). The temporal structure of spoken language understanding. *Cognition, 8,* 1–71.

Sajavaara, K., & Lehtonen, J. (1980). Language teaching and the acquisition of communication. In K. Sajavaara, A. Räsänen & T. Hirvonen (Eds.), *AFinLA Yearbook 1980* (Publications of the Finnish Association of Applied Linguistics No. 28, pp. 25–35).

Second Session:
Second Language Speech Production

Chair: K. Ruder

CHAPTER 5

Second Language Speech Production: Factors Affecting Fluency

KARI SAJAVAARA
University of Jyväskylä

Multilingualism and multilingual societies are more numerous in the world than unilingualism and unilingual societies, which implies that acquisition of second languages must be quite common. Acquiring language(s) is a most normal phenomenon. Why is it then necessary, or even reasonable, to discuss the problem of second language speech production? The reason is the well-known fact that while language acquisition in natural settings, whether L1 or L2, leads without any special problems to thorough internalization of the language(s), foreign language teaching results in nativelike fluency in exceptional cases only.

If "second language" refers to all languages acquired after L1, the task of describing second language speech production is enormous, since it covers a multitude of phenomena from informal L1-like acquisition to the most formal learning in classroom settings. At one end of the continuum we have total acquisition, which results in nativelike performance without any distinguishable trace of non-L1 disfluency; at the other end, language behavior is based entirely on explicit memorization of rules and attempts at their application, which is successful under favorable circumstances only. The problems involved range from various teaching-induced factors of the "non-natural" way of learning foreign languages in the classroom to socio-psychological criteria present in face-to-face situations leading to naturalistic acquisition.

Theorizing around the problems of second language speech production also involves the entire complex of problems embedded in the interrelationship between the linguistic code, on the one hand, and communication, human interaction, speech processing as a whole, and memory and perception, on the other. It is understandable that the linguist's attention has been centered on the linguistic code to the extent that categories and phenomena abstracted for a linguistic analysis of the code have often been transferred over to the analysis of human communication. Grammar has moreover been granted an autonomous status prior to everything else—even at the cost of the other important system belonging to the code, namely, the lexicon. Most of the discussion of the human being's ability to acquire and use languages has been based on this idea of the autonomous status of grammar. Too little attention has been given to the use of language, the ways in which people are able to cope with their communicative needs, establish social contacts, and express their feelings in their mother tongue or in second languages.

In most research related to language, a grave defect is the basic assumption that problems of communication, or problems of language teaching, can be dealt with in terms of a formal theoretical model or a single scientific discipline. Problems that are at least partly non-linguistic cannot be solved by reference to linguistic theories alone. In the last few years, particularly after the disintegration of the TG framework, a certain trend has been noticeable away from the primacy of grammar. Various approaches to communicative competence have been posited alongside grammatical competence (for a recent review, see Canale & Swain, 1980). This has involved a certain change in the general attitude toward the question of what language is and how it is used.

There is another reason that a theoretical linguistic model cannot be sufficient for the purposes of the description of second language speech processing. Linguists' descriptions of languages are static; they represent the final product of language acquisition since they are abstractions derived by linguists from available language data. For such descriptions languages are normally treated as verbal codes and no links are usually established with the dynamism of the contexts in which they are used for communication or other purposes (cf. Sajavaara & Lehtonen, 1979). Second language processing needs to be described against a dynamic representation of the processes of human interaction and language learning and acquisition. The learner is never exposed all at once to a language in its entirety. Similarly, language use involves various dynamic aspects of human interaction and communication, which should be integrated into the description of second language proficiency. In communication situations, moreover, language users themselves dynamically construct the building blocks of communicative success (see Jordan & Fuller, 1975). This "communication game" involves basic rules which are known to everybody, but the strategy and tactics are chosen in correlation to the needs arising in a given situation. Any models of human information processing, or the development of systems to deal with such processing, in which the participants are described as passive automatons, or as a kind of assembly line, are bound to be defective in that they neglect the active role of the participants as problem-solvers.

In this paper it is impossible to give a thorough survey of the factors that affect second language speech production. Therefore, a number of areas of particular relevance have been chosen to illustrate second language speech production as representative of speech production in general. The following aspects will be discussed: communication and interaction, speech processing, second language acquisition and L1 influence on L2.

COMMUNICATION AND INTERACTION

For communication and language behavior to take place, a communicative situation is required in which there is a minimum of two participants in a specific setting. The participating individuals bring a number of elements into the situation which cannot be excluded from any discussion of human speech production, whether of L1 or of L2. Any idealization of the material that excludes them means a serious distortion of the true state of affairs—of which we already have enough examples. An individual always has a goal of some sort, and to reach this goal makes use of a range of processing heuristics that combine his experience in previous situations with whatever practical means are available. The speaker's behavior cannot be separated from a complex of speaker-internal factors which include, at a global level, the speaker's will, intention, and needs, and a variety of emotive and affective variables. These include attitudes and performance capability, which is not constant and varies under the influence of personality factors, processing load, and a number of external factors. The external factors that influence the speaker's performance involve the other participants' internal factors—their goals, needs, and intentions—and the time available, the setting, including aspects of discourse history and simultaneous events, and the participants' "common history" and shared knowledge (most of these "external" factors have their speaker-internal reflections).

The practical means available to a speaker, which could be called the tactics of message processing, consist of more or less automated processes/programs and various kinds of strategies. The borderline between processes/programs and strategies can never be very strict but can be drawn roughly along the line dividing unconscious and conscious ways of carrying out different tasks of communication (cf. Færch & Kasper, 1980).[1] The distinction that Færch and Kasper (1980) make is promising: "Strategies are *employed* by the individual (agentiveness), in opposition to processes, which *take place* in the individual." This distinction, even with a hazy borderline, has important consequences for the treatment of second language speech processing. If strategies involve conscious procedures on the part of the speaker, such procedures can also be interfered with, or manipulated (cf. Færch & Kasper, 1980), which means they can also be activated by overt teaching; on the other hand, processes, by definition, are not open to overt manipulation, and require indirect methods for their alteration.

It is impossible to understand speech production and reception unless the starting point is interaction, the "game" of verbal exchanges carried out by interlocutors. In addition to the initial goal, the speaker's message is influenced

---

[1]The term "communication strategy" is used in interlanguage terminology primarily for the means speakers use when their L2 system fails them. Færch and Kasper do not use the term in this way.

by expectations about what the listener may already know/believe/think; about the listener's assumed attitudes and feelings; the listener's reactions to the message (the parties know that they want, or do not want, to communicate something and it is in their common interest to build upon this assumption, which results in their willingness, or unwillingness, to understand each other); mutual agreement or disagreement on attitudes or opinions; and shared knowledge as well as expected information (see Bayless & Tomlin, 1977).

In most cases there is no way of knowing how successful a message has been in respect to the original intentions of the speaker. This depends on a multitude of factors, which are basically the same as those functioning at the production end and there are too many incalculables for one to be sure to what extent, if at all, a hearer's interpretation corresponds to what was originally intended by the speaker. Fortunately, approximations are sufficient in most cases and communication can go on undisturbed. The idea, so common that the meanings in language are fixed, or are universal for members of a particular speech community, is an abstraction.

Most discussions of second language speech processing are handicapped by the fact that researchers do not pay any attention to the socio-psychological functions of language. Language users' second language performance is viewed as unidirectional. What are called communicative processes/strategies are mostly characterized by a "virginal" abstraction of the speaker's production away from its proper context: interactional communication. (Some researchers do remember, it is true, to point out that they are intentionally disregarding interaction.) The communication process can be divided, in accordance with Rehbein (1976), for instance, into phases which include analysis of the situation, goal formulation, planning, and realization (cf. Færch & Kasper, 1980), but in L2 literature such phases are treated as if their implementation were unproblematic, aside from various difficulties that might arise in the speaker alone. When interaction in context is taken into account, problems may arise for at least two reasons:

1. The listener's reactions may interrupt the processes of communication or may make it necessary for the speaker to interrupt the communicative strategies in progress for reasons such as: (a) The speaker may realize that the strategy being followed is ineffective (something has been analyzed incorrectly and the message does not reach the interlocutor), (b) the interlocutor reacts to the message in ways which have not been predicted by the speaker, (c) something takes place outside the speaker-hearer dyad that affects the hearer and results in reactions on the part of the speaker, and (d) the speaker decides to abandon the original message or plan in view of expectations about further developments in the situation.

2. Under normal circumstances, what we are able to observe is the final product of a combination of processes and strategies, and generally there is no way of

knowing whether this product is the realization of the original goal or the result of adjustments made in the course of production.

It goes without saying that in view of what has been said above, it is necessary to give up Shannon-and-Weaver type models of communication as models of human interaction and communication. The signal which is coded by the speaker and transmitted to the hearer for decoding carries only part of the message. A more comprehensive model of the speech chain is given in Figure 1. Language is used by individuals for definite purposes which are related to the speaker-hearer's intentions in some specific time and environment. Any elements that make up part of an utterance, or other behavioral phenomenon, are situation-specific (cf. Lyons, 1977). Interaction in a communicative situation resembles a problem-solving task in which a variety of critieria are used by the interactants to reach an agreement (in the extreme case there is no common language and a *lingua franca* has to be developed, see Jordan & Fuller, 1975). Instead of the speaker encoding a message and then the hearer decoding it, both parties are faced with the problem of reaching an agreement on the content: the speaker has to give enough cues, verbal and non-verbal, for the hearer to be able to reconstruct the message. The speaker must relate, what is going to be said, to knowledge of the world and expectations about what will take place in the hearer. The hearer is also active, not passive, recipient: the hearer's task is to make use of the cues transmitted by the speaker and correlate them with other parameters in order to create the most probable interpretation and draw conclusions about how the speaker expects to alter or call up knowledge. Under normal circumstances, all these procedures require several consecutive cycles.

It is more than obvious that many things can go wrong or interfere in these processes and strategies even in L1 communicative acts. The chances of speech production being handicapped in these respects are multiplied in L2 because there the system is affected by the nature of second language acquisition/learning, on the one hand, and the interrelationship between L1 and L2, and possible L3s, on the other.

A MODEL OF MESSAGE PROCESSING

The Finnish-English Cross-Language Project, which was undertaken in Jyväskylä in 1974, has been concerned with integrating knowledge about human information processing with information about language acquisition and cross-languistic data. The theoretical aspects of this work have recently been presented in the model of message processing (Sajavaara & Lehtonen, 1984), shown in Figure 2. The following discusses the model in terms of the present topic.[2]

---

[2]This section of the present paper is a revised and extended version of Sajavaara & Lehtonen, 1984. I wish here to acknowledge my debt to my colleague, Professor Jaakko Lehtonen.

Figure 1. A dynamic model of the speech chain from the perspective of the total communication process. (Messages flow in both directions.) (From Lehtonen & Hurme, 1980)

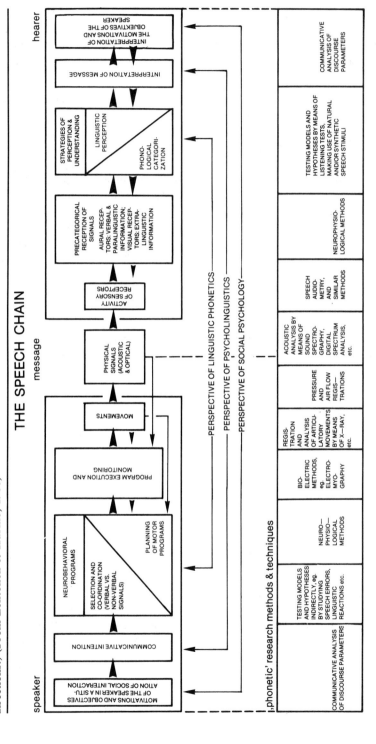

50

Figure 2.   A simplified model of message processing. (From Sajavaara & Lehtonen, 1980)

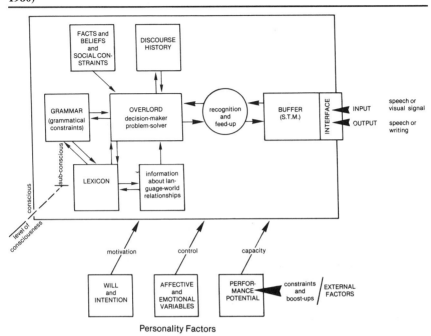

A description of the processes activated when people are planning utterances, or processing the utterances they hear, calls for a model that describes the phenomena and processes required for communicative success. According to Carroll, Tannenhaus, and Bever (1978), Flores d'Arcais (1978), and Marslen-Wilson, Tyler, and Seidenberg (1978), more emphasis than has been needs to be placed ''on the role of surface perceptual cues used by the perceiver to construct 'functional propositional units' '' (Marslen-Wilson et al., 1978).

A distinction can be made between a linguistically oriented approach and a communicatively oriented one: A linguistically oriented approach aims at explaining how a linguistic representation is derived from speech input; a communicatively oriented approach describes how the hearer deciphers the speaker's intentions in context.

Formerly language competence was primarily understood to refer to an internalized knowledge of the verbal code, but today it is far more difficult to make statements about what it is to know, or not know, a language. The fact that a learner is able to recognize the phenomena in a system abstracted by a linguist does not necessarily mean that the learner can use them in natural speech communication. In language teaching, what is called ''communicative'' is concerned mainly with the production of grammatically well-formed sentences, and a "communicative" language teaching method actually means teaching grammar "communicatively," not teaching communication.

Structural linguists have applied an atomistic method to the description of languages which split the language code into subsystems. Structures and items fundamental in such analyses were regarded as basic elements in language production. It was assumed that the constructs of linguistic description were also units relevant to the production and perception of messages or to the process of language learning. Such an assumption is unfounded (cf. Slobin 1979). These constructs have changed radically with developments in linguistic theory. As Wode (1980) has pointed out, the only thing that is common to all linguistic theories is the fact that they do not represent the processing and acquisition of languages.

A reference model for language processing is a descriptive model and involves a choice between structural and operational models of language and the chain of speech (cf. Lehtonen, 1978; see also Davis, 1978; Levelt & Flores d'Arcais, 1978). A structural model describes language as a set of rules abstracted from language data; in a dynamic approach rules are regarded as descriptions of regular structures in the language and not as models for the mental processes involved in speaking and listening (cf. Clark & Clark, 1977). An operational model describes language in action.

One of the misleading features of structural models is their hierarchical construction. In speech perception linguistic information is not processed hierarchically through levels of grammar going from the concrete level of presentation to phonology and syntax, and then on to more abstract content. Instead, the hearer makes simultaneous use of phonological, syntactic, pragmatic, and other knowledge by means of a time-sharing system (cf. Lea, 1980). There are cues for all these levels in the flow of acoustic speech waves but the information necessary for information processing is not present in the actual speech signal alone, and a great deal must be inferred from context or discourse history. These factors are also present in message production, which also cannot be seen in terms of hierarchical steps leading from higher linguistic levels to phonology and actual physical speech. In reception the main function of lexicon, syntax, and phonology is constraint: they reduce the number of potential guesses necessary for the identification of the acoustic speech input (for a more detailed analysis of the functions of phonology in speech reception, see Lehtonen & Sajavaara, 1980). This knowledge-driven process is primary, and simultaneous with the secondary, input-driven analysis (cf. Lindsay & Norman, 1977). Through a retroactive reworking effect, a word or a sequence of words may be changed in response to the subsequent context. Since such processes are, for the most part, not accessible to consciousness, only the single, final option is usually perceived, not the preceding choices.

Human communication is dependent on a variety of factors (see Figure 2). Grammar and lexicon are combined with discourse history, facts and beliefs, social constraints, and information about language-world relationships. They feed information to the "Overlord," or "Problem-Solver," which makes decisions about the recognition and content of messages received and the features to be fed into messages to be produced.[3] The functioning of the Overlord is highly dependent on the data, available in the data bank, whether conscious or subconscious; the recognition and feeding in of new information can take place only in reference to previous knowledge. In addition, there are a number of intervening variables which include will and intention, affect and emotion, and performance potential. All of these may function differently in different kinds of external situations (see Sajavaara, 1978a). The final outcome is a compromise between data, task demands, and available capacity. The response buffer in Figure 2 is a functional entity which "mediates both the storage of sequences of phonemically coded items during short-term memory tasks, and the storage of pre-planned sequences of impending speech in normal speech production" (Ellis, 1979). Short-term memory and the response buffer together are responsible for the chunking of the speech chain—the division of material into units which can be processed within the constraints of memory capacity. The interface deals with the reception and actual transmission of linguistic data and in a very broad sense governs the articulatory organs, their motor programs, and the processes of hearing.

As is evident by now, the communicative approach implies a reorientation toward grammar. References to grammar include the characteristics of the communication mechanism which make it possible for a speaker to produce a grammatically acceptable utterance and to interpret the information embedded in a text in a predictable way. Such grammatical rules are not necessarily neurobehavioral structures, but they have to be, in some way, represented in them (cf. Buckingham & Hollien, 1978; see also Lehtonen, this volume). Communicative competence involves the proper use of the mechanism described in Figure 2. It can be achieved through natural communication only (cf. Krashen, 1978; Widdowson, 1979); formal teaching in the classroom leads to "pseudo-competence," knowledge about grammatical constraints in the form of generalized rules. It is sufficient for the simulation of acceptable language behavior only in particular situations (see Sajavaara, 1978a).

The most interesting and problematic section of the model is the interrelationship between the lexicon and grammar. According to Marslen-Wilson and Welsh (1978), every lexical memory item or "word" can be defined as an intersection of procedures operating over a range of cognitive dimensions (cf.

---

[3]This should not be interpreted as a solution to the "Black Box" problem. It has only been transferred to a slightly deeper level. The model presented here is only a representation of the problem points in language processing and an attempt to correlate linguistic elements to other elements. It does not represent the flow of data in the processing mechanisms, and thus the arrows indicate relationships only (see Lehtonen, this volume).

Ellis, 1979; Morton, 1979), and an appropriate access code activates the entire range of processing procedures. A ''word'' activates, for example, certain frequent and prefabricated phrases, word combinations, grammatical constraints, selectional restrictions, semantic concepts and fields (cf. Miller & Johnson-Laird, 1976), etc. Thus, from the processing point of view, words, in this sense, are primary, and the language ''machine'' is not entirely dissimilar to what was given up as a finite state grammar by early TG grammarians (Chomsky, 1957; see Lehtonen, this volume). ''Word'' is here used as a pretheoretical label for a processing unit which includes all the information concerning the word's use in utterances and its relationships to other words within and outside utterances. It may be that all of language competence is embedded in memory in the form of such lexical items (Marslen-Wilson & Tyler, 1980). Since the speaker-hearer perceives final outcomes only, formal teaching, with its adherence to linguistic constructs, may seriously handicap metalinguistic observations.

Second language users experience problems for several reasons (cf. Færch & Kasper, 1980): A rule—an instruction belonging to a program—which is part of the language user's internal system (a) may not be retrievable, (b) it may be inaccurate, wrong, or in the case of foreign language teaching, contrary to the speaker's intuitions. (c) The rule may belong to the language user's system but the user refuses, for some reason, to apply it fully or in all appropriate communication situation. This includes Krashen's (1978) ''Monitor under-users,'' who are characterized by not applying rules even when they know them, and Færch and Kasper's (1980) strategy of formal reduction, where an inadequate linguistic system makes it necessary for speakers to make do with ''less of their interlanguage repertoire than is in fact at their disposal.'' It may also be that the speaker wants to avoid errors or facilitate speech production in order to reach higher levels of fluency without distorting the message. (d) The rule necessary for the execution of a plan may not have been acquired at all. This may result from the fact that the learner has not yet reached the stage in the acquisition process where this rule normally is acquired. It may be that the rule has not been taught, or cannot be taught because its exact formulation is not possible in the present state of knowledge, or is so complex that it is functionally unwieldy. It also may be, simply, that the learner is unable to internalize explicitly formulated rules. (e) The language user exaggerates the importance of monitoring and controlling of the processing mechanism (Krashen's ''Monitor over-users''), and makes an attempt to apply explicit rules under all circumstances.

In L2 production the above problems increase the further away one moves from naturalistic L1-type language acquisition because the system is bound to be correspondingly defective and dependent on explicit formal properties; it also becomes more fragile and more liable to malfunction due to external factors, since greater performance potential is normally required for second language processing. Speech behavior at a normal rate is usually possible only if most of the programs needed are available as automatic processes. A great deal can be explained by means of Levelt's (1977) skill theory. The execution of complex tasks such as language processing requires attention, but capacity is limited. Initially complex tasks require large amounts of effort and energy, but after certain lower-level tasks have become automatized, more capacity is available for higher-level planning and subtasks which have not been automatized. The attentional capacity of the speaker-hearer is not constant and increases with task difficulty to a peak, from which it suddenly begins to decline again. Unless plans and programs necessary for the execution of a task are "acquired," to use Krashen's (1978) dichotomy between acquisition and learning, the planning device will have to resort to "learned" items, which require more processing and greater capacity. It is self-evident that the system as a whole strives for efficiency, which is not, however, the same as economy of surface features (see Sajavaara, 1978a). Insufficiency of whatever information the Overlord needs, results in a failure of language production and a need for repairs. Insufficient automation can be compensated for by increased capacity or low task demands (or by functional or topic reduction, see Færch & Kasper, 1980). Unsuccessful operation of the speech production device may also be due to dispersion of attention resulting from other simultaneous tasks, emotional states, high loads on problem-solving capacity, and other factors (Laver, 1973; Levelt, 1977).

One of the most important conclusions to be drawn from the preceding concerns the high degree of task-dependency of speech production and perception. There are very few factors that remain constant under all circumstances, from speaker to speaker, and with the same speaker, and numerous factors are open to variation in relation to a multitude of other factors.

SECOND LANGUAGE ACQUISITION

Several approaches to the theory of second language acquisition have been developed so far (for surveys, see Bausch & Kasper, 1979; Schumann, 1979). Only a few can be listed here. We have Krashen's Monitor Model (Krashen, 1978), Schumann and Stauble's Acculturation Model (Schumann, 1978), and Selinker and Lamendella's neurofunctional perspective (Selinker & Lamendella, 1978). Hatch's (1977) input studies contain a considerable amount of new information. There is also Bialystok's (1978) model of second language acquisition, and work on universal tendencies in language acquisition by Wode and his collaborators (Wode, 1979). Data relevant to theories of second language acquisition have also been produced by research programs concerned with aspects of bilingualism, such as the "Pidgin-Deutsch" and ZISA projects (see Dittmar, 1978; Meisel, 1980), and the "OISE" programs of Canada; and with cross-language problems—and Danish PIF project, for example, (Færch, 1979) and the Finnish-English project (see Sajavaara & Lehtonen, 1979). There is still a long way to go, however, before arriving at an integrated picture of the entire process of language acquisition, particularly as concerns the interrelationship between formal aspects of language and other developmental features (see Wode, 1979). Recent literature on second language acquisition (e.g., Hakuta & Cancino, 1977; Hatch, 1977) is mainly concerned with learners acquiring languages in natural settings, while there is very little data about foreign languages in formal classroom settings.

Successful naturalistic language acquirers are more concerned with communication than with form (see Fillmore, 1976). Caretakers pay attention to learners' messages, not to their grammar (Snow & Ferguson, 1977; Waterson & Snow, 1978). In some recent work on how people acquire second languages, a distinction has been made between conscious language learning (memorization of rules) and unconscious acquisition which results from exposure to the target language (see d'Anglejan, 1978; Bialystok, 1978; Krashen, 1978). This should not be seen as a strict dichotomy but as a continuum which has two extremes: total acquisition, which results in native-like performance, sufficient for the production of acceptable L2 strings under favorable circumstances (cf. Sajavaara, 1978a). In addition to type of exposure, the age of the learner, the type of the rule system, and the level of acculturation also affect the outcome. Children before the "critical age" normally only acquire; later, people can both acquire and learn. In rule systems which relate to semantics, notional categories, pragmatics, and sociolinguistic rules, higher requirements must be set for acquisition, and there are rules which can be only acquired, since they cannot be specified clearly enough for learning (see Gingras, 1978; Krashen, 1978). Optimal acquisition requires a high level of acculturation and integrative motivation; a total lack of both may block acquisition entirely (Schumann, 1978). Adults may learn a great deal of information about a language, but they may also acquire an ability to use the language for communication in a way that resembles the acquisition of L1. Conscious learning is not necessary for acquisition and, when present, does not necessarily lead to acquisition, either. In formal teaching situations learners may acquire something without it being overtly taught—or despite its being taught.

Figure 3 is a simplified model of parameters present in language acquisition. Language contact is needed for input. Intake is regulated by a "socio-affective filter," which is controlled by a variety of social and personality factors, on the one hand, and knowledge about the language and the world, on the other. The filter can be opened by integrating the learner both psychologically and socially with the target group and, obviously, by adding to the learner's knowledge about the world. The importance of the mother tongue may be greater here than has been assumed, because if competence is a superior skill lying beyond the level of proficiency, a great deal of what is important in communication can obviously be transferred from this competence, which has been acquired in connection with L1 acquisition. It is important to remember that both the conscious and subconscious perception of what makes the world (including language) is governed by previous experiences. Previous knowledge is a yardstick that measures everything that is perceived and passed on to memory.

Figure 3. A model of language learning and acquisition processes. (From Sajavaara & Lehtonen, 1984).

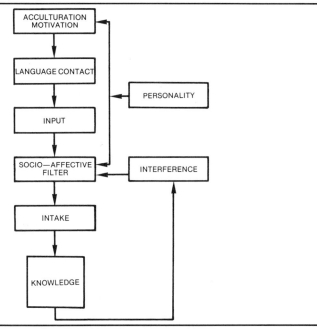

Most work on language teaching based on the isolation of autonomous levels of description gives the impression that learners have the ability to create concrete representations on the basis of the abstractions which are taught to them. In language acquisition the true state of affairs is the reverse: learners build up their language systems on the basis of the input of the concrete representations to which they are exposed. Thus the system actually goes from the concrete to the abstract, and not vice versa. Foreign language teaching methodologies derived from structuralist principles imply that a learner has the ability to synthesize the abstract categories isolated by linguistic analysis into a coherent and functional communicative system. As was pointed out above, typical structuralist or generativist teaching materials are built upon analytical structural drills under the assumption that after the learner has automatized the structures or transformational rules of each grammatical level, it will be possible to synthesize the categories in natural situations of language use and produce fluent speech by automatically applying the hierarchical procedures described earlier in this paper. This has been the theoretical motivation for pattern-practice drills, which are an extreme example of the isolation of categories. Lamendella (1979) questions the validity of drills for the facilitation of second language acquisition:

> Pattern-practice drills lead to Foreign Language Learning in which acquired behavioral subroutines for phonology and grammar may be evoked automatically only in

further classroom exercises. Conversational interactions for such learners typically require conscious direction, with speech behavior produced under the direction of the cognition hierarchy. In consequence, the students' performance does not reliably lead to communicative success. (Lamendella, 1979, p. 18)

Most of Lamendella's criticism can be generalized to apply to any language teaching methodology or any research on language teaching that resorts to analytical and atomistic theories.

Language teaching has traditionally been built upon the idea of the primacy of production, and tradition was followed even in the days of the grammar-translation method. There are a number of reasons, however, why more attention should now be paid to reception as a basis for improving production (cf. Krashen, 1978; see also Gingras, 1978). Why is it important to consider aspects of understanding speech and written texts when dealing with language acquisition? There are at least two reasons: (a) Language teaching aims at the correct use of the "machinery" described in Figure 2. (b) The process of speech reception is the channel through which linguistic and other information reaches the learner in a language-learning situation; if it does not function properly, there can be no intake.

In communicative situations people assume several roles. For foreign language speakers the roles are more restricted than for native speakers: the typical situation is that of a stranger talking to a stranger, and most of the social criteria found for L1 do not apply to the L2 speaker, whose social role is reduced to that of simply a foreigner. A native speaker will have expectations quite different from those in normal L1 settings. A foreigner may be given, for instance, more time for the formulation of a message, and the native speaker may switch over to "foreigner talk." The conversational mechanisms which govern the interchange of textual roles, the turn-taking system, may not function in the same way they function in full-scale L1 situations: a native speaker talking to a non-native speaker is more prepared to finish the non-native's utterances or give reformulations when there are hesitations. A non-native seldom achieves symmetrical parity with a native (Ventola, 1977). A non-native tends to retain the participatory role of a respondent, and is likely to be less active and more willing to cede the role of the discourse initiator to the native. It is to be expected that a non-native's role as a foreigner and respondent will influence reactions to what can be described as "parameters of fluency."

L1 INFLUENCE ON L2

The question of L1 influences on L2 processing has been subject to many exchanges of opinion. It was the initial impetus for constrastive analysis and is one of the problems that come up constantly in connection with error analysis and interlanguage studies. Too often the basic issue has been simplified to the question of whether or not L1 influences L2. Here, as elsewhere, a simple dichotomy is misleading. It should not be discussed as an either-or problem at all but should be treated as a continuum. There are different kinds of influence at different levels of learning, and it varies between learners. On the other hand, there are global and universal characteristics that seem to operate generally in language processing and language acquisition (that the two are closely interrelated as should be obvious from what has been said above). Space does not allow for a detailed discussion of the entire issue but some major aspects will be taken up below.

According to Krashen, speech performance is always initiated by means of the acquired system, and the learned system is available as a monitor to edit the output. In acquisition-poor environments a speaker must rely on L1 competence as a performance initiator. The initial L1 string is then ''translated'' into an L2 string, whose grammaticality and acceptability depend on the availability of ''rules,'' as described above, and on the nature of the constraints present. Under optimal circumstances the L2 string is initiated and processed on the basis of the acquired L2 system without the interference of the Monitor. Most L2 speakers are located somewhere between the two extremes: at least occasionally they have to rely on L1 systems for speech processing. This is the case when an L2 unit has not been acquired and the Monitor fails to give the right answer. L1 influence on surface strings may be due to the fact that (a) the string has been initiated by the acquired L1 system and the Monitor has not been able to correct the string, (2) the Monitor lacks the correct ''rule'' and an L1 rule is used as a repair, or (3) strings originally initiated with correct L2 acquired systems are mutilated by the learned systems (see Sajavaara, 1978b). The L1 and L2 acquired and learned systems are closely interlinked, and both systems are referred to several times during speech production, which may be one of the reasons for highly variable performances by the same speaker in different situations.

Most of the previous research in this area has dealt with the final product, the surface string. There is an urgent need to develop methodologies to study the stages before the actual utterance is produced. Such techniques might include prevented audiomonitoring, delayed auditory feedback, shadowing techniques, and masking noise. The ability of present tests to reveal ''critical'' points in the interlanguage speech channel is still rather limited. One natural way of approaching the problem is through the analysis of a student's speech production in natural situations of language use. Deviations from the target in the production of features that are known to function as cues for the processing of utterances will reflect corresponding difficulties in perceptual processing. Similarly, if some native-language features break through the pronunciation of L2, the student may be expected to apply the same cues when trying to process L2. Some quite unexpected elements may be confused with each other. A Finn may meet difficulties in the fortis/lenis distinction of English consonants as a result of the long/short distinction between Finnish vowels; changes in the stress pattern of words may actually be errors in the pronunciation of certain sounds; and so on. Differences in the ways in which two languages signal higher-level information such as syntactic patterns, lexical units, or textual features can result in interference in speech communication; for example, the process by which a lexical item is detected in English is different from that used in Finnish (see Karlsson, 1977). More information is needed about discourse planning as it is revealed, for instance, in speech errors in L1 and L2. Systematic errors can be expected to reveal aspects of the processes before the final product. The Jyväskylä project has developed a method for the study of discourse which makes it possible to describe real-time discourse. In this way we have access to the analysis of the distribution of speech performance in time, which is particularly important in the analysis of discourse dynamics and studies in which information about reaction time, time of hesitation, location of pauses, and other such features, is needed. It is possible to record and analyze simultaneous speaking turns (e.g., simultaneous starts, feedback moves of listeners, completions) and the chronemics of discourse in general. Phenomena to be studied include language behaviors in different interactional settings, ability to use different channels of communication to convey messages and intentions, and ability to understand and interpret messages transmitted by other interactants. Two approaches using a communicative perspective are provided by our pilot studies. One is the analysis of speakers' linguistic and non-linguistic behavior in non-interactive communicative situations such as reading texts of varying complexity or free delivery of speech during different narrative tasks (see Lehtonen, 1978; and Sajavaara & Lehtonen, 1978). The other approach is the description of the communicative behavior of native speakers and non-native students and schoolchildren in interactional situations. Particular emphasis is placed on differences in fluency between non-native and native speakers (see Sajavaara & Lehtonen, 1978, 1979; Sajavaara, 1977).

Too much attention in interlanguage studies has probably been paid to the transfer of individual structures from L1 to L2. Felix (1978) has pointed out that the effect of L1 knowledge on the acquisition of L2 has not been globally investigated. There are indications that if there is any L1 interference at all in the naturalistic acquisition of L2, it occurs in the form of sporadic erroneous performance and does not result in productive interim stages of acquisition (Felix, 1978). Felix makes it quite clear that the situation is far more complex than has generally been assumed. It seems to be important, first of all, to make a distinction between the transfer of individual structures and the similarity/dissimilarity of acquisitional sequences. Individual structures do get transferred from L1, depending on factors such as the type of acquisition/learning and the learner's expectations about the interrelationship of L1 and L2, while differences between the acquisitional sequences of L1 and L2 are, according to Felix, a direct reflection of the L2 acquirer's linguistic repertoire. The interrelationship here lies at a much deeper level than the surface or near surface categories that have normally been the subject of interference studies.

Wode (1980) points out that there are some global characteristics that apply to all acquisitional types (L1, L2, L3, relearning, FLT): decomposition of target structures, reliance on prior knowledge, and individual variation. These occur in varying degrees in different acquisitional types. On the other hand, several researchers (e.g., Corder, 1967) have pointed out that the acquisition of L1 and L2 differ profoundly because, for example, the state of the learner at the initiation of learning is different. With the exception of simultaneous acquisition of two languages, the L2 acquirer also builds upon L1 knowledge and makes use, in most cases, of different and more developed cognitive and mental capacities. Keller-Cohen (1979) points out that "the child's prior experience with language seems to lead him to look for global properties of language such as large analytic units linked to clear contexts." Keller-Cohen also shows that children do not as easily identify structures not corresponding to structures in L1 (see also Schachter, 1974). This is consistent with what is known about learning, perception, and memory in general. Learning can be regarded as addition to knowledge, and new knowledge must be integrated with previously acquired knowledge: "There must be a suitable set of background knowledge and memory structures before any particular new knowledge can be properly acquired" (Lindsay & Norman, 1977). Thus, native language programs guide second language acquisition and second language production. In Finnish, for example, the word is an important processing unit in that the suffixes that are embedded in it give cues about the syntactic and semantic analysis of the entire message. In Germanic languages, and English in particular, most of the same information is found in independent morphemes adjoined to the head word or neighboring it in word order (cf. Karlsson, 1977). In Finnish the processing of linguistic structures is linear, using word stems and endings (i.e., morphotactic forms) while in English the same process is governed by both lexical words and function words that belong to the same syntactic unit, which have to be held in short-term memory. In Finnish sentences are processed word for word, while in English prosodically marked chunks make up the processing units.

Even if we have to give up the early contrastivist assumption that the distance between L1 and L2 determines the degree of learning difficulty, distance is still of some importance; but even more important is the learner's mental image of the correlation between the structures of L1 and L2. Ringbom (1979) writes:

> At the very outset of their studies, Swedes already seem to have some basic intuitive knowledge of English automated, in that much of their mother tongue knowledge is of direct relevance to their English studies. This automated knowledge can easily be extended to an automated knowledge of a related language. The grammatical categories of English are familiar to Swedes and much of its vocabulary at least vaguely recognizable . . . the linguistic knowledge Finns have automated in their mother tongue is of comparatively little use for learning English . . . the result of lacking automation is wrong comprehension of very staccato speech with disturbing pauses. (p. 81)

Ringbom's work with Finns and Swedish speaking Finns learning English as L2 has clearly indicated that there are L2 production problems that directly relate to the distance of the two languages (see Palmberg, 1979; see also Sharwood Smith, 1979).

Influence from L1 is seen in varying degrees at different levels of analysis, from phonology to pragmatics. To a certain extent the influence is a function of the acquisitional stage, on the one hand, and the degree of optionality of the items in question (because phonological constructs are more or less obligatory this may be one reason that phonology is the first to be affected by foreign influences). Individual variation is also considerable. In addition to variation due to "environmental" factors, such as exposure to L2, age, type of rule system, and acculturation (see Sajavaara, 1978b), variation may also be due to stylistic shifts and shifts due to attention and degree of formality (Tarone, 1979).

CONCLUSION

It should be evident from the present discussion that the reasons for problems in second language speech production may be multifarious. Good linguistic or communicative competence is not always realized in fluent speech: one person may master the finest nuances of literary expression and yet be incapable of good speech performance; another person, whose command of structure and vocabulary is restricted, may carry on efficient speech communication with great skill.

At least two aspects seem to be combined in fluency: linguistic acceptability and smooth continuity of speech. Fluency equals the communicative acceptability of the speech act, or "communicative fit," and expectations concerning this fit vary according to the situation. Learning to speak fluently does not always imply an uninterrupted flow of speech that is sequentially and grammatically irreproachable. The "good" speaker "knows" how to hesitate, how to be silent, how to self-correct, how to interrupt, and how to complete expressions or leave them unfinished. Speech must meet the expectations of the speech community and represent normal, acceptable and relaxed language behavior. In this way, knowing a language, that is, knowing how to use a language for communicative and other purposes, involves a number of social and cultural skills in addition to language skills. This is also important for the treatment of second language perception and production.

REFERENCES

Bausch, K.-R., & Kasper, G. (1979). Der Zweitsprachenerwerb: Möglichkeiten und Grenzen der "großen" Hypothesen. *Linguistische Berichte, 64,* 3–35.

Bayless, R., & Tomlin, R. (1977, October). *The role of expected information in the analysis of English texts.* Paper presented at the NWave Conference, Washington, D.C.

Bialystok, E. (1978). A theoretical model of second language learning. *Language Learning, 28,* 69–83.

Buckingham, H., & Hollien, H. (1978). A neural model for language and speech. *Journal of Phonetics, 6,* 283–297.

Canale, M., & Swain, M. (1980). Theoretical bases of communicative approaches to second language teaching and testing. *Applied Linguistics, 1,* 1–47.

Carroll, J.M., Tannenhaus, M.K., & Bever, T.G. (1978). The perception of relations: The interaction of structural, functional, and contextual factors in the segmentation of sentences. In W.J.M. Levelt & G.B. Flores d'Arcais (Eds.), *Studies in the perception of language* (pp. 187–218). New York: John Wiley & Sons.

Chomsky, N. (1957). *Syntactic structures.* The Hague: Mouton.

Clark, H.H., & Clark, E.V. (1977). *Psychology and language: An introduction to psycholinguistics.* New York: Harcourt Brace Jovanovich.

Corder, S.P. (1967). The significance of learner's errors. *IRAL, 5,* 161–170.

d'Anglejan, A. (1978). Language learning in and out of classrooms. In J.C. Richards (Ed.), *Understanding second and foreign language learning* (pp. 218–236). Rowley, Mass.: Newbury House.

Davis, S.M. (1978). Audition and speech perception. In R.L. Schiefelbusch (Ed.), *Bases of language intervention* (pp. 43–66). Baltimore, Md.: University Park Press.

Dittmar, N. (1978). Ordering adult learners according to language abilities. In N. Dittmar, H. Haberland, T. Skuttnabb-Kangas & U. Teleman (Eds.), *Papers from the first Scandinavian-German symposium on the language of immigrant workers and their children* (pp. 119–147). Roskilde: Universitetscenter.

Ellis, A.W. (1979). Speech production and short-term memory. In J. Morton & J.C. Marshall (Eds.), *Structures and processes* (Psycholinguistic Series 2, pp. 157–187). London: Paul Elek.

Færch, C. (1979). *Research in foreign language pedagogy: The PIF project* (Anglica et Americana 7). Copenhagen: University of Copenhagen.

Færch, C., & Kasper, G. (1980). *Processes and strategies in foreign language learning and communication.* Unpublished manuscript.

Felix, S.W. (1978). *Linguistische Untersuchungen zum natürlichen Zweitsprachenerwerb.* München: Fink

Fillmore, L.W. (1976). *The second time around: Cognitive and social strategies in second language acquisition.* Ann Arbor, Mich.: University Microfilms.

Flores d'Arcais, G.B. (1978). The perception of complex sentences. In W.J.M. Levelt & G.B. Flores d'Arcais (Eds.), *Studies in the perception of language* (pp. 155–186). New York: John Wiley & Sons.

Gingras, R.C. (1978). *Second language acquisition and foreign language teaching.* Arlington, Va.: Center for Applied Linguistics.

Hakuta, K., & Cancino, H. (1977). Trends in second language acquisition research. *Harvard Educational Review, 47,* 294–316.

Hatch, E. (1977). *Second language learning. Bilingual education: Current perspectives/Linguistics.* Arlington, Va.: Center for Applied Linguistics.

Jordan, B., & Fuller, N. (1975). On the non-fatal nature of trouble: Sense-making in lingua franca talk. *Semiotica, 13,* 11–31.

Karlsson, F. (1977). Morphotactic structure and word cohesion in Finnish. In K. Sajavaara & J. Lehtonen (Eds.), *Contrastive papers* (Jyväskylä Contrastive Studies 4, pp. 59–74). Jyväskylä: University of Jyväskylä.

Keller-Cohen, D. (1979). Systematicity and variation in the non-native child's acquisition of conversational skills. *Language Learning, 29,* 27–44.

Krashen, S. D. (1978). The Monitor Model for second-language acquisition. In R.C. Gingras (Ed.), *Second language acquisition and foreign language teaching* (pp. 1–26). Arlington, Va.: Center for Applied Linguistics.

Lamendella, J. (1979). The neurofunctional basis of pattern practice. *TESOL Quarterly, 13,* 5–19.

Laver, J. (1973). The detection and correction of slips of the tongue. In V.A. Fromkin (Ed.), *Speech errors as linguistic evidence* (pp. 132–143). The Hague: Mouton.

Lea, W.A. (1980). *Trends in speech recognition.* Englewood Cliffs, N.J.: Prentice-Hall.

Lehtonen, J. (1978, December). *The theory and methodology of speech science and contrastive analysis.* Paper presented at the 16th International Conference on Polish-English Contrastive Linguistics, Boszkowo, Poland.

Lehtonen, J., & Hurme, P. (1980). The speech chain and the theory of speech. In P. Hurme (Ed.), *Voice, speech, and language: Reports and reviews* (Papers in Speech Research 2, pp. 1–27). Jyväskylä, Finland: University of Jyväskylä. Institute of Finnish Language and Communication.

Lehtonen, J., & Sajavaara, K. (1984). Phonology and speech processing in cross-language speech communication. In S. Eliasson (Ed.), *Theoretical issues in contrastive phonology* (pp. 85–99). Heidelberg: Julius Groos.

Levelt, W.J.M. (1977). Skill theory and language teaching. *Studies in Second Language Acquisition, 1,* 53–70.

Levelt, W.J.M., & Flores d'Arcais, G.B. (Eds.). (1978). *Studies in the perception of language.* New York: John Wiley & Sons.

Lindsay, P.H., & Norman, D.A. (1977). *Human information processing.* New York: Academic Press.

Lyons, J. (1977). *Semantics* (Vols. 1–2). Cambridge: Cambridge University Press.

Marslen-Wilson, W.D., & Tyler, L.K. (1980). The temporal structure of spoken language understanding. *Cognition, 8,* 1–71.

Marslen-Wilson, W.D., Tyler, L.K., & Seidenberg, M. (1978). Sentence processing and the clause boundary. In W.J.M. Levelt & G.B. Flores d'Arcais (Eds.), *Studies in the perception of language* (pp. 219–246). New York: John Wiley & Sons.

Marslen-Wilson, W.D., & Welsh, A. (1978). Processing interaction and lexical access during word recognition in continuous speech. *Cognitive Psychology, 10,* 29–63.

Meisel, J.M. (1980). Strategies of second language acquisition. *Wuppertaler Arbeitspapiere zu Sprachwissenschaft, 3,* 1–53.

Miller, G.A., & Johnson-Laird, P.N. (1976). *Language and perception.* Cambridge: Cambridge University Press.

Morton, J. (1979). Word recognition. In J. Morton & J.C. Marshall (Eds.), *Structures and processes* (Psycholinguistic Series 2, pp. 107–156). London: Paul Elek.

Palmberg, R. (Ed.). (1979). *The perception and production of English: Papers on interlanguage* (AFTIL 6). Åbo: Åbo Akademie. Department of English.

Rehbein, J. (1976). *Planen I-II* (Series A, Paper Nos. 38–39). Trier: University of Trier, Linguistic Agency.

Ringbom, H. (1979). The English of Finns, Swedes, and Swedish Finns: Some concluding remarks. In R. Palmberg (Ed.), *The perception and production of English: Papers on interlanguage* (AFTIL 6, pp. 77–85). Åbo: Åbo Akademie. Department of English.

Sajavaara, K. (1977). Contrastive linguistics past and present and a communicative approach. In K. Sajavaara & J. Lehtonen (Eds.), *Contrastive Papers* (Jyväskylä Contrastive Studies 4, 9–30). Jyväskylä: University of Jyväskylä.

Sajavaara, K. (1978a). The Monitor Model and monitoring in foreign language speech communication. In R.C. Gingras (Ed.), *Second language acquisition and foreign language teaching* (pp. 51–67). Arlington, Va.: Center for Applied Linguistics.

Sajavaara, K. (1978b, December). *The Monitor Model and contrastive analysis.* Paper presented at the 16th Conference on Polish-English Contrastive Linguistics, Boszkowo, Poland.

Sajavaara, K., & Lehtonen, J. (1978). Spoken language and the concept of fluency. In L. Lautamatti & P. Lindqvist (Eds.), *Focus on spoken language* (Special issue of Language Centre News, pp. 23–57) Jyväskylä: Language Centre for Finnish Universities.

Sajavaara, K., & Lehtonen, J. (1979, August). *Prisoners of code-centred privacy: Reflections on contrastive linguistics and related disciplines*. Paper presented at the First Nordic Interlanguage Symposium, Hanasaari, Espoo, Finland.

Sajavaara, K., & Lehtonen, J. (1980). Language teaching and the acquisition of communication. In K. Sajavaara, A. Räsänen & T. Hirvonen (Eds.), *AFinLA Yearbook 1980* (Publications of the Finnish Association of Applied Linguistics No. 28, pp. 25–35).

Schachter, J. (1974). An error in error analysis. *Language Learning, 24,* 204–215.

Schumann, J.H. (1978). The acculturation model for second language acquisition. In R.C. Gingras (Ed.), *Second language acquisition and foreign language teaching* (pp. 27–50). Arlington, Va.: Center for Applied Linguistics.

Schumann, J.H. (1979, August). *Three theoretical perspectives on second language acquisition*. Paper presented at the First Nordic Symposium on Interlanguage, Hanasaari, Espoo, Finland.

Selinker, L., & Lamendella, J. (1978). Two perspectives on fossilization in interlanguage learning. *Interlanguage Studies Bulletin, 3,* 143–191.

Sharwood Smith, M. (1979). Strategies, language transfer and the simulation of the second language learner's mental operations. *Language Learning, 29,* 345–361.

Slobin, D.I. (1979). *Psycholinguistics* (2nd ed.). Glenview, Ill.: Scott, Foresman & Co.

Snow, C., & Ferguson, D.A. (Eds.). (1977). *Talking to children.* Cambridge: Cambridge University Press.

Tarone, E. (1979). Interlanguage as chameleon. *Language Learning, 29,* 181–191.

Ventola, E. (1977). *On the structure and management of casual conversations.* Unpublished master's thesis, Macquarie University, Sydney, Australia.

Waterson, N., & Snow, C. (Eds.). (1978). *The development of communication.* New York: John Wiley & Sons.

Widdowson, H.G. (1979). *Explorations in applied linguistics.* London: Oxford University Press.

Wode, H. (1979). *Studies in second language acquisition* (Occasional Papers No. 11). Singapore: SEAMEO Regional Language Centre.

Wode, H. (1980). Language acquisitional universals: L1, L2, pidgins, and foreign language teaching. *AFinLA Yearbook 1980* (Publications of the Finnish Association of Applied Linguistics No. 28).

CHAPTER 6

Natural Language Development: Acquisitional Processes Leading to Fluency in Speech Production*

HARALD CLAHSEN

Gesamthochschule Wuppertal

Children that acquire their mother tongue in everyday social interaction are able to speak fluently without ever having been instructed in the grammar of their language. Natural second language (L2) acquisition can, in certain cases, also result in nativelike competence. Only in exceptional cases, however, does foreign language teaching produce the ability to communicate fluently in the target language, even when grammatical rules have been explained to the learner. The explication of grammar by itself does not trigger language learning processes. There are obviously other factors which enable a learner in natural settings to acquire fluent skills in the target language.

Sajavaara (this volume) maintains that L2 fluency can only be achieved if the learner has *automatized* the required linguistic operations. This is a central notion within skill theory which Levelt (1977) applied to problems of second language acquisition. L2 speech production is seen as a hierarchically structured task which requires a program for its realization. One of the most important prerequisites of skilful speaking is that such programs are available in long term memory; this is especially true for lower level plans such as the articulatory patterns of words and phrase structures. Programs belonging to the learner's permanent cognitive equipment are said to be automatized. Automatized lower level patterns require less processing capacity, and allow the speaker to focus more on higher level decisions such as topic choice and intonation pattern. On the basis of the preceding assumptions Sajavaara holds that L1 acquisition occurs under the optimal conditions for internalizing linguistic operations. Foreign language teaching, on the other hand, does not lead to an automatized linguistic repertoire,

*This paper was written in connection with the research project ZISA. I want to thank all the members of the research group, and especially Jürgen Meisel, Günter Neis, Armin Mester and Frank Struwe for their corrections and helpful remarks. I remain, of course, responsible for all remaining shortcomings.

"because the system is bound to be correspondingly defective and dependent on explicit formal properties" (p. 83).

If the preceding is one of the main reasons for the limited success of foreign language teaching, then it is necessary to study in detail the strategies and learning processes leading to automatization in natural language acquisition. In the following I try to make a contribution to the discussion of this problem. In particular, I will discuss some of the results of the Wuppertal project on natural L2 acquisition as well as those in my own work on L1 acquisition.

WUPPERTAL RESEARCH PROJECTS ON NATURAL LANGUAGE DEVELOPMENT

Our research group, ZISA, is studying the untutored acquisition of German as a second language by adult foreign workers. Three years ago we carried out a cross-sectional study consisting mainly of free conversations with 45 Spanish, Italian, and Portuguese women and men. Currently a longitudinal study is being done using primarily the same techniques and methods. 12 people will be interviewed over a period of approximately two years, beginning as soon as possible after their arrival in Germany. The linguistic analysis will focus on syntactic problems, but morphological and lexical properties will receive more attention than they did in the cross-sectional study. In another study, Pienemann (1979) carried out a longitudinal study on child second language acquisition using the methods developed by our research group. I have tried to supplement these works with a study on the acquisition of German as a first language in which I have observed male twins (from age 18 months to 42 months) and their sister (age 13 months to 29 months) for a period of more than two years.

Preliminary results from these studies (see Clahsen, 1980a; Meisel, 1980b) allow us to make some tentative claims about the similarities of L1 and L2 language learning processes in natural settings. Here, I present two of the parallels between L1 and naturalistic L2 acquisition which might be regarded as conditions for attaining fluency in speech production.

DEVELOPMENTAL STAGES IN LANGUAGE ACQUISITION

Since the work of Bloom (1970) and Brown (1973) it has been acknowledged that L1 acquisition can be described as a strictly ordered developmental sequence. The Kiel project (Wode, 1976) and our own studies have shown that there are developmental stages in naturalistic L2 acquisition as well. In terms of skill theory, this similarity suggests that lower-level plans have to be learned in a fixed sequence in order to become automatized. This hypothesis is based on "what is known about learning, perception, and memory in general. Learning can be regarded as addition to knowledge, and new knowledge must be integrated with previously acquired knowledge" (Sajavaara, this volume, p. 61).

With respect to the problem of automatization it is necessary to discover the principles which underly the integration of linguistic knowledge in natural language acquisition. For this purpose I will compare the sequence in which certain German word order phenomena are acquired in three different types of language learning—adult L2, child L2, child L1.

The main findings of the ZISA cross-sectional study were developmental sequences in some syntactic rules in adult L2 acquisition (Clahsen, 1980b). These sequential stages are confirmed by recent findings from the longitudinal study.

Leaving aside details, the sequence in which verb placement is acquired can be described as follows:

(I)   None of the standard word order rules are applied, and the linear order of constituents is NP$\begin{Bmatrix} \text{AUX} \\ \text{MOD} \end{Bmatrix}$ V (NP) (PP):

(1)

ich	ankomme	hier	an	Wuppertal.
I	arrive	here	in	Wuppertal.

(II)   Learners use a rule, Particle Placement, which has the effect of moving non-finite parts of verbal elements to sentence final position:

(2)   mit   mein bruder ich <u>habe</u> sieben monat <u>gewohnt.</u>
       with my   brother I   have seven months stayed.

(III) Subject-Verb Inversion is applied:

(3)   in die große schule <u>kann man</u> englisch lerne.
       in the great school can   one English learn.

(IV)   A rule, V-End, is used which only applies to embedded clauses and moves the finite verb into final position:

(4)   aber früher habe ich viel   gesäuft, wie ich meine sorgen <u>gehabt habe.</u>
       but earlier have I   much drunk,   as I   my   sorrows had   have.

Each of these standard German word order rules marks just one developmental stage. Note, as shown in the examples, that the learner belonging to a stage x_i defined by a rule r_i applies all of the rules $r_{i-1}, r_{i-2} \cdots r_{i-n}$ characterizing the previous stages and does not use any of the rules $r_{i+1}, r_{i+2} \cdots r_{i+m}$ which would define the subsequent stages. We use this criterion derived from implicational scales when defining a strictly ordered developmental sequence (Meisel, Clahsen & Pienemann, 1979). Since Pienemann's (1979) longitudinal study of three eight-year-old Italian girls confirms these stages, we assume, that this developmental sequence represents the way in which German is acquired as a second language by adults and children with a Romance language as L1.

With respect to German as a first language, Clahsen (1980a) found a developmental sequence for the position of verbal elements. It is beyond the scope of this paper to discuss the sequence at length. What I want to do here is to examine whether the rules which define stages (I)–(IV) in L2 acquisition are learned in a similar sequence in L1 acquisition. In L1 acquisition:

(I′)   There is no fixed linear order of constituents.

(5)   *sitzen bein.*
       sit leg.
       "I sit on the leg."

(6)   *boden bürs.*
       floor brush.
       "I brush the floor."

(II′)   Verbal elements containing non-finite parts such as particles appear regularly in final position; finite verbs are still placed in final as well as in second position; preference, however, is given to final position.

(7)   *deckel drauftun.*
       cover onput.
       "I put on the cover."

(III′)   All finite verbs occur in sentence second position and verbal elements containing finite and non-finite parts now appear in discontinuous word order:

(8)   *die schere hat Julia.*
       the scissors has J.

(9)   ein schiff muss du   erst   jetzt bauen.
       a   ship   must you firstly now build.

(IV′)   As soon as the first embedded clauses appear, V END is applied.

(10)   kuck, was ich in mein tasche hab.
       look, what I   in my   pocket have.

An obvious similarity between L1 and L2 acquisition of German word order rules is that they both follow a strictly ordered developmental sequence. This is a result which one would have expected in the light of other studies on the acquisition of grammar. Another similarity between the two developmental sequences is that when the learners reach the last stage they have acquired Standard German word order for both matrix and embedded sentences. This result corroborates the hypothesis that systematic integration of new grammatical rules with previously acquired systems is one of the main conditions for successful language acquisition.

In spite of these similarities, each of the developmental stages in the two acquisitional types differ in certain respects. The L2 learners start their developmental careers with a very specific assumption about the position of verbal elements in German: they transfer the underlying word order of their mother tongues to the target language (Meisel, 1980b). Children learning German as L1, however, initially seem to follow the more general hypothesis that there are no word order restrictions for verbs at all. The next stage in L1 acquisition is also characterized by a very broad generalization, namely placement of all verbal elements, especially those containing non-finite parts, in sentence final position (Roeper, 1973; Miller, 1976). At stage (III') children acquire a rule which is structurally identical to a "Verb Second" transformation which has been repeatedly assumed in generative linguistics (Bierwisch, 1963; Roeper, 1973) to be the most general and simple description of the peculiarities of German syntax. To sum up, the overall strategy of L1 learners is to assume the most general hypothesis which is consistent with the linguistic input.

In contrast to this line of development, L2 learners start out with a specific assumption about German grammar which has its origin in the learner's knowledge that sentences have to be constructed according to certain formal syntactic rules. In the course of the subsequent stages they acquire each of the specific rules of German syntax separately.

Up to this point two ways of attaining standard German word order have been demonstrated. As far as I can see, it is premature to consider one of the developmental sequences as more effective than the other. In this respect the process of learning a language can be compared to that of learning to play chess; a beginner may ask about each of the chessmen's moves separately, or ask instead more general questions such as, "How do the more important pieces move as opposed to the pawns?" Both strategies may lead the beginners to the automatization of the chessmen's moves, which is prerequisite to playing chess skilfully.

Apart from learners' different hypotheses about German syntax there are certain restrictions which are adhered to in both L1 and L2 acquisition. As noted above, L2 learners initially place all verbs in second position. This regularity holds even for those verbal elements which contain non-finite parts (example 1), where standard German requires discontinuous word order. In L1 acquisition verbal elements of this kind are placed in sentence final position (7); discontinuous word order is not acquired until stage (III'). Although these complex verbal elements appear in different positions in the two acquisitional types, the learners' hypotheses share one similarity: separation of finite and non-finite parts is not carried out in the initial stages.

Another example of the same kind concerns the acquisition of Inversion. Strangely enough, L2 learners acquire mastery of this operation comparatively late, though it exists in their mother tongues, too. Similarly, L1 learners apply Verb Second at the beginning of stage (III') only to structures where the subject is the first constituent in the sentence. If an adverbial has been topicalized, the finite verb appears after the subject.

Discontinuous word order and Inversion seem to be extremely complex language learning tasks. The factor that causes difficulty is that semantic units are interrupted and reordered. Slobin (1973) has shown that there is a tendency in early child language to retain underlying semantic units at the surface level. With respect to Inversion, Slobin (1978) maintains that the verb and its object constitutes a kind of perceptual gestalt which resists interruption. In addition, Meisel (1980b) shows that Inversion constitutes a major difficulty for learners and also for native speakers. As an explanation he suggests that the separation of the verb from its object is at least a contributing factor for this complexity.

What I would like to claim is that language learning tasks and the resulting problems are equally complex in L1 and L2 acquisition, irrespective of the language learners' different generalizations. Once again this seems to be like learning chess: no matter how you try to learn the game, the knights' moves, for instance, remain more complex than those of the king.

If Meisel's rather speculative remarks are confirmed, we will have an explanation of the underlying principles according to which linguistic knowledge is internalized in natural language acquisition. Learners tend to prefer linguistic plans which correspond more or less directly to underlying semantic structure. It is only later in development that linguistic phenomena are acquired which are more complex in terms of linguistic processing, that is, in which underlying semantic units have to be reorganized. As shown above, the preference for performative simplicity does not lead learners to completely identical hypotheses about the structure of the target language; there are rather two lines of development both resulting in automatized linguistic knowledge about German word order.

STRATEGIES OF SIMPLIFICATION

In this section I will point to another very general aspect of automatization in natural language acquisition. Consider utterances like (11), (12) and (13), which are taken from the three types of unguided language development:

(11) (child L2 acquisition, Pienemann, 1979)
      warum Ø   machen aua?
      why   Ø you make   ouch?
(12) (adult L2 acquisition, Clahsen, 1980b)
      dann Ø   immer deutsch sprechen.
      then Ø we always German speak.
(13) (L1 acquisition)
      diese gleise Ø   mamma.
      these rails Ø bought mommy.

As indicated in the translations, either the subject NP (11, 12) or the predicate (13) is missing. One might possibly interpret these deletions as the result of incomplete acquisition: the learners have not yet realized that subject and predicate are obligatory constituents in German. But if we look at the entire developmental sequence, this interpretation turns out to be wrong, since deletions like (11), (12), and (13) do not appear in the initial stages. The hypothesis favored here, on the other hand, is that such deletions may occur as a consequence of the learner's attempt to avoid structures which constitute complex learning tasks. Clahsen (1980a) shows that at the beginning of L1 acquisition a verb is only deleted if it is redundant and its meaning can be inferred from other parts of the utterance, as in (14):

(14) hase Ø   lieb.
      hare Ø/ is nice.

As soon as children start to place verbs in front of the subject (+ Inversion) even non-redundant verbs are missing. Exactly at the time when Verb Second including Inversion has become obligatory, these deletions decrease to zero.

Pienemann (1979) shows a similar connection between subject deletion and Inversion in natural L2 acquisition. During the first 40 weeks of acquisition, when Inversion was not applied, there were no missing subjects either. Immediately before acquiring the rule subject deletions appeared. In the following 10 weeks learners used both, but as soon as Inversion was acquired as a rule, subject deletions decreased to zero again.

As it will be analyzed here, deletions not only accompany, but also prepare for the acquisition of Inversion. During a period of uncertainty a learner systematically reduces the number of obligatory contexts for the application of the rule by deleting one of the two constituents involved in the structural description. As mentioned above, Inversion can be regarded as a complex learning task. As a result, this operation cannot be automatized immediately—note that it takes learners some time before they apply Inversion obligatorily. During this transitional period the complexity of the task is reduced by diminishing the number of contexts. After having automatized Inversion, there is no need anymore for simplifying these structures, and the deletions vanish.

This example shows that a careful distinction should be made between a learner's internalized grammatical plans and the strategies for executing these plans (Clark & Clark, 1977; Meisel, 1980a). Surface structure errors cannot be directly interpreted as indicating insufficient acquisition of grammatical rules. Rather errors can have a positive function in language learning. In the process of automatizing complex grammatical plans, certain strategies of deletion are used which no doubt lead to deviations from the standard norm, but which vanish as soon as their preparatory function is accomplished.

SUMMARY

The starting point of this paper was Sajavaara's assumption that the lack of an automatized linguistic repertoire is one of the major reasons for foreign language students' inability to communicate fluently in the target language. As a consequence, detailed studies were called for of the processes by which learners in naturalistic situations attain automatization of their linguistic knowledge. On the basis of the Wuppertal projects on language acquisition two general characteristics of language learning processes in everyday interactions were presented:

(1) In spite of the general preference for performative simplicity, different hypotheses about the structure of the target language are stated in L1 and L2 acquisition, both resulting in automatized linguistic knowledge about German word order.

(2) During the acquisition of complex linguistic operations learners make use of strategies of simplification which help them to automatize their linguistic repertoire.

In this paper I have claimed that there is a greater chance of attaining fluency in a reasonable amount of time if foreign language teaching syllabusses are based on developmental information of the kind shown in 1 and 2 above.

REFERENCES

Bierwisch, M. (1963). *Grammatik des deutschen Verbs*. Berlin: Akademie Verlag.

Bloom, L. (1970). *Language development: Form and function in emerging grammars*. Cambridge, Mass., London: M.I.T. Press.

Brown, R. (1973). *A first language: The early stages*. Cambridge, Mass.: Harvard University Press.

Clahsen, H. (1980a). Variation in der frühkindlichen Sprachentwicklung. *Michigan Germanic Studies, 6*, 219–246.

Clahsen, H. (1980b). Psycholinguistic aspects of L2-acquisition: Word order phenomena in foreign workers' interlanguage. In S.W. Felix (Ed.), *Second language development: Trends and issues* (pp. 57–79). Tübingen: Narr.

Clark, H., & Clark, E. (1977). *Psychology and language: An introduction to psycholinguistics*. New York: Harcourt Brace Jovanovich.

Levelt, W.J.M. (1977). Skill theory and language teaching. *Studies in Second Language Acquisition, 1*, 53–70.

Meisel, J.M. (1980a). Etapes et itinéraires d'acquisition d'une langue seconde. *Champs Educatifs, 1*, 48–58.

Meisel, J.M. (1980b). Strategies of second language acquisition: More than one kind of simplification. *Wuppertales Arbeitspapiere zu Sprachwissenschaft, 3*, 1–53.

Meisel, J.M., Clahsen, H., & Pienemann, M. (1979). On determining developmental stages in natural second language acquisition. *Wuppertaler Arbeitspapiere zu Sprachwissenschaft, 2*, 1–53.

Miller, M. (1976). *Zur Logik der frühkindlichen Sprachentwicklung: Empirische Untersuchungen und Theoriediskussion*. Stuttgart: Klett.

Pienemann, M. (1979). *Der Zweitspracherwerb ausländischer Arbeiterkinder*. Unpublished doctoral dissertation, Gesamthochschule Wuppertal.

Roeper, T. (1973). Connecting children's language and linguistic theory. In T.E. Moore (Ed.), *Cognitive development and the acquisition of language* (pp. 187–196). New York: Academic Press.

Slobin, D.I. (1973). Cognitive prerequisites for the development of grammar. In C.A. Ferguson &

D.I. Slobin (Eds.), *Studies of child language development* (pp. 175–208). New York: Holt, Reinhart & Winston.

Slobin, D.I. (1978). *Universal and particular in the acquisition of language.* Unpublished manuscript.

Wode, H. (1976). Developmental sequences in naturalistic L2 acquisition. *Working Papers on Bilingualism, 11,* 1–31.

CHAPTER 7

Indexicality in Language and "Nonverbal Communication"

STARKEY DUNCAN, JR.
University of Chicago

As one who was beginning work on interaction during the time when advocates of context-free grammar were solemnly claiming the absolescence of all other approaches, I especially appreciate Professor Sajavaara's wide-ranging paper. The emphasis is squarely on language acquisition and language use in the context of both social conduct and individual information processing. I shall confine my remarks on Professor Sajavaara's paper to that aspect with which I have some research experience: the relation between language and interaction. I regard it just as implausible to claim that language proficiency can be adequately described without reference to situations of use—that is, interaction—as it is implausible to claim that conversation can be adequately described without reference to the linguistic code.

In the interest of fairness, one must point out that linguists have not been alone in their traditional efforts to study in isolation one aspect of a larger communicative whole. During the time that many linguists were vigorously refining the notion of a context-free grammar and applying it to language description, other investigators mainly experimental social psychologists—were rapidly developing the study of so-called nonverbal communication. The typical study of "nonverbal communication" not only focused on such things as body motion and voice quality to the exclusion of linguistic phenomena, but also attempted to understand isolated actions, such as gaze direction and filled pauses, to the exclusion of other nonverbal actions. The consistency of this extreme isolationist approach to interaction research was complete when investigators chose to ignore even the most fundamental insights of the rich legacy of linguistic research. It was as if investigators of nonverbal communication could not recognize that linguists had been concerned with at least some aspects of the communicative process for several hundred years. Linguists, on the other hand, could not recognize the deeply social nature of language acquisition and use. As a consequence, nonverbal researchers undertook to reinvent the wheel. In a neighboring province linguists were struggling to perfect a semi-circular device.

Contemporary investigators have before them the task of integrating the two separate areas of inquiry. Each area can make unique contributions to a more integrated research paradigm. At the least, linguists have long considered techniques of describing the structure of sequences of meaningful events. However, as Professor Sajavaara clearly points out, linguists must appreciate the fact that language co-occurs with other important communicative actions in interaction sequences. In my opinion, social psychologists must relax their obsession with nonverbal communication as a handy indicator of personality traits and realize that, even if this perspective is useful for some questions, it cannot be productively pursued apart from adequate descriptions of interaction structure.

Pressing issues for research on language use and interaction are very basic ones. I believe that most relevant phenomena relating to the conduct of interaction remain to be discovered. It is a most fertile area for innovative anthropological linguists. Experimental studies of hypothesized interactional phenomena have scarcely been considered by psycholinguists. In studies of interaction structure the debate has hardly begun on the relative merits of alternative approaches to describing that structure, while in linguistics this central question appears to be more open than ever before as linguists continue to expand the boundaries of their area. I am particularly concerned with issues of methodology, such as, for example, the sorts of evidence that are appropriate to support hypotheses of interaction structure.

Professor Sajavaara mentions many phenomena rarely encountered in linguistic grammars that we have observed to be fairly common elements in the videotapes that we have made of two-person conversations between speakers of American English. Examples would be (a) proper type and timing of auditor "back-channel" actions, such as "yeah," "m-hm," and head nods; (b) completing a speaker's sentence by the auditor; (c) the speaker's completing a sentence with a gesture; (d) the orderly exchange of speaking turns; and (e) initiating and reciprocating smiling. Finally, in some cases in which the speaker apparently believes the auditor fully understands what is to be said, the speaker may simply abandon a sentence before it is complete and move to the next one. All of these seem unexceptional to the participants and undisruptive to the flow of the interaction.

If we accept, if only momentarily and for purposes of argument, the desirability of more integrated research on language and nonverbal communication, then we must consider the functional basis on which such integration is possible. If language and nonverbal communication both occur in interaction but serve very different communicative functions, then more integrated study would seem misdirected; each element of interaction might appropriately be studied in its own right. Although this is a most complex topic, I would like to mention for purposes of discussion what I take to be the general direction of a response.

It seems to me that language and nonverbal communication are joined through the notion of indexicality. For a definition of indexicality, I shall draw extensively on the work of Silverstein (1976). For him, an indexical sign assigns values to one or more social categories applicable to the interaction situation in which it is used. The relation between the indexical sign and the social categories is described by a "rule of use": "a general function that describes the relationship between speech context, given as a set of variables, some of which must have specific values, and some portion of the utterance, some message fraction" (Silverstein, 1976, p. 26).

The indexical function of signs is sharply distinguished from the referential function, defined "as communication by propositions—predications descriptive of states of affairs—subject to verification in some cases of objects and events, taken as representations of truth in others" (p. 14). As Silverstein points out:

> It is this referential function of speech, and its characteristic sign mode, the semantico-referential sign, that has formed the basis for linguistic theory and linguistic analysis in the Western tradition (p. 14).
>
> All of our analytic techniques and formal descriptive machinery have been designed for referential signs, which contribute to referential utterances in referential speech events. . . . When we speak of linguistic categories, we mean categories of the referential kind. (p. 15)

While linguistics has concerned itself almost entirely with the referential aspect of language, indexicality is pervasive in language use. Silverstein suggests that "the sign modes of most of what goes on in the majority of speech events are not referential." He provides a number of examples of indexicality, ranging from the exotic to the mundane. More exotic would be the "mother-in-law" vocabulary of Dyirbal (Dixon, 1972), a language of the Australian aborigines. Dyirbal contains two sets of lexical items, one for everyday use and one for use when one's mother-in-law is present in the speech situation. Use of either set of vocabulary items clearly indexes one aspect of the relationship between the speaker and members of the audience. More mundane would be the operation of past tense in English, where the verb indexes a specific relation between the speech event and some time prior to the utterance. Similarly indexical is the operation of the English deictics "this" and "that."

Silverstein suggests that there are pure indexical expressions, mixed indexical-referential expressions, and pure referential expressions. My belief is that, while there may be pure indexical expressions, it is unlikely that there are any pure referential expressions. It seems likely that the use of any convention indexes one or more elements of the social situation, so that all convention-based action has an indexical aspect.

In any event, for the purpose of this discussion it is important to point out that various indexical tasks are accomplished in different ways by different languages. Let us say that a speaker makes a referential statement and wishes (or is obliged) also to indicate an assessment of its veracity. Depending on the language, this indexical business may be accomplished inflectionally, lexically, nonverbally, or through some combination of these means.

Indexicality is commonly associated with nonverbal communication. For example, facial expressions are often said to index in a very direct way the emotional state of the participant. Public interest in nonverbal communication seems to stem primarily from the belief that through unwitting nonverbal actions a participant may index certain "true," inner states that would otherwise remain hidden. Less titillating, perhaps, was our hypothesis (Duncan & Fiske, 1977) of the category "transition readiness" for participants in the conversations we observed. Through the use of certain signals using actions in syntax, intonation, paralanguage, and body motion, participants were said to index their relative readiness to proceed either to the next interaction unit within the speaking turn, or to an exchange of the speaking turns, depending on the signal used. (It would appear that nonverbal communication contributes in a much more specialized and narrow way to the referential aspect of communication.)

Both language and nonverbal communication are deeply involved in the essential indexical process. In some cases language and nonverbal communication may redundantly index the same social categories; in other cases, the two modalities may be accomplishing quite different indexical tasks. In any event, it would seem that careful, systematic study of indexical expression—itself a sharp departure from an exclusive concern with the referential aspect of language— would be an especially productive avenue for integrated linguistic-nonverbal research.

I believe that the indexical process is continuously served in two distinguishable aspects of the interaction process: (a) the choice and ratification of conventions, and (b) stylistic or strategic variations in the performance of conventions chosen and ratified by the participants. For example, I assume that within the Anglo-American culture of the interactants on our videotapes, there are a number of different conventions for dealing with the exchange of speaking turns and related phenomena. Assuming for the moment the accuracy of our hyopthesized signals and rules, it appears that a single convention was chosen by all the participants we have observed. This particular convention presumably indexes certain characteristics of the participants, their relationship to each other. and other aspects of the interaction situation. Once the convention is adopted in the interaction, it can be used to index other social categories, such as the transition readiness mentioned above, a participant's status as speaker or auditor, and the degree to which the auditor is successfully following the speaker. Thus, both choice and performance of convention contribute to the indexing of social categories by participants. I shall comment further on this notion as we discuss Professor Tannen's paper later this week.

In the research literature there are a number of manifestations of interest in aspects of the indexical process. I shall briefly mention a few of these as examples, time constraints precluding more detailed discussion:

1.   There has been interest by linguists, sociolinguists, and psychologists in such phenomena as language style, use of "formal" and "informal" per-

sonal pronouns, and forms of address. In each case, efforts are made to describe the social categories indexed by a given form.

2. Several authors have commented on the process of "metacommunication," in which participants define and comment on the type of interaction that is taking place, such as "joking," "play," "formal," and the like. I take it that "metacommunication" in this sense refers to a special and rather small subset of indexical relations.

3. As mentioned above, all of the nonverbal-communication research literature is concerned with indexicality in one form or another. It is worth noting, however, that the kind of state involved in the transition-readiness hypothesis is rather different from the assortment of emotional states typically associated with nonverbal communication. Once again, the subset of emotional states seems rather small within the total set of social categories indexed in interaction.

4. Finally, there has been considerable interest recently in the use of deictics in both language and gestures.

This cursory list, taken together with Silverstein's examples, may begin to suggest the type, if not the range, of indexical phenomena. It seems reasonable to suggest that in most, if not all, language communities, both language and nonverbal actions continuously convey a rich and complex array of indexical information. The context of this information, the manner in which it is conveyed, and the respective contributions of language and nonverbal communication—these issues present a major challenge to contemporary investigators.

REFERENCES

Dixon, R.M.W. (1972). *The Dyirbal language of North Queensland.* Cambridge: Cambridge University Press.

Duncan, S.D., Jr., & Fiske, D.W. (1977). *Face-to-face interaction: Research, methods and theory.* Hillsdale, N.J.: Lawrence Erlbaum.

Silverstein, M. (1976). Shifters, linguistic categories, and cultural description. In K.H. Basso & H.A. Selby (Eds.), *Meaning in anthropology* (pp. 11–55). Albuquerque: University of New Mexico Press.

CHAPTER 8

A Note on Second Language Speech Production

JÜRGEN M. MEISEL
Gesamthochschule Wuppertal

Second language speech production is obviously too vast an area to reasonably be discussed as a whole. Even when using Kari Sajavaara's presentation (this volume) as a starting point for the discussion, one suffers from having to make a choice, since an overview touches upon a great number of interesting points worth treating in more detail. In this brief paper I will, after some general remarks, restrict the discussion to one aspect of the topic; I will suggest that Sajavaaara's assumption that "successful naturalistic language acquirers are more concerned with communication than with form" (p. 56) cannot capture some of the intricacies of the relation between social-psychological parameters and second language development.

ON THE RELEVANCE OF LINGUISTIC DESCRIPTIONS FOR AN ANALYSIS OF SPEECH PRODUCTION

To begin with, I want to point out that I disagree in at least one aspect with the general approach taken by Sajavaara: in accordance with an increasing number of recent publications, a distinction is made between "structurally oriented" and "communicatively oriented" research. One might agree that there has been an overemphasis on formal properties of language in the past which should be counterbalanced. Nevertheless, it is regrettable that some of Sajavaara's statements now seem to imply that the study of formal properties should be replaced by the study of communicative aspects of language development and use.

I must admit though, that throughout Sajavaara's paper it has not been entirely clear to me exactly what his position is with respect to this problem. Criticism is never addressed to a specific publication or author; names are given only for those authors whose views support Sajavaara. To give an example, it might very well be argued that linguistic descriptions alone cannot be sufficient to explain language use; but, when put this way, the claim is a trivial one with which most linguists would easily agree, and is one of the basic assumptions underlying all psycholinguistic research. On the other hand, it is hard to see what might be meant by the expression, a "theoretical linguistic model" cannot be sufficient; I would contend that any non-theoretical model would fail even more miserably. Furthermore, it is obviously incorrect to say that "linguists' descriptions of languages are static," for there are non-static and even dynamic (which is not necessarily the same) models available.[1] My suspicion is that the distinction between a "linguistically oriented" and a "communicatively oriented" approach is rather artificial, and that the sometimes violent attacks against the former are directed at a straw man.

Admitting that interaction should be the starting point for an analysis of speech production does not imply that speakers, in executing speech plans, do not use units which correspond to linguistically defined entities. It seems to me that in view of the evidence collected by psycholinguistic research over the past twenty years, a statement like the following is untenable:

> It was assumed that the constructs of linguistic description were also units relevant to the production and perception of messages or to the process of language learning. Such an assumption is unfounded. (Sajavaara, p. 52)

This could only be maintained if interpreted as an argument against the exclusive relevance of such descriptions; as has been pointed out by Ingram (1971) and many others, algorithmic competence models can hardly account adequately for processes of language use.[2] A less trivial interpretation of the statement, however, implies that structurally defined segments of speech—syllables, constituents, including the sentence, abstract underlying structures and surface structures, rules, etc.—are irrelevant for speech production. Such a view, it appears to me, cannot be backed up by referring to Clark and Clark (1977). On the contrary, Clark and Clark favor what is called the "skeleton and constituent model," in which special importance is given to almost all units of linguistic description, from distinctive features up to surface structures of sentences. This includes arguments in favor of a more abstract theory of "words" than seems to underly Sajavaara's claim to the effect that words "are primary and the language 'machine' is not entirely dissimilar to . . . a finite state grammar" (p. 54).

It is not impossible that I myself am fighting a straw man, since Sajavaara's "model of message processing" apparently does allow for the inclusion of linguistic structures. But statements such as the one quoted are, at the least, misleading, and it seemed safe, therefore, to emphasize the possibly trivial claim that constructs of linguistic description are relevant units in the production and perception of messages.

---

[1] I will refer here to only one of a number of such approaches to language, that taken by scholars like Charles-James N. Bailey and Elizabeth Traugott; for an overview, see Bailey, 1981.

[2] For an application of this argument to natural L2 acquisition see Meisel (1980a).

SOCIAL-PSYCHOLOGICAL FACTORS IN THE FORMATION
OF LEARNER TYPES

The first point I want to make deals with natural second language acquisition and is concerned with the relation between social-psychological factors and the learners orientation, and the resulting kinds of L2 production. Sajavaara believes that language acquisition in natural settings, whether L1 or L2, leads "without any special problems to thorough internalization of the language(s)" (p. 45) and to nativelike performance, whereas foreign language teaching very rarely achieves this goal. The explanation he offers can be summarized, I believe, as follows: (1) "a high level of acculturation and integrative motivation" (p. 56) results in (2) the successful L2 acquirer being primarily interested in communication, as opposed to form; (3) as a consequence, L2 is acquired unconsciously, and this again (4) leads to nativelike production, whereas conscious language learning normally only makes possible the production of grammatical strings under favorable conditions.

Much of this is corroborated by our own research dealing with the acquisition of German by adult workers who have immigrated from Italy, Spain and Portugal.[3] Data from cross-sectional as well as from longitudinal studies indicate, however, that the relation between social-psychological factors, speakers' orientation, their approach to acquisition and/or learning of L2, and second language speech production is by no means as straightforward as it might appear. To begin with an evaluation of the end-product: in the case of working class immigrants to various countries of Europe and North America, there can be no question of "nativelike fluency without any special problems"; rather, this would be the exceptional case. As for the "good" or "successful" learner, I must admit that I do not quite know what these qualifications refer to. Sajavaara apparently uses them as denoting "communicatively successful," but defining the terms in this way would beg the question. The crucial aspect of good and successful L2 speech seems to be "fluency"; unfortunately, we are not given a sufficiently precise explanation of this term either. Only in the very last paragraph of the paper is there an indication that fluency "does not always imply an uninterrupted flow of speech that is sequentially and grammatically irreproachable," contrary

---

[3]This work was carried out by our research team, ZISA (Zweitspracherwerb italienischer und spanischer Arbeiter), established at the Gesamthochschule Wuppertal in 1974 and transferred to the Universität Hamburg in 1980. All the members of the team over the last years have contributed to our discussions; I therefore want to thank the present and former members for their contributions, especially Harald Clahsen and Manfred Pienemann. The cross-sectional study was financially supported by the Minister für Wissenschaft und Forschung des Landes Nordrhein-Westfalen (research grant of the Stiftung Volkswagenwerk (1978–1982)). The preliminary results of these projects are summarized by Clahsen, Meisel, and Pienemann.

to what one might have suspected from the preceding argumentation. This, however, leaves us with the following definition:

> Fluency equals the communicative acceptability of the speech act, or "communicative fit," and expectations concerning this fit vary according to the situation.

If I interpret this correctly, successful L2 acquisition is defined as resulting in fluency of speech production, which in turn depends on situational factors (including the listeners' expectations), thus allowing for non-perfect utterances according to the criterion of situational adequacy.

Our own findings concerning immigrant workers' acquisition of German strongly support Sajavaara's claim that some learners are more concerned with communication, whereas others appear to pay more attention to formal aspects of language. We did not find, however, a simple relation of cause and effect between these approaches to L2 and social-psychological factors on the one hand, and successful acquisition on the other. This has to do with the fact that not all L2 acquirers are interested in meeting the expectations of the L2 speech community, and those who are do not necessarily maintain this interest to the same degree over longer periods of time. Sajavaara misses this point by simply extending the inter-actionist viewpoint from L1 to L2 and by overemphasizing the necessity of adjusting one's speech to the listener's knowledge, beliefs, attitudes, feelings, etc. The learner's performance is not only a "compromise between task demands and available capacity," although these are certainly crucial factors; the learner's own needs also strongly influence the decision of what solution is to be preferred in the attempt to achieve this compromise. In the early stages of natural L2 acquisition, the learner is necessarily what has been called a "cultural outsider," and "the need to communicate functional information [as opposed to social information],[4] by the most efficient means available, exerts an initial pull towards an optimal state of simplification" (Littlewood, 1975). The question, however, is whether more complex needs ever arise or whether the learner ever has the opportunity or ever wishes to be anything else than a cultural outsider. As long as there is no aspiration to become a cultural insider, speech need not "represent normal, acceptable and relaxed language behavior" (Sajavaara, p. 63), since what would normally stigmatize the native speaker is merely taken "as the outward sign of his role as a foreigner" (Littlewood, 1975). To use the metaphor Sajavaara (1977, and this volume) repeatedly refers to, communication—linguistic and otherwise—is a game where some of the rules may be ignored or may at least be occasionally violated by the players: they are playing without competing.

---

[4]One should not quarrel, at this point, about the adequacy of a model which distinguishes between social and functional information. All, or most, models of language functions make a distinction of this kind, although they frequently break it down into a more sophisticated list of diverse functions. There seems to be little disagreement, however, about the fact that L2 learners at some point neglect some of these functions so that they can "get the message across."

The consequence of the learner's restricted repertoire of communicative roles is not only, as pointed out by Sajavaara himself, that the native speaker's expectations differ from those in normal L1 settings. The learner also has a choice between different strategies which might make possible the above mentioned "compromise" in speech production, and this choice depends, among other things, on the learner's orientation towards either segregation from the target language community or integration with it. In case of the first option, there is no need to strive to meet the normal expectations of an L1 listener; the second option, however, forces the learner to behave linguistically like a native speaker, abandoning the privileges of the cultural outsider.

In what way will this affect second language speech production? Sajavaara points out, basing his assumption on Levelt's (1977) skill theory, that nativelike speech behavior requires that the "programs needed are available as automatic processes." Quite frequently in L2 production this is not the case—or at least not to a degree which would allow coping with the more complex tasks of language processing. The compromise, thus, can only be reached by simplifying one's speech. We have, on different occasions (Meisel, 1980b; Meisel, Clahsen & Pienemann, 1979), discussed structural properties of simplification processes, some of which correspond to the list of "problems" given by Sajavaara. It would go beyond the constraints on this paper to give more details; one point, however, should be emphasized: simplification is defined as a *process* of speech production and perception; merely listing surface characteristics of interlanguage varieties would not be an adequate treatment of it. Instead, simplification can be explained as the choice of cognitively less complex solutions to problems of language processing. Cognitive complexity, in turn, is defined in terms of principles such as Slobin's (1973) "operating principles." I have tried to show (Meisel, 1980b) that L2 acquirers, not unlike children acquiring a first language, prefer solutions which are in accordance with such operating principles (e.g., Slobin's Operating Principle D: "Avoid interruption or rearrangement of linguistic units," and Operating Principle E: "Underlying semantic relations should be marked overtly and clearly.") This holds true even in cases where L1 and L2 share the same kind of structure (e.g., subject-verb inversion in interrogatives), and which should be expected to represent easy learning tasks if positive transfer was an adequate way of accounting for processes underlying L2 production. The choice of less complex solutions can be further motivated by Slobin's (1977) observation that language learners at early stages tend to follow the first two of four "charges": (1) be clear and (2) be processible; only later do they "attend more closely to the third and fourth charges as well" (Slobin, 1977): (3) be quick and easy, and (4) be expressive. The latter two fulfill more communicative needs and correspond to what has been called above "social information"; this brings us back to the question whether such needs necessarily arise for all L2 learners.

It has been implicit in the foregoing discussion that the development of such needs is not merely a matter of "earlier" or "later" in the process of L2 acquisition; a non-assimilatory orientation may never allow an interest in social information to develop. This has led Meisel, Clahsen, and Pienemann (1979) to postulate a model of L2 acquisition which predicts that even if learners continue to acquire new rules, thus passing through a sequence of developmental stages, one will find different interlanguage varieties at each stage, depending on the degree and on the kinds of simplification used by the learners. This latter point about simplification leads to the problem of judging fluency in L2 speech, and to the role of social-psychological factors in the acquisition of fluency. I have argued elsewhere (Meisel, 1977, 1980b) that at least two kinds of simplification have to be distinguished according to different functions in the course of L2 development: (a) elaborative simplification, which can be interpreted as a learning aid that facilitates the next step towards the target grammar. This is supported by Sajavaara who writes that speakers may "facilitate speech production in order to reach higher levels of fluency without distorting the message"; speakers may even avoid structures which are already at their disposal (Meisel, 1980b; Sajavaara, this volume). (b) Restrictive simplification, which facilitates the use of the internalized linguistic competence without necessarily contributing to its further elaboration. Both kinds of simplification may occasionally lead to identical structural patterns, for "simplicity" is defined in terms of cognitive complexity, and the two kinds merely differ in their functions. Which of these functions is operative can normally be determined only by the developmental context. It is the choice of the one kind of simplification rather than the other, I want to claim, which is strongly influenced by social-psychological factors, such as the desire to assimilate, among others. This claim is corroborated by the findings of our research group (Meisel, 1980b). 45 learners in our cross-sectional study were grouped according to language internal criteria distinguishing between users of predominantly restrictive simplification and nonusers. These groupings were matched against the results of an analysis of the social-psychological data on the 45 learners.[5] The analysis consisted of groupings on the basis of 35 variables per person by means of a clustering algorithm; a factor analysis was used to represent the relations between the variables, the principle goal being to determine group differentiating factors; the validity of the groupings was checked by using a discriminant analysis. Matching the linguistic groups with the social-psychological groups produced very encouraging results; the discriminant analysis revealed a reliability of 95% for the separation of the linguistic groups; it thus strongly supported the relevance of the given language internal groupings (= kinds of simplification) for the distribution of the social data.

At this point I see a major disagreement between our findings and the claims made by Sajavaara. Our distinction between learners using restrictive or elab-

---

[5]The computerized analysis was designed and executed by Michael Artmann, Universität Münster.

orative simplification does not correspond to Sajavaara's distinction between acquirers primarily interested in communication, and those primarily interested in form. Rather, one can find speakers that focus on the communication in the group of learners preferring restrictive simplification, and learners using elaborative simplification who are "monitor over-users" in Krashen's (1978) terminology. In other words, "a high level of acculturation and integrative motivation" need not result in primary interest in communication and in nativelike production. On the contrary, just because of their anxiety to meet the expectations of the L2 speech community, some learners who are oriented towards assimilation tend to avoid all risks; they are mainly concerned about the target norm even if they have to pay for this with considerably reduced communicative force, and occasionally restrict themselves to monostylistic performance. On the other hand, lack of an assimilatory motivation need not lead to non-fluent speech. Some learners of this kind produce stylistically more variable speech which—in spite of frequent grammatical deviation—is intuitively judged by native speakers as more "normal, acceptable and relaxed language behavior."

To sum up, we support Sajavaara's claim that some learners are more concerned with communication, and that others concentrate on formal aspects of language. This partitioning, however, does not correspond to the distinction between an assimilatory and non-assimilatory orientation, although a learner's orientation does allow predictions about the kinds of simplification surfacing in the learner's speech. Most, or even all, learners use simplifications at some point in L2 development; some may never give these up, even as they procede through different stages of L2 acquisition. But it is apparently an entirely different matter whether a person tends to avoid any possibility of making an error (for example, by restricting speech to minimal expansions of phrase structure rules and by avoiding all possible variation), and whether someone makes use of a large grammatical repertoire, even if this causes a number of errors. This distinction between learners, I would contend, cannot be explained by means of social-psychological factors, but rather by the personality of the learner and other individual differences; the question of whether a person likes to take risks or not seems to be more relevant than "level of acculturation and integrative motivation." I suspect that it is the risk-avoiding type of learner who corresponds to Krashen's "monitor over-user." As for establishing criteria for L2 speech production fluency, I would like to support the view that fluency might be defined in terms of "communicative acceptability." This implies, however, that the idea of a cause-and-effect relation between social-psychological variables and successful acquisition of fluent L2 production has to be given up.

REFERENCES

Bailey, C.-J.N. (1981). Theory, description, and differences among linguists. Or, what keeps linguistics from becoming a science. *Language and Communication, 1*, 39–66.

Clahsen, H., Meisel, J. M., & Pienemann, M. (1983). *Deutsch als Zweitsprache: Der Spracherwerb ausländischer Arbeiter.* Tübingen: Narr.

Clark, H.H., & Clark, E.V. (1977). *Psychology and language: An introduction to psycholinguistics.* New York: Harcourt Brace Jovanovich.

Ingram, E.A. (1971). A further note on the relationship between psychological and linguistic theories. *International Review of Applied Linguistics, 9,* 335–346.

Krashen, S.D. (1978). The Monitor Model for second language acquisition. In R.C. Gingras (Ed.), *Second language acquisition and foreign language teaching* (pp. 1–26). Arlington, Va.: Center for Applied Linguistics.

Levelt, W.J.M. (1977). Skill theory and language teaching. *Studies in Second Language Acquisition, 1,* 53–70.

Littlewood, W.T. (1975, August). *The transmission of functional information and social information in learners' speech.* Paper presented at the AILA Congress, Stuttgart.

Meisel, J.M. (1977). Linguistic simplification: A study of immigrant workers' speech and foreigner talk. In S.P. Corder & E. Roulet (Eds.), *The notions of simplification, interlanguages and pidgins and their relation to second language pedagogy* (pp. 88–113). Genève: Droz.

Meisel, J.M. (1980a). Etapes et itinéraires d'acquisition d'une langue seconde. *Champs Educatifs, 1,* 48–58.

Meisel, J.M. (1980b). Strategies of second language acquisition: More than one kind of simplification. *Wuppertaler Arbeitspapiere zu Sprachwissenschaft, 3,* 1–53.

Meisel, J.M., Clahsen, H., & Pienemann, M. (1979). On determining developmental stages in natural second language acquisition. *Wuppertaler Arbeitspapiere zu Sprachwissenschaft, 2,* 1–53.

Sajavaara, K. (1977). Contrastive linguistics past and present and a communicative approach. In K. Sajavaara & J. Lehtonen (Eds.), *Contrastive Papers* (Jyväskylä Contrastive Studies, 4, 9–30). Jyväskylä: University of Jyväskylä.

Slobin, D.I. (1973). Cognitive prerequisites for the development of grammar. In C.A. Ferguson & D.I. Slobin (Eds.), *Studies of child language development* (pp. 175–208). New York: Holt, Rinehart & Winston.

Slobin, D.I. (1977). Language change in childhood and history. In J.T. Macnamara (Ed.), *Language learning and thought.* New York: Academic Press.

CHAPTER 9

Production Strategies in L2 Performance

MANFRED RAUPACH
Gesamthochschule Kassel

Several of the preceding papers have demanded that psycholinguistic research account for all relevant factors in human communication. Comparable tendencies to expand research domains in the direction of communicatively oriented research can be observed in other disciplines as well. The interests of different disciplines thus tend to converge, so that finally no clear boundaries can be drawn between, for example, psycholinguistic, sociolinguistic, and pragmalinguistic points of view. In discussing language production models, therefore, one should set forth precisely what one expects from them at the outset.

The main interest of existing work in second language (L2) production models derives from the need for a new theoretical framework that accounts for a psycholinguistically oriented approach to foreign language learning and teaching. It is above all the notion of "strategy" that, in consequence of an approach claiming to be "focused on the learner," has attracted the attention of many writers (e.g., Bialystok, 1979; Færch & Kasper, 1980; Hamayan & Tucker 1979; Porquier, 1979; Selinker, 1972; Sharwood Smith, 1979; Tarone, Cohen & Dumas, 1976; Váradi, 1980). Hence, Kari Sajavaara is quite in line with this tendency when he stresses the importance of strategies by accepting a distinction between processes, which take place in the individual and are, by definition, not open to overt manipulation, and strategies, which are employed by the individual and, thus, can be activated by means of "overt teaching."

In the following I want to offer some comments on the concept of strategy and on the requirements it should meet in a model of L2 production.

Owing to the influence of cognitive psychology, the notion of "strategy" has come to be used in research on second language processing, although rather loosely and sometimes controversially. Studying the processes of learning or attaining a concept, Bruner, Goodnow, and Austin (1956) developed the idea of "strategies of decision-making," which referred to the regularities learners show in their pattern of decisions in the acquisition, retention, and utilization of information. Strategies have as one of their main objectives the property of minimizing the cognitive strain in concept formation. They change with the nature of the concept being sought, with the situation, with the consequences of behavior, and other factors. The question of whether the subject is or is not conscious of the strategy used is of no particular interest. In full agreement with Bruner et al., Gilmartin, Newell, and Simon (1976) and Simon (1979) define strategies, or programs, as "intervening variables between task environment and performance." In their information processing model of human memory, strategies have the genuine function of controlling the use of memory storage and processing time. If the constraints built into the model and the strategies used are correctly specified, the best performance of the model is claimed to be close to the best performance of humans in the same task. Thus it seems possible, with this type of model, to predict human performance on a new task, one of the challenging research questions being: How does a person create new and better strategies from previous ones? This view implies the statement that strategies are modifiable by learning and at least partially under the voluntary control of the subject.

In psycholinguistic research, the term strategy used in connection with language behavior refers to certain behavioral inductions that are involved in the perception/production of speech in L1 performance.[1] The exploration of these decoding/encoding operations serves primarily to verify hypotheses about the "psychological reality" of structures and rules in transformational grammars (Bever, 1970). It is generally accepted that strategies in the defined sense do not necessarily follow the sequence of transformations that are established in the linguistic analysis of a sentence. Bever illustrates this point in a detailed discussion of perceptual strategies such as segmentation, semantic labeling and sequential labeling.[2] Bierwisch (1975) comments more particularly on production strategies and arrives at the formulation of some requirements that are essential for the development of production models.[3] In current research on the acquisition

---

[1]It is evident that a more ambitious discussion of the concept of strategy would have to take into account a set of definitions that have been developed in other disciplines. One might think of Bernstein's (1971) "speech variants," which have been taken up under the name of "verbal strategies" by Hawkins (1977), and others, and which are described as "patterns of linguistic choices which are specific to a particular context" or of Starkey Duncan's definition given during this conference as a "product of choice in the frame of conventions."

[2]Considering the relation between a particular strategy ("Strategy A," a segmentation strategy) and a transformational grammar, Bever (1970) gives the following clarification:

Clearly, Strategy A presupposes the distinction between internal and external structural relations. But there is no obvious way in which the grammatical transformations may themselves be transmuted into subcomponents of Strategy A. Rather Strategy A is implemented on the basis of knowledge of the possibility that a particular external form class sequence could correspond to an internal structure; the possible external sequences are, of course, enumerated by the transformations, but not necessarily in a way that can be directly utilized in the process of perception. (p. 292)

[3] Bierwisch, by analizing errors in spontaneous speech, finds support for his assumptions concerning the relations between strategies and rules, and attributes certain specific characteristics such as *Verdichtung* and *Verkürzung,* to the strategies that do not hold for linguistic transformations.

and teaching of second languages, as it is presented in the paper of Sajavaara, the term strategy has been used with at least two fundamentally different meanings. One group of researchers, among them Meisel and Clahsen, has adopted the psycholinguistic notion, extending the suggestions of Bever, Bierwisch, and others to the description of production strategies in L2 and to the developmental stages in the process of natural second language acquisition. Their discussion centers on the relations that exist, in the framework of a transformational grammar, between syntactic rules and strategies. In this approach the problem of the learner's consciousness or awareness in the use of certain strategies is not a crucial one, quite in contrast to the concerns of a second group of researchers who, like Sajavaara, postulate the existence of "overt teachable strategies" in L2 processing. Most of the investigators belonging to this second group have concentrated on the learning and teaching of L2 in the "formal classroom setting," and not in a "natural setting," as Sajavaara puts it. It seems to be characteristic of their definition of a strategy that the notion of "problem" forms an integral part of it: "The essential thing is that strategies can only be applied when something is acknowledged to be problematic" (Jordens, 1977). The interest in research on learning and teaching an L2 has resulted not so much in a discussion of the theoretical status of strategies within a model of L2 production, but rather in lists of observed or postulated production strategies of L2 learners. Based on the highly detailed discussion of Færch and Kasper (1980), the following classes of strategies can be set up:

1. Formal reduction strategies. These are strategies that help the learner "to avoid producing non-fluent or incorrect utterances." In activating formal reduction strategies, the learner decides to "communicate by means of a 'reduced' system"; for example, by simplification.
2. Functional reduction strategies. These are strategies that result in "goal reduction." The learner decides to abandon or modify the original intention and reduces the communicative goal in order to avoid a problem. Subtypes of functional reduction strategies are: topic avoidance, message avoidance, and meaning replacement, as well as modal and personality reductions, by which the learner "conveys a distorted picture of his personality" (Harder, 1980).
3. Achievement strategies. These are strategies that help the learner in reaching a communicative goal by expanding the learner's communicative resources. These problem-solving (not problem-avoiding) strategies may include, according to some authors, strategies aimed at solving retrieval problems. They embrace non-verbal strategies such as mime and gesture, as well as cooperative strategies involving direct or indirect appeals to the interlocutor. The main subtypes are, however, code-switching from L1 to L2, inter- and intralingual transfer and the so-called interlanguage based strategies that result in (over)generalization, paraphrase, word coinage, and restructuring.

In contrast to the previously mentioned psycholinguistic conception, in which strategies are related mainly to syntactic and semantic aspects of sentences, the overview given here implies a much broader understanding of strategies, including among other things the speaker's intention and non-verbal behavior. Models that are to account for variables of this kind would necessarily have to incorporate not only strategies of L2 production, but communication strategies in general. There are additional requirements the concept of strategy must meet if it is to reflect a fuller understanding of the mental processes involved in second language performance and if, as suggested in Sajavaara's paper, the concept is expected to help prepare the ground for improving a learner's fluency.

The interpretation of language processing, particularly second language processing, as a series of procedures such as decision-making, hypothesis-testing and problem-solving connects the concept of a strategy in an L2 production model with definitions developed in cognitive psychology and in psycholinguistics, as they were summarized above. Apart from this general aspect, however, certain distinctions prove to be especially relevant for L2 production:

1. Sajavaara's distinction between "more or less automated processes" and conscious procedures like strategies. This distinction turns out to be crucial if strategies are claimed to be "activated by means of overt teaching."
2. The distinction between global and local strategies, or strategies and tactics (Leontiev, 1973).[4] As stated above, one property of strategies as they are conceived in cognitive psychology is their flexibility. This is true, in the first place, for local strategies. In connection with L2 production, these strategies are assumed not only to change with the task, the situation, the outcome of behavior, and so on, but to be constantly exposed to revision, old strategies being completely abandoned in favor of new ones.
3. The distinction between strategies coming from autonomous internal developments and those which are imposed from outside. The former depend on the degree of proficiency the learner has reached in the acquisition process. They may mark a necessary intermediate phase in the learner's activation of interlanguage. It must be questioned whether attempts to work on them by "overt manipulation" are successful, or even advisable.
4. In cognitive psychology, the performance of humans or of models can obviously be classified qualitatively; this enables the researcher to make judgments about the effectiveness of underlying strategies. With reference to L2 production, judgments of this kind are much more intricate. In fact, classifications like those of Færch and Kasper reveal that most of the strategies pointed out in connection with L2 production are misleading: either

---

[4]For the distinction between high-level decisions, occasionally equated with strategies (Sharwood Smith, 1979), and automated lower level decisions see Levelt, 1977; also, Miller, Galanter, & Pribram, 1960, and their definitions of plans, strategies and tactics.

they result in non-nativelike performance—true of all reduction strategies, such as code-switching and (over)generalization—or they cause the speaker to relinquish the original utterance intention by avoidance strategies. So, what are the best strategies to teach?

5. The distinction between acquisition or learning strategies on the one hand and production or communication strategies on the other. A description of the relations between these two types is another objective for research on second language processing.

6. The distinction between language-specific and learner-specific strategies. In view of the enormous variety of strategies different learners display in their second language performance, one of the most demanding problems consists in determining which strategies are language-specific or representative of certain groups of learners, and which ones are idiosyncratic. Since individual learners activate a multitude of strategies that remain unexplained, if not unnoticed, this final distinction involves a crucial methodological problem; that is, finding out how production strategies can best be revealed.

To conclude, the notion of ''overt teachable strategies'' may come from premature expectations on the part of those concerned with foreign language teaching, rather than being the result of empirical reflections on L2 production. The adoption of existing psycholinguistic concepts of strategies can obviously only account in part for the specific strategies in L2 production. We are still in need of more insight into the mental processes that are involved in L1 and L2 performance; our production models should reflect more thoroughly the fundamental differences that exist between these two modes of communication.

REFERENCES

Bernstein, B. (1971). A critique of the concept of compensatory education. In B. Bernstein (Ed.), *Class, codes and control* (vol. 1, pp. 190–201). London, Henley, & Boston: Routledge & Kegan Paul.

Bever, T.G. (1970). The cognitive basis for linguistic structures. In J.R. Hayes (Ed.), *Cognition and the development of language* (pp. 279–362). New York: John Wiley & Sons.

Bialystok, E. (1979). The role of conscious strategies in second language proficiency. *The Canadian Modern Language Review, 35,* 372–394.

Bierwisch, M. (1975). Psycholinguistik: Interdependenz kognitiver Prozesse und linguistischer Strukturen. *Zeitschrift für Psychologie, 183,* 1–52.

Bruner, J.S., Goodnow, J.J., & Austin, G.A. (1956). *A study of thinking.* New York: John Wiley & Sons.

Færch, C., & Kasper, G. (1980). Processes and strategies in foreign language learning and communication. *Interlanguage Studies Bulletin, 5,* 47–118.

Gilmartin, K.J., Newell, A., & Simon, H.A. (1976). A program modeling short-term memory under strategy control. In C.N. Cofer (Ed.), *The structure of human memory* (pp. 15–30). San Francisco: Freeman.

Hamayan, E.V., & Tucker, G.R. (1979). Strategies of communication used by native and non-native speakers of French. *Working Papers on Bilingualism, 17,* 83–96.

Harder, P. (1980). Discourse as self-expression and the reduced identity of the L2 learner. *Applied Linguistics, 1,* 262–270.

Hawkins, P.R. (1977). *Social class, the nominal group and verbal strategies,* London, Henley, & Boston: Routledge & Kegan Paul.

Jordens, P. (1977). Rules, grammatical intuitions and strategies in foreign language learning. *Interlanguage Studies Bulletin, 1,* 53–70.

Leontiev, A.N. (1973). Le principe heuristique dans la perception, la production et la compréhension du langage. *Bulletin de Psychologie, 26,* 260–269.

Levelt, W.J.M. (1977). Skill theory and language teaching. *Studies in Second Language Acquisition, 1,* 53–70.

Miller, G.A., Galanter, E., & Pribram, K.H. (1960). *Plans and the structure of behavior.* New York: Holt, Rinehart & Winston.

Porquier, R. (1979). Stratégies de communication en langue non-maternelle. *Travaux du Centre de Recherches Sémiologiques, 33,* 39–52.

Selinker, L. (1972). Interlanguage. *International Review of Applied Linguistics, 10,* 209–231.

Sharwood Smith, M. (1979). Strategies, language transfer and the simulation of the second language learner's mental operations. *Language Learning, 29,* 345–361.

Simon, H.A. (1979). *Models of thought.* New Haven, London: Yale University Press.

Tarone, E., Cohen, A.D., & Dumas, G. (1976). A closer look at interlanguage terminology: A framework for communication strategies. *Working Papers in Bilingualism, 9,* 76–90.

Váradi, T. (1980). Strategies of target language learner communication: Message adjustment. *International Review of Applied Linguistics, 18,* 59–71.

CHAPTER 10

On Fluency in Second Language Speech

JOCHEN REHBEIN
Ruhr-Universität Bochum

In reading Sajavaara's paper on "Second Language Speech Production: Factors Affecting Fluency" one is surprised by the fact that very little is directly said about "fluency." This is probably due to the intention of the author to deliver a research report and to sum up a large number of "factors" (or "variables") relevant to language production in general and, as such, to fluency in particular. Such an intention reveals a methodological problem not only in this paper but in most language acquisition research. The "multitude of factors" in second language production—how do they work in real communication? Even though the model may be "dynamic," could one derive interpretations of real instances of the interplay of these factors from models like the one given here. Some of the factors are relevant in some situations of speech, others are not—how can one impose order on the anarchy of factors? Confronted with a real segment of talk produced in a second language, how can we find out which factor is involved in what way? I think the "factor" model of research common to psychology, and sociology, and to psycholinguistics and sociololinguistics as well, must be submitted to methodological questioning (cf. also the component model of Leeson, 1975).

In the following I shall try to outline some hypotheses on fluency in second language speech and make a plea for starting from documents of actual speech production (e.g., transcriptions), and for following an interpretative method of analysis. A similar course is adopted by Dechert (1980), Fillmore (1979), Raupach (1980) and Sajavaara and Lehtonen (1980).

MONITORING ACTIVITIES AND GLOBAL PREFABRICATION

The first hypothesis is related to the processing of planning and uttering activities.

This study resulted from an investigation of verbal capabilities of the second immigrant generation in Germany and was supported in part by the "Grundschulprojekt Krefeld." I am grateful to Ayşe Öktem and Halis Benzer for their help in transcribing the recordings.

The following examples originate from Turkish speakers' German speech, the first three ((E1)–(E3)) from an experiment in which Turkish pupils were asked to reproduce a short story read to them in German. After having futilely tried to reproduce it in German, they were given the same story in Turkish and were asked to reproduce it in their mother tongue; in a subsequent step, they were able to retell the story in their second language German. Within the same experiment, a group of German pupils produced retellings in German. (For conventions of transcription, see Ehlich & Rehbein, 1976.)

(E1)

```
 ⎡ Y                                               (( 4s ))  In eina Schule
 | HJ  Versuch's nocheinma auf Deutsch!
1 ⎣

 ⎡ Y   . . . wa ((5s)) ein kleina . . eh . . . Geldbetrak ((7s)) ge-
 | HJ  hm̆                        hm̆
2 ⎣

 ⎡ Y   klaut.        Für den Diebschtahl (( 5s )) kännen fünf . .
 | HJ          genau!                                            hm̄
3 ⎣

 ⎡ Y   Kinda (( 6s )) Sie ßind f/eh acht Jahre alt.
 | HJ                                      hm̄hm̄ (genau)
4 ⎣

 ⎡ Y   (( 8s )) Sie waren während (( 6s )) / in der Pause. (( 5s )).
 | HJ                              hm̄hm̄
5 ⎣

 ⎡ Y   . ((5s)). und in der Klasse . (( 25s )). gesehen (( 6s )) Da sag-
 | HJ  hm̄hm̄                          hm̄hm̄
6 ⎣
```

In this example one can easily perceive the overlong pauses (time indicated in seconds) between separate fragments of produced talk; the child is an "over-user" of the monitoring process, in Krashen's (1978) terms. We see that the activities of speaking and monitoring (the latter including planning and control activities) are rigorously separated. But no monitoring indicators are interactionally given by the child, and very few repairs can be noticed. Let me, now, briefly discuss some hypotheses concerning fluency.

(A) Fluency of speech means that uttering and planning/controlling are to be
executed at least partly simultaneously.

Consider lines 5–6 of the transcript. The sentence "Sie waren während/in der
Pause und in der Klasse gesehen" ("They were observed during/in the break in
the classroom.") passed through three pauses, but was finally completed. This
means that the speaker, however roughly, in some way globally planned the
utterance in advance (during the 8 seconds prior to the start of the sentence), but
she also needed further planning and control time while processing different parts
of the utterance. Let me derive another hypothesis from this observation:

(B) Fluency depends on the activity of planning an entire utterance in advance;
therefore, a second language speaker must sort out or create in advance a global
scheme for the utterance which allows him or her to build in different parts of
speech while proceeding. (Some proposals relevant to this are made by Fillmore, 1979.) In general, global planning and local, or segmental, planning are
carried out by both native speakers and second language learners. But the
planning of segments is simpler when the native language is used, as evidenced
by the speech of the preceding child in Turkish:

(E1′)

$$\begin{array}{l} \text{Y} \quad \text{öğretmende} \; (\; (\; 3s \;) \;) \; \text{hm} \; (\; (\; 3s \;) \;) \; \text{bes tane sihirli değnek} \\ 1 \end{array}$$

$$\begin{array}{l} \text{Y} \quad \text{çikarmis demişki, bunlar . . de/äh sihirli değnekler} \\ \text{H} \qquad\qquad \text{hm} \\ 2 \end{array}$$

$$\begin{array}{l} \text{Y} \quad \text{demiş} \; (\; (\; 4s \;) \;) \; \text{bu beş kişiye vermiş birer tane, demiş} \\ 3 \end{array}$$

$$\begin{array}{l} \text{Y} \quad \text{ki bunları yarın sabaha kadar} \; (\; (\; 2s \;) \;) \; \text{äh.e.} \; (\; (\; 2s \;) \;) \\ 4 \end{array}$$

$$\begin{array}{l} \text{Y} \quad \text{burıya getireceksiniz demiş} \; (\; (\; 4s \;) \;) \; \text{bunlar almışlar,} \\ \text{H} \qquad\qquad\qquad\qquad\qquad \text{hm} \\ 5 \end{array}$$

$$\begin{array}{l} \text{Y} \quad \text{eve gitmişler.} \\ 6 \end{array}$$

Here, duration of pauses is shorter, and within-utterance pauses do not occur.

Another observation concerning (E1): Those utterances with which the speaker establishes references are usually produced in uninterrupted units of speech;
these reference procedures seem to be "anchoring points" within the production

process; prepositional phrases, in particular, ("In eina Schule . . . ," "Für den Diebschtahl . . .") are used in this way in the text; it is plausible that anchoring points are self-constructed means of mastering the task of reproducing the story; they form "fluent pieces of talk" in themselves, so to speak. In other cases, these anchoring points are repeated in the following utterance (e.g., "Lärer," "ausgeteilt" in (E2)) so that they serve as new starting points.

REPAIRS AND PRESTARTS

The next example, from an eleven-year-old Turkish girl, is from the same experimental situation:

(E2)

1 | G   Und der Lä/die Lären hat gesacht, daß/äh die Lärer

2 | G   hat das . .ehm . . . . ((click)) Zauberstäbe/eh . .für Zau-

3 | G   berstäbe genommen und die hat das für Kinder ge/äh
  | HJ   hm̄m̄

4 | G   ausgeteilt ((4s)) ausgeteilt

(E2') is the girl of (E2) in Turkish during the same experiment:

(E2')

1 | G   ondan öğretmende demiş ki . .bende beş tane demiş değnek
  | var

2 | G   sihirli değnek demiş . . onu masaların üstünden almış . . .

3 | G   demiş ki bu beş tane sihirli ma/ma/şim/değnek demiş . . .

4 | G   hepsi äh kimin demiş hırsız olduğunu gö/gösterecek demiş . . .

From a grammatical point of view, the speech in (E2) is no better than that in (E1), but it is uttered "communicatively" and appears very fluent. The reason for the impression of fluency is that repairs are often structured in ways not found in (E1):

1. pause
2. "ehm"/"eh" (to establish/continue/hearers' expectations)
3. pause
4. first effort (part of a word or of a tentative version)
5. self-interrupt
6. improved version (usually the final version)
7. new start

This repair mechanism shows the "monitor" at work, but not in an egocentric use, as Krashen (1978) has described it, but, paradoxically, a communicative one, since it includes the interlocutor in the speaker's own planning process; it is like thinking aloud. It does not interrupt the fluent flux of speech and shows that the hypothesis that speaking and planning must be carried out at the same time is supported. One might say that applying the repair mechanism above is a second language strategic counterbalance to compensate for deficiencies in fluent production which prevents the interlocutor from interrupting or turning away (cf. Sajavaara, this volume; the work of repair mechanisms in foreign language classroom discourse has been analyzed in detail in Rehbein, 1978). There is yet another tendency one comes across if one studies (E1). Y does not complete most of the utterances she starts, and breaks off what she is saying in order to start her next utterance. This means that she does not reach one utterance goal before focusing on the next one, that she does not continue to focus on the utterance in process, and "prestarts" with the next one. It is to be inferred that her planning activity interferes with her verbalization, for otherwise she would have used a linguistic means to indicate a change of focus. The result here is a kind of pseudo-fluency, because the hearer is obliged to change to a new focus before having reached the goal provided by the foregoing one (cf. Chafe's [1980] terms here, too).

The phenomenon described above is due to the specific second language situation of the immigrant child. As far as fluency in her native language is concerned, it is well established and very regular (cf. (E1')). In her native language, this child does not recur to repair mechanisms in order to compensate for word searching and other such processes, and she does not break off an utterance before having ended it. All in all, this child's German speech shows the difficulty of planning next steps of speaking and of executing preplanned pieces of talk. Thus, one may propose that fluency in a second language requires the capability of handling *routinized complex speaking plans*. The task that has to be fulfilled by a fluent second language learner requires not only the work of categorizing what one wants to say, but also the verbalization of categorized knowledge along the lines of specific plans and patterns of communicative order.

NATIVE LANGUAGE FRAGMENTATION

Let us look at the fluent German speech of an eleven-year-old native German girl retelling a story:

(E3)

Und ⟨ (1.7s) ⟩ der Lehrer, der hatte dann so ⟨(1.35s)⟩ fünf S/äh Zauber-
stäbe ⟨ (1.3s) ⟩ und ⟨ (2.7s) ⟩ äh hat die/hat dann ⟨(0.5s)⟩ fünf ⟨ (0.2s) ⟩
äh Kindern ⟨ (0.4s) ⟩ das dann gegeben immer ⟨ (1.6s) ⟩ und dann
⟨ (1.3s) ⟩ . das Kind, das den⟨(.1s)⟩ . äh Stab um eine Fingerbreite v/äh
verlängert ⟨ (0.7s) ⟩ hatte, das sollte dann der Dieb gewesen sein ⟨(0.7s)⟩ und

Interpretation of (E3) relies on the use of an oscillomink print, as did the discussions of previous examples. In this example, one is impressed by the regular sequences of speech production. In going through the lines one can find three separated chains of verbalization:

1. *der Lehrer, der hatte dann fünf äh Stäbe*
2. *äh hat die dann fünf äh Kindern das dann gegeben immer*
3. *das Kind, das den äh Stab um eine Fingerbreite v/äh verlängert hatte, das
   sollte dann der Dieb gewesen sein.*

These three utterances, or utterance segments, are fragmentized by several pauses ranging from one long pause within the first series up to three short pauses in the second. The first long pause comes close to being a stumble, while the other pauses are bridged by prosodic features characteristic of a single unit of speech. Thus non-fluency and the long pause within the first verbalization series seems to be caused by the process of remembering the number five (*fünf*).

Following the ideas of Chafe (1980), I take the three parts of the preceding discourse as being separate utterances. Chafe finds that verbalization is realized by ''perchings'' or ''spurts'' which are planned and meant as whole units of speech (these units are speech act units and not identical to sentence or clause units). All speech elements within such a unit follow a central focus of speech. This focus is common to speaker and hearer. Fluency is a (context-bound) ratio of the duration of inner-unit pauses to the complexity and length of speech elements within it. ''Context bound'' means that various self-interruptions, repairs, deliberation pauses, and other features, are granted by the hearer (and therefore not taken as indications of non-fluency). The context of the above discourse was a story retelling session in which special expressions such as numerical concepts, special objects, names, intricate actions, and series of events demanded extended planning within the verbalization itself.

Let us look, now, at a specific feature which regularly occurs in story tellings and retellings. This is the framing of an element such as *und, und dann* by two pauses. Such elements are specific markers which bind pieces of spoken information together in a flow of speech. What discoursive elements like these really do is to open a new discourse space in which a new process of focusing is possible (cf. Rehbein, 1977, 1980). Thus, they are *routinized fluency markers.*

It becomes clear now that "fluency" cannot be considered a phenomenon restricted to speech production alone, although it is often measured or assessed as such. Speakers must take into account elements of the context in which they are speaking and acting; they must orient themselves according to the expectations of hearers, the type of discourse being carried on (cf. von Essen, 1979), and a number of general hearer activities. ("hearer's planning"; Rehbein, 1976, 1977). The above examples refer to narrative retellings in an interview. Other situations call for the prefabrication of other forms for fluent, rapid speech.

FORMULAIC SECOND LANGUAGE SPEECH

The following example is taken from an informal bilingual interview with a Turkish worker who, at the time, had been in Germany for 8 years.

(E4)

Und dann keine Wohnung ((0.9s)) albe Wohnungsamt komm da ((0.8s)) imma komm ((0.8s)) Yunanisch Frau ((0.4s)) Hm̄ ((0.7s)) Keine Wohnung ((0.8s)) Ausländer ((0.9s)). Keine Wohnung . . Keine Wohnung ((1.1s)). Undann ((1s)). Hausmeister, ne? ((0.7s)) Firma da, alle ((1.1s.))

This speaker's production is characterized by short segments of speech uttered every 700–900 milliseconds, separated by short pauses. The segments, consisting of two to four words, function as speaking units, or "processing units," to use Sajavaara's term, and form semantically complete wholes. They do not seem to refer explicitly to any foregoing or following word (although this is not quite the case). All in all, the production shows a certain type of fluent speech.

What kinds of expressions are used by the foreign speaker in (E4)? As far as the example goes (and as is confirmed by the whole of the interview from which this excerpt is taken) the utterances consist of "formulae" frequently occurring in oral speech situations and appear to have been acquired by the speaker in untutored ways of learning. The formulae are used by the speaker to express various contents (e.g., "*keine Wohnung*") and to realize different speech activities. One might say that this speaker uses verbalizing routines in order to realize different utterance goals.

Let me draw a very brief conclusion from this example. In many cases speech formulae may help learners produce fluent speech, which is one of Fillmore's

(1979) chief hypotheses about fluency. However, speech formulae can also prevent learners from developing nativelike fluency. The speech excerpt in (E4), for example, would be assessed by a German native speaker as broken, not fluent, speech, although it might be considered fluent according to objective time measures. Another hypothesis about fluency follows from this: Different and separate segments of speech are bound together by extended "frames"; new points of focus must be guided by a central focus; segments of linear, ordered speech are subsumed under larger units of speech. In speaking, a "segmentizing plan" must organize the different segment plans if the spoken discourse is to be fluent.

The kind of linear ordering we have found in (E4) allows the second language speaker to compensate for non-fluency, to some degree, and makes possible the post hoc construction of an utterance scheme which links several, not simply two, neighboring segments of speech together, yielding a kind of post hoc fluency.

CONCLUSIONS

After a discussion of some methodological problems in Sajavaara's approach, I have presented some hypotheses about fluency in a second language. The hypotheses derived from interpretations of recorded speech. They are that:

1. "Fluency" means that the activities of planning and uttering can be executed nearly simultaneously by the speaker of the language.
2. The activity of monitoring can enhance fluent speech.
3. "Fluency" is context dependent in so far as it changes according to the speaker's evaluation of the hearer's expectations; the expectations are inferred through several mediums of perceiving, but they meet their boundaries in culture specific presuppositions about the structure of speakers' knowledge.
4. There are "compensatory strategies" which second language learners can use to counterbalance non-fluency. These are the use of:
    (a) communicatively explicit word searching devices, repair mechanisms, etc.;
    (b) unbroken series of speech formulae (although the impression given may not be one of fluent speech);
    (c) elements in the preceding utterance as anchor points for the current one.
5. "Fluency" involves adequate planning of separate segments of speech, each with its own focus, and global planning of larger discourse units, and more complex speech actions.
6. There are three kinds of discourse segmentation relevant to fluency:
    (a) Partitioning of discourse sections;
    (b) Partitioning of discourse segments;

(c) Segmentation of the utterance itself. This last type of segmentation will not be accorded the honor of fluency by native hearers.

REFERENCES

Chafe, W.L. (1980). Some reasons for hesitating. In H.W. Dechert & M. Raupach (Eds.), *Temporal variables in speech* (pp. 169–180). The Hague: Mouton.

Dechert, H.W. (1980). Contextual hypothesis-testing procedures in speech production. In H.W. Dechert & M. Raupach (Eds.), *Towards a cross-linguistic assessment of speech production* (pp. 101–121). Frankfurt: Lang.

Ehlich, K., & Rehbein, J. (1976). Halbinterpretative Arbeitstranskriptionen (HIAT). *Linguistische Berichte, 45,* 21–41.

Essen, O. von (1979). *Allgemeine und angewandte Phonetik* (5th ed.). Berlin: Akademie-Verlag.

Fillmore, C.J. (1979). On fluency. In C.J. Fillmore, D. Kempler & W.S.-Y. Wang (Eds.), *Individual differences in language ability and language behavior* (pp. 85–101). New York: Academic Press.

Krashen, S.D. (1978). Individual variation in the use of the monitor. In W.C. Ritchie (Ed.), *Second language acquisition research* (pp. 175–183). New York: Academic Press.

Leeson, R. (1975). *Fluency and language teaching.* London: Longman.

Raupach, M. (1980). Cross-linguistic descriptions of speech performance as a contribution to "contrastive psycholinguistics." In H.W. Dechert & M. Raupach (Eds.), *Towards a cross-linguistic assessment of speech production* (pp. 9–22). Frankfurt: Lang.

Rehbein, J. (1976). *Planen II: Planbildung in Sprechhandlungssequenzen.* (Series A, Paper No. 39.) Trier: University of Trier, Linguistic Agency.

Rehbein, J. (1977). *Komplexes Handeln: Elemente zur Handlungstheorie der Sprache.* Stuttgart: Metzler.

Rehbein, J. (1978). *Reparative Handlungsmuster und ihre Verwendung im Fremdsprachenunterricht.* Unpublished manuscript, Seminar für Sprachlehrforschung, Ruhr-Universität Bochum, Bochum.

Rehbein, J. (1980). Sequentielles Erzählen: Erzählstrukturen von Immigranten bei Sozialberatungen in England. In K. Ehlich (Ed.), *Erzählen im Alltag* (pp. 64–108). Frankfurt: Suhrkamp.

Sajavaara, K., & Lehtonen, J. (1980). The analysis of cross-language communication: Prolegomena to the theory and methodology. In H.W. Dechert & M. Raupach (Eds.), *Towards a cross-linguistic assessment of speech production* (pp. 55–76). Frankfurt: Lang.

Third Session:
Cognition and Production

Chair: R. Posner

CHAPTER 11

Toward a Cognitive-Based Model of Language Production

KENNETH F. RUDER
AMY FINCH
University of Kansas

How often have we heard the phrase "He doesn't know what he is talking about"? Implied in such a cliché is the notion, at the least, that an individual is capable of producing language he doesn't fully comprehend. Such a view, however, is not consistent with prevailing thought on the potential relationships between comprehension and production in the process of acquiring a language. Indeed, it is almost inconceivable even to imagine that one could produce an utterance and not comprehend what he had produced.

A commonly held view of language production, albeit somewhat simplified, is that language production is the product of the interaction between a motor component (articulatory or gestural) and comprehension; that is to say, that the term "production" implies a comprehension component. To extend such a definition even further, the recent literature in language acquisition and language training has focused heavily on the claim that in the process of acquiring a language, comprehension precedes production. Although this seems to be the primary viewpoint, the literature also suggests that the relationship between comprehension and production will vary with production preceding comprehension for some linguistic structures (e.g., word order).

The prevailing thought in current psycholinguistic literature, then, seems to favor the notion that comprehension and production are both performance modes tapping the same underlying process. Such views do acknowledge a developmental lag between comprehension and production, with comprehension preceding production when such a lag occurs. Production, however, is viewed as tapping the comprehension component as well; that is, what the child produces,

The preparation of this paper, as well as some of the research reported herein, was supported in part by Grants HD 00870 and HD 00183 from the National Institute of Child Health and Human Development to the Bureau of Child Research, University of Kansas, and by Grant HD 07066 from the National Institute of Child Health and Human Development to the Kansas Center for Mental Retardation and Human Development.

the child must comprehend. Within such a viewpoint, a model of language production must not only acknowledge a comprehension component but must include it as well. A model of language production must also account for the discrepancy found in the developmental literature which suggests that there may be various relationships between comprehension and production, which depend on such aspects as the structures being learned and the context of the situation. We will also see that besides accounting for the above relationship, a model of language production must account for the relationship between language and cognition. In this paper, we shall review some of the more prevalent views regarding the comprehension and production relationships, as well as the language and cognition relationship, with an aim toward developing a consistent view of language production—consistent in that it will handle not only developmental data showing differential performance between comprehension and production modes, but in that it will also handle neurolinguistic data on adult aphasia which indicate that comprehension and production are separate processes. To put this discussion in perspective, we will first provide a general description of the comprehension and production processes.

PERSPECTIVES ON COMPREHENSION AND PRODUCTION COMPONENTS

When one discusses the relationship of comprehension to production, and vice versa, it is almost always done with respect to the competent adult language user. A problem with this approach is that the competent adult displays such a complete integration of behavior that it is difficult to separate component parts from the integrated whole. As a result, much of the discussion to follow will be based on data from individuals who are not competent language users: children in the process of acquiring a native language and members of disordered populations who have suffered some language loss and/or are learning language. It is in these cases that the breakdown of functional language behavior allows us to make inferences regarding the components of competent communicative performance.

Functional language behavior in the context of a communication event must, at the very least, consist of the integration of three general components—conceptual organization, receptive language, and productive language. There is no question but that the behavior of normal children and adults is integrated and organized. This integration is manifested in a variety of ways: in the correspondence between many of their responses to real objects and the words they use to represent those objects, and in the relationship between the speech they are able to understand and the speech they are able to produce. Integration is also seen in the relationships within the linguistic system. People who are able to understand a sentence such as "The plate is not here?" will most often be able to understand a sentence such as "The plate is here." or "Where is the plate?". Moreover, if we ask individuals to write an answer to a question and they do so correctly, we will not be surprised if they can answer the same question orally; nor if they can select the correct answer on a matching or multiple choice task. At an even more primitive stage, if we ask a small child his or her age and the child holds up three fingers, we will not be surprised that at another time the child says "Three" in response to the same question.

While it is easy to give examples of the integration of behavior among normal older children and adults, it is also easy to give examples of the failure of the development of this type of integrated behavior among young children and mentally handicapped people. Among pathological groups we may find people who are able to understand much speech but able to produce little. Or we may find people who seem to respond appropriately to most of the objects in their environment, but who exhibit little or no receptive or productive language. By the same token, we may find individuals whose language reception and expression are limited because of impoverished conceptual organization.

Within the developmental literature several investigators have tried to explain the discrepancy between comprehension and production. Huttenlocher (1974) has explained the differences between comprehension and production in saying that "the first involves recognition of words and recall of the objects, acts and relations for which they stand, where the latter involves recognition of objects, acts and relations and recall of words that stand for them." She used this difference to account for the fact that comprehension was more advanced than production. Huttenlocher further indicated that this discrepancy between comprehension and production might be due to retrieval difficulties: "It is easier to retrieve object-information on the basis of a word than it is to retrieve word-information on the basis of an encounter with an object." This statement is based on the assumption that there are differences in relative distinctiveness of memories for objects/events and memories for words, and that there are differences between the mental processes of recognition and recall.

Clark (1978) has also described the differences between the processes of comprehension and production:

The processes of language comprehension and language production make different demands on the language user. In comprehension, listeners try to interpret what they have heard from other speakers. This process, in children, is supported by the actual physical setting of the utterance combined with the children's general knowledge about the objects, events, or relations present. In contrast, in production, speakers try to convey particular meanings to others. This process, unlike comprehension, receives no direct support from the setting, since what is said depends on the speaker's intention. Instead, it is supported by the child's ability to retrieve from memory the appropriate linguistic or nonlinguistic devices for conveying what he wants to convey. (p. 953)

Although both Huttenlocher and Clark seem to be approaching the comprehension-production discrepancy from only one direction, that comprehension precedes production, Bloom (1974) has indicated that depending upon the communication situation, production might precede comprehension. In explaining this position she suggested that "the mental representation that gives rise to an utterance is cognitively less complex than the search for an 'existing' perceptual schema that is triggered by hearing speech." She further explained "that what an individual knows about an event will determine his ability to both speak and understand messages that code that event and, further, either the event in actual context or the mentally represented event will always be a richer source of information about messages than a linguistic signal alone." Thus, production may precede comprehension in those situations where the child does not have an immediate nonlinguistic context to help with the interpretation of a message.

The three general components—conceptual organization, receptive language, and productive language—are stressed in the above discussions both when the integrated competent language user is talked about, and as well when the child in the process of learning language is discussed. These components may be useful in understanding the integration of behavior, referred to above, which we consider an important aspect of a competent language user.

THE COMPREHENSION COMPONENT

When one begins to evaluate language comprehension, there is also an evaluation of certain aspects of the child's conceptual organization. For example, if a hearer follows the command "Jump!", it is likely that the hearer has organized or categorized the set of movements involved in jumping, and could probably jump in imitation of someone else jumping. This would indicate that at a nonverbal level, another person's jumping and the hearer's own jumping were related. Moreover, if the hearer responded appropriately to the command, "Show me a cup!", performance on a nonverbal matching task involving cups might also be expected. Moreover, the hearer might respond to the various cups in a task by demonstrating a knowledge of their function by acts of drinking, scooping or stirring. While it is possible to operationally distinguish conceptual organization, comprehension, and production, these three undoubtedly share common underlying processes. In particular, if one subscribes to the view that language maps a conceptual base, then the cognitive component must be an integral part of the comprehension process. By definition, language comprehension refers to the understanding of linguistic symbols which represent cognitive orientations to the surrounding world.

Just as cognitive organization is an integral part of the comprehension process, so too can comprehension be viewed as an integral part of language production. Cognitive organization can be tested and/or demonstrated, as previously mentioned, without recourse to either comprehension or productive language skills, whereas testing of language comprehension skills involves some measure of linguistic and cognitive behavior. Similarly, the prevailing view in the language intervention literature is that language comprehension skills can be evaluated without recourse to productive language. Most views of language production, however, suggest that a child's productive language mirrors the child's receptive skills, with the implication that comprehension precedes production (Fraser, Bellugi & Brown, 1963). Carried one step further, this view also implies that language is learned via the receptive mode—comprehension. Such a view underlies the approach to language teaching taken by Winitz and Reeds (1975). Their program rests on the assumption that intensive training in the comprehension of a language leads to speech and language production without any need of teaching speech directly.

Although still controversial, the bulk of the evidence suggests that comprehension precedes production in normal language development (see Nelson, 1973; Ingram, 1974; Winitz & Reeds,1975). In fact, Nelson (1973) in her longitudinal study reports that:

> The early tests of language comprehension at fifteen and twenty months and of imitation at twenty months all predicted language maturity at two years, and for this purpose comprehension at fifteen months was impressive as noted earlier. It appears that one can predict from the child's response to language at 13–15 months his relative production status at 2 and 2½ years. . . . It indicates the probable importance of covert language processing prior to language production as an organizing factor and emphasizes the need for further study. (p. 79)

Ingram (1974) takes a slightly different view in that he feels the empirical issues are really the nature of comprehension and production, and of the gap between them, rather than whether comprehension precedes production. Ingram does stress the importance of the role of comprehension in language learning. Winitz and Reeds (1975), as previously mentioned, take the strongest stand in regard to comprehension and production. They take the position that comprehension learning leads automatically to production unless there are performance constraints. They also take the position that production mirrors comprehension, although they do recognize that intervals of variable length often exist between comprehension and production.

The relationship between comprehension and production is a complex one, at best. Chapman (1974) has recently summarized four different versions of this relationship. To condense her summary even further, these four views of the comprehension/production relationship can be stated as: 1) Comprehension precedes production as the general rule, b) comprehension of some linguistic forms, such as pronouns (Ingram, 1974), precedes the production of those forms; while c) for certain forms (word order signaling subject and object), productive control is achieved before comprehension; and d) whether comprehension precedes or follows production is dependent upon the presence or absence of cues from the immediate context. The latter view is a complex one which indicates that a variety of possible relationships might exist between comprehension and production on the basis of contextual cues, and that such relationships are not static, but subject to change at any point in developmental time.

THE PRODUCTION COMPONENT

Language production, in its simplest form, refers to the act of speaking. It refers to the use of words to request, name, or describe linguistic or non-linguistic events. Productive language, then, is meaningful and is a speech event. Both components are essential to what one generally considers a productive language event. Speech without meaning will generally be referred to as echoic and/or jargon verbal behavior. Meaning expressed by means other than speech (gestures, paralanguage, etc.) is generally thought of as a communication system outside the domain of "linguistic" analysis.

Such a simplistic view of language assumes that language production is the sum of a comprehension component plus a verbal component, that language production is subsumed by language comprehension. Stated differently, what the individual produces, the individual must comprehend. It is also sometimes assumed that if a person lacks productive language, there must also be a lack of conceptual organization and receptive language. This is frequently not true. Both clinical observations and research data clearly indicate that children can exhibit rather extensive conceptual organization and language receptivity without being able to produce language (Lenneberg, 1966; Spradlin, 1963). The broadest view of language production, then, implies that it mirrors comprehension and cognitive skills. The developmental progression from comprehension to production has been questioned recently by Chapman and Miller (1975) in a study which demonstrated production of syntactic forms for which the subjects displayed no comprehension. Rice (1980) cites a similar phenomenon in the acquisition of color terms.

Language production, then, must be more than an echoic, meaningless imitation, although at the same time full comprehension of what is produced is not a prerequisite of what might be considered language production. This latter point is an issue of considerable disagreement, as we will delineate later in this paper. It is not the only bone of contention regarding what is to be considered the domain of language production.

Central to many discussions of language production is the role of pauses and/or hesitation phenomena in defining the domain of language production. Generally, in speaking of language production, our first perception is of the "flow of speech" and of the linguistically analyzable parts of speech which comprise the spoken message (words, subjects, predicates, functors, contentives, etc). However, the notion "flow of speech" obscures a very real facet of the production process, namely that speech does not generally "flow smoothly." The stream of speech is frequently disrupted by pauses, vocal fillers, false starts and other hesitations. The role that such phenomena play in language production must be considered in any complete theory of language production. In depth discussion of pauses and hesitation in language production, however, is beyond the scope of this paper. The purpose of the present paper is not to provide a complete model of language production, but rather to examine the role that cognition might play in such a model of language production, and particularly how cognitive processes might interact with the comprehension and productive processes of the integrated language user.

COGNITION AND THE INTEGRATION OF LANGUAGE BEHAVIOR

Let us look more carefully at the processes that are involved in the integrated language use of a competent language user. In order to do this, we will take the telegraphic sentence "Boy kick horse." and trace the processes involved within each domain. First, let us look at the processes involved at the conceptual level. To start with, the user must make a complex set of discriminations. If this sentence is to be used appropriately (in either comprehension or production), "the boy" must be clearly differentiated from other objects. The act of kicking must be discriminated from the act of hitting, touching, caressing and all other actions. Horses must also be discriminated from all other objects.

Second, if the sentence "Boy kick horse." is to have maximum use for a child, the child must have developed concepts or categories for boys, kicking actions, and horses. That is, the concept of "boy" cannot be restricted solely to a specific boy. Likewise, the concept of "kick" must include a wide range of acts involving striking an object with the foot. The same can be said of horses. Finally, the child must clearly discriminate the relationships between concepts— boys kicking horses versus horses kicking boys.

Each of the above processes can be demonstrated in non-verbal tasks. Both discrimination and categorization can be demonstrated by a child's performance on matching tasks. For example, the child might be shown a picture of a boy and required to select all the boys from a set of choices including women, girls, men, and other objects. The same procedure could be carried out for pictures involving horses and the act of kicking. Finally, a similar technique could be used to demonstrate that the child could discriminate the directionality of kicking. That is, the child would be given a set of pictures of horses kicking boys and boys kicking horses. The task is to match or group them into piles demonstrating the two relations.

Let us assume that the child demonstrates the conceptual organization necessary to use our simple telegraphic sentence, "Boy kick horse." In order to process this linguistic message in the comprehension mode, processes corresponding to those involved in conceptual organization must be posited for interpreting auditory signal. Ideally, the subject should discriminate the word "boy" from such words as "toy," "coy," "joy," "buy," "boat," and "bow." Conversely, the child should classify or treat as equivalent all nonphonemic variants of the word "boy." For example, the subject should respond the same way to the word "boy" said in a loud, low pitched voice as to the word "boy" said in a weak, high pitched voice. The same type of discrimination and categorization should also be shown with the words "kick" and "horse." Finally, the child should be able to discriminate between the sentences "Boy kick horse," and "Horse kick boy," and non-sentences such as "Kick horse boy." Note that while all of the discriminations and classifications involved in conceptual organization were non-auditory, all of the discriminations and classifications just described are auditory.

One might speculate that if a child had the necessary conceptual organization and could discriminate, categorize, and respond differentially to word order on the auditory level, there could be no trouble with auditory comprehension. This may not be true. A child might be able to demonstrate discrimination, categorization, and organization through matching tasks at the conceptual level. The child might also show these processes at the auditory level through verbal imitation, in not saying, for example, "Horse kick boy" in response to the stimulus "Boy kick horse." But still, the child might fail on an auditory language reception task because of a failure to make appropriate associations between auditory and conceptual organization.

Appropriate language production (or inappropriate use, as the case may be) involves a complex set of interrelations among the three components of integrated language behavior which we have been discussing. It requires, first of all, a congruence of conceptual organization and language comprehension. Verbal language production must reflect this congruence. This is, by definition, necessary in a competent language user. In practice, however, it may be difficult to judge congruence or incongruence among the three components strictly on the basis of verbal production. An echoic child, for example, may produce a perfectly grammatical and apparently meaningful sentence and yet not be able to comprehend and/or organize the underlying meanings or intent expressed by the sentence. That is, the verbal production may be nothing more than an echoic verbal imitation of something the child has heard in the past. The verbal productions of mynah birds or parrots fall into this category—the verbal production of languagelike utterances without understanding of the underlying linguistic or cognitive features represented by the utterance.

A further word of caution regarding the use of productive language to infer comprehension and/or cognitive skills is reflected in studies by Chapman (1978), Chapman and Miller (1975) and Rice (1980). Cited in these studies are instances in which the child produces language behaviors in specified contexts but does not display comprehension abilities commensurate with production skills.

As should be apparent from this brief overview of the components of an integrated language system, the status of the various components of a functioning communication event is confusing, to say the least. There seems to be agreement that at least three general components of a functional communication system must be considered in any theoretical framework concerning the nature of a comprehension or production model of language behavior. These components are a) the comprehension component, b) the production component and c) the cognitive component. Consideration of these components within a general model of language production requires a review of the literature examining two important relationships, one between comprehension and production and the other between language and cognition. The information from these two areas will be integrated with the suggestion that cognitive based models of language may need to address the issue of different levels of conceptual organization for language production and language comprehension. Since most of the data for these relationships derive from studies of first language acquisition, that literature will be the focus of review. An attempt will be made to integrate relevant data from neurolinguistic studies in the discussion of a tentative model of language production that follows our discussion of the relationship between language comprehension, language production, and cognitive abilities.

PRIMACY OF COMPREHENSION

"Most writers agree that the child understands the language of others considerably before he actually uses language himself" (McCarthy, 1954). This statement sums up the traditional viewpoint that what the child produces, the child must necessarily comprehend.

This viewpoint has had support from various researchers. One of the first studies to systematically study the relationship between comprehension and production was by Fraser, Bellugi, and Brown (1963). They used ten grammatical contrasts to compare comprehension with two forms of production, imitation without a referent and elicited production with a referent. Their subjects consisted of twelve children 37 to 43 months of age. They found that imitation exceeded comprehension, which exceeded production ($I > C > P$). Although they discussed the fact that the probabilities of chance success were not necessarily the same across the tasks, their final conclusions indicated that production was less advanced than comprehension.

The results of the Fraser et al. (1963) study were further substantiated by Nurss and Day (1971). Nurss and Day used four-year-old children from two different socio-economic levels and two races. Using the ICP test (Fraser et al., 1963) they found that the higher status children performed significantly better than either group of lower class children on all three tasks of imitation, comprehension, and production. However, the three groups of children performed in a similar way in that comprehension scores were higher than production scores.

The above two studies seem to support the traditional viewpoint that comprehension precedes production. However, Baird (1972) and Fernald (1972) questioned the results of the Fraser et al. study on the basis of the probabilities of chance success and the scoring procedure used. Baird found that in order to use direct comparisons between tasks such as comprehension and production, "it is necessary that the chance success rates be equal across tasks or otherwise be under experimenter control.'' Since the probabilities of chance success were not the same across tasks for the Fraser et al. study, their results are subject to question.

Fernald's study was similar to Fraser et al.'s, but used two different scoring procedures. When using the Fraser et al. scoring procedure, Fernald obtained the same results as they had, with imitation preceding comprehension and comprehension preceding production. However, when he used a revised scoring system which tended to equalize the probabilities of chance success between comprehension and production, there was no consistent relationship between comprehension and production. Although the total correct production score was slightly higher than the total correct comprehension score, the relationship varied depending on the grammatical contrast, with production better than comprehension on some items, and comprehension better than production on others.

Another group of studies which suggest that comprehension precedes production have dealt with children's ability to follow commands. These studies have found that children in the telegraphic stage using two- and three-word utterances respond more consistently to commands which are well-formed than to commands which are telegraphic. Shipley, Smith, and Gleitman (1969) investigated children's responses to commands which varied in completeness. While they found that the telegraphic group responded better to well-formed commands, their holophrastic group—children using single-word utterances—preferred one-word and telegraphic commands. They interpreted these results as a basis for not using spontaneous speech as a direct indication of a child's linguistic competence. They stated that ''the child is more 'competent' with language than his early speech would by itself imply''; in other words, comprehension is more advanced than production.

The results for the telegraphic group have been replicated (Petretic & Tweney, 1977; Ruder, Smith & Murai, 1980). However, these studies have found that holophrastic children also responded more consistently to well-formed commands. The differences in the results have been explained as differences in determining length of utterance, in presentation of stimulus items, and in scoring procedures. Overall, the above studies support the viewpoint that comprehension precedes production, especially in children in the telegraphic stage of development.

Although studies which have investigated children's responses to commands have found that comprehension precedes production, they have made no effort to present commands corresponding to children's spontaneous speech. In other words, the commands used were not taken from utterances actually spoken by individual children. Thus, these studies have only shown that general comprehension may precede production. These studies have also not controlled for contextual cues. The children may have used contextual cues to help them understand the commands. For example, in responding to the command ''Give me the spoon'' the child may have only understood ''give'' and ''spoon''; since the object was present the child could have recognized ''spoon'' upon hearing it and then given it to the experimenter without understanding all of the words in the command. Both Chapman (1978) and Bloom (1974) have indicated that comprehension in context may precede production in context, but that production may precede comprehension out of context. Context may be nonlinguistic and linguistic. Thus, depending on the situation, there may be cues which are (a) both nonlinguistic and linguistic, (b) nonlinguistic only, or (c) linguistic only. Production of language is not bound by these cues, but comprehension is. Thus, investigators studying the relationships between comprehension and production must take into account these types of context and their effects upon the two processes.

Other studies which have supported the viewpoint of comprehension preceding production have come from the training literature. Winitz (1978) stated that ''the psychological channel for language learning is comprehension; production, when it occurs, simply contributes to the communication process, but it is not the primary channel for language acquisition.'' This supports a training paradigm which emphasizes comprehension (cf. Winitz & Reeds, 1975). However, Winitz (1978) has indicated that although production is not a major factor in language acquisition, it might be an important component which speeds up the acquisition of language comprehension.

Ruder, Herman, and Schiefelbusch (1977) investigated the primacy of comprehension in language acquisition. They reported that comprehension training alone was not sufficient to result in the production of a variety of lexical items. Although comprehension training did result in some ability to produce the items, production was limited and lagged behind comprehension performance. They found that comprehension training followed by imitation training facilitated production the most.

Huttenlocher (1974) and Benedict (1979) have conducted longitudinal studies to investigate the relationship between comprehension and production. Both studies found that comprehension was more advanced than production in the early stages of development, 9 to 21 months of age. However, they found that there was no simple one-to-one correspondence between the words that a child understood and those that the child produced. Thus, the spontaneous production of words may or may not match the words which are comprehended. Huttenlocher (1974) also found no evidence of overextensions—the use of a word in a broader sense than that found for adults (e.g., ''dog'' for ''horse'') in comprehension, even though this did occur in production. Both studies, therefore, concluded that there was an asymmetry between comprehension and production in both qualitative and quantitative respects, with comprehension exceeding production.

Overall, the primacy of comprehension has not been totally supported. Although a few studies have shown that comprehension precedes production, there are other studies which have shown no consistent relationship between these processes. It also appears that there may be differences in the relationship between comprehension and production depending upon the nonlinguistic and linguistic information available.

COMPREHENSION AND PRODUCTION: INDEPENDENT PROCESSES

The independence of comprehension and production has been demonstrated primarily in the training literature and adult neurolinguistic literature. These two fields have one important point in common—they both deal with disordered populations (although one relevant training study was carried out with normal children as subjects-Rice, 1980).

Guess (1969) provided one of the first language training studies that investigated the possibility that comprehension and production were two separate classes of linguistic behavior which could be established independently of each another. Guess taught two mentally retarded adolescents to receptively identify the plural morpheme while also testing their use of it. He did not find a generalization from receptive training to expressive use. Guess then taught productive use of the plural and reversed training on receptive identification of the morpheme. The reversal training did not affect subjects' production of the morpheme. Guess concluded that receptive comprehension was functionally independent of expressive speech and suggested that comprehension and production could be two separate and "functionally independent classes of behavior." However, he went on to suggest that receptive training may have facilitated productive training. This latter suggestion seems to be contrary to the statement of the independence of the two behaviors.

Guess and Baer (1973) further investigated the relationship between comprehension and production by teaching pluralization rules concurrently in both the comprehension and production modes. In conducting their study they taught different allomorphs of the plural in the two different performance modes (plural form -s in production, and -es in comprehension). They looked at the generalization of the plural allomorphs to the opposite modality (-s in comprehension; -es in production). They found that three of their four subjects did not generalize from either modality to the opposite one. They concluded that "automatic generalization between receptive and productive language is not necessarily an inevitable result of training." However, they further stated that "the interdependence or independence of receptive and productive language is open to unexpected individual differences." Some children showed generalization from one modality to the other, while others showed only partial or no generalization. Thus, these results seem to point to the independence of comprehension and production, in many, as well as the interdependence of the processes in some individuals.

Recently, Keller and Bucher (1979) examined the patterns of cross-modality generalization during the training of lexical items in six mentally retarded children. Although their results indicated that the children acquired receptive responses more rapidly than productive responses, they found more generalization from production to comprehension than from comprehension to production. Keller and Bucher concluded that their results supported the independence of comprehension and production since noun labeling could be established in either modality independently. However, caution must be used in interpreting these results since several methodological problems seem apparent. Although a multiple baseline single-subject design was used, no continuous baseline on the second behavior was used during the training of the first behavior; counterbalancing of the training procedures was not used, and no replication was completed. Other procedural difficulties include the use of two different training procedures and the possibility that productive training involved incidental receptive training, whereas receptive training did not include any productive training. This latter problem would bias the results of generalization from productive training to comprehension.

Rice (1980) found similar patterns of independent as well as dependent development of comprehension and production during training of color terms. She used two groups of children. One group used a color sorting strategy for equating objects while the second group did not. Rice found that the children who did not use the color sorting strategy were able to produce the color terms appropriately but could not comprehend them. These children could recognize that color was an attribute of the objects but could not recognize that color could be a means of equating objects. The group that used a color sorting strategy generalized from production training to comprehension. Rice hypothesized that "perhaps it is necessary for recall that the original information be stored as a criterial attribute." She concluded that "the particular production and comprehension tasks presented in this study would have tapped into different levels of conceptual organization with production tasks not requiring categorical equivalence of color and comprehension tasks requiring such conceptual information." Rice further speculated that production may precede comprehension "when the underlying nonlinguistic relationship is such that is is more difficult to recall than the word." This is the opposite of Huttenlocher's (1974) hypothesis that object-knowledge is easier to recall than word-knowledge. Rice indicated that further investigations of the relationship between cognition and the two performance modes of comprehension and production are necessary.

Additional evidence supporting the independence of comprehension and production comes from the adult aphasia literature. The localizationist position argues that every behavior/ability can be traced to a specific area in the brain which has responsibility for that behavior (Brookshire, 1978).

One of the most extensive investigations and descriptions of the relationship between an area of the brain which suffers injury and the behavioral symptoms which result, comes from the Boston Veterans Hospital and Boston University.

The resultant classification system is known as the Boston classification system and represents a localizationist viewpoint (Bookshire, 1978; Goodglass & Kaplan, 1972). A primary feature of this classification scheme is that depending on the site of a lesion a patient may exhibit a comprehension or production problem with the other modality being left relatively intact. Thus, an aphasic patient may exhibit comprehension deficits without concomitant production deficits, or production deficits in which comprehension processes are left intact.

Recent investigations (Bradley, Garrett, & Zurif, 1980; Caramazza and Zurif, 1978; Zurif, 1980) have provided some counterevidence to the above dichotomy and the independency of comprehension and production. Caramazza and Zurif (1978) compared comprehension for complex sentences in three types of aphasia (Broca's, Wernicke's, and Conduction). They found that the Conduction and Broca's aphasics responded with much difficulty when they had to rely only on syntactic knowledge to understand sentences. However, they had no difficulty understanding sentences which could be decoded on the basis of semantic and world knowledge. The Wernicke's aphasics performed at a higher level and seemed to be insensitive to syntactic or semantic factors.

Zurif (1980) reported on a study by Bradley et al. (1980). Their results further substantiated the comprehension difficulties in Broca's aphasics and indicated that comprehension and production may not be as independent as was initially thought. Therefore, although much of the aphasia literature historically has thought of comprehension and production as being independent behaviors, more recent research has indicated that they may be related, with comprehension skills being similar to production skills.

Overall, the above training studies and neurolinguistic findings from aphasia present contradictory evidence. On the one hand, they do establish that it is possible to train a subject in either modality without first establishing the response in the opposite modality, and they also indicate that trauma of some kind may affect one process without affecting the other. However, all studies showed some generalization to the opposite modality for some individuals. This seems to indicate that comprehension and production may be related in some individuals. Bloom (1974) has stated that comprehension and production ''represent mutually dependent but different underlying processes, with a resulting shifting of influence between them in the course of language development.'' The above studies seem to support this viewpoint better than the independence viewpoint.

Rice (1980) has also suggested that comprehension and production tasks may be tapping different underlying nonlinguistic information. If this proposal is correct, then the fact that comprehension or production may be trained independently may not be unreasonable. The degree of independence between the two processes may depend upon the integration of the cognitive underpinnings. Thus, if the cognitive underpinnings are not integrated, researchers may find comprehension preceding production in some cases, production preceding comprehension in other cases, and the accomplishment of either comprehension or production with the other process.

INTERACTIONIST VIEWPOINT

Recent research (Chapman & Miller, 1975; deVilliers & deVilliers, 1973; Keeney & Wolfe, 1972; Wetstone & Friedlander, 1973) which has investigated the relationship between comprehension and production has challenged the traditional viewpoint that comprehension precedes production. Bloom (1974) has stated that part of the problem in studying this relationship is the fact that in evaluating comprehension the children's responses are multidetermined. Thus, what the child does depends upon knowledge of words and syntactic structure, the linguistic context, the nonlinguistic context, and general knowledge of the world. Bloom further stated that comprehension and production "represent mutually dependent but different underlying processes, with a resulting shifting of influence between them in the course of language development. . . . the developmental gap between comprehension and speaking probably varies among different children and at different times and may often be more apparent than real."

Ingram (1974) discussed the viewpoint "that comprehension does precede production, and that it could never be any other way. . . . that comprehension ahead of production is a linguistic universal of acquisition and that the empirical issues involved here are not this claim but rather the nature of comprehension and production and the gap between them." Ingram stated that the traditional viewpoint was not that language comprehension must be complete before production begins, nor that comprehension of a specific grammatical form or construction must be complete before production; rather, the traditional viewpoint is that some comprehension of a specific grammatical form or construction must occur before production.

The differences between Bloom's and Ingram's viewpoints regarding the relationship between comprehension and production may be more apparent than real. Ingram argued that evidence from child language acquisition, such as overextensions, the discrepancy between the order of appearance of grammatical forms and constructions in the two performance modes, and the observation that comprehension equals production in some cases, does not contradict his viewpoint. He states that the only claim it makes is that first words/constructions must have also been noticed or understood to some extent before they are produced.

Bloom and Ingram have thus both indicated that the relationship between comprehension and production is a complex one. Although they come from different viewpoints, they both suggest that there may be a shifting influence between the two performance modes. Recent research in word order, noun-verb agreement and word meaning substantiates this point of view.

Keeney and Wolfe (1972) investigated production, imitation, and comprehension of subject-verb agreement by children 3;0 to 4;11 years of age. They found that although the children used correct subject-verb agreement in their own utterances, and even corrected ungrammatical sentences when imitating them, they did not understand the relation between verb inflections for number and the meaning of singular and plural. However, the results of the comprehension tasks on which they based this conclusion were not clear cut and may have involved skills, such as metalinguistic skills, that were beyond the children's capability. In support of Keeney and Wolfe are findings from deVilliers and deVilliers (1973) and Chapman and Miller (1975) who obtained similar results in their investigations of children's use of word order in both comprehension and production. These studies found that production preceded comprehension in that the children were able to use appropriate word order in their own speech but could not use this information alone to comprehend reversible active and passive sentences. DeVilliers and deVilliers (1973) found a marked improvement in the ability to use word order information in comprehending reversible active sentences from Early Stage 1 (MLU 1.0 to 1.5) to Late Stage I (MLU 1.5 to 2.0), but the children did not use this information on reversible passive sentences until Stage IV (MLU 3.0 to 3.5).

Chapman and Miller (1975) concluded that their results supported Bloom's (1974) idea that comprehension and production were different underlying processes. The strategies the children were using for encoding an event appeared to be different from the strategies used to comprehend utterances. It also appeared that production based upon a mentally represented event was easier for the child than comprehending an utterance on the basis of linguistic information only.

Wetstone and Friedlander (1973) investigated children's reliance on word order during comprehensive tasks. They, too, found that production preceded comprehension. They concluded that "although comprehension may proceed more rapidly than production in the initial stages of language development, there may come a point when the child may produce more fluently than he can comprehend."

Roberts (1979) also investigated the comprehension and production of word order in children during Early (MLU 1.0 to 1.5) and Late Stage I (MLU 1.5 to 2.0). In contrast to the above studies he found that Early Stage I children do appear to use word order in comprehension tasks. However, their use of word order tended to be related to specific verbs. He found that Late Stage I children tended to comprehend word order in all three verb contexts tested, whereas Early Stage I children only did so for one or two verb contexts. The discrepancy between these results and deVilliers and deVilliers (1973) and Chapman and Miller (1975) may have been due to the dependent variable measured (latency of response), the specific verb contexts used, and the fact that child-as-agent responding was controlled. Roberts concluded that his results support Ingram's (1974) contention that partial comprehension precedes production.

The third area in which investigators have found production preceding comprehension is in the acquisition of word meaning. Blank (1974) described the acquisition of *why* and *how*. She stated that the child's preferred avenue of learning, in which comprehension precedes production, is inadequate in the acquisition of *why* and *how*. Thus, the child is forced to acquire the meaning of these words through a different process—and must produce the terms before comprehending them. She further stated that the child's ability to rely on sensorimotor skills (action, imitation, and imagery) was probably responsible for the common finding that comprehension preceded production. However, in acquiring the meaning of words, such as *why* and *how*, these sensorimotor skills were inadequate.

Nelson and Bonvillian (1978) and Leonard, Newhoff, and Frey (1980) also found a discrepancy in the acquisition of word meanings in that individual children showed different patterns of learning. They found that some children followed a traditional pattern of comprehension preceding production while others followed a pattern of production preceding comprehension. Nelson and Bonvillian held that neither pattern was developmentally more mature.

The most recent evidence on the relationship between comprehension and production demonstrates that it is a complex relationship which varies depending on the demands of the situation. Much of this literature supports Bloom's (1974) hypothesis that the relationship varies during the course of language acquisition, with comprehension preceding production in some tasks, and production preceding comprehension in others.

One of the most significant contributions of more recent research in comprehension and production has been the suggestion that there may be different conceptual organizations underlying these two performance modes. Blank (1974) indicated that the cognitive underpinnings which lead to comprehension preceding production might not be adequate in some situations, so that the child has to utilize a production strategy in order to determine the meaning of some language concepts. Rice (1980) further speculated that there may be different underlying conceptual organizations for comprehension and production.

The fact that cognition or underlying nonlinguistic skills are important in the acquisition of language has been stressed throughout the most recent literature in child language. However, the important question which arises out of the comprehension/production literature revolves around the relationship of cognition to comprehension versus production.

THE RELATIONSHIP BETWEEN COGNITION AND LANGUAGE

The relationship between cognition and language has recently received emphasis in the area of child language. The discussion centers around the question of whether or not, and to what extent, the child's learning of language involves mapping these skills onto pre-existing nonlinguistic cognitive structure. The literature also discusses the ages at which language can affect cognitive growth, and when cognition affects language growth. A brief review of the different viewpoints on this relationship will be presented.

STRONG COGNITIVE HYPOTHESIS

One of the most prevalent theories on the relationship between language and cognition is the strong cognitive hypothesis (Macnamara, 1972; Sinclair-de-Zwart, 1973). According to Macnamara, children learn language "by first determining the meaning which the speaker intends to convey to them and by then working out the relationship between the meaning and the language." Macnamara further states that the child discovers the syntactic structures of language with the aid of meaning and cognitive skills which make it possible to note regularities in linguistic input.

Both Macnamara and Sinclair-deZwart find that the child relies on a set of cognitive strategies which helps in the task of relating symbols to the speaker's intention. Sinclair-deZwart (1973) discusses the Piagetian viewpoint that the child brings to the task of learning language a set of universal cognitive structures which have developed during the sensorimotor period of development. She holds that the universal linguistic aspects which have been noted in child language are made possible because of the universal cognitive structures acquired by children. Thus, "the infant brings to his language acquisition task not a set of innate linguistic universals, but innate cognitive functions which will intimately result in universal structures of thought. . . ."

Although Macnamara stated that his focus was on the comprehension of language and early developing strategies, he did not differentiate specifically between comprehension and production. However, researchers who tend to support the strong cognitive hypothesis (Clark, 1973, 1978; Nelson, 1974; Nelson, Rescorla & Gruendel, 1978) have recently emphasized the differences between comprehension and production. Nelson et al. (1978) have hypothesized that much of word-concept development takes place in comprehension and that the close match between underlying cognitive aspects and the meaning of a word will be in comprehension, not production. Thus, there is some indication that the processes of comprehension and production tap different cognitive underpinnings of language.

Although those who support the strong cognitive hypothesis do not state that language can never influence cognitive growth, they feel that this influence does not occur during the early years of language development. Thus, Macnamara (1972) indicates that once the child progresses in language, the use of language can facilitate the development of thought.

INDEPENDENCE OF COGNITION AND LANGUAGE

The independence viewpoint states that language and cognition derive from independent sources and follow independent courses of development. Although it is not explicitly stated, most of the research on syntax which followed Chomsky's (1957) model, implies such a position. As Bates et al. (1977) have indicated, "the acceptance of a Chomskian grammar as a psychologically real model of language inevitably resulted in the position that language and cognition could not be derived ontogenetically from one another." This nativistic position suggested that both linguistic structures and cognitive structures develop independently out of species-specific innate mechanisms.

Vygotsky (1962) also held the view that thought and language have different beginnings. He maintained that the relationship between thought and speech undergoes many changes. "Progress in thought and progress in speech, are not parallel. Their two growth curves cross and recross. They may straighten out and run side by side, even merge for a time, but they always diverge again." He felt that there was both a pre-intellectual stage of speech development and a pre-speech phase of thought. According to Vygotsky, "the most important discovery is that at a certain moment at about the age of two the curves of development of thought and speech, till then separate, meet and join to initiate a new form of behavior." Although cognition and language are thought to develop independently, there is an indication between the two at some point in development at which time "thought becomes verbal and speech rational." This view of the relationship between cognition and language does not separate comprehension and production, although the nativist position did classify them as performance modes which could be affected by many factors, including memory, distractions, perceptual aspects, and competence.

INTERACTIONIST POSITION

Bowerman (1976, 1981) and Schlesinger (1974) have proposed an interactive approach which stresses that language "builds on the developing cognitive repertoire and in turn shapes it" (Schlesinger, 1974). Bowerman (1976) argues that although cognitive development may pace the acquisition of language forms and constrain the ways in which these forms are used, language nevertheless may introduce new concepts and interact with cognitive growth to determine the acquisition of certain other concepts. She believes that this interaction may occur even during the early growth period of language development. According to this view, the child may have to develop a certain level of cognitive maturity before acquiring the skills needed for learning a specific concept. However, at this point the child may begin to note how the concept is marked linguistically, and begin to produce this meaning in speech in its unmarked form. Through the child's ability to notice linguistic devices and early developing uses of the meaning of the concept, language interacts with cognitive development to firmly shape and establish it.

The majority of the data in support of the interactionist position comes from production data (Bowerman, 1976, 1977; Braunwald, 1978). Thus, it is difficult to evaluate the relationship between cognition and comprehension under this viewpoint. However, Bowerman (1977) argues that linguistic input is important in the child's development of language, and that it may activate the child to search for similarities among stimuli in the environment. She finds that there is a "complex interaction in word acquisition between children's own predispositions to categorize things in certain ways and their attention to the words of adult language as guides to concept formation." Thus, it seems likely that comprehension in some way is important in the interactive approach, and that it provides one mode through which concepts may be developed. However, it is not specifically stated that the relationship between cognition and production is necessarily the same as the relationship between cognition and comprehension.

The literature regarding the relationship between cognition and language must be evaluated in light of the child's acquisition of language. Therefore, the different positions regarding this relationship must be able to account for child language acquisition. The strong cognitive hypothesis has usually been supported by the fact that the child is aware of certain concepts before beginning to mark them formally in speech. Thus, new forms are first expressed by old functions, and new functions are first expressed by old forms. For instance, the child learns a concept such as "more than one" nonlinguistically, and may begin to express this in language without marking it formally (e.g., *more cookie* instead of *more cookies*). However, the strong cognitive hypothesis cannot account for the changes which take place in the encoding of concepts such as the plural since the same basic meaning is being expressed. Thus, why does the child continue to master a formal linguistic device to express the same basic meaning for which the necessary cognitive knowledge has already been developed? If the child has the cognitive underpinnings for this expression, why aren't they linguistically marked from the start? Could there be various linguistic underpinnings which are necessary for specific aspects of language development?

This latter question is what Cromer (1974, 1976) and Slobin (1973) have addressed. They have posited a weak cognitive hypothesis which states that although cognitive structures and operations are important in understanding language acquisition, they are not sufficient in and of themselves to explain this process. The weak cognitive hypothesis indicates that the child must also "possess certain specifically linguistic capabilities in order to express these meanings in language" (Cromer, 1976).

Although these linguistic capabilities may be important in the language acquisition process, it could also be that the child doesn't have the complete cognitive underpinnings during the initial stages. Thus, through the use of unmarked forms, language interacts with cognitive development to firm up the cognitive underpinnings. It is this interactive approach which seems to account for most of the data in child language. Thus, the child may begin to express meanings by using forms which are already available. Through the use of these forms and the ability to note the various concepts contained in the language heard (cf. Ingram's partial comprehension hypothesis), the child develops the full cognitive underpinnings as well as the formal linguistic devices that go with the form.

If we accept the notion that cognition and language interact at some level during the course of development, the next step is to begin to expand this relationship to the two performance modes of comprehension and production. As the literature indicates, there appear to be a variety of relationships between comprehension and production, with these relationships dependent upon the linguistic and nonlinguistic information available.

Chapman (1974) indicated that much of the controversy regarding the relationship between comprehension and production revolves around imprecise definitions of these two performance modes. She indicated that individuals studying this relationship "specify the scope of one's claim by stating which forms are being studied as well as what cues are available to the child." Thus, the relationship between comprehension and production tends to vary depending upon the linguistic constructions and forms studied and depending upon the linguistic/nonlinguistic context; comprehension may precede production when nonlinguistic cues are available but may follow production when contextual cues are not available. Possible cues affecting comprehension may be

> the syntactic-semantic analysis assigned to the sentence; the observed relations among objects and events in the immediate environment; the relations among objects and events previously mentioned in the conversation; or the usual relations among the mentioned objects and events in the listener's past experience. (Chapman, 1974)

Bloom (1974) has also argued that intention to speak and contextual support were factors affecting production.

Huttenlocher's (1974) description of what differentiates comprehension and production may prove helpful in sorting out the underlying cognitive skills for each. Comprehension is said to involve recognition of words and recall of the objects, acts and relations for which they stand; production, on the other hand, involves recognition of objects, acts and relations and recall of words that stand for them. Huttenlocher's position is that production is more difficult than comprehension because of retrieval problems. Therefore, she speculates, object-knowledge is easier to retrieve on the basis of a word than word-knowledge is on the basis of an object. Huttenlocher has used the retrieval process as support for comprehension preceding production, whereas Rice (1980) has used it to show how production may, in fact, precede comprehension. (Although later in development word-knowledge may be easier to recall than object-knowledge, depending on the information encoded in the object-knowledge.) It is this position that Rice (1980) supported for color terms. The object-information in her study involved knowledge that color could be a means of equating objects. She stated that this knowledge was more difficult to acquire than object-information involved in knowing that a particular object was a distinct entity. Thus, some of the children in her study were able to recognize the relationship and recall the word (production) but were unable to recall the relationship when they heard the word (comprehension).

TOWARDS A COGNITIVE-BASED MODEL OF PRODUCTION

If nothing else, the preceding discussion raises the possibility that language production is a separate process from comprehension. Such a notion is not entirely novel. The aphasia literature at least as far back as the mid 1800's has viewed language as being composed of receptive components and expressive components (Lesser, 1978). Paul Broca in 1861 described a pathological condition in which articulation was severely impaired while comprehension of spoken language was apparently unaffected. On the other side of the coin, the literature also discussed disturbances which affected receptive skills, with productive skills being relatively intact (Goldstein, 1948).

Much of aphasia theory and practice, even in contemporary times, has been predicated on the assumption that the receptive and expressive components (comprehension and production components) were separate processes. A third component, frequently referred to as "inner speech," has been used as an explanatory device to relate the separate processes of production and comprehension. Thus, a disturbance on the input side of this model would result in a receptive (sensory) aphasia, while the inner speech and expressive components would remain unaffected. Similarly a disturbance on the output side could result in a productive (Broca's) aphasia, with inner speech and the receptive component remaining intact. Disturbances of inner speech, however, would necessarily affect both receptive and expressive components.

The power of the preceding model lies in the "inner speech" component. Definitions of inner speech range from the vague "black box" phenomena utilized in early behavioristic psychology to the "inner speech form" described by Humboldt (1907). The "black box" conception is descriptively inadequate and requires no further mention. Humboldt describes "inner speech form" as the structure of language which reflects the special way in which the people who speak a particular language view the world and as the internalized rules of a specific language which a people use to communicate their feelings, ideas, and so on, to their fellowman.

Inner speech, as typically utilized in most aphasia literature, differs from inner speech form in that it reflects a universal process of relating language form to cognitive processes, whereas inner speech form deals primarily with cultural and language specific forms. Inner speech, in this context, was defined (Goldstein, 1948) as the totality of processes and experiences which occur when we are going to express our thoughts, or other matters in language production, and when we perceive heard sounds as language. This definition of inner speech is important from several perspectives, in the context of our discussion of a model of language production. First of all, the model implies that language comprehension and language production are separate processes, but that they are related through the sharing of the same inner speech mechanism. The aphasia model of language comprehension and production is based, in this respect, in part on the observations of Vygotsky (1962), which differentiate between the acquisition of the spoken word and the comprehension of that word. Concerning the acquisition of language production, the child first speaks in words which are later combined into phrases and sentences. Acquisition thus proceeds from the less complex to the more complex, as far as external performance is concerned. On the receptive side, Vygotsky views the acquisition of word meaning as taking an opposite developmental direction in which words initially have broad general sentential-like meaning, and only later does the child perceive the meaning of individual words (Goldstein, 1948). Inner speech, in this view, serves the purpose of "mental orientation of conscious understanding" (Goldstein, 1948) and ultimately serves as the relational bridge between understanding and speaking.

The second perspective of importance relates to the conception of inner language as being a single process, identical for both comprehension and production. In this sense, the aphasia model is consistent with the behavioral view of language comprehension and production as being related through a single process of mediation (Osgood & Sebeok, 1965). The mediation model differs from the aphasia model in one important aspect. The mediation model, as proposed by Osgood and Sebeok, views comprehension and production processes as mirror images of each other related by the mediation process. The aphasia model views comprehension and production as distinct processes capable of independent function. The data presented by Martin (1970) on differences in the encoding and decoding of hesitation phenomena can be viewed as further support for the two processes functioning separately even within language competent adults.

In the literature just reviewed, the data seem to argue against a mirror image model of production and comprehension. Moreover, the data relating cognitive functioning to comprehension and production processes suggests strongly that the cognitive organization for each may differ. Consider, for example, what is required for an individual to auditorially process a language signal. Sensory processing of this signal is a temporal task, that is, speech is presented to the listener in a linear fashion. Decoding the signal is likewise a linear task. Comprehension results from the convergence of a number of operations carried out on segments of the signal (phonological and morphological processing) and relating these to prior experiences and frames of reference (cognitive features).

Language production, on the other hand, is not simply a matter of applying decoding rules in reverse. For one thing, when perceiving a situation to be talked about, we usually have a number of options regarding what to say about it. As Vygotsky (1962) has pointed out, the entire situation is uncertain and in fact, the speaker may choose to omit certain aspects of the situation entirely. In general, the speaker must select from a set of possible cognitive structures those most suitable to the communicative intent at the moment. These cognitive structures may involve established categories derived from prior experience, the cognitive structures relating most directly to the immediate context, and the structural choices available to the speaker for inclusion in the message conveyed. A model of language production must, therefore, include a component which is responsible for the selection of the cognitive structure which underlies the meaning and intent of the language production.

A model of language production which adheres to these constraints has been proposed by Schlesinger (1977). His model attempts to explicate the processes by which a speaker expresses intentions via language utterances. A central feature of his model is that it includes a component involving semantic representations. The semantic representations are formalized as I-markers (input markers) since they provide the direct input to the mechanism which produces utterances. A set of realization rules relates the I-markers to spoken utterances. Schlesinger's model has as a basic premise that the structures underlying speech must be conceptual in nature.

The nature of the cognitive categories underlying language production (and comprehension, for that matter) remain largely unspecified. More and more, however, there seems to be a convergence of thought on the categorical nature of the cognitive structures underlying language. Schlesinger, for example, speculates that the categorization imposed by I-markers may be expected to exert sufficient influence on cognitive development, that is, the child is prone to perceive the world in terms of the categories provided by that particular language. Schlesinger also allows for the possibility that concepts can be formed independent of language and may not have a direct language reference.

Especially pertinent to the present view of the cognitive basis for language production is the explicit provision in Schlesinger's model for a language based concept, once arrived at, to be employed in some instances and not others. The model implies that I-markers and their underlying semantic representations may influence the way we think, but that the individual will not totally be at the mercy of the categorization. An important fact of language and cognition in its interaction with the organism is that the individual is seemingly able to perceive each of various objects going under the same ''name'' as something unique and notice how they differ from each other.

This latter feature of the I-marker language production model is especially pertinent to our previous discussion of the apparent difference in cognitive structures underlying the acquisition of comprehension and production of color terms (cf. Rice, 1980). The fact that children could produce the name of a color but not comprehend it requires a careful consideration of what knowledge was necessary in order to perform correctly on the training task. First, the children needed to be able to discriminate color values in order to perform the tasks. Both groups (the color-concept users, those who sorted by color, and the non-color-concept users, those who did not sort by color) were able to discriminate the color values as demonstrated by a matching task. The children also needed to know that multi-attribute objects could be equated on the basis of color. The color-concept subjects demonstrated this knowledge on the sorting task whereas the non-color-concept subjects did not. Therefore, one difference between the groups was that one group was able to use color as a critical attribute for class membership. In order to respond correctly on the production tasks, the subjects only needed to know that each object was a specific color, without realizing that the objects could be equated on the basis of the same color. The children also needed to know that "color" called for a color term, and needed to be able to recognize the color of the particular object presented. The last requirement for the production task was the ability to recall which color term corresponded to the colored object presented.

In order to respond correctly on the comprehension tasks the children needed to understand commands (e.g., "Give me . . .") and prenominal adjectives (e.g., "The red one"). All of the children demonstrated these skills by following commands such as "Give me the cup" and "Give me the big/little one." The children also needed to recognize the color term and hold it in memory as they tried to recall the relation for which the term stood, "i.e., the complex interrelationship between the color term 'red' and the color properties of objects" (Rice, 1978). The color-concept-users were able

to both recognize (on production tasks) and recall (on comprehension tasks) the relationship between the color terms and the color properties of the objects. They also knew that color could be used as a criterial attribute for equating objects. The non-color-concept subjects only performed correctly on the production tasks indicating the ability to recognize the relationship but not recall it. They did not demonstrate knowledge of color as a criterial attribute. (Rice, 1978, p. 88–89)

The subjects could manage the production tasks without knowing that color could be a criterial attribute for equating objects. However, this knowledge appears to be very important for correct performance on the comprehension tasks. When asked to "Give me the red one," the child has to recognize the word "red" and recall the relationship for which it stands. Subjects who did not use color as a means for equating objects were unable to perform correctly on the comprehension tasks. It was posited that the comprehension failure was tied to the lack of conceptual knowledge (how to form groups of objects alike in their coloredness), or, more precisely, to the inability to recall the relationship. If the children did not know the relationship among the objects, they could not recall it. It is hypothesized that under this particular set of training circumstances, the co-existence of correct production with incorrect comprehension is accounted for by the underlying cognitive organization (Rice, 1980; Ruder & Rice, 1978). Such a view is consistent with the notion advanced in Schlesinger's (1977) model, that the cognitive structure reflected by the I-marker in production need not be the same structure tapped in a comprehension task.

To summarize, our review of literature, particularly that from the field of aphasia and child language acquisition, has led us to posit several important considerations which we feel a model of language production must account for. First of all, comprehension and production must be viewed as separate processes. Encoding and decoding processes, in particular, cannot be viewed simply as mirror images depending on whether we are discussing input or output. The model of language production described by Schlesinger (1977) is a cogent example of the application of the "independence" principle to a working model of language production. One may argue about the explanatory adequacy of the particular model; it does, however, acknowledge the separate, if not independent, nature of comprehension and production processes.

A second consideration, is that a model of language production include more than a description of the motor component (i.e., articulation). A viable production model must consider the variables of semantic representation, cognitive structure, and syntactic organization, in addition to phonological production.

A third consideration derived from this review requires that a production model acknowledge the interaction of the comprehension and production components during communication. As suggested earlier, in the ideal communication event comprehension and production processes may be inseparable in that what the speaker produces, the speaker also comprehends, and conversely, what is comprehensible is producible. In much of the language production research with adults, underlying comprehension has been assumed, and this assumption may in large part be responsible for the view that comprehension and production are dependent components, with production subsuming comprehension, and comprehension preceding production in language acquisition. While such an observation seems to run counter to considering comprehension and production as separate components of communication, there are data in support of this observation, and an adequate model of language production must consider these data as well as those supporting separate functioning.

The fourth, and perhaps the most crucial consideration arising from this discussion, is that a model of language production acknowledge the potential for and existence of different cognitive structures underlying comprehension and production. Such a consideration is essential if we wish to account for production without comprehension and the independence of the comprehension and production processes in aphasia. Moreover, the inclusion of separate cognitive structures for comprehension and production can account not only for data which supports the independence of the two communicative functions, but also for their apparent interdependence in many instances. Thus, the literature on language acquisition indicated that there is variation, aside from individual differences, in the relationship between comprehension and production. Guess and Baer (1973) and Rice (1980) both found independence of comprehension and production in some children, and interdependence in others.

If one views the cognitive structures underlying comprehension and production as separate but overlapping, the congruence between comprehension and production can be viewed as tapping overlapping cognitive structures. Furthermore, to account for the discrepant comprehension and production performances of first language learners at various stages of development, one might posit a system of converging cognitive structures such that, initially, the cognitive structures may be entirely distinct, and result in differences in performance between production and comprehension. As the cognitive structures converge, the gap between comprehension and production is diminished, eventually to a point at which comprehension and production functions are entirely congruent. This pattern of development has been supported by Rice (1980) in that children who used a color sorting strategy generalized from production training to comprehension, whereas those who did not use this strategy did not generalize from one process to the other.

Such a view of overlapping and converging cognitive structures provides a mechanism to account for the discrepancy between comprehension and production in the previously cited studies. Such a view is also not inconsistent with the I-marker model of production advanced by Schlesinger (1977). Even though it is not an explicit feature of his description, inclusion of such a cognitive component would enhance the model's explanatory adequacy.

It should be recognized, at this point, that the considerations for a language production model advanced in this paper apply equally well to any model of language comprehension. While these considerations are tentative in nature at this time, they form a basis for research. Data from such research can only help to refine our views of language production and its relationship to comprehension. The obstacles to such research efforts, particularly in devising ways to assess the cognitive structures underlying comprehension and production, may be monumental. We should consider this a challenge; in accepting this challenge we take an important step toward explaining the processes involved in acquiring a language and remediating language impairment.

REFERENCES

Baird, R. (1972). On the role of chance in imitation-comprehension-production test results. *Journal of Verbal Learning and Verbal Behavior, 11,* 47–77.

Bates, E., Benigi, L., Bretherton, I., Camaioni, L., & Volterra, V. (1977). From gesture to the first word: On cognitive and social prerequisites. In M. Lewis & L. Rosenblum (Eds.), *Interaction, conversation, and the development of language* (pp. 247–307). New York: John Wiley & Sons.

Benedict, H. (1979). Early lexical development: Comprehension and production. *Journal of Child Language, 6,* 183–200.

Blank, M. (1974). Cognitive functions of language in the preschool years. *Developmental Psychology, 10,* 229–245.

Bloom, L. (1974). Talking, understanding, and thinking. In R.L. Schiefelbusch & L.L. Lloyd (Eds.), *Language perspectives: Acquisition, retardation, and intervention* (pp. 285–311). Baltimore, Md.: University Park Press.

Bowerman, M. (1976). Semantic factors in the acquisition of rules for word use and sentence construction. In D.M. Morehead & A.E. Morehead (Eds.), *Normal and deficient child language* (pp. 99–179). Baltimore, Md.: University Park Press.

Bowerman, M. (1977, July). *The structure and origin of semantic categories in language learning child.* Paper prepared for Fundamentals of Symbolism, Symposium N. 74 of the Wenner-Gren Foundation for Anthropological Research.

Bowerman, M. (1981). Language development. In H.C. Triandis & A. Heron (Eds.), *Handbook of cross-cultural psychology.* Vol. 4: *Developmental psychology* (pp. 93–185). Boston: Allyn & Bacon.

Bradley, D.C., Garrett, M.F., & Zurif, E.B. (1980). Syntactic deficits in Broca's aphasia. In D. Caplan (Ed.), *Biological studies of mental processes* (pp. 269–286). Cambridge, Mass.: M.I.T. Press.

Braunwald, S.R. (1978). Context, word and meaning: Toward a communicational analysis of lexical acquisition. In A. Lock (Ed.), *Action, gesture and symbol: The emergence of language* (pp. 485–527). London: Academic Press.

Brookshire, R. (1978). *An introduction to aphasia* (2nd ed.). Minneapolis, Min.: BRK Publishers.

Caramazza, A., & Zurif, E.B. (1978). Comprehension of complex sentences in children and aphasics: A test of the regression hypothesis. In A. Caramazza & E.B. Zurif (Eds.), *Language acquisition and language breakdown: Parallels and divergencies* (pp. 145–161). Baltimore, Md.: Johns Hopkins University Press.

Chapman, R.S. (1974). Discussion summary: Developmental relationship between receptive and expressive language. In R.L. Schiefelbusch & L.L. Lloyd (Eds.), *Language perspectives: Acquisition, retardation, and intervention* (pp. 335–344). Baltimore, Md.: University Park Press.

Chapman, R.S. (1978). Comprehension strategies in children. In J.F. Kavanagh & W. Strange (Eds.), *Speech and language in the laboratory, school, and clinic* (pp. 308–327). Cambridge, Mass.: M.I.T. Press.

Chapman, R., & Miller, J. (1975). Word order in early two- and three-word utterances: Does production precede comprehension? *Journal of Speech and Hearing Research, 18,* 355–371.

Chomsky, N. (1957). *Syntactic structures.* The Hague: Mouton.

Clark, E.V. (1973). What's in a word? On the child's acquisition of semantics in his first language. In T.E. Moore (Ed.), *Cognitive development and the acquisition of language* (pp. 65–100). New York: Academic Press.

Clark, E.V. (1978). Strategies for communication. *Child Development, 49,* 953–959.

Cromer, R.F. (1974). The development of language and cognition: The cognition hypothesis. In B. Foss (Ed.), *New perspectives in child development* (pp. 184–252). Baltimore, Md.: Penguin.

Cromer, R.F. (1976). The cognitive hypothesis of language acquisition and its implications for child language deficiency. In D.M. Morehead & A.E. Morehead (Eds.), *Normal and deficient child language* (pp. 283–333). Baltimore, Md.: University Park Press.

deVilliers, J., & deVilliers, P. (1973). Development of the use of word order in comprehension. *Journal of Psycholinguistic Research, 2,* 331–341.

Fernald, C. (1972). Control of grammar in imitation, comprehension, and production: Problems of replication. *Journal of Verbal Learning and Verbal Behavior. 11,* 606–613.

Fraser, C., Bellugi, U., & Brown, R. (1963). Control of grammar in imitation, comprehension, and production. *Journal of Verbal Learning and Verbal Behavior, 2,* 121–135.

Goldstein, K. (1948). *Language and language disturbance.* New York: Grune & Stratton.

Goodglass, H., & Kaplan, E. (1972). *The assessment of aphasia and related disorders.* Philadelphia: Lea & Febiger.

Guess, D. (1969). A functional analysis of receptive language and productive speech: Acquisition of the plural morpheme. *Journal of Applied Behavior Analysis, 2,* 55–64.

Guess, D., & Baer, D. (1973). An analysis of individual differences in generalization between

receptive and productive language in retarded children. *Journal of Applied Behavior Analysis,*
6, 311–329.

Humboldt, W. (1907). Über die Verschiedenheit des menschlichen Sprachbaues und ihren Einfluß
auf die geistige Entwicklung des Menschengeschlechts. *Bd. VII der Gesammelten Schriften.*
Berlin: Königlich-Preußische Akademie der Wissenschaften.

Huttenlocher, J. (1974). The origins of language comprehension. In R. Solso (Ed.), *Theories in*
cognitive psychology: The Loyola Symposium (pp. 331–368). Potomac, Md.: Lawrence
Erlbaum.

Ingram, D. (1974). The relationship between comprehension and production. In R.L. Schiefelbusch
& L.L. Lloyd (Eds.), *Language perspectives: Acquisition, retardation, and intervention* (pp.
313–334). Baltimore, Md.: University Park Press.

Keeney, T., & Wolfe, J. (1972). The acquisition of agreement in English. *Journal of Verbal*
Learning and Verbal Behavior, 11, 698–705.

Keller, M., & Bucher, B. (1979). Transfer between receptive and productive language in developmentally disabled children. *Journal of Applied Behavior Analysis, 12,* 311.

Lenneberg, E. (1966). The natural history of language: A psycholinguistic approach. In F. Smith &
G.A. Miller (Eds.), *The genesis of language* (pp. 219–252). Cambridge, Mass.: M.I.T.
Press.

Leonard, L., Newhoff, M., & Frey, M. (1980). Some instances of word usage in the absence of
comprehension. *Journal of Child Language, 7,* 189–196.

Lesser, R. (1978). *Linguistic investigations of aphasia.* London: Arnold.

Martin, J.G. (1970). On judging pauses in spontaneous speech. *Journal of Verbal Learning and*
Verbal Behavior, 9, 75–78.

Macnamara, J. (1972). Cognitive basis of language learning in infants. *Psychological Review, 79,* 1–
13.

McCarthy, D. (1954). Language development in children. In L. Carmichael (Ed.), *Manual of child*
psychology (2nd ed.) (pp. 492–630). New York: John Wiley & Sons.

Nelson, K. (1973). Structure and strategy in learning to talk. *Monographs of the Society for Research*
in Child Development, 38 (Serial No. 149).

Nelson, K. (1974). Concept, word, and sentence: Interrelations in acquisition and development.
Psychological Review, 81, 267–285.

Nelson, K.E., & Bonvillian, J.D. (1978). Early language development: Conceptual growth and
related processes between 2 and 4½ years of age. In K.E. Nelson (Ed.), *Children's language*
(Vol. 1, pp. 467–556). New York: Gardner Press.

Nelson, K., Rescorla, L., & Gruendel, J. (1978). Early lexicons: What do they mean? *Child*
Development, 49, 960–968.

Nurss, J., & Day, D. (1971). Imitation, comprehension and production of grammatical structures.
Journal of Verbal Learning and Verbal Behavior, 10, 68–74.

Osgood, C.,& Sebeok, T. (1965). *Psycholinguistics.* Bloomington: Indiana University Press.

Petretic, P., & Tweney, R. (1977). Does comprehension precede production? The development of
children's responses to telegraphic sentences of varying grammatical adequacy. *Journal of*
Child Language, 4, 201–209.

Rice, M. (1978). *The effects of children's prior nonverbal color concepts on the learning of color*
words. Unpublished doctoral dissertation, University of Kansas, Lawrence.

Rice, M. (1980). *Cognition to language: Categories, word meanings and training.* Baltimore, Md.:
University Park Press.

Roberts, K. (1979). *The comprehension and production of word order in early stage I.* Unpublished
doctoral dissertation, University of Kansas, Lawrence.

Ruder, K., Herman, P., & Schiefelbusch, R.L. (1977). Effects of verbal imitation and comprehension training on verbal production. *Journal of Psycholinguistic Research, 6,* 59–72.

Ruder, K., & Rice, M. (1978). *Comprehension and production: A study in the acquisition of color terms* [film]. Lawrence, Bureau of Child Research, University of Kansas.

Ruder, K., Smith, M., & Murai, H. (1980). Response to commands revisited again. *Journal of Child Language, 7,* 197–203.

Schlesinger, I.M. (1974). Relational concepts underlying language. In R.L. Schiefelbusch & L.L. Lloyd (Eds.), *Language perspectives: Acquisition, retardation and intervention* (pp. 129–151). Baltimore, Md.: University Park Press.

Schlesinger, I.M. (1977). *Production and comprehension of utterances.* Hillsdale, N.J.: Lawrence Erlbaum.

Shipley, E., Smith, C., & Gleitman, L. (1969). A study in the acquisition of language: Free responses to commands. *Language, 45,* 322–342.

Sinclair-deZwart, H. (1973). Language acquisition and cognitive development. In T.E. Moore (Ed.), *Cognitive development and the acquisition of language* (pp. 9–25). New York: Academic Press.

Slobin, D.I. (1973). Cognitive prerequisites for the acquisition of grammar. In C.A. Ferguson & D.I. Slobin (Eds.), *Studies of child language development* (pp. 175–208). New York: Holt, Rinehart & Winston.

Spradlin, J.E. (1963). Language and communication of mental defectives. In N.R. Ellis (Ed.), *Handbook of mental deficiency* (pp. 512–555). New York: McGraw Hill.

Vygotsky, L. (1962). *Thought and language.* Cambridge, Mass.: M.I.T. Press.

Wetstone, H., & Friedlander, B. (1973). The effect of word order on young children's responses to simple questions and commands. *Child Development, 44,* 734–740.

Winitz, H. (1978). A reconsideration of comprehension and production in language training. *Allied Health and Behavioral Sciences, 1,* 272–315.

Winitz, H., & Reeds, J. (1975). *Comprehension and problem solving as strategies for language training.* The Hague: Mouton.

Zurif, E. (1980). Language mechanisms: A neuropsychological perspective. *American Scientist, 68,* 305–311.

CHAPTER 12

Kinds of Production

FLORIAN COULMAS

Universität Düsseldorf

Grammar is as disappointed not is a grammar is as disappointed. Grammar is not as grammar is as disappointed. (Gertrude Stein)

For some years we have been witnessing the fall of the ideal speaker-hearer and the rise of the actual language user. This process is most apparent in the way that psycholinguistic models of language behavior no longer accept or take for granted the idealizations of theoretical linguistics. During the sixties and early seventies, psycholinguistics seemed to be primarily concerned with testing hypotheses that grew out of transformational grammar. Now, even within the transformationalist camp, the priorities and demands of grammars should depict as accurately as possible people's actual linguistic knowledge and behavior.

As part of this development, psycholinguistic and neurolinguistic models of speech and language have attained deeper theoretical significance, and rightly so, as I see it. Linguistic capabilities depend on neural, psychic, and social properties of the human species, and it is at least questionable whether theoretical models of language should completely ignore these properties. In my view, comprehension and production are processes which ought to be studied not as supplemental to linguistic structure, but as preconditions to understanding the interplay of structure and function in language.

Before considering the relationship between comprehension and production, and before setting out to devise a model of production, we need to answer the question of what linguistic production is, or, less ambitiously, what we mean by "production." However, I do not intend to quibble about words; I am not interested in terminology. What I would like to do here is not to attempt a definition of the term "production," but rather to mark off the diversity in the object of our discussion. It seems to me that we can hardly start to discuss relationships between X and Y before we agree about what X and Y are. Thus, my aim is a modest one. The only thing I want to do is present a framework, or rather a list of different kinds of linguistic activities, that might be subsumed under the general heading of "production."

MODE OF OUTPUT

First of all, we must account for two different modes of output: oral and written. There is oral production and written production, and although this distinction has been largely ignored in linguistic circles, a number of recent studies (e.g. Olson, 1980; Tannen, 1980) have shown that it is a simplistic misconception to consider written language merely as a permanent copy of spoken language. By and large, talking and writing fulfill very different functions, and oral and written outputs are accordingly different in many respects. To mention only the most obvious one, while every normal human being is a native speaker of some language, the art of writing is by no means universal, and is mastered only rudimentarily by many. Hence, many people exhibit great discrepancies between oral and written production.

Spoken and written language differ not only with respect to their physical manifestation but also, and more importantly, with respect to the underlying planning strategies. Linguistic production addressed to a co-present interlocutor has to meet requirements that are different from those placed on a text whose interpretation cannot rely on a common situational context. Hence, highly skilled speakers may perform poorly if asked to produce in writing. The relations between spoken and written language are a complex issue which cannot be discussed in a limited space. Suffice it to note that a model of production must take into account the various distinctions between oral and written output and the corresponding planning strategies.

MOTIVATION

The next distinction to be considered refers to motivation. By "motivation" I mean the impulse leading to linguistic production. The distinction I want to make is between spontaneous and elicited production. These are only rough and ready categories, but they represent an important parameter for differentiating kinds of production.

How to elicit spontaneous speech is a well-known and much discussed methodological problem in linguistic fieldwork (e.g., Labov, 1971). The solution to this problem, which is sometimes considered a paradox, is not what I am after here. I mention it only because it demonstrates that there is a difference between spontaneous and elicited speech that linguists find important. This difference has to do with awareness, or the relative attention payed to one's own linguistic behavior. It is a well-established fact that this is an important sociolinguistic variable. However, there are other aspects of the distinction which are perhaps more important for a psycholinguistic model of production. There are speakers who are limited entirely to elicited speech in their linguistic behavior; they do not speak spontaneously. While these are pathological cases, their performance is a kind of production, however degenerate or impaired it may be. The extreme form of reduction to elicited production is the pathological phenomenon known as "echolalia" (see H. Whitaker, 1976, for a lengthy discussion). Patients suffering from this syndrome, when addressed, repeat whatever their interlocutor says. It is, I believe, an interesting question, in what sense and to what extent utterances of this kind qualify as linguistic production.

There is evidence that echolalic patients display a communicative attitude towards their interlocutor (Whitaker, 1976). They do not echo everything they hear, only that which is addressed directly to them, although there is also evidence that they do not understand what they are saying. There must, however, be some kind of linguistic processing going on which not only enables them to reproduce linguistic stimuli but also to correct grammatical errors that occur in the stimuli. For if such patients are presented a sentence containing a mistake, for instance, in person or number agreement, they repeat the sentence in its grammatically correct form. If this is not production proper, we will have to state where else it begins.

In my view, it is quite misleading to ask whether or not comprehension and production interact; it is not a simple yes-no question. The observations reported in the aphasia literature seem to indicate that one must think in terms of multiple levels of production. The levels differ with respect to relative awareness and the involvement of conscious cognition. To some extent, the levels vary with what I have referred to here as motivation. In any event, the difference between elicited and spontaneous production correlates with a variety of other factors. Speakers whose actual performance is reduced to elicited utterances, catatonic patients, for instance, do not necessarily suffer from any language deficit. On the other hand, spontaneous speech is, of course, no proof at all that there are no language problems. The points I want to make are simply that production varies with respect to a variety of interesting properties, depending on whether it is spontaneous or elicited, and that this contrast is therefore deserving of attention in the construction of models of production.

TASK

A production model must be able to account for different types of tasks. Here, again, I want to propose a crude distinction that seems of some importance. Although linguistic behavior can reflect a multiplicity of tasks, I will confine myself to pointing out differences between those involving production, on the one hand, and "reproduction" on the other.

Consider the differences between presentations to scientific conferences which are read to the audience and those which are not. In the first case, thought and wording are carried out beforehand, the result being a reproducible product. In the second case, the thinking is (presumably) done beforehand, and some of the wording, but to a considerable extent the actual linguistic expression is made up on the spot. Can we capture the differences between these two kinds of presentation by describing one as production proper and the other as "reproduction," a derivative form of production? The reader may slightly alter a text in reproducing it aloud, and the non-reader may recall and use previous formulations. In either case there is both production and reproduction.

What about actors who recite long and elaborate texts from memory that were produced by somebody else? Are they only reproducing? If an actor forgets part of a speech, a prompter may provide assistance by reading the part from a book, whispering the words so that the actor can, in turn, reproduce them for the audience. Obviously, there are many differences between the two kinds of reproduction: the actor reproduces from memory, the prompter relics on the written source. The prompter's task may be more reproductive than that of the actor; but it is not entirely simple, since the prompter must be ready to provide the appropriate words at any time. Does this task involve no production at all? In some cases an actor's task is to convey an impression of spontaneity and authenticity, and make it appear that what is said is not spoken by rote. For a TV-announcer, in contrast, there is no need to camouflage the reproductive nature of his or her performance. Thus, even within the class of reproductive linguistic tasks there is a wide range of variation.

A very elaborate kind of reproduction can be seen in typing to dictation. It is always stunning to see how rapidly a skilled typist can transform an acoustic input into a written output. And obviously, linguistic processing must be going on, because otherwise the output would never conform to the orthography of the written language. This kind of linguistic reproduction is very similar to shadowing; only the mode of output is different. However, this is not merely a "technical" difference in the "hardware." The "software" is also different, since the written reproduction of an acoustic input involves an additional program that maps phonetic representations of utterances onto orthographic representations. The converse program handles reading aloud. In both cases, reproduction involves many elements of production, and it is not altogether clear exactly what the differences between the two are. Clearly, the notion of reproduction means, among other things, that the sender of a message is not identical with its original producer, although a repeated message can become the repeater's own message when, for example, an oath is repeated by someone as a means of taking the oath.

Unlike an oath, many prefabricated expressions are the common property of the speech community. Their use strains memory, rather than computation, because they are conventionalized means of mastering recurrent communicative tasks. In this respect they are quite different from utterances for which an appropriate form for the message had to be constructed. A detailed treatment of the multiple functions of prefabricated expressions is impossible here. Notice, however, that they abound in everyday speech, and that they represent reproducible chunks of language whose employment relieves the productive mechanisms of speech—on the morpho-syntactic level, at least. What this shows is that linguistic performance on a hierarchy of levels. Different kinds of communicative tasks can be characterized as being, to a greater or lesser extent, productive or reproductive. The same holds true for the linguistic means by which these tasks are carried out.

EXECUTION

An additional distinction is related to that between production and reproduction. It does not, however, concern the communicative task, but rather its execution. Following recent research by Bolinger (1976), Van Lancker (1975), Krashen and Scarcella (1978), Whitacker (1979), and Coulmas (1980, 1981), I propose, in this connection, to distinguish between two aspects of the execution of linguistic activity: the creative and the automatic.

If a shop assistant says "Can I help you?" to a customer, the utterance is almost completely automatic. The clerk uses the same phrase many times every day. When production consists of formulaic speech, it is largely automatic. But, on the other hand, the distinction between creative and automatic is not bound to a distinction between types of expressions. While it is correct that the production of prefabricated expressions relies on automatized skills, these skills are not restricted to such expressions. Rather, it seems that large parts of grammar are removed from conscious control under normal circumstances, and, as such, automatic when used in production. Many utterances involve both creative and automatic aspects of production. The composition of a complex sentence for the expression of a complex thought is a creative process requiring careful planning, but not every part of the composition is carried out at a level of brain function which requires that we pay attention to it. That the semantic relations come out right is a matter of creative and consicous planning; but that the morphosyntactic surface structure conforms to the grammar of the respective language is largely achieved by automatized programs for the implementation of surface-near rules.

To know a language fluently is to be able to use it—or rather, its lower level grammatical rules—automatically. Drills in foreign language training, for example, serve the function of providing a certain degree of automatization and thus enable the speaker to withdraw attention from *how* something is to be put into words and to pay more attention to *what* is to be said. Not every part of grammar is susceptible to automatization. It seems that we must assume a descending order of types of grammatical rules with respect to their automatization. Thus, the phonetic component, which determines the actual form of the output, is by and large automatic, and the same holds true for a good deal of morphosyntax. Those parts of grammar that are close to cognition, on the other hand, are not subject to automatization. All utterances can be characterized as being more on the creative side or more fully automatic. Many ready-made phrases require no creative effort at all. However, the execution of most linguistic acts involves both creative and automatic aspects of production. The goal of matching psychological reality in a production model can not be attained unless the distinction between these two aspects of production is properly taken into account.

GENRE

To continue the list of distinctions relevant for a psycholinguistic model of production, let us consider now a communicative aspect of production which, for lack of a better term, I lable *genre*. Linguistic utterances can be auto-communicative or allo-communicative. Allo-communicative utterances, in turn, can be addressed to one or more interlocutors. Accordingly, I propose a triple distinction between *monologue, dialogue,* and *polylogue.* Obviously, innumerable utterances of the same form can and do occur in each of these genres. Yet, it cannot be taken for granted that genre does not affect production. If, for instance, the same person does the talking and the listening, this may not be very entertaining, but at least the speaker can be sure of his or her audience. In contrast with this auto-communicative monologue, a speaker participating in dialogue or polylogue must always be careful to get the interlocutor's attention. Moreover, the speaker has to apply various strategies which the auto-communicator can safely ignore in order to acquire and keep a speaking turn. These strategies are also suspended in allo-communicative monologues such as public speeches and announcements. Further differences between monologue, dialogue, and polylogue that may have a bearing on production concern the sequential organization of utterances, their thematic and functional relations, their explicitness, and so on. However, in what ways production varies with respect to these factors is a question to be investigated empirically, rather than to be dealt with here, where it can only be mentioned in passing.

COMPETENCE

It is quite obvious that I cannot give an exhaustive catalogue here of types of linguistic production. Nor can I hope to touch upon the majority of properties pertaining to different aspects of production, for our knowledge of what is and is not relevant here is very incomplete. But it is clear that some discussion involving the speaker's linguistic competence must not be left out. The final distinction to be made here is very important and concerns native and non-native competence: What are the main differences between them? Presumably, the differences are all a matter of degree—but they can be very extensive. While the native language of a normal speaker lends itself readily to the expression of whatever comes to mind, one's expressive possibilities may be drastically limited under the conditions of non-native control of a language. Many speakers are non-native speakers of some language, but those speakers who are equally competent in more than one language are less numerous. For the majority of bi- or multilinguals there is a marked difference between the native language and one or more second languages. For one thing, the necessary automatization discussed above can only be achieved by practice. Thus, even though one's knowledge of a language may be highly developed, production may be a conscious effort if the speaker is not used to employing the particular tool of that language. Further, the asymmetry of comprehension and production is likely to be more pronounced in non-native competence. We do not know how languages are stored in the brain, but it is certain that this asymmetry is not, or not only, a matter of retrieval problems. In foreign language usage it is particularly obvious that the occurrence of unknown lexical items can be compensated for by various kinds of inference. Their meaning can be inferred and learned from context, but they cannot be produced unless they have been previously heard. Similarly, many idiomatic expressions do not present any problem for comprehension, but they cannot be produced correctly without having been learned.

A point that may be brought out in non-native speech is the likelihood that production precedes comprehension, and that the relation between comprehension and production is a matter of gradation. Consider the case of a speaker with no knowledge of English who repeats an utterance such as "Go to hell!" after somebody else. Is the imitator swearing or not? What about religious congregations praying in Latin or Hebrew? Are those members who mumble the words without knowing the language not praying? Their efforts would then be entirely amiss.

There are, in other words, types of production that do not presuppose comprehension. Or rather, there are different types of comprehension. The fact that I know that I can convey a message by means of an expression *XYZ* does not imply my knowledge of the internal structure of *XYZ*. Thus, the speaker above who swears in English may very well know what the expression does without understanding what it means. Even after learning English this speaker may never analyze the expression and recognize its internal structure. The speaker may only understand that the expression is unfriendly, and use it in order to convey unfriendliness. The speaker may thus treat "Go to hell!" as a holistic unit, and produce it as such.

The interaction of production and comprehension in non-native speech is, of course, only one of the issues whose discussion can shed light on linguistic production in general. Many others call for a more thorough treatment than can be given here. A most intriguing question, for example, is how languages are stored in the brain. How much storage space they require? How do they relate to a first language, and to each other? Differences between the rate of speech in the native and non-native language can be illuminating here, as can the study of speech disorders in the polyglott (cf. Paradis, 1977). Another topic of interest is the effect on production of a speaker's emotional attitude toward a language. This attitude will be significant on a socio-psychological as well as individual level. In another area, much research has been devoted to interference between different linguistic systems. However, in terms of a psychological interpretation of interference, many questions remain.

Obviously, not all of the psychologically interesting aspects of non-native production can be referred to here, and such is not the purpose of these remarks. My interest in this section has been simply to point out the significance of the distinction between native and non-native competence for a psycholinguistic model of production.

CONCLUSIONS

The task of devising a production model for language is a difficult one. The object of such a model is very complex in itself, and it comprises a wide range of different phenomena. In the above I have presented a list of preliminary distinctions which a production model must take into consideration.

A production model is supposed to provide for an answer to a number of important questions, among them:

- Does production (logically) presuppose comprehension?
- Does comprehension (developmentally) precede production?
- Are production and comprehension symmetric processes?
- Do comprehension and production always interact? If so, how?

Without wishing to dispute the importance of such questions, it is my contention that they can only be posed sensibly if the type of production at issue is reasonably specified. The distinctions enumerated above, and graphically summarized below, should help to do this.

Figure 1. Types of Production: Some Psycholinguistically Relevant Distinctions

Competence	Mode of Output		Motivation		Task		Execution		Genre		
	oral	written	spontaneous	elicited	productive	reproductive	creative	automatic	monologue	dialogue	polylogue
native											
non-native											

Examples

non-native elicited oral polylogue reproduction:
  collective liturgical Latin prayers
native spontaneous written monological creative production:
  diary writing
native spontaneous oral monological automatic production:
  interjections/exclamations: *Good Lord! Hell!*
non-native elicited oral dialogue reproduction:
  response to teacher question in foreign language drill

REFERENCES

Bolinger, D.L. (1976). Meaning and memory. *Forum Linguisticum, 1,* 1–14. (Reprinted in G.G. Haydu (Ed.), *Experience forms* (pp. 95–111). The Hague: Mouton, 1979.)

Coulmas, F. (1980). Introduction: Conversational routine. In F. Coulmas (Ed.), *Conversational routine: Explorations in standardized communication situations and prepatterned speech* (pp. 1–17). The Hague: Mouton.

Coulmas, F. (1981). Spies and native speakers. In F. Coulmas (Ed.), *A festschrift for native speaker* (pp. 355–367). The Hague: Mouton.

Krashen, S., & Scarcella, R. (1978). On routines and patterns in language acquisition and performance. *Language Learning, 28,* 283–300.

Labov, W. (1971). Methodology. In W.O. Dingwall (Ed.), *A survey of linguistic science* (pp. 412–491). College Park, Md.: University of Maryland.

Olson, D.R. (1980, June). *Written language and literal meaning.* Paper presented at Symposium on The Development and Use of Writing Systems, Bielefeld, West Germany.

Paradis, M. (1977). Bilingualism and aphasia. In H. Whitaker & H.A. Whitaker (Eds.), *Studies in neurolinguistics* (Vol. 3, pp. 65–121). New York: Academic Press.

Tannen, D. (1980). Spoken and written language and the oral/literate continuum. *Proceedings of the Sixth Annual Meeting of the Berkeley Linguistics Society* (pp. 207–218). Berkeley, Ca.: Department of Linguistics, University of California.

Van Lancker, D. (1975). *Heterogeneity in language and speech: Neurological studies. (Working Papers in Linguistics No. 29).* Los Angeles, University of California, Linguistics Department.

Whitaker, H. (1976). A case of the isolation of the language function. In H. Whitaker & H.A. Whitaker (Eds.), *Studies in neurolinguistics* (Vol. 2, pp. 1–58). New York: Academic Press.

Whitaker, H.A. (1979, August). *Automatization: A neurolinguistic model.* Forum lecture presented at the 1979 Summer Institute of the Linguistic Society of America, Salzburg.

CHAPTER 13

Understanding the Relationship between Comprehension and Production

JANICE M. KEENAN AND BRIAN MACWHINNEY

University of Denver

St. Augustine, in his *Confessions,* says that he learned language by noting how people spoke about different objects and by then trying to accustom his mouth to matching those sounds. Such has been the common folk wisdom on the relationship between comprehension and production: comprehension is viewed as the primary source of learning to produce language. As Ruder and Finch (this volume) clearly illustrate, however, the recent literature in developmental psycholinguistics shows how clever researchers can make something that has seemed to the general public quite straightforward now appear to be both complicated and wrong.

There are three ways in which this reversal of the common folk wisdom has been achieved. One way is to imply that production does not depend upon comprehension through claims such as that with which Ruder and Finch began their paper, namely the statement, "He doesn't know what he is talking about." If we examine those cases in which this statement might be applied, we typically find that a term such as "foresight" has been covertly substituted for the term "comprehension." Thus, it is not the case that the utterance has not been understood by its speaker; rather the speaker has failed to appreciate the consequences or implications of what was said. Does this mean, then, that there are no cases in which we can say "He doesn't understand what he is saying" and not be talking about foresight? Perhaps the statement could be applied to an aphasic victim with a lesion in Heschl's Gyrus—the auditory cortex. But, if a normal person had on earmuffs, thereby approximating the state of this type of aphasic, we would simply say "He cannot hear what he is saying" rather than "He doesn't understand what he is saying."

A second way in which the folk wisdom has been subverted is by the pro-

Preparation of this paper was supported by a grant from the Institute of Education, NIE-G-78-0173, to the first author.

liferation of attempts to demonstrate the primacy of production over comprehension—attempts which only succeed by disabling normal comprehension. Thus, studies like those of Chapman and Miller (1975) and Chapman (1978) achieve their effect, at least in part, by depriving the subject of the normal contextual support for comprehension. They succeed in showing that comprehension without contextual support may be inferior to production. In such studies the removal of contextual support is viewed as a way of measuring pure comprehension. Unfortunately, the unnaturalness of the resultant task may lead to underestimates of competence, and, as a result, these findings may tell us little about the normal relations between comprehension and production.

The third way of reversing the folk wisdom also involves demonstration of the primacy of production over comprehension. But these demonstrations involve a type of experimental manipulation that is just the opposite of that mentioned above. Instead of making the comprehension task abnormally difficult, the production task is made abnormally easy. An example of this is Rice's (1980) study. By making the production task simpler, she demonstrated that production can precede, or exceed, comprehension. In the extreme case, production is reduced to mere imitation and comprehension is elevated to a series of elaborate metacognitive judgments and predictions.

The point of this discussion has been to underscore our basic agreement with Ruder and Finch's analysis of the methodological problems involved in studying primacy relations between comprehension and production. As these examples have demonstrated, one can support any hypothesis regarding the relation of comprehension and production simply by either redefining the terms or by manipulating the requirements of the task. Clearly, what is needed at this point is a framework within which to view these various manipulations.

Ruder and Finch argue that comprehension and production are separate processes which are nonetheless intimately related in both language learning and in everyday use. In truth, it is hard to imagine, given what we now know about comprehension and production, how anyone could disagree with their conclusion. For all practical purposes it can be taken as an established fact that comprehension and production are separate processes which are nonetheless intimately related. The problem that faces the field is not verifying this proposition. Rather, the problem is specifying, in even the sketchiest terms, what the nature of the relationship is and how the two interrelate in actual behaviors.

One way to proceed in this endeavor is to break down production and comprehension into their component processes. Such an analysis will allow us to see the structural similarities between the two and thus will permit detailed specifications of their relatedness. It also has the additional benefit of providing a framework in which to view the cognitive requirements of the various task manipulations used to study language development.

In the remainder of this paper we will attempt to outline one possible analysis of the component processes in comprehension and production; and we will show

how this framework can be used to distinguish between various types of comprehension and production tasks or behaviors. Although this framework seems to be consistent with everything that we know about comprehension and production, our goal is not to argue for the particulars of this account. Rather, we present it only as an attempt to illustrate the type of discussion that is now needed in this area.

A FRAMEWORK FOR COMPREHENSION AND PRODUCTION

Space limitations require us to limit our discussion of this framework to the simplest case—the acquisition of lexical items. Our comments in this regard are an elaboration of some proposals first published in MacWhinney (1978).

We will use the terms *reception* and *expression* to refer to what many authors call comprehension and production. Our preference for these terms is based on the fact that "production" is often used to refer only to articulatory processes, whereas "expression" refers to the entire chain of processing from the formation of a communicative intention to the generation of articulatory movements. Similarly, "comprehension" is often used to refer only to post-auditory processing, whereas "reception" refers to both audition, parsing, and deeper comprehension.

Within both expression and reception, we can talk about three basic stages or processes in lexical acquisition. These three stages are: a) functional acquisition, b) formal acquisition, and c) mapping acquisition. We will examine these three types of learning first for reception and then for expression.

Reception

We assume that there are three processes involved in receptive acquisition: (a) the acquisition of a receptive function, that is, a concept; (b) the acquisition of an auditory form, and (c) the acquisition of a mapping from the form to the function. The first step in lexical acquisition is the receptive acquisition of a function. Many of the child's receptive functions or concepts arise directly from interactions with the material world. Thus, children develop the idea of a "tree" by seeing trees. Other concepts arise from children's interactions with their caretakers and playmates in the context of games and rituals (Wittgenstein, 1958).

Parallel with the acquisition of a receptive function is the acquisition of a form. Form acquisition occurs while the child listens to speech. Thus, the child that hears the sound /dawg/ repeatedly will acquire it as a new form. During listening, forms (in this case, the sound of words) may be stored with varying strength. Forms that have been heard repeatedly and clearly will be the strongest. Forms that have been heard only indistinctly or only on occasion will be weaker. Most forms will be so weak that they will be lost between hearings. Note that knowledge regarding the shape of a form does not require knowledge about the meaning of the form. Thus, it is reasonable to talk about the learning of the forms of words as the acquisition of a set of unknowns.

In the third type of receptive acquisition, the unknown is identified. This occurs by developing an association that relates the form to a meaning. For example, a child may map /dawg/ onto the meaning "four-legged, furry creature." In some cases a form may be present for some time before the corresponding function is acquired. More often a function is present and the child is waiting to match it to a form. When a salient form occurs in the context of the occurrence of the function, it will be acquired, and mapping of the form onto a function will follow directly.

Expression

Expressive acquisition is also assumed to involve three processes: a) acquisition of an expressive function, b) acquisition of an expressive form, and c) acquisition of a mapping from the function to the expressive form. At each stage expression can rely on prior developments in reception. However, receptive abilities alone are not enough to ensure expressive competence.

The first process in expressive lexical acquisition is the formulation of an intention to communicate. The intention may be to label something, to request some action, to engage in social interaction, or to convey information. Before the child tries to express an intention, the communicative function is acquired, at least to some degree, through reception. However, there are many things in this world that we recognize but seldom wish to talk about. Such functions are present receptively without being present expressively.

The second type of expressive acquisition involves the acquisition of an expressive form. Thus, once the child has formulated an intention to say something, such as the intention to say that something is a member of the "furry and four-legged" class, it may turn out that the child has no formal way of expressing this function. Acquisition of expressive forms often derives from imitation. But in order to imitate, the child must have a way of taking auditory forms and converting them to articulatory forms. As the child phonology literature clearly shows (Ferguson, Peizer & Weeks, 1973), this is not an automatic process. Rather, the child must devise an articulatory program in each new case. Once this program is devised, it may then be acquired as a new unit.

The third type of expressive acquisition involves forming an association between a meaning (and/or an intention) and an expressive form. For example, given the meaning "furry, four-legged creature," an intention to communicate, and the expressive form /dawg/, the child learns to get from the meaning to the form. Note that this type of learning involves acquisition of a pathway that goes in a direction that is opposite to that learned in reception. Note, too, that both the form and the function must be available before the child can control the mapping.

The Relation Between Reception and Expression

Given this brief sketch of the components of reception and expression, we are now in a position to go beyond the vague statement that production and comprehension are separate but related processes. We can now say how they are related. Reception and expression are related in that a) both involve the acquisition of functions or meanings, b) both involve the acquisition of forms, and c) both involve the acquisition of mappings between forms and meanings. Because they involve different forms and different mappings, however, the cognitive and physiological requirements of the two will clearly differ (Benedict, 1979; Huttenlocher, 1974).

We can also use this framework to specify how expression is dependent on reception in acquisition. In most cases the child first acquires a receptive form and then uses this form as the basis for the creation of an expressive form. However, in certain rare cases, a child may have expressive use of a word without appearing to understand it (Benedict, 1979; Huttenlocher, 1974). To see how this can occur, recall that there are three processes involved in expression acquisition: (a) acquisition of communicative intentions, (b) acquisition of expressive forms, and (c) acquisition of mappings from meanings to forms. Of these three, only the first two are dependent on reception. Communicative intentions are the expressive counterparts of concepts that emerge first in receptive processing. Similarly, expressive forms are compiled on the basis of the corresponding receptive forms. However, the mapping of a communicative intention onto an expressive form does not depend on reception.

Since not all of the expressive processes are dependent on reception, the child may have different expressive and receptive vocabularies. This is because even though acquisition of expressive forms presupposes receptive forms, acquisition of expressive mappings does not presuppose complete receptive mappings. Thus, a child can have expressive, but not receptive, use of a form whenever the child has developed an expressive, but not a receptive, mapping. This could occur, for example, when a child hears a form and learns to develop an expressive form from this receptive form, but never develops a usable mapping of the receptive form onto a meaning. Then the child is in a situation where there is an intention to communicate a meaning but no mapping from this meaning onto an expressive form. Because the child also has an expressive form available that is not tied down to a meaning, this form can be used to develop a mapping from the intended meaning onto this form. As a result, the child can show expressive use of a form without properly understanding it. Note, however, that because the expressive mapping is developed independent of reception, it is possible (even likely) that in these instances the child's use of the form may not coincide with adult usage of the form.

The proposed framework can also be used to account for the differences among types of lexical learning behaviors or tasks. Table 1 summarizes six different results of the application of the component processes of reception and expression. For each level of behavior the processes are listed in the order in which they must occur. Furthermore, the six levels of behavior are themselves listed in the order in which they could be observed if somehow we could tap into

Table 1.   Six Levels of Lexical Acquisition

Level	Component Processes
1. perceptual learning	receptive function acquisition
2. discrimination learning; identification	receptive function acquisition receptive form acquisition
3. echoic imitation	receptive form acquisition expressive form acquisition
4. lexical comprehension	receptive function acquisition receptive form acquisition receptive mapping
5. comprehending imitation	receptive function acquisition receptive form acquisition expressive form acquisition
6. lexical production	receptive function acquisition receptive form acquisition receptive mapping expressive function acquisition expressive form acquisition expressive mapping

lexical acquisition at each step along the path of development of a given lexical form.

The first level is essentially nonlinguistic. It involves the acquisition of a perceptual concept—some cluster of perceptions that has become stabilized in memory.

The second level involves nothing more than the acquisition of an auditory form. Of course, it is difficult to measure such acquisition directly, so experimenters usually teach the child to attach some overt, nonlinguistic response to the newly acquired form. In other words, the child is given discrimination training. An example of this is the receptive training Guess (1969) used to teach mentally retarded adolescents to respond to the plural.

In Guess's (1969) study there was also a group which received training in the production of plurals. That group seems to have been operating on Level 3, echoic imitation. They picked up the sound of the plural and learned to transfer it into the corresponding expressive form.

Guess (1969) found that his receptive training did not facilitate expressive use and that, furthermore, his expressive training did not lead to an improvement in receptive processing. Our analysis allows us to see why both types of generalization failed to occur. Referring to Table 1, we can see that Level 3 relies on a process, expressive form acquisition, that is not involved in Level 2. Thus, it is no surprise that Level 2 training did not result in Level 3 performance. In contrast, one would expect Level 3 training to facilitate Level 2 performance. But, recall that Level 2 performance depends on discrimination training. Thus, the expressive training group failed to show reception because they had not been trained to respond to the plural as a stimulus.

In the normal process of language acquisition children seem to spend little time on these three levels. Rather, they move quickly to Level 4, where they take receptive forms and map them onto underlying meanings. Comprehending imitation (Level 5) seems to be an intermediate step between acquisition of lexical comprehension (Level 4) and acquisition of lexical production (Level 6). In comprehending imitation the child begins to acquire an expressive form. This level is followed, often quite imperceptibly, by the acquisition of full productive competence (Level 6), which includes the control of the mapping from meaning to expressive form.

As previously noted, this analysis of types of lexical acquisition has been offered only as an illustration of how we might better be able to understand the relation between production and comprehension and the relation between various types of production and comprehension tasks. Hopefully this type of approach will help to move us away from the definitional issues in this area and toward the investigation of the relations between comprehension and production.

REFERENCES

Benedict, H. (1979). Early lexical development: Comprehension and production. *Journal of Child Language, 6,* 183–200.

Chapman, R. (1978). Comprehension strategies in children. In J.F. Kavanagh & W. Strange (Eds.), *Speech and language in the laboratory, school, and clinic* (pp. 308–317) Cambridge, Mass: M.I.T. Press.

Chapman, R., & Miller, J. (1975). Word order in early two- and three-word utterances: Does production precede comprehension? *Journal of Speech and Hearing Research, 18,* 355–371.

Ferguson, C., Peizer, D., & Weeks, T. (1973). Model and replica phonological grammar of a child's first words. *Lingua, 31,* 35–65.

Guess, D. (1969). A functional analysis of receptive language and productive speech: Acquisition of the plural morpheme. *Journal of Applied Behavioral Analysis, 2,* 55–64.

Huttenlocher, J. (1974). The origins of language comprehension. In R. Solso (Ed.). *Theories in cognitive psychology: The Loyola Symposium* (pp. 331–368). Potomac, Md.: Lawrence Erlbaum.

MacWhinney, B. (1978). The acquisition of morphophonology. *Monographs of the Society for Research in Child Development, 43,* Nos. 1–2.

Rice, M. (1980). *Cognition to language: Categories, word meanings and training.* Baltimore: University Park Press.

Wittgenstein, L. (1958). *Philosophical investigations.* New York: MacMillan.

CHAPTER 14

Development of Language and Thought and the Production-Comprehension Controversy

R. W. RIEBER
City University of New York

Ruder and Finch attempt to reconcile conflicting points of view on an issue fundamental to the field of psycholinguistics. In the discussion of their paper we will first summarize their position and then proceed to clarify and elaborate upon some of the difficulties inherent in these general issues, as well as their attempt to resolve these issues.

In "Toward a Cognitive-Based Model of Language Production," authors Kenneth Ruder and Amy Finch extensively review studies representing the more prevalent views concerning the relationship between comprehension and production in language. The purpose of their review is to arrive at one model of language performance able to account for and to subsume the three main models of language performance suggested by earlier literature. The first of these earlier models is based upon the theory that comprehension must precede production, the second upon the theory that comprehension and production are independent processes, and the third model, upon the theory that the two processes in some way interact.

In order to reconcile the contradictions implied in these three models, the authors introduce cognitive theory from the body of cognitive literature that has generally remained separate from the body of literature concerning comprehension and production. According to the cognitive based model of language production the authors propose toward the end of the paper, a cognitive component underlies both comprehension and production and can be used to explain the relationship between these two components.

In reviewing the literature concerning the "primacy" model, the authors summarize several studies. That of Winitz and Reeds (1975) represents the strongest position regarding this model. Winitz and Reeds claim that "comprehension learning leads automatically to production." Ruder and Finch go on to cite three separate studies all of which further refine this model by stating that comprehension precedes production, particularly in the telegraphic stage of speech development in children. Finally, the authors make passing reference to studies which show that "no consistent relationship" exists between the two speech components and conclude that the primacy model has not definitively been proved.

In the next section of the paper, Ruder and Finch review the literature supporting the theory that comprehension and production are independent processes. The first group of studies in this section is based on language training experiments, while the second group is based on adult aphasia research. In both groups the studies deal with "disordered" populations. Since the language of these populations is characterized by lack of integration, comprehension and production are more readily observable as separate components than they are in the speech of competent adult speakers. Ruder and Finch conclude that the first group of studies regarding child training present contradictory evidence. While the studies do show that one can train a child in either comprehension or production without necessarily establishing a response in the opposite component, the studies also show "some generalization to the opposite modality," indicating that the components are somehow interrelated. In the second part of this section, the authors review the literature concerning Broca's, Wernicke's, and Conduction aphasia in adults. They conclude that while, in the past, these studies have been thought to prove the independence of speech components, more recent studies in this area have indicated that the components may be related; that the skills involved in language comprehension may be similar to those involved in language production.

The next section of the paper is concerned with the third model, describing the relationship between comprehension and production, and states that the two components in some way interact with each other. The most important study the authors cite is that of Bloom (1974) who postulates that the components "represent mutually dependent but different underlying processes, with a resulting shifting influence between them in the course of language development." Blank (1974) and Rice (1980) both carry Bloom's position one step further by introducing cognitive theory to explain Bloom's "underlying processes." Ruder and Finch conclude this section stating that "the important question which arises out of the comprehension/production literature revolves around the relationship of cognition to comprehension versus production" (p. 125). The remainder of their paper examines this question.

The central question in the next section is whether or not the acquisition of language in children involves mapping language skills onto pre-existing nonlinguistic structures. The three main models researchers have proposed to answer this question parallel the three previously discussed models used to explain the relationship between comprehension and production. The "strong cognitive hypothesis," for instance, is analogous to the "primacy" model, and states that the child bases language learning upon a set of universal cognitive structures. Ruder and Finch point out that recently researchers who support this theory have indicated that cognitive underpinnings for comprehension may be different from those for production.

According to the independency model discussed in the next section, thought and language have different beginnings. This position was implicit in Chomsky's (1957) model of deep structure, but finds little support today.

Having summarized the major literature concerning the three models of language production, the authors proceed to clear the ground for their discussion of a cognitive model of production by pointing out that researchers need to precisely define the language structures and cognitive skills they are measuring. Using Huttenlocher's (1974) study of word- versus object-knowledge retrieval as an example, they suggest further that researchers should conduct studies relating comprehension and production tasks to pertinent conceptual information.

Ruder and Finch give greatest support to the third cognitive model they discuss in this section. According to the "interactionist position, 'language' builds on the developing cognitive structure and in turn shapes it." Proponents of this position ask supporters of the strong cognitive position these provocative questions: "Why does the child continue to master a formal linguistic device such as the plural to express the same basic meaning for which the necessary cognitive knowledge has already been developed?" and "If the child has the cognitive underpinning for this expression, why aren't they marked linguistically from the start?" According to the interactionist model, language interacts with cognitive development to consolidate underlying cognitive structures. Ruder and Finch endorse this position, and, in the last section of the paper, try to show how the interactionist cognitive model can be related to the speech components of comprehension and production.

In the last section of the paper, the authors propose a cognitive model of speech production. Their model runs counter to that of Osgood and Sebeok (1965) which describes comprehension and production processes simply as mirror images of each other related by a mediation process. Ruder and Finch find support for their interactionist model in Schlesinger's (1977) model. Schlesinger postulates that cognitive structures are categorical in nature, and that a child tends to perceive the world in terms of the categories characteristic of the particular language, but that the child can also form concepts independently of the language's categories.

On the basis of their review of literature, Ruder and Finch make several proposals pertinent to further research in language production. First, comprehension and production must be viewed as separate processes. Second, a model of language production must include more than a description of "the motor component." Third, comprehension and production must be viewed as interacting during communication. The most important as well as the most original proposal the authors make is that which states that different cognitive structures underly comprehension and production, and that the cognitive structures converge during progressive stages of language acquisition. This model accounts for the discrepancies between the models of comprehension and production earlier cited.

Our main objection to this paper rests upon a fundamental theoretical-epistemological issue. By describing comprehension and production as separate but interacting components, Ruder and Finch fail to recognize that these components are integral parts of a single mental process, or gestalt. This produces an ambiguity or confusion in their meaning of the concept of separateness. The only way to reconcile the discrepancy between separate and some degree of interaction would be to make it clear that separateness exists only as an abstraction utilized by the scientist to take apart the gestalt in order better to understand its function. Within this frame of reference, we can talk about elements of a whole as if they were separate from their dynamic interacting function within the organism. By engaging in this elementalization process, we are attempting to find how and why this element is a manifestation of an inner gestalt process or operation that is phenomenologically experienced as a gestalt. Furthermore, we are attempting to find its place in the homeostatic union between the whole and the sum of its parts. Theoretically, coordinations or interactions must take place between any of Fry's (1969) levels of the communicative process (semantic, lexical, morpheme, phoneme, or motor control.) The interaction of the levels in Fry's model is a good example of the body-mind interaction unity. Ruder's model fails adequately to take into account this important unification principle.

In order to account for the discrepancies between the various theories of comprehension and production of language cited in this paper, it would be useful first to understand the epistemological problems inherent in the various explanations given by the authorities in the field. The first important problem that should be considered is how comprehension and performance of language and thought may be best understood within a developmental perspective. Within this framework it is quite clear that the terms of language and cognition are often used as abstractions that imply that they are separate entities in the mental operations of the organism, whereas in reality they are best understood as processes or functions of an interacting psychophysical gestalt. No conclusive answer can be given at this time as to what this dynamic psychophysical gestalt consists of and how it works. Nevertheless, it appears clear from our perspective that the most useful theoretical framework would be one which attempts to understand the reciprocal relationships between language and thought as a functional dialectical operation. Moreover, from a primarily diachronic perspective, it would seem to be important that we appreciate the role that development plays in shaping the psychological understanding of language-cognitive performance and language-cognitive comprehension.

To begin with, the important problem is to define the two concepts we are dealing with—production and comprehension. These two concepts may be easily defined in a general sense, but when one has to define them more specifically in terms of context and in terms of the organism's development in time, qualitative and quantitative criteria in one's definition are crucial.

Ruder and Finch fail to point out the important related issue of the symbolic or semiotic functions intrinsically involved in the complex relationship between comprehension and performance. Although disagreement may exist among many authorities as to the nature of symbolic function during development, it is our opinion that symbolic function serves as a mediating device between actions (i.e., pre-verbal comprehension-intelligence) and representation (i.e., verbal production-intelligence). There is even greater controversy among authorities as to the origin or moment of acquisition of language and thought in the course of its ongoing development. Basic to the understanding of the concepts described above is the issue of continuity versus discontinuity. In order to clarify where and when continuity versus discontinuity may be useful in one's description of the development of the human organism, it is most important to specify and be aware of the epistemological differences that emerge when one describes a particular event in time. Furthermore, it is crucial that we appreciate the differences that really matter when we are describing similar things at various levels of abstraction. For example, Bates and Camaioni (1976) refer to a level of comprehension and/or production such as the "proto-indicative" and "proto-imperative." At this level, comprehension and performance are qualitatively and quantitatively different from that which takes place in a similar vein when the child is capable of producing its first word. During the latter period, it is possible that some children may simultaneously acquire comprehension and production of a single concept.

Therefore, it is apparent that comprehension and performance mean different things and function in different ways at different levels of abstraction. These are clearly differences that make a difference, and one should not fail to take this important distinction into consideration. If one considers the qualitative changes that occur in children in terms of the process of their mental construction of the real world, the concept of this continuity can be most useful. For example, between the ages of four and six, the child readily engages in what psychologists sometimes refer to as magical thinking, that is, an understanding of cause and effect relationships in a nonlogical manner. On the other hand, at about seven years of age children begin to establish as part of their understanding of the real world a more logical relationship between cause and effect. Another basic issue which is very much related to this concerns the relationship between inner language as opposed to interpersonal communicative discourse. Without a solid basis for inner language events, children would not easily develop interpersonal communication. In this sense, we may better understand inner language as a by-product of the child's personal representations of its own world. Furthermore, we may also more clearly understand the child's interpersonal world where cultural determinants play a significant role.

If we are to continue to make progress in this field we must take into account all of the considerations mentioned above and deal with them in such a way as to appreciate the holistic function of the development of mental operations in the human organism.

REFERENCES

Bates, E.V., & Camaioni, L. (1976). *La communicazione nel primo anno di vita*. Torino: Boringhieri.

Blank, M. (1974). Cognitive functions of language in the preschool years. *Developmental Psychology, 10*, 229–245.

Bloom, L. (1974). Talking, understanding, and thinking. In R.L. Schiefelbusch & L.L. Lloyd (Eds.), *Language perspectives: Acquisition, retardation and intervention* (pp. 285–311). Baltimore, Md.: University Park Press.

Chomsky, N. (1957). *Syntactic structures*. The Hague: Mouton.

Fry, D.B. (1969). The linguistic evidence of speech errors. *Brňo Studies in English, 8*, 69–74.

Huttenlocher, J. (1974). The origins of language comprehension. In R. Solso (Ed.), *Theories in cognitive psychology: The Loyola Symposium* (pp. 331–368). Potomac, Md.: Lawrence Erlbaum.

Osgood, C., & Sebeok, T. (1965). *Psycholinguistics*. Bloomington: Indiana University Press.

Rice, M. (1980). *Cognition to language: Categories, word meanings and training*. Baltimore, Md.: University Park Press.

Schlesinger, I.M. (1980). *Production and comprehension of utterances*. Hillsdale, N.J.: Lawrence Erlbaum.

Winitz, H., & Reeds, J. (1975). *Comprehension and problem solving as strategies for language training*. The Hague: Mouton.

CHAPTER 15

Psychological Processes in Discourse Production

WALTER KINTSCH
University of Colorado

Psychology has recently rediscovered its interest in reading comprehension, partly in response to a national malaise: the literacy problems in our schools. The reading problem has been joined by an equally disturbing writing problem. The development of a psychology of writing, of writing problems, and of teaching writing has acquired a certain urgency. Others, of course, have been concerned with these issues for a long time, and psychology is clearly a latecomer in this area. The question is, what does it have to offer. There are no concrete achievements to point to yet, which is hardly surprising, given the lack of work on writing until very recently, but there is promise.

Since classical antiquity there have been treatises on good writing, on style, and on teaching writing. What distinguishes the psychological approach to writing from these continuing efforts? Not more than a small, but important shift in perspective: from a concern with text structure and the writer's abilities, to the actual process of discourse production. Psychologists attempt to model writing from what they know about the basic cognitive operations, explicitly taking into account human processing limitations. It is precisely through knowing what these limitations are and how they affect the outcome of the writing process that psychological theories attain predictive power, and, we hope, will open up new ways of looking at writing and writing problems.

It seems desirable to place some general constraints on the development of a psychological theory of writing. First, such a theory should be closely related to a corresponding theory of comprehension. This is not to claim anything as primitive as that writing is merely comprehension in reverse; obviously, there are significant task differences, but the two behaviors are complementary, and it would be pointless to try to understand one without the other. Comprehension is a component of writing, because the writer, in editing and monitoring his output, must comprehend what he writes. In this essay I propose to investigate writing

Preparation of this report was facilitated by Grant MH 15872 from the National Institute of Mental Health.

processes against the background of the theory of text comprehension of Kintsch and van Dijk (1978).

The second constraint is even more important. An enormous, ancient body of knowledge already exists on writing; a psychological theory will have to deal with it, somehow. Let us not re-invent the wheel. The task is to make use of rhetoric (journalism, copywriting, advertising) not to neglect it, or to disguise well known facts as new discoveries. A good theory is one that assures that psychology and related disciplines can take advantage of each other. They should not be independent of each other, nor should one subsume the other. There is, moreover, another body of scientific knowledge that is relevant for a theory of writing: the laboratory work on memory and cognitive processes. Many psychologists, when they start working on complex processes, disregard the laboratory results and the theories based on them as too simpleminded, and insist on starting from scratch once again. Here, I want to propose the opposite strategy: to build a theory of the writing process cumulatively, building both on the list-learning paradigms of the psychological laboratory and on the analytic and descriptive tradition of rhetorics.

The Flower and Hayes Model.

Indeed, there is something else to build upon: the recent work on writing within the cognitive science framework. There is not much as yet: an interesting program to write stories by computer in the Yale tradition (Meehan, 1976), a review by Black (1982), and a few attempts at psychological modeling: Bruce, Collins, Rubin, and Gentner (1978) and Flower and Hayes (1979), who provide a useful foundation for the present model; and experimental work by Voss, Vesonder, and Spilich (1980), who are concerned more with one of the subprocesses of text production than with a general model of writing, as will be discussed below.

Flower and Hayes provide a task analysis of the writing process (as such, this is not very different from Bruce et al.), and substantiate it via protocol analysis. They are able to show that the processing stages they discuss have distinct psychological characteristics, and they develop a methodology that can be used effectively in the exploration of the writing process (Atlas, 1979). I propose to use Flower and Hayes' basic analysis of writing into subprocesses, and conceive of my task as modelling (some of) these subprocesses in sufficient detail so that they become more than mere names for unanalyzed global processing units.

Flower and Hayes distinguish three major subprocesses of writing: planning, translating, and editing. The planning process is subdivided into three components: generating ideas, organizing, and goal setting (the latter is a control process that decides when to schedule generating, organizing, translating, or reviewing). Two components of the editing process are also distinguished: an automatic editing that interrupts other ongoing activity, and a more systematic reviewing process. They show that these sub-processes can be distinguished in various ways (for example, by means of the written products of each, notes from the generation process, outlines from organization, and well-formed sentences from the translation process). But they do not go into sufficient detail about how these subprocesses work.

I am going to concentrate here on the subprocesses of generating and organizing. I cannot at this point present detailed formal models, but merely a program for how such models can be developed within the framework of the Kintsch and van Dijk theory of comprehension. I shall say very little about translating, indicating only how these processes would fit into the general framework.

A note is in order as to the domain of writing processes to which the present model will be applied. The model is general, but for a start I would like to neglect the truly creative aspects of writing—writing something that has never been said or thought of in quite that way before by the writer, or even by anyone else. I want to come back to that, but first consider the kind of writing that is for the most part reformulation of familiar ideas—writing a textbook, an essay or an editorial; the college student writing a theme on "Religion" or a story on "A baseball game."

ON GENERATING IDEAS

Flower and Hayes have very little to say: the generating process derives its first memory probe from information about the topic and the intended audience; as items are retrieved, associative chains are formed, which are broken whenever something not useful to the writing task is retrieved.

What do writers have to go on, beyond the empty page staring into their face, when they start writing? First of all, a topic that they want to write on. This topic may be very vaguely defined ("religion"), or it may be quite specific ("Discuss Marx's statement that religion is the opium of the people"). These two topics differ in the amount of constraint they impose upon the idea generation process. Often, a more constrained generation episode may follow a less constrained one, as in the case where the general topic "religion" is successively refined in writing an essay, but transitions from very specific to quite general topics also occur. The topic only partly controls the idea generation process. There are other important constraints: the type of text being generated (a story for the *New Yorker,* a textbook chapter, an editorial), and closely connected with that, the readers for whom the text is being written. Note that writers try to communicate with their audience, however indirectly, and that this process is therefore regulated by the Gricean conventions that govern all human communication (Grice, 1975): for example to say what is relevant, not to say too much, or too little, to say it so that it can be understood. Indeed, because of the remote relation between reader and writer, a writer must observe special, more stringent conventions than a speaker who has the advantage of personal contact (cf. for example,

Hirsch, 1977; Rubin, 1980). Thus, we have two kinds of constraints to consider: the topic, and conventions about text type and audience. What they constrain is the search for ideas in the writer's knowledge base.

We have to make some assumptions, therefore, about the nature of that knowledge base. Knowledge is part of a person's long-term memory (LTM). Various models of LTM have been proposed, ranging from almost random, minimally organized (Landauer, 1975) to intricately structured (in terms of conceptual hierarchies, scripts, frames, schemata). However, there may be disadvantages to conceiving of scripts and schemata as LTM structures; instead, one may think of them as being constructed when needed for some purpose in a particular context. This construction process makes use of information in LTM, of course, but the information is not in itself tightly organized and is structured only on demand for the purposes of a particular task. The relevant relations among units of information must be stored in LTM, but there are always multiple relations and hence many potential structures; when we construct a frame from this rich set of possibilities, we pick one particular pattern of stored LTM relations suitable for our task. Imagine a huge road map of the U.S. as a two-dimensional analogue of LTM: all paths are potentially there, but if we want to go from Denver to San Francisco via Atlanta, a particular path lights up, as in a subway map. In that sense, frames are constructed from LTM, if and when they are needed. There is not only one fixed frame, but in complex situations, a number of alternatives; flexibility is gained from mere rote elements.

In comprehending discourse, for instance, one does not pull a frame out of LTM, ready made, and then plug text propositions into the slots of that frame, but one constructs a frame suitable for organizing a particular text, using relevant knowledge. Script application, in the sense of Schank and Abelson (1977), is a special case where the relevant knowledge (about a procedure) is fairly simple and leaves few options (there is only so much one can do in a restaurant under normal conditions); but consider the reader who reads an essay on "religion": there is no frame to be pulled out to guide the reading, but there is much loosely organized knowledge about religion that can be used to construct suitable frames ("facts" in the Kintsch & van Dijk, 1978, terminology) in interaction with the text.

We conceive of LTM as a huge propositional network that is organized only in the sense that certain relationships exist among the propositional nodes (for example, they may have common arguments), and in the sense that related propositions are somehow close to each other. A spatial metaphor is useful here. The memory network is like the universe. In a multi-dimensional space, there are galaxies of knowledge on this or that, with subclusters like star systems. There is a lot of local structure there, as well as some very specific relations within a knowledge cluster, but if observed from enough distance, all we have is a locally uniform space, dense in some regions, full of holes in others. Holes may be filled when new knowledge is acquired through learning, and where there are nothing but holes in one person's knowledge system, others have grown a thicket of nodes. But in some unspecified way these nodes are grown so that related nodes are deposited in neighboring regions of the space. (Landauer, 1975, has described a mechanism that assures that contemporaneous experiences are stored more or less together.) Thus, the knowledge space contains an area where information can be found that has to do with "religion" (including personal, spatio-temporally tagged episodic nodes), and, at some distance from it, a space for "Quantum Theory"—a vast void for most people. How can information regarding some more or less well specified topic be retrieved from such a knowledge base?

Obviously, people do not have a procedure to search their knowledge spaces systematically. Otherwise, given enough search, they would always find any piece of information that is actually stored. What the exact processing limitations are that make such a procedure impossible is unknown.

How people actually go about retrieving information from memory has been studied quite extensively in the context of list learning tasks. Most memory specialists today subscribe to some version of a generate-edit theory. The nature of the retrieval cue is crucial for the generating process (Tulving, 1979); extensive use is made of inter-item associations in generating (Anderson & Bower, 1972); through a process of pattern completion the retrieval cue recovers the to-be-called item (Kintsch, 1974); the editing process which weeds out inappropriately generated items can be highly complex and task specific (Mandler, 1979). A model of recall in a list learning task which embodies all these features has recently been proposed by Raaijmakers (1979). It is the best and most complete model of recall available today, both because it has been worked out formally and in detail, and because it embodies the important principles mentioned above which have emerged from 20 years of study of this experimental paradigm. I shall investigate the applicability of the RS model to a new task: the task of retrieving information from memory within certain constraints, i.e., the process of generating ideas in writing.[1]

There are two problems. One must decide where and how to look for an idea in the vast knowledge space, and then actually produce it. For the second problem—the actual memory search—the RS theory provides a ready-made solution, as I shall show below.

---

[1]The term "memory" is used here in a very broad sense, in accordance with its use in experimental psychology: it comprises all kinds of information stored in the brain, from personal experiences, to general knowledge, to procedures and strategies. Non-psychologists often find this use of the term puzzling, and object to such statements as "ideas in writing are generated from memory." But no harm is done, as long as one understands in what sense "memory" is used in that phrase.

On the Construction of a Retrieval Cue and the Establishment of a Search Set.

The question is, where to look for information in memory, or, less meta-phorically, what questions to ask and in what order to explore them.

LTM is to be probed with a *retrieval cue*. This cue has several components. First, there are the contextual features, paramount in list-learning tasks. They are less important now, but can not be neglected (the familiar writing environment, versus the idea that finally pops up in the shower; today's headache). Next, there are the constraints imposed by the intended test type and audience. Certain searches can be excluded on the basis of such considerations, without actually having to examine their outcomes. Finally, and most importantly, there are the content specifications of the to-be-generated ideas. These may be extremely general, as in the "religion" example, in which case all sorts of ideas will be generated that will be difficult to organize, or they may be very specific, as in the "opium of the people" example, which will generate fewer ideas, but in such a way that they will be easier to organize.

Thus, we have a retrieval cue and could go on searching for ideas with that cue. But a whole new set of problems emerge at this point, for no text is written on the basis of one generation episode. Many memory searches are needed, and the question arises how these are controlled. What are the search strategies writers use? Are some better than others, and why?

How do people construct an outline for what they are going to write on (a search plan, not an outline for the final product, which would be a macrostructure)? The principle is clear: consider some proposition A that is currently in the writer's short-term store (it would be the topic at the beginning of the process). It has certain relations to other propositions in the knowledge structure, say V, W, X, Y, and Z. A search plan is obtained by deciding to explore X next, or X, Y and Z in that order. What governs such decisions?

There are many questions and almost no answers. The additional constraints mentioned above concerning text type and audience certainly play a role; they might, for example, exclude alternatives V and W right away as inappropriate. But beyond that, we know very little. Each node in a search tree represents a decision to continue the search in a certain way in the face of many alternatives. When do people explore a search tree in depth, when do they make a breadth-first search? Some pathways seem obligatory (for instance, the pro and contra in the delights of opium). How does the level of constraint interact with the choice to follow up the search in a particular way (as when X is a well-constrained path, and Y is vague)? Most importantly, what effects do human processing limitations have on their search strategies? Are short-term memory limitations a factor, and if so, how are they overcome through the use of external memory devices?

There seem to be at least two promising ways to investigate such questions. First, through the observation of actual human search processes in writing, using protocol analysis or experimental procedures. For instance, P.G. Polson (personal communication, 1980) has described search behavior in a problem solving task as depth-first to a certain level, followed by an exploration of other branches to the same level, with repeated reiterations. Polson speculates that this search pattern reflects an adaptation to short-term memory limitations: a depth-first strategy makes the least demands on short-term memory capacity, but elaborating a path too far has its dangers, because possible constraints from other branches are neglected in the process. To what extent is such a search strategy specific to the highly constrained problem-solving task used by Polson? As a second example, consider a study by Atlas (1979), who had subjects generate ideas to answer a letter. Expert writers exhibited considerable planning in this task, in contrast to novices. Clearly, such methods could be used to investigate empirically the kind of search strategies writers employ in the idea generation process.

But the empirical investigation must be supplemented theoretically. Theories of information retrieval and search processes provide a starting point (e.g., Winston, 1977). They are not psychological theories, however, because they fail to consider human capacity limitations and the nature of the human knowledge base. Nevertheless, an exploration of the formal properties of search processes may be instructive and eventually lead to a psychological theory of memory search strategies. How is the search to be guided, by means-ends analysis or by productions? If the latter, how are the productions themselves to be controlled— by recency, by importance? Do people make use—or should they—of the heuristics that computer scientists employ to make searches more efficient (disaster cut-off, futility cut-off, feed-over)? Given that the knowledge base is infinite for all practical purposes, how is it possible for depth-first searches to be used successfully? How do short-term memory limitations affect breadth-first strategies? At present, there is no model that would permit us to answer such questions.

Another problem concerning search strategies is suggested by an observation made about comprehension strategies (Miller & Kintsch, 1980): when people have a choice, they tend to select the largest possible unit to organize a text. That is, if there is a suitable frame, that is used; but if no frame fits the text, people still organize the text, but in terms of smaller, propositional units. Is there a corresponding phenomenon in the idea generation process? Is it the case that, at each stage in the process, people favor the most general retrieval probe?

But let me return from the unexplored work of psychological search strategies, setting this problem aside for future research. Suppose that we have our retrieval cue with which to probe the memory system and that it is constituted as was hypothesized at the beginning of this section: some contextual cue, information about text type and audience, and some specification of the content of the to-be-retrieved memory node. For the most part, with the exception of the context cues, the constitution of the retrieval cue is under the writer's control. From now on the idea generation process is automatic, and two things happen: the retrieval cue defines a *search set,* and ideas are then generated from that set.

The following assumptions are made about establishing a search set. The retrieval cue is directly related to one or more propositional nodes in LTM. These nodes are automatically contacted. Their number depends on the specificity of the information in the retrieval cue: there may be only vague and general constraints (once more, the "religion" example provides an illustration in which case many nodes with the argument RELIGION will be activated), or there may be highly specific constraints (the "opium of the people" topic would activate only a small subset of the nodes from the previous example). Each activated node has a neighborhood of some fixed size. The union of the neighborhoods of all activated nodes constitutes the search set.

The number of nodes in the search set thus depends on two factors: the number of nodes contacted by the retrieval cue, which produces a set of possibly overlapping semantic neighborhoods; and secondly the density of the knowledge space which determines how many nodes are actually found in these semantic neighborhoods. Thus, the level of constraint imposed by the retrieval cue and the density of the knowledge space in the area of the search jointly determine how many nodes will be included in the search set. The tighter the constraints, the fewer nodes will have to be searched; the denser the nodes in the knowledge space, the more there are to be searched. The important point is that the size of the search set is outside the subject's direct control: given a retrieval cue and a knowledge base the search set is constituted automatically.

How the Search Proceeds and What Sort of Ideas are Recovered.

The search itself is automatic, too, and follows the principles of the episodic memory retrieval model of Raaijmakers (1979). The only difference is that we are now looking for information that is defined in a different way. In a list-learning task, the goal is to recover words that are associated with a particular kind of context tag; here, the search is for information that is related to the retrieval probe in terms of content and other criteria (text type and audience).

In Raaijmakers, the items of the study list constitute the search set. They are associated with each other and with a context cue. Here, the search set is defined by the semantic neighborhoods contacted by the retrieval cue; again the items in the search set are interassociated, but they are not normally associated with the present context cue. If the search set contains $n-1$ memory nodes, plus the retrieval cue, we obtain an interassociation matrix $\{s_{ij}\}$ of size $n \times n$. The search, according to Raaijmakers, has two components. First an item is selected, which occurs with a probability proportional to its relative strength of association to the retrieval cue. A sampled item is not necessarily recoverable, however, because not enough information may be stored at a particular memory node to make recovery possible. In other words, the pattern completion process may fail. The probability that it succeeds depends in the model on the absolute strength of the association between the item and the retrieval cue.

If an item is not successfully recovered, the search continues until a certain number of failures to recover anything have occurred. (This number is probably quite small—see Flower & Hayes, 1979.) At that point, the generation episode is terminated. If a recovery attempt is successful, the search continues, but two changes are made: first of all, the recovered item is now added to the retrieval cue, so that the new search is doubly constrained, by the original probe as well as the already generated information; secondly, the association between the sampled item and the retrieval cue is incremented by some amount $\emptyset$. Thus, as more memory nodes are recovered, the nature of the retrieval cue keeps changing in that it is always redirected somewhat by the last item. At the same time, however, the whole associative structure is dynamic, too: the items already once sampled grow stronger and are resampled with an increased likelihood which is equivalent to decreasing the sampling probabilities for the ideas that the writer has not yet thought of.

The Raaijmakers model is mathematically formulated, in detail. There is no point in reproducing here this formulation. We can simply accept it wholesale with only minor modifications. One of them concerns the editing process which recovered ideas undergo before they are actually produced. A decision model based on signal-detection theory seems appropriate here: the suitability of each recovered idea is evaluated against some criterion derived from the content as well as the type- and audience-specifications of the original memory probe.

But so what? What can this model do for us? Can it be tested experimentally, as the Raaijmakers original can be tested with list-learning data? That depends on what kinds of data we can obtain. But even now, the model explains qualitatively a number of interesting phenomena about writing. Start with interference: one tries to think of something, but the mind keeps going down the same well-travelled track, and it is on the beach or in the shower (significant individual differences here!) that the crucial idea finally comes. Increasing the associative strength between sampled items and the retrieval cue accounts for this output interference, and changes in the contextual components of the probe for the shower-effect. Retroactive and proactive interference occur because certain associations are formed that are maladaptive for a task—they lead the search process astray.

A large search set (not sufficiently constrained by the probe) will decrease the probability of sampling an item in the set, while a small, highly constrained set will improve it, for the same reasons that allow Raaijmakers to predict the list length effect in recall. There are many non-intuitive questions that can be explored with this model, such as those concerning the interaction between level of constraint and density of the knowledge space (and hence learning effects). Furthermore, the strength and distribution of inter-item associations is another factor that interacts with the previous ones in ways that simply cannot be computed without a precise model.

It may also be useful to explore the temporal characteristics of the idea generation process, taking up the Bousfield and Sedgewick (1944) tradition in a new context. We can make, for instance, predictions about the rate of idea generation in relation to the number of ideas generated.

Another question is, are we going to find an analogue in writing to the part-list cueing effect in recall? Finally, and most importantly, how does the search process interact with search planning? Can one identify which strategies are good under which conditions (knowledge density, probe specificity)?

I would claim that the model seems fairly rich and promising, worth working out in detail. Note that it is a very global model. It abstracts from the content detail of semantic memory models (''A robin is a bird'') in favor of global, crude statistics like the density of the knowledge space. It is looking at retrieval from afar!

ORGANIZATION

Again, Flower and Hayes' (1979) characterization of this stage is inadequate: they describe five elementary operators—identify first or last topic; order with respect to previously noted topic; find subordinate topic; find superordinate topic; identify category. Organizing, it is claimed, is done by these operators. Clearly, there is much more to organizing a text than this.

The question is, how ideas, once generated according to a search plan, are organized. The search plan used to generate ideas need not be the same as the final organization of the text. In general, there will be reorganizations as new relationships among ideas are discovered.

The top levels of the final organization eventually become the macrostructure of the text, while the lower levels form the microstructure. The output of the organization process, therefore, is the textstructure, ready to be put into words by the translation process. Of course, no strictly sequential stages are implied by the model: idea generation, organization, and translation may be scheduled in many different ways. At one extreme, all ideas might be generated first, then organized, and then translated into words. At the other extreme, a single idea may be generated at a time, related to whatever is already written, and expressed in words. What sort of process scheduling writers use under what conditions is pretty much an open question at this point.

What are the principles by means of which a set of ideas can be organized? There are two sources that can provide the necessary constraints to organize a text. They are not independent, but it is quite useful to distinguish them. Both content and form may provide a basis for organizing a text. The very nature of the ideas that are to be organized may determine the organization. Ideas are always interrelated in some way, directly or indirectly, in the long-term memory structure. Sometimes these interrelationships are strong, direct, and quite unique. This is, for instance, the case in the memory systems called scripts. If a script applies, it is usually quite clear what is to follow what; indeed there are not many choices (disregarding literary techniques). There is only one straightforward organization for a given content. An example of this type of organizational strategy has been described by Voss et al. (1980). They asked subjects to generate an account of a half-inning of a fictitious baseball game. While different subjects generate quite different ideas in this task, the organization of the ideas is pretty much determined. Given the constraints of the task, subjects must start out with a description of the setting of the game (which teams are playing, who is at bat, what inning, what score, plus some optional material like names of the pitcher and first batter). Thereafter, the description of the game consists of a sequence of game states, rigidly ordered, and of actions which provide the transitions between these states. These actions can be described in considerable detail (see Spilich, Vesonder, Chiesi, & Voss, 1979), and characterized as to their level of specificity and importance. But the main point here is that, given the states and the actions, this content fully determines a unique organization.

Only in rather extreme cases is the content so all-powerful as in the example above, however. More frequently, content admits to many alternative organizations. Fortunately, the writer has available additional, formal rhetorical strategies for organizing material. Consider as a second example the essay on "Religion is the opium of the people." Suppose a writer has generated a number of ideas on this topic by the processes described in the previous section and now sets out to organize them. (Again, not all generation has to be done before organization, and it is quite possible that organizational strategies may also influence the search strategies in the generation process.) The organizing task here is much more difficult than in the case of the essay on baseball. In the baseball case, the total number of different ideas that can be generated is not huge. After all, only so many things can happen in a game. Furthermore, their interrelationships are highly constrained, either by causal or temporal relations. In the religion essay, on the other hand, the number of different ideas that can be generated is much larger, and the relationships among the ideas are diverse and complex. Rhetorical strategies are needed to impose a structure on this material. Suppose, for example, that a writer decides on the overall structure of an argument. We assume that the writer has internalized a series of strategies for organizing an argument. What these strategies are, we can take from rhetoric books. Thus, for instance, following Aristotle, a writer would immediately organize material into three major subsections: statement of the issues, assembly of evidence, and conclusion. The first question would be, what is the proposition to be argued? In the present case, this is given. Is the proposition clear, and if not what are the issues involved? What is the common ground? It does not matter that different writers, depending on the nature of their knowledge base and their attitudes, might identify very different issues. The only important consideration here is that in every case, this structure provides them with a way of organizing their ideas. The writer can then go on, asking what the facts in the case are, how they are related to the issues, and how they are to be evaluated. In this way, an overall frame for the to-be-generated text is constructed: the proposition is elaborated into issues, and facts are related in orderly ways to the issues. Finally, the question becomes, what does the evidence mean in relation to the argument? Again, various ideas can be assigned a function in the overall structure, or, if that is not possible, they may be rejected at this stage of the process. The writer has some more choices at this point: to employ persuasion as part of the argument, or to check the argument for fallacies. In either case, the writer can take recourse to further strategies to achieve these sub-goals. Thus, although the content relations were too complex to provide a ready-made structure for this essay, the rhetorical relations can do the job.

How seriously such a model deserves to be taken depends mostly on how well it is possible to specify the rhetorical strategies that writers use to organize a text. This ought to be a feasible task, since we have a long tradition in rhetoric to go on. However, there are many questions. Have rhetoricians really considered everything that is relevant to a psychology of writing? What is an appropriate formalism for expressing these strategies? How is their use controlled? I can do no more here than provide a few suggestions.

I am concerned mostly with expository texts and arguments, less with non-technical description and narratives, though similar principles apply there. That is, I am interested in what sort of rhetorical strategies are available to help organizing an essay, an editorial, a theme, or a chapter in a textbook.

Strategies may be applied recursively. A writer may decide on one overall form for a text—that of an argument, for example. But as this form is elaborated, other structures may be embedded: terms are defined or illustrated, classifications are made, contrasts or similarities are established, the components or the functionings of some complex system are analyzed; definitions may occur within definitions, and contrasts within contrasts. Thus, the eventual complexity of the essay is in no way predetermined, and its structure is flexible and changeable. Strategies must be highly redundant in order to be applied successfully, but they need not be unambiguous, logical, or mutually exclusive. The formalism that is probably best suited for expressing such strategies is a production system. I shall indicate here what some of the rhetorical productions might be for organizing expository text, without concern for precise formulations, nor for the control structure that would be necessary to make such a system function. Basically, what I am doing is to formulate as productions some rhetorical rules taken from Brooks and Warren (1949) and Pitkin (1977).

Let $X, Y, \ldots$ be concepts, propositions, or strings of propositions. On the left side of the productions are stated some conditions; when they apply, the actions on the right side are taken. The actions always consist of organizing the text propositions, that is, of constructing a frame within which these propositions can be embedded:

1. Y identifies (i.e. specifies in space/time) X → term X + identification Y
2. Y illustrates (i.e. is prototype of) X → term X + illustration Y
3. Y defines X → term X + genus V + differentiae W
   compare X,Y
   contrast X,Y

   $\cdots$

4. $X_1, X_2, \ldots \in X, \bigvee X_i = X, \bigwedge X_i = \emptyset \to$ classify X into X_is
5. X is similar to Y in terms of Z and Z is significant → compare X,Y
6. X is dissimilar to Y in terms of Z and Z is significant → contrast X,Y
7. X and/or Y → coordinate X,Y
8. X is physical whole with parts Y → list parts and relations among parts
9. X is process or operation with stages Y → list stages and relations among stages
10. X is physical cause or logical consequence of Y → cause + consequence
11. X is a complex with components Y → list components and interrelations
12. X intensifies Y → X + Y
13. X qualifies Y → X + Y
14. X specifies time of Y → X + Y
15. X specifies place of Y → X + Y
16. X specifies manner of Y → X + Y
17. X specifies significance of Y → X + Y
18. X evaluates Y → X + Y
19. X is a problem to be solved by solution Y → (to be expanded analogously to the definition example)
20. X is a question answered by Y → (to be expanded analogously).

Strategies 19 and 20 are not worked out here in detail, because just as in the case of definitions, any of the other strategies may be used to solve a problem or answer questions.

Consider how the strategies might be used to organize a text. Let us try a minitext with only two ideas: "It is springtime and the transients gather in Central Park." Strategy 14 applies, and we obtain the organization

$\begin{cases} \text{it is springtime} \\ \text{the transients gather in Central Park} \end{cases}$

The case is of course trivial: with only two ideas, there is surely no need for an organizational strategy. But suppose that instead of a single time proposition, a long string of propositions had been generated describing spring in Boulder, the snow in the mountains, the warm sun below, and then equally many propositions about the gathering of the transients in the park. Now Strategy 14 comes in handy. It provides a framework with two slots to organize the text. Within each slot, propositions may be further organized by means of other strategies that might apply. If the text is short, this is not necessary: we can get by with relatively crude means, such as relating the propositions in each slot only via argument repetition. Thus, we obtain a text representation structured in terms of a frame (with possible embeddings) and with propositions related by argument repetition in the slots of the frame. And there is something more that Strategy 14 does for the writer in our example: it tells how to express in words the relation between the time slot and the assertion slot in the writer's frame—a topic to be discussed below under "Translation."

The list of 20 strategies presented above is no more than a suggestion for how this problem can be approached. It is inadequately formalized, probably incomplete, and certainly not detailed enough. For instance, at least two kinds of contrast need to be distinguished: positive-negative (*not x, but y*) and concession-assertion (*x, yet y*). These distinctions need to be made because they are relevant for the translation process: different verbal expressions must be used in the two cases.

At the beginning of this section, two principles for organizing ideas were described: exploiting the constraints inherent in the ideas, and the use of rhetorical strategies. Although this distinction was useful, it is, strictly speaking, superfluous, for it is obvious now that the content-dependent organization is just a special case of rhetorical structure. Consider Voss's "baseball" example. Strategies 10 (causal analysis) and 14 (temporal sequence) are sufficient to organize the ideas generated here, for actions in the game cause certain game states, which are followed by other actions, and so on, until the final goal state, the end of the half-inning, is reached. What is so special here is merely the relational impoverishment of the idea set: causal and temporal relations are just about the only ones possible, if one complies with the experimental instructions to describe the game action. Thus, although it is certainly convenient to talk about a baseball script, the notion is really superfluous: the script can be generated when we need it from a flexible, loosely organized knowledge base.

TRANSLATION

Translation, the third major component of the writing process, could and deserves to be treated in at least as much detail as Generation and Organization. Again, we have a large body of knowledge to draw upon: while we relied on memory models and rhetoric before, we now can make use of linguistics and psycholinguistics (e.g., MacWhinney, 1984). I shall not do that in this paper, however, and restrict myself to some rather general observations.

We assume that at this point the writer has available both the macro- and microstructure of the text, that is, its complete semantic representation. The microstructure consists of propositions, interrelated by various semantic relations which we approximate by argument repetition, and further organized into frame units. These filled-in frames are called "facts" in Kintsch and van Dijk. The macrostructure consists of the most relevant and significant facts, hierarchically organized. This is what the writer needs to put into words now.

Several problems must be distinguished. There is first of all the task of signaling to the reader which portions of the text are macrorelevant, and what sort of a macrostructure coincides best with the writer's intentions. The strategies by means of which comprehenders try to reconstitute the writer's organization, or construct their own, are discussed in Kintsch and van Dijk. Presumably they correspond very closely to the production strategies of the writer.

Next, there is a whole set of problems concerned with translating the microstructure of the text into words. Translation strategies at the paragraph, sentence, and word level need to be distinguished. A great deal of linguistic and psycholinguistic work is relevant here (considerations of style, for example). The rhetorical organization strategies described above also have translation components associated with them. For instance, Strategy 12, which distinguishes between an assertion and its intensification, has the following conventional expressions associated with it: $x -$ indeed y, $x -$ in fact y, $x -$ even y, not merely $x -$ but y, $x -$ if not y; and in negative expressions: not $x -$ let alone y, $x -$ to say nothing of y, $x -$ not to mention y (see Pitkin, 1977). Similar lists of connectives can be compiled for the other strategies. Thus, organization constrains translation.

Recent work by Kozminsky (in preparation) illustrates how specific models of the translation process can be developed. Kozminsky's problem is to organize and connect six sentences, each dealing with a significant aspect of a stockmarket report (sales, dividends, etc). Thus, the ideas are given and already translated into words, but they need to be put into a reasonable order and linked by sentence connectives. Kozminsky solves the problem by specifying the relevant knowledge base and organizational strategies. The knowledge base reflects the stockmarket analyst's assumptions about the causal relations and correlations among the six market indices. This intercorrelation matrix defines several possible paths through the six-dimensional feature space. If a particular path is selected, the connectives between adjacent sentences can be generated by a few strategies: what is relevant in reading these stock reports is the evaluation of the stock implied by each sentence, especially whether it is positive or negative. In terms of this evaluation, each sentence pair is either a contrast, comparison, coordination, intensification, or regression. Therefore, the strategies listed in the previous section apply, and since they carry with them a choice of possible sentence connectives, one of the possible connectives can be chosen. Thus, from a list of six sentences, Kozminsky obtains a properly ordered, cohesive text.

Kozminsky's work (and also Atlas's, 1979, mentioned before in another context) illustrates a promising research strategy: to isolate from the huge problem of text production manageable subcomponents and to study these in detail, both experimentally and theoretically. Attempts to test the model as a whole would be futile.

EDITING AND REVIEW, AND PROCESS CONTROL

These are the two last components of a process model of writing, neither of which can be considered here. Flower and Hayes have done some important descriptive work on these problems, but of course most of the questions remain for further research: What are the conditions that trigger editing and review? How do they interact with the various search and organization strategies? How should they be used? How can they be used, given the flexibility and versatility of recent computer editing systems? What are the conditions that transfer control from Generation to Organization to Translation, and vice versa? When are some control strategies to be preferred to others? Most of all, a more systematic approach is needed to investigate these problems than the random sampling of questions I have given here.

CREATIVITY

It is important to say a few words here about the creative aspects of writing, if for no other reason, than to show that this important problem falls, at least in principle, within the domain of the model. So far, I have restricted the model to noncreative writing: within certain constraints, the writer generates ideas from LTM and connects them along established lines (a kind of regurgitation).

In creative writing (as always, I am more concerned with the creation of ideas, rather than the way they are expressed), there is an additional processing component. The ideas generated from LTM are connected along new lines that do not simply retrace relations already established in LTM. Instead, new relations among ideas are inferred, and, indeed, new ideas are formed. (Formally, this amounts to the same thing, since both relations among ideas and ideas are represented as propositions.)

One needs to describe a system of transformation operators, inference rules, or analogical processes that govern the generation of new propositions from old ones. This has been done for limited domains, such as set inclusion hierarchies, but there is room for more research. In terms of experimental paradigms to study these processes, problem solving and analogical reasoning suggest themselves, for it is not sufficient that some old idea be retrieved from LTM, instead a new one must be formed.

If we thus distinguish between the reproduction and the production of ideas, what properties of LTM provide a friendly environment for production? Materska (1976) has shown that reproduction and production (experimentally defined) are not always correlated positively. When reproduction reaches a very high level, production may in fact be inhibited. In terms of the present model, what is responsible for this inhibition effect—very strong, dominant associations? Since the same memory system is used in both tasks, what are the characteristics that permit a more efficient use of that system for one task than for the other?

CONCLUSION

There are too many questions without answers. The purpose of this essay was to show that the theoretical framework suggested here might eventually yield answers to these questions. I have here not a theory, but a program for building and exploring one.

REFERENCES

Anderson, J.R., & Bower, G.H. (1972). Recognition and retrieval processes in free recall. *Psychological Review, 79,* 97–123.

Atlas, M.A. (1979). *Addressing an audience: A study of expert-novice differences in writing* (Technical Report No. 3) Washington, D.C., Document Design Project.

Black, J.B. (1982). Psycholinguistic processes in writing. In S. Rosenberg (Ed.), *Handbook of applied psycholinguistics: Major thrusts of research and theory* (pp. 179–216). Hillsdale, N.J.: Lawrence Erlbaum.

Bousfield, W.A., & Sedgewich, C.H. (1944). An analysis of sequences of restricted associative responses. *Journal of General Psychology, 30,* 149–165.

Brooks, C., & Warren, R.P. (1949). *Modern rhetoric.* New York: Harcourt Brace Jovanovich.

Bruce, B., Collins, A., Rubin, A.D., & Gentner, D. (1978). *A cognitive science approach to writing* (Technical Report No. 89). Cambridge, Mass., Center for the Study of Reading.

Flower, L.S., & Hayes, J.R. (1979). *A process model of composition.* (Technical Report No. 1). Washington, D.C., Document Design Project.

Grice, H.P. (1975). Logic and conversation. In P. Cole & J.L. Morgan (Eds.), *Syntax and semantics: Vol. 3. Speech acts* (pp.41–58). New York: Academic Press.

Hirsch, E.D., Jr. (1977). *The philosophy of composition.* Chicago: University of Chicago Press.

Kintsch, W. (1974). *The representation of meaning in memory.* Hillsdale, N.J.: Lawrence Erlbaum.

Kintsch, W., & van Dijk, T.A. (1978). Toward a model of text comprehension and production. *Psychological Review, 85,* 363–394.

Kozminsky, E. In preparation.

Landauer, T.K. (1975). Memory without organization: Properties of a model with random storage and undirected retrieval. *Cognitive Psychology, 7,* 495–531.

MacWhinney, B. (1984). Grammatical devices for sharing points. In R.L. Schiefelbusch & J. Pickar (Eds.), *The acquisition of communicative competence.* (pp. 323–374). Baltimore, Md.: University Park Press.

Mandler, G. (1979). Organization and repetition: Organizational principles with special reference to rote learning. In L.-G. Nilsson (Ed.), *Perspectives on memory research* (pp. 293–327). Hillsdale, N.J.: Lawrence Erlbaum.

Materska, M. (1976). Relations between productive and reproductive utilization of information at different stages of learning. *Polish Psychological Bulletin, 7,* 115–123.

Meehan, J.R. (1976). *The metanovel: Writing stories by computer* (Research Report No. 74). New Haven: Yale University, Computer Science Department.

Miller, J.R., & Kintsch, W. (1980). Readability and recall of short prose passages: A theoretical analysis. *Journal of Experimental Psychology: Human Learning and Memory, 6,* 335–354.

Pitkin, W.J., Jr. (1977). X/Y: Some basic strategies of discourse. *College English, 38,* 660–672.

Raaijmakers, J.G. (1979). *Retrieval from long-term store.* Nijmegen: Stichting Studentenpers.

Rubin, A.D. (1980). *A theoretical taxonomy of the differences between oral and written language.* In R.J. Spiro, B.C. Bruce & W.F. Brewer (Eds.), *Theoretical issues in reading comprehension: Perspectives from cognitive psychology, linguistics, artificial intelligence, and education* (pp. 411–438). Hillsdale, N.J.: Erlbaum.

Schank, R., & Abelson, R. (1977). *Scripts, plans, goals, and understanding.* Hillsdale, N.J.: Lawrence Erlbaum.

Spilich, G.J., Vesonder, G.T., Chiesi, H.L., & Voss, J.F. (1979). Text processing of domain related information by individuals with high and low domain knowledge. *Journal of Verbal Learning and Verbal Behavior, 18,* 275–290.

Tulving, E. (1979). Relation between encoding specificity and levels of processing. In L.S. Cermak & F.I.M. Craik (Eds.), *Levels of processing in human memory* (pp. 405–428). Hillsdale, N.J.: Lawrence Erlbaum.

Voss, J.F., Vesonder, G., & Spilich, G.J. (1980). Text generation and recall by high-knowledge and low-knowledge individuals. *Journal of Verbal Learning and Verbal Behavior, 19,* 651–667.

Winston, P.H. (1977). *Artificial intelligence* (1st ed.). Reading, Mass.: Addison-Wesley.

CHAPTER 16

How Linguistic Is Cognition?

DOROTHEA ENGEL-ORTLIEB
Universität Hamburg

Kintsch's presentation of psychological processes in discourse production marks a turn toward production processes in cognitive psychology. The question of "how to write an article" is the starting point for elaborating a program of discourse production which covers the generation of ideas (what to say), their cognitive organization (how to say it) and their expression in ("translation into") language. Theoretically this approach is based on the list-learning paradigm of experimental psychology, on ancient rhetorical prescriptions for "good style," and on a tentative production model of cognitive science. Kintsch's main interest is written discourse.

The preceding approach to discourse production must be very careful not to mix up theoretically distinct levels of linguistic description:

1. List-learning paradigms are word-level paradigms. Can they actually be transferred to the discourse level?
2. Rhetorical prescriptions are instructions for language use in discourse. Can they be integrated with list-learning paradigms?
3. Written language already has the status of a metalanguage, which is learned at school and derived from the natural spoken language of native speakers by prescriptive rules. Typical production phenomena such as hesitations, corrections, repetitions, empty phrases, stereotyped expressions, and so on, do not occur in written language, yet they have a tremendous impact on patterns of discourse production.

Kintsch, as a cognitive psychologist, says much about the generation of ideas and their organization, but little about their translation into language. It is obvious that there must be a knowledge base from which to generate ideas. The interesting questions are: How is this knowledge base, rooted in LTM, structured, and how can information be retrieved from it. LTM, according to Kintsch, is a potentially structured propositional network. Retrieval of information depends on a variety of retrieval cues working together for idea generation. Once these cues are set to work, the process of memory search is automatic—which is to say, unexplained. Retrieval cues can be topic specific—contextual features, associative strength—and communication specific—the expectations of the writer/reader within a communicational network which includes choice of text type.

It is standard procedure to model memory processes on the basis of recall. An input of words, sentences or discourse is compared with its immediate, or delayed, (re)production under experimental conditions. Changes in output are taken as an indication for memory processes. The generation of ideas and their organization are now an inherent part of the comprehension process (input and knowledge base have to be compared) and also part of the production process (the knowledge base has to be turned into output). The question is: Is not Kintsch's model of idea generation applicable to memory processes in general, comprehension as well as production? In other words, is it specific enough to capture the uniqueness of the production processes? It is certainly not specific enough to distinguish writing processes from the processes of speaking. Chafe (1980), with a very different approach, starts with hesitation patterns in spoken language and uncovers a wide range of interrelationships between cognitive and linguistic processes in discourse production. He is able to explain similarity and differences of written and spoken language in cognitive processing (Chafe, 1984).

One of the most striking discoveries in cognitive psychology, for me, was the discovery of the chunking process by Miller (1956). The hierarchically organized chunking process seems to be one of the fundamental principles of cognition as well as of language, and the close relationship between language and cognition appears to me to be based on sharing this organizational principle. This shared process allows transfer from one state to the other. Chafe's research shows that the translation process from cognition to language only comes into play at a very detailed level of the hierarchy. Research on discourse processing with aphasics shows that high level chunking on the discourse level (in terms of story schemata) is still possible, even though concrete linguistic specifications are missing.

The above hierarchy is also recognized by Kintsch in the distinction between micro- and macrostructure, and in coherence patterns formed by argument repetition or frame units. Nevertheless, Kintsch's approach to discourse is more atomistic than holistic, bottom to top, and cuts a text into pieces—propositions and components of propositions—before embedding them in larger units with the help of formal technical rules.

The dominance of form over content which characterizes Kintsch's approach to discourse is once again reflected in his incorporation of rhetorical elements into discourse processing; he presents a list of 20 operations for constructing frames for embedded propositions. Only a few of these (8—whole/parts; 9—stages; 10—logical consequence; and 11—complex components) might be applicable to actions. Kintsch's approach automatically favors expository discourse and neglects narrative, which becomes vivid through content-dependent holistic patterns of realization which focus on an actor and move from lower to higher levels of chunking, and back, as shown by story schemata. In this sense, the report of a base ball game is not the same as a narrative.

As long as LTM is described as a propositional network, no theoretical distinction is possible between cognition and language, because the cognitive network is described linguistically. There is also no distinction possible between linguistic material as the input to a memory task and experiential knowledge which is stored in LTM. This is one reason that Kintsch's model of idea generation is too general. If cognition and language share the same organizing principle, this does not mean that they are the same at all levels or states. According to Chafe, cognition seems to operate more on (content-dependent) higher level chunks, and language seems to operate more on (content- or form-dependent) lower level chunks. A predominant role for form and language in a theory of cognition can, therefore, easily lead to a theory too linguistic to still be cognitive.

REFERENCES

Chafe, W.L. (1980). The deployment of consciousness in the production of a narrative. In W.L. Chafe (Ed.), *The pear stories: Cognitive, cultural, and linguistic aspects of narrative production* (pp. 9–50). Norwood, N.J.: Ablex.

Chafe, W.L. (1983). Integration and involvement in spoken and written language. In T. Borbé (Ed.), *Semiotics Unfolding,* Vol. 2 (pp. 1095–1102). (Proceedings of the Second Congress of the International Association for Semiotic Studies, Vienna, July 1979). Berlin: Mouton.

Miller, G.A. (1956). The magical number seven, plus or minus two: Some limits on our capacity for processing information. *Psychological Review, 63,* 81–97.

CHAPTER 17

Constraints on Psychological Processes in Discourse Production

SUSAN KEMPER
University of Kansas

Professor Kintsch has argued that psychological theories and research can provide a framework for studying writing. He has focused on three processes: the generation of ideas, the organization of text structure, and the translation of these ideas into words. He suggests that psychological models of the structure of LTM, of search and retrieval processes, and of production systems can elucidate these processes. Kintsch, in restricting himself to expository texts, has, however, neglected an important aspect of writing and a source of constraints on the writing process. He acknowledges that the search of LTM may be constrained by retrieval cues determined by the intended audience and text type, as well as the topic of the text. The information that is retrieved, in turn, constrains the organization of the text and this organization, Kintsch suggests, constrains the translation process. However, Kintsch has neglected the writer's goals and motives. Such goals and motives, as well as the medium of the text (newspaper articles vs. novels), and the intended audience (professional colleagues vs. children) may well constrain how LTM is searched for relevant information, how this information is organized, and how it is translated into words.

Speech act theory (Austin, 1962; Searle, 1969) may be used as a starting point for describing the goals of writers. Searle's (1975) taxonomy of speech acts suggests that we may distinguish five general types of text acts:

1. Representatives: texts that undertake to represent a state of affairs (past, present, future, or hypothetical). This class might include: letters, novels, histories, and newspaper articles.
2. Directives: texts that are intended to get the reader to do something. Directives include: advertising, persuasive arguments, editorials, sermons, and instructions.
3. Commissives: texts that commit the writer to a course of action such as contracts and ultimatums.
4. Expressives: texts that express the writer's feelings or emotions, including diaries, eulogies, hymns of praise, or meditations.

5. Declaratives: texts that bring about or institute a new state of affairs, including legal decisions and laws.

Each of these types of text acts may be associated with a set of preconditions necessary for the satisfactory performance of the intended act. These preconditions, in turn, may constrain the processes of idea generation, text organization, and translation.

For example, consider a writer who intends to produce a magazine article on the general topic of baseball. Such an article might be written in order to persuade young men and women to play baseball (a directive text) or to express the author's personal pleasure in watching baseball (an expressive text). Each of these goals can be associated with a distinct set of preconditions:

1. In the case of the directive text, these preconditions specify that: (a) the writer would prefer young men and women to play baseball (the sincerity condition), (b) the author believes the intended audience is able to play baseball and would not normally do so (the preparatory condition), (c) the article is an attempt by the author to get the audience to play baseball (the essential condition), and (d) the article describes some future actions of the audience (the propositional content condition).
2. In the case of the expressive text, these preconditions are less restrictive: (a) the writer must enjoy watching baseball (the sincerity condition) and (b) the text must describe the author's enjoyment (the propositional content condition); they do not place any restrictions on the present or future actions or beliefs of the audience.

Such preconditions can be used by the writer to direct the search of LTM and to restrict the retrieval of information. For example, the preconditions for the directive text will constrain the search process to retrieve information about the benefits of sports in general and baseball in particular (physical fitness, sportsmanlike conduct, self-discipline, competitive spirit). Those for the expressive text constrain the search process to the retrieval of information regarding exciting double-plays or controversial decisions witnessed by the author. In the first case, these constraints would block the retrieval of information about the unsportsmanlike conduct of professional managers, while those in the second case would exclude information about the long-term financial security or upward mobility of baseball players.

The author's goals expressed as preconditions necessary to fulfill different types of textual acts can be fruitfully incorporated in psychological models of information search and retrieval processes. Such preconditions can specify the retrieval cues employed or determine thresholds or criteria for the retrieval of different types of information.

So too, these preconditions may determine the macro-structure of the text. In conjunction with the kinds of rhetorical strategies outlined by Kintsch, writers may have strategies available for subserving different goals by different organizational formats.

The same facts, recollections of baseball games played and watched, can form the basis for a directive text or for an expressive text. The facts of murder may be organized into a newspaper article (a representative text) or a legal brief for the prosecution (a directive text), or a confession of guilt and remorse (an expressive text). Grimes's (1975) covariance predicates (i.e., antecedent-consequence structures) may be characteristic of directive texts that state the author's beliefs and the potential benefits (or costs) for the audience. Macro-structures such as story grammars (Mandler & Johnson, 1977) or causal chains (Schank, 1975) may be prototypical or representative texts. Expressive texts may consist of event or state descriptions plus the author's evaluation of these events or states, as in Labov and Waletzky's (1967) high-point analysis schemata.

It is with respect to the process of translation that the use of speech act theory and authors' intentions may be most useful. Stylistic properties of texts may be constrained by what the author is trying to do. The use of irony, of metaphor, of hyperbole, or of colloquial speech, may reflect the author's goals and strategies for meeting the preconditions necessary to fulfill the goals. For example, Booth (1974) suggests that the use of irony (and its extended form satire) is a powerful tool for establishing agreement between author and reader. The author invites the reader to go beyond the literal interpretation to the ironical reading and in so doing implies that the reader, like the author, is so intelligent and well-informed as to reject the literal interpretation. Thus, irony may be used in persuasive texts in order to fulfill the essential condition; it conveys the implication that the reader who agrees with the author in terms of the ironical reading should agree with the author in terms of the general topic as well. Other stylistic properties of texts may well reflect strategies for achieving different goals.

As an example of how an author's goals may constrain the processes of generation, organization, and translation, let us examine an essay by Poe. Poe's (1902) essay "The Philosophy of Composition" sketches the steps involved in the writing of "The Raven." Poe describes ten steps:

1. The choice of a sentiment or effect to be represented: melancholy.
2. the determination of the optimal length: 100 lines, as that is the maximum that can be read at a single sitting.
3. the selection of a technique to convey that effect: a brief refrain that is repeated in novel contexts.
4. the determination of the character of the refrain: a single word that involves a sonorous vowel (long o) and a pronounceable consonant (r).
5. the selection of a word to fit the choice of effect and the criteria in step four: "Nevermore."
6. the determination of a reason for the monotonous repetition of this word: uttered by a non-reasoning creature capable of speech—a raven.

7. the selection of a concrete topic to fit steps 2 and 5: a lover's meditation on the death of a beautiful woman.
8. the selection of the precise form to incorporate the refrain: a question-answer format.
9. the selection of the rhythm, metre, and length of the stanzas to convey melancholy.
10. the determination of the details of the plot.

Poe's essay, if he is to be believed, demonstrates that each step in the creation of a poem is constrained by the author's goals. The ideas, their organization, and their wording were carefully designed to represent a melancholy state of affairs.

Literary critics have repeatedly warned against committing the "intentional fallacy" (Wimsatt & Beardsley, 1954) in the interpretation of texts. It is committed whenever the critic evaluates the author's goals and motives rather than the text per se. To neglect the role of author's intentions in the actual writing process may be a more serious fallacy. Although authors may have mixed motives, and their texts may both, for example, inform and persuade, their goals in writing surely influence the content, structure, and wording of their texts. By examining how these goals constrain generation, organization, and translation processes, psychologists may be better able to develop models of writing and to identify components of writing failure.

REFERENCES

Austin, J.L. (1962). *How to do things with words*. Oxford: Clarendon Press.

Booth, W.C. (1974). *A rhetoric of irony*. Chicago: The University of Chicago Press.

Grimes, J. (1975). *The thread of discourse*. The Hague: Mouton.

Labov, W., & Waletzky, J. (1967). Narrative analysis: Oral versions of personal experience. In J. Helm (Ed.), *Essays on the verbal and visual arts* (pp. 12–44). *(Proceedings of the 1966 Annual Spring Meeting of the American Ethnological Society.)* Seattle, London: University of Washington Press.

Mandler, J.M., & Johnson, N.S. (1977). Remembrance of things parsed: Story structure and recall. *Cognitive Psychology, 9,* 111–151.

Poe, E.A. (1902). The philosophy of composition. In J.A. Harrison (Ed.), *The complete works of E.A. Poe* (Vol. 14, pp. 193–208). New York: Crowell.

Schank, R.C. (1975). The structure of episodes in memory. In D.G. Bobrow & A. Collins (Eds.), *Representation and understanding: Studies in cognitive science* (pp. 237–272). New York: Academic Press.

Searle, J.R. (1969). *Speech acts: An essay in the philosophy of language*. Cambridge: Cambridge University Press.

Searle, J.R. (1975). A taxonomy of illocutionary acts. In K. Gunderson (Ed.), *Language, mind and knowledge* (pp. 344–369). Minneapolis: University of Minnesota Press.

Wimsatt, W.K., & Beardsley, M.C. (1954). The intentional fallacy. In W.K. Wimsatt (Ed.), *The verbal icon: Studies in the meaning of poetry* (pp. 3–18). Louisville: The University of Kentucky Press.

CHAPTER 18

The Life Story: A Temporally Discontinuous Discourse Type

CHARLOTTE LINDE

Structural Semantics

The purpose of this paper is to show that discourse units like the narrative are used to form higher level units, one of which, the life story, is temporally discontinuous, that is, is told over an indefinite number of separate occasions. The principles which speakers use to construct these life stories coherently is the particular focus of the investigation.

LEVELS OF LINGUISTIC ANALYSIS

In this section, I will present what I see as a taxonomy of the best-known linguistics proposals for dealing with the analysis of spoken language beyond the level of the sentence. The structure of this taxonomy comes from researchers' varied assumptions about the properties of their object of study. The purpose of presenting this taxonomy is not to criticize any of the approaches mentioned, but rather to locate the present work within its intellectual context. I believe that all these approaches contribute something valuable to our understanding. For an object of study so complex as language and its use, only multiple perspectives can hope to give us knowledge which is sufficiently rich and precise.

I am grateful to Eleanor Rosch and Dan Slobin for introducing me to autobiography as an important area of investigation. My interest in discourse analysis and my understanding of how to do it are due to William Labov. Much of my understanding of the nature of text and the process of understanding it comes from conversations with A.L. Becker and Livia Polanyi. I have also been greatly aided by comments and suggestions by Gelya Frank, Veronika Ehrich, George Lakoff, Willem Levelt, and James Weiner; I would like to thank them all. Larry Selinker has taken me further in the direction of conceptual and stylistic clarity than I had thought possible. Finally, I would like to thank Joseph Goguen for his criticism, help and support throughout this project.

I am grateful to the English Language Institute of the University of Michigan, and to Mrs. Eleanor Foster for help in the preparation of this paper.

My primary debt is to the people who told me something of their lives, and whose lives are here treated dispassionately as objects for analysis. I hope that I have somewhat redressed any apparent separation between them and myself by using fragments of my own stories as well.

Is There a Linguistic Hierarchy?

One very common assumption, made of by most of the work described in this section is that there is a linguistic hierarchy of types of units. For example, a sequence of morphological units makes up a word or lexical unit, a sequence of sentences makes up a discourse unit, and so on. For the last relation, there is some question as to whether the relationship is a strictly hierarchical one, or whether we should prefer a description in terms of an instrumental relation, in which the units on one level provide the means for the expression of units on the next level. An example would be the distinction between the notion "interrogative sentence" and the notion "question," where the first provides an instrument for the expression of the second. (I owe this distinction to Fillmore, 1980, and Morgan, undated). The relation between sentences and discourse units appears to have characteristics of both the hierarchical and the instrumental relation.

The assumption that there is a hierarchy of linguistic units is not shared by everyone who works with questions of language and language use. Most notably, the school of conversational analysis represented by Sacks, Schegloff, Jefferson, etc, concentrates on the question of how observed order and regularities in a conversation are produced by the participants (For example, Sacks, Schegloff & Jefferson, 1974; Schegloff & Sacks, 1973). This requires a detailed analysis of the moment to moment details of construction, without recourse to abstract linguistic entities as determinants of the speakers' behavior. This view could be seen as conflicting with the notion of a hierarchy of linguistic units. However, I see the relation between the two types of analysis as complementary, roughly analoguous to a syntagmatic approach (the conversational analysts) and a paradigmatic approach (the discourse analysts).

What are the Units of the Hierarchy?

Given that one assumes a hierarchy of linguistic units, the next level up from the sentence has generally been assumed to be a temporally continuous unit. For example, the narrative has been the prototypical case for discourse analysis (Labov & Waletzky, 1967; Labov, 1972; Wolfson, 1976; Polanyi, 1978; Tannen, 1979; Linde, in press). The narrative is temporally continuous, that is, a typical narrative is told in the course of a single occasion of talk, and an interruption is clearly a break which must be repaired in some way. Temporal continuity of the narrative means that the narrative is a bounded unit. We know when the speaker is and is not engaged in telling a narrative, with some degree of negotiation at the boundary zones. (Sacks 1974; Polanyi, 1979)

Other discourse units on the same level as the narrative have been studied. Some examples are:

1. The spatial description (Linde, 1974; Linde & Labov, 1975). The study of apartment layout descriptions shows a structure analogous to the narrative—

a pseudonarrative in which non-temporal information is given a temporal organization. The boundaries are equivalent to those of the narrative.

2. The task description (Grosz, 1977). In this study an expert on the repair of a water pump answers the questions of an apprentice repairing it. The interaction was shown to be tree structured, and the boundaries could be defined as a consequence of this structure.

3. The plan (Linde & Goguen, 1978). A study of the Watergate tapes showed that there are sections of these political discussions in which the president and his advisors were engaged in the social activity of planning. These planning sessions showed clear boundaries. The initial boundary was marked by a statement of the goal of the plan, and the final boundary was marked by an evaluation of the probable success of the plan, the degree of the speaker's commitment to the plan, and by a general evaluation of the nature of the situation. The plan itself was shown to be tree structured.

4. The explanation (Weiner, 1979). Descriptions of income tax decisions and plan evaluations from the Watergate data were used to study the structure of explanation. Explanation, too, was shown to be formally tree structured.

Levels above the Discourse Unit

A number of researchers have attempted to explore the question of the nature and structure of the level above the discourse unit. The best known program of research has been Hymes's notion of levels of description for the ethnography of speaking (Hymes 1968, 1972). In Hymes's terms, the narrative, description, joke, and so on, is a "speech act," which is contained within some larger "speech event." The speech event is a socially determined occasion for a certain type of talk, such as a conversation, a therapeutic interview, and classroom lesson. The work of Labov and Fanshel (1977) on the therapeutic interview is to some extent located on this level, as is much of Gumperz's work on conversational misunderstanding (Gumperz, 1977, 1980).

The Life Story: A Temporally Discontinuous Discourse Type

The work mentioned in the preceding section assumes that the level superordinate to the discourse unit must be a single, temporally continuous stretch of speech. The assumption allows us to identify and investigate a number of entities which appear to have social reality for the participants. If we relax the requirement for temporal continuity, we are enabled to recognize another discourse type which has some social reality—the life story.

In the following definition of "life story" I will attempt to render precise and accessible to analysis a notion which we use as members of this culture. Just as items like "sentence," "story," and "conversation" were folk notions before their investigation and description by linguistics (or her older sister, rhetoric), so "life story" is a common notion. Intuitively, we believe that we "have" a life story, and that any normally competent adult has one. This non-technical notion of life story means something like "The events that have made me what I am," "What you must know to know me." For the present work, I will give the following definition:

> A life story consists of the coherence and discoherence within and among those individual stories and other discourse units in the sub-sequence of all stories and other discourse units told by an individual during that individual's entire lifetime which satisfy the following criteria:
>
> 1. The stories or other discourse units contained in the life story make a point about the speaker, not about the way the world is.
> 2. The stories have extended reportability. That is, they are tellable over the course of a long period of time.
> 3. They are most likely to be told in a social situation involving the creation of a greater level of intimacy, or the maintenance of an established state of intimacy.

Let us examine this definition in some detail. The first point is that an entire life story is constantly added to and changed in the course of a lifetime, so that to have a record of an entire life story would require of all the talk ever produced by a given speaker. This is in principle possible to gather, but in practice impossible. A discussion of how to break this apparent methodological deadlock will be found below.

The next point is that not all stories told by a speaker form part of the speaker's life story. One criterion for inclusion of a story as part of a life story is that its evaluative point is directly about the speaker or some event framed as relevant because it happened to the speaker, not because it makes some evaluative point about the way the world is in general. That is, I would want to consider as part of my life story a story about what happened to me when I was in the hospital, but not similar events told as a story about what's wrong with hospitals.

Given that a story is framed as making a point about the speaker and the things that have happened to the speaker, a further criterion for inclusion is that it have extended reportability. Extended reportability means that a story can be told again and again over a long period of time. Thus, the story of a career decision, or a divorce, or a major illness is relevant and reportable over a major portion of life, while a story about the funny thing the guy in the health food store said this afternoon is reportable for a day or two, at most, as a story about what happened to me (although it may retain extended reportability as a story about what health food store people are like).

Among the stories which fit these criteria will be those stories which we tell in the course of a relationship at points where intimacy is increasing. For example, I recently participated in a conversation with someone who told me a story about his divorce and struggles over child custody. I then told him a story about my own divorce. This exchange of stories can be described in a number of ways. One description is that by telling the story of my divorce, I was establishing myself as someone who has suffered similarly and so is capable of understanding. Another description is that the exchange of stories marked a certain stage of intimacy in our relation. Or one could say that the exchange created the intimacy. Which of the latter two descriptions one prefers depends on one's ontological aesthetics—the extent to which one is willing to populate one's world with explanatory entities like "intimacy." In either case, there were also markers in the conversation like "It's nice to get to know you better" which give some warrant for analysing the exchange in terms of increased intimacy. The point is that the stories which participate in such exchanges definitely form part of the life story.

Another important point is that in addition to individual stories, the life story may also contain other discourse units such as chronicles and explanations. These are discussed in detail later. These discourse units appear to be subordinate in frequency and importance to the story, which is the primary discourse unit of the life story, but they do occur.

A final point is that life stories are not defined simply as a particular subset of stories (or sub-sequence, since the order of the stories is relevant), but as the coherence and discoherence as they are discussed in the section on coherence. The crucial point is that a life story is not simply a collection of stories, but involves the relations among them as well. This is what permits the life story to express our entire sense of what our lives have been about, without our ever necessarily forming a single narrative organizing our entire lives.

The definition given above is objective, or external, in the sense that it would be possible, in principle, to pick out and study the object I have defined. I also conjecture that this object would correspond closely to our internal, subjective notion of a life story. This subjective life story is accessible to investigation by introspection, and consists of the ongoing stories we tell ourselves to organize our own understanding of our lives.

Studying the Life Story.   Clearly it would be impossible in a practical sense to study the life story as I have defined it. We might hope to get some representative sampling by recording a week of someone's conversation, or one day per month for five years, but even data like this would fail to capture the changing quality of a life story, because it focuses on the stories comprising the life story, rather than on the coherences within and among them.

A life story is constantly changing, not only by the addition of new material, but by reinterpretation of old material as well. We change our stories for each new hearer, we change a given story for a given hearer as our relation to that hearer changes, we change our stories as new events occur which change our understanding of past events, and we change our stories as our point of view, ideology, or overall understanding changes and reshapes our history.

An image which may help to clarify the type of entity I am trying to define is a cloud of butterflies moving across a garden. Some butterflies drop out and others join in, each butterfly is constantly changing its own position slightly within the cloud, and the entire cloud is moving.

Is it then possible at all to study such a unit? It very much depends on what questions we want to ask. The answer is probably no if we wish to study the entire life story or to determine the characteristics of those stories which are included in it, and those which are not. However, I take as my goal the discovery of the principles of construction and coherence which speakers use to form the individual stories comprising the life story, as well as the principles of coherence which they use to relate these individual stories. Since these principles are very general, in order to study them, it is necessary to have as data only a representative portion of a speaker's life story. A cross-section of a speaker's life story, even one taken at a single moment in time, will contain enough stories and their relations to permit the study of the creation of coherence.

THE DATA

The data which I have used come from oral interviews on choice of profession. Choice of profession is used since, at least for middle class professional speakers (who furnish the data for this study), it is a necessary part of a life story. One need only recall how often one is asked ''What do you do?'' to realize that professional choice is an essential part of our account of ourselves. Professional choice was also chosen since it is less emotionally charged than accounts of major illness, divorce, religious conversion, and other experiences, and so is easier to elicit in the course of a single interview.

The interview begins with the question ''What is your profession?'' (unless I am already known to know it) and then asks ''How did you arrive at that?'' or ''How did you become a _____?'' In general, the interview elicited multiple accounts, sometimes overlapping, sometimes contradictory, of the speaker's professional choice and its relation to the speaker's overall understanding of his or her life.

Validity

In using interview data, there is always a question about its relation to spontaneous conversation. One rough way to check the relation is simply to listen to the exchange of stories, since one is involved in it as both listener and speaker. This check suggests that the present interviews are quite representative.

Another indication of the validity of the data is that many of the speakers proffer alternate accounts without further prompting. Some of these further accounts are offered immediately; others follow after a noticeable period of silence by the interviewer. Such silence on the part of the interviewer is not neutral, of course. Rather, it is a strong indication to the speaker that more is required. However, silence does not invariably produce this effect. Particularly when the speaker has just produced a unit with definite boundaries, like an apartment description, silence will elicit a meta-comment like "Is that what you wanted?" Because the unit is finished, it is difficult or impossible for the speaker to continue on the same level of discourse, and so the discourse goes up to a level of meta-comment. However, we do not find this pattern in the choice of professional interviews. Because it is common to give multiple accounts, silence elicits further accounts, rather than a question about closure.

A final factor which indicates that the interview is closely related to everyday exchanges is that a number of speakers spontaneously mention that friends have recently asked similar questions. All these reasons suggest that the data elicited by this interview form part of the life stories of the speakers, and can therefore be used to study the principles of construction of life stories.

THE DISCOURSE UNITS FOUND IN THIS DATA

We may now turn to the discourse units which comprise the interviews. These are the narrative, the explanation, the chronicle, and the question-answer pair.

The Narrative

The first, and perhaps most basic of the discourse units is the narrative. Narrative as a technical term is taken from Labov's analysis of the narrative (Labov, 1972; Labov & Fanshel, 1977; Labov & Waletzky, 1967). In this analysis, the defining property of a narrative is that it is a sequence of past tense main clauses in which the order of the clauses is taken as matching the order in which the events referred to are presumed to have occurred. Almost all narratives contain more than just narrative clauses. Syntactically, they will include an optional abstract, an orientation section, narrative clauses, and an optional coda.

The optional abstract summarizes the story, often giving the point in advance, or indicating what kind of story it is. Almost all narratives contain orientation clauses. These are clauses which establish the characters, the time, the place, and the circumstances of the narrative. They may be placed at the beginning of the narrative, or be somewhat interspersed with the narrative clauses. The narrative clauses then follow, forming the backbone of the story; these are, as we have seen, simple past tense main clauses whose order is taken as the order of events. The final narrative clause may optionally be followed by a coda, signaling the end of the narrative. This may be a pure ending marker, like "That was it," or it may give the effects of the events narrated, or bring the sequence up to the present.

These units are all sequential, forming, with some reversals and overlaps, the beginning, middle, and ending of a narrative. But narratives also contain an element which can not be assigned to a linear place in the string, and which, apparently, can be placed anywhere. This is the evaluation, the means the speaker uses to convey the point of the story, the reason it is worth telling. Evaluation may be overtly and externally expressed as in a sentence like "I think that's

Figure 1.   The Parts of a Narrative

The Clause	Its Function
That was more or less an accident.	Evaluation of entire story
Uh, I started out in Renaissance studies	Orientation
but I didn't like any of the people I was working with	Orientation/Evaluation
and at first I thought I would just leave Y and go to another university.	Narrative (main verb — *thought*)
But then a medievalist at Y asked me to stay or at least to reconsider whether I should leave or not	Narrative
and pointed out to me that I had done very well in the medieval course that I took with him and that I seemed to like it	Narrative (absence of subject for *pointed out* indicates that the verb is closely tied to the previous verb, is part of the same event and may be simultaneous with it)
and he was right.	Evaluation
I did.	Evaluation
And he suggested that I switch fields and stay at Y.	Narrative
And that's how I got into medieval literature	Coda —— summarizes the story and marks the ending.

pretty good." It may be expressed through lexical choice. For example, "We went home to my house" is purely a narrative clause, but "We all finally made it home to my house" clearly has evaluative force as well, implying that the deed was difficult and took a long time to accomplish. Even simple repetition may have evaluative force, as in "He looked and he looked and he looked for her." It would be impossible to list here the entire range of syntactic and semantic devices which can have an evaluative effect. Labov (1972) and Polanyi (1978) have detailed many such devices.

In order to make this analysis of narrative structure clearer let us now examine one of the narratives which forms a part of the interview data. In Figure 1, the left hand column contains the clauses of the narrative, and the right hand column shows the function of the clauses. The speaker has finished telling how she got into English Literature, and has just been asked how she got into her particular field of research. This example is structurally relatively simple, but it gives a good indication of what the narratives of professional choice look like.

The Chronicle

Another discourse unit found in the data is the chronicle, a unit related to the narrative, but not identical to it. To my knowledge, the chronicle has not previously been reported in the literature. As a working definition, a chronicle is a telling of a sequence of events whose function is to fill in the major happenings of a given period of time. In ordinary conversation, chronicles seem to be given when the speaker needs to fill in information not known to the hearer. Thus, at the reunion of friends, we hear chronicles used to answer questions like "What have you been doing with yourself for the past two years?" Chronicles are also exchanged when people are getting to know each other and need to recount what they feel are the major events of their lives and the chronology of these events.

Example 1 is a chronicle which immediately follows a narrative about how the speaker left college and began working in a bank, ending with a strong evaluation of that job as a wrong decision. The example then fills in the time from the point of leaving that job to enter the army up till the present moment.

> (1)   Uh, the other decisions, I made a decision out here (California) to, to, to not go into the theater uh out here, in Asia. Went into the service and then went a year abroad. Decided while abroad not to go into movies or the theater. And so made the decision there and came back and didn't know quite how to get into city work, so in terms of deciding to be a teacher, again, it was the first and most realistic avenue I saw of getting into poverty work at all. Wasn't, it *certainly* wasn't that I wanted to be a teacher, I always saw it as a temporary thing and never more than when I got involved in it. But um then I made a very deliberate decision to get out of teaching and into the community housing group, and ver-, a very *wrenching* decision to leave the community s-, group and join the city bureaucracy. And then a very easy decision to get the fuck out of the city bureaucracy.

There are a number of points to be noted about the structure of Example 1. First, it makes use of the "narrative presupposition." That is, just as in the narrative, the order of narration is to be understood as the order of events. Thus, in this example, we are to understand that going into the service preceded teaching, teaching preceded the community housing group, and the community housing group preceded the bureaucracy. The second point is the absence of the other elements of the narrative form. There is no abstract, no orientation section, and no coda or conclusion. The third and most striking difference is in the use of evaluation. In this example, and in all the chronicles I have examined, there are evaluations of each individual event, but the sequence as a whole is unevaluated. This contrasts with the use of evaluation in narrative, where all the evaluations in a narrative tend to build toward a single evaluative point. This difference is motivated by the differences in the use of the narrative and the chronicle. In telling a narrative, the speaker must create some justification for telling it or face a devastating "So what?" response. In telling the chronicle, the speaker need not create a justification because the information being given has already been demanded, either by the hearer, or by the speaker's and hearer's understanding of the situation. Since the purpose of the telling is already known to be the filling in of chronological sequence, a further purpose is not necessary. The investigation of the chronicle requires further research, but this description should serve to identify the chronicle as one of the discourse units present in the data of this study.

The Explanation

A third discourse unit found in the data is the explanation, which is discussed in Weiner (1979) and Goguen, Weiner, and Linde (1983). Explanation, here, means a particular discourse unit, not an action of the speaker. That is, we may tell a story to justify some action, and it will thus function as an explanation. But the explanation as a discourse unit has a particular structure which distinguishes it from other discourse units.

The explanation begins with a statement of some proposition to be proved, and then follows it with a sequence of reasons, often multiply embedded reasons for why the proposition is to be believed. Example 2 is typical, by no means as long or as logically elaborate as many found in this data. It is given by the same speaker who told the narrative in Figure 1. Immediately after this narrative, I asked "Do you think it (medieval literature) was the right choice?" The speaker then answered this question with an explanation showing that the choice between medieval literature and Renaissance literature, which she had at first considered, in fact made no real difference. That is, Example 2 is a proof of the equivalence of medieval and Renaissance literature.

> (2)   Sometimes I don't think it makes any difference. I don't think I could've ever specialized in a very late field and been happy, I mean, I think if I had been in the nineteenth or twentieth centuries, I would've gotten bored and probably turned in desperation to literary theory, which is what a lot of people do. Um now that seems to me like a horrible sin, but it might have happened.
>
> As for the difference between medieval or Renaissance or seventeenth century, I don't think it makes much difference. Um I'm very happy being a medievalist and now I couldn't imagine switching, but if I had liked the people in the Renaissance and had stayed in it I would never have imagined switching either. So, um you know, I mean it was a right choice because it led to a job and it led to good friends and it led to a good career and a lot of satisfaction, but uh in other circumstances I think staying in the Renaissance would have led me to the same place.

The explanation begins with the statement of the equivalence *I don't think it makes any difference.* The speaker then establishes the relevance of this equivalence by showing that the apparently possible alternatives—nineteenth and twentieth century literature—need not be considered. She then restates the equivalence: *As for the difference between medieval or Renaissance or seven-*

teenth century, I don't think it makes much difference. She then shows that in two particular respects the choice of either field would have led to the same place. These are (a) that she can not imagine switching from medieval to Renaissance literature, but that in an alternate world, she would have felt the same way about Renaissance literature; and (b) that the choice of medieval literature has led to a satisfying life, but that the choice of Renaissance literature would have led to the same sort of life. Thus, the equivalence of the two choices in these two respects, which by the conventions of interpretation we must take to be the relevant respects, establishes that the choice of one of the two makes no difference. (An analysis of the formal structure of natural explanations and their relation to formal reasoning will be found in Weiner, 1979, and Goguen, Weiner, & Linde, 1983.)

The Use of Explanations.   To understand the role of explanations in life stories, we must examine some issues relating to the use of explanations—when do speakers use them, and what sorts of propositions do they use them to prove? Roughly speaking, explanations appear to be used to establish propositions about which the speakers are uncertain or uncomfortable. Explanations are not given as a first account in answer to a question. First accounts are almost invariably narratives. The explanations come as subsequent accounts, usually in response, not to the question, but to something brought up by the speaker. This relationship between discomfort and the subsequent position of explanations can be seen in an examination of those cases in which speakers overtly indicate that the proposition to be proved is one about which they have doubts. For example, there is one sequence in which a speaker begins by stating that going into the Marines was a waste of time. When I questioned him about this evaluation, the sequence in Example 3 ensued.

(3)   a   CL: How'd you get into the Marines?
       b   HL: I (pause) volunteered. But uh _____
       c   CL: Yeah I know, that's how it's done.
       d   HL: (Laughs) Yeah, well I wanted to be with the best or *some*
                   bullshit reason. I had a roommate in high school that did it.
                   I'm very uncomfortable about it.

This sequence immediately precedes an explanation in which the proposition proved is *It was a mistake, but, you know, you can't spend two years anywhere and not learn something.* This is then followed by a fairly unconvincing explanation, and then an evaluation of the explanation as unconvincing. This is a very overt example of an explanation being used in a situation of ambivalent feelings, but to some degree, this appears to be the case in most uses of explanations. For example, the explanation of 2 immediately follows the narrative in Figure 1. This narrative has as its abstract *That (the choice of medieval literature) was more or less an accident.* We may note here that although the speaker does not indicate that there is anything wrong with an accidental choice of field, in fact our knowledge as members of the culture tells us that this is somewhat problematic, going against our sense of a competent person being an active agent, in charge of his or her own life. I believe that the speaker takes some account of the possibility of her account being seen as problematic by following it with an explanation of why the choice in fact made no difference, and therefore, by implication, argues that the accidental character of the choice is not actually a problem. Indeed, there is a widespread use of this pattern; all the stories in the data which present some event as accidental are followed by some account which shows that in some way the accident was not really an accident. (A fuller discussion of this will be found in Linde, forthcoming.) More generally, we may say that the form of logical reasoning found in explanation is not our first mode of presenting experience; it is the mode we employ once things have begun to go wrong.

Question-Response Pairs

Narrative, chronicles, and explanations are the three major discourse units found in the data of this study. They are units whose structure is primarily imposed by the speaker. But there are also sections in the interview whose structure is dictated by the interviewer, rather than by the speaker. These are chains of questions and responses, like the chain in 4.

(4) CL: OK. Tell me what your profession is.
   JF: I'm a copy editor of scientific and technical publications. Production editor.
   CL: And uh how'd you arrive at this job?
   JG: I've been doing it for *years*. I started out proofreading and ended up an editorial assistant and it just growed.
   CL: And how'd you, how'd you get into the whole field?
   JG: Um I started out freelancing in um, with people that my father knew while I was in college. No, actually my first proofreading was summer school, between high school and college.
   CL: And how'd you get into it as a full time job?
   JG: It was the thing to do. When I decided not to go into graduate school.
   CL: Mm hmm. Why?
   JG: Um I always knew I could um correct grammar fairly easily and mark things up and then from the first job I got it seemed interesting enough to stay in.

The central question posed by a sequence like this is the nature of the principles required to describe why each answer is in fact a response to the question. This problem has been attacked by Labov and Fanshel (1977) and by Goffman (1976), but it remains appallingly open-ended. For the purposes of this work, it suffices to identify such question-response pairs, or chains of pairs, as one of the discourse structures present in the data. A detailed analysis of their structure is not attempted since I have made very little use of them in the analysis of the life stories; they are not very revealing of the structuring principles used by the speakers themselves.

THE CONSTRUCTION OF COHERENCE

Thus far, I have proposed the life story as a temporally discontinuous linguistic unit, composed of narratives, explanations, and chronicles, and the coherences within and among them. The explication of these coherences requires the notion of "coherence principle," a term which I have taken from A.L. Becker (1979). Becker distinguishes textual issues of coherence, reference, spontaneity, and intent. For the present discussion, his distinction between coherence and reference is most relevant. Coherence involves the relations of words, phrases, sentences, and larger units of the text to one another, while reference involves the relation of units in the text to items in a non-textual domain. Such a distinction permits us to work with what we have, which is the text itself.

As Becker has shown, the philosophically deepest coherence principles are those structuring principles of a particular language which its speakers take to be iconic; facts about the world rather than facts about language. For speakers of English, as for speakers of Indo-European languages generally, tense is taken as iconic, a true picture of a non-linguistic world in which time really exists. We find this, on the morphological level, in the fact that tense marking is an obligatory category. On the discourse level, we find it in what Labov has called the narrative presupposition—the necessary interpretation that if two main clauses are presented sequentially, the event referred to by the second follows the first, temporally, unless specific lexical markers are used to counteract the narrative presupposition. Thus, the narrative presupposition forces us to interpret 5 as a different sequence of events than 6.

(5)   I got very nervous and backed my car into a pole.

(6)   I backed my car into a pole and got very nervous.

The narrative presupposition is also the linguistic foundation for the theory of causality which this culture takes as unquestionably true of the world. In its crudest form this theory states that a temporal sequence will be interpreted as a causal sequence, unless there are very strong injunctions to the contrary. That is, under normal circumstances, post hoc, ergo propter hoc. Thus, in reading 5 we assume that the nervousness caused the accident, where in 6 we assume that the accident caused the nervousness. In the larger discourse unit of the narrative, there need not be a causal relation between each event and the next, but the entire temporal sequence will be taken as causal. As Becker has shown, in Javanese texts, for example, there are complex and sophisticated texts built around principles of significant coincidence which do not make use of causality as a structuring principle. The causality implicit in western narratives is a result of the structures of particular languages, rather than a necessary truth either about the world or the human mind.

The Coherence Principles of Life Stories

The foregoing discussion deals with the linguistic creation of causality in English. Given this level of causality, we may now turn to an examination of a more specific and detailed level of coherence principles which organize the life stories. In giving an account of one's life, one faces the problem of establishing a chain of causality which is neither too thin nor too thick. Too thin an account suggests that one's life has proceeded at random, discontinuously. Too thick an account suggests that the speaker implicitly accepts a deterministic or fatalistic theory of causality. Neither of these extremes is generally acceptable, and is subject to correction. The correction may be made by the speaker, by following a deterministic account with an accidental one, or vice versa. That is, speakers often perform a sort of philosophical wobble around a socially determined equilibrium. The speaker who does not maintain this equilibrium, may be subject to correction by the hearer.

Adequate Causality. Adequate causality means a chain of causality which is socially accepted as a good reason for some particular state or action. Its adequacy comes from cultural and subcultural beliefs about proper lives, and also from the particular speaker's cleverness or ineptness in framing his or her story. In this data I have found two forms of adequate accounts; these are based on character traits, or on multiple non-contradictory accounts. In other data, we would no doubt find further types of adequate accounts; the two found here should serve as examples of adequacy. *Character Traits as an Adequate Account.* Speakers appear to take character traits as primitive, referring to them as obvious causes for career decisions. Indeed, it seems intuitively correct that statements like "I was always good at it" or "I always was the kind of person who liked that sort of thing" are good explanations for career choice, and need not themselves be explained. We need not give an account of why we have the character traits that we do, although some explanations in terms of family circumstances, or parents' traits are possible.

An example of the use of character traits can be seen in 7. It comes from the speaker of the narrative in Figure 1, and is the first account she gives of how she arrived at her profession.

(7a) I seemed to be very good in reading and analyzing books and writing, so I became an English major

(7b) and from then on since I knew I would go as far in whatever I chose as I possibly could go, getting a Ph.D. became a necessity

Two character traits are invoked as reasons, one explicitly named and the other referred to implicitly. The first is ability; the second, in 7b, is determination or ambition. These are taken by the speaker as wholly adequate; in all her subsequent accounts she gives no further attention to the issue of why she chose literature. Her later narratives and explanations work with the somewhat less adequate accounts of why she chose her particular field of study, but the choice of literature is unquestioned, having been adequately motivated. *Richness of Account.* An account is "rich" when it contains many reasons which differ, but do not contradict one another. Examples are too long to give in detail here, but a brief description of one such example may suffice. A particularly rich account is given by a speaker who holds a degree in 17th century literature and teaches courses on the relations of science and the humanities, and on medical ethics. Her first reason is essentially chance "That was almost by dint of being in a certain place at a certain time." This is followed by an account in terms of family history—her father was a writer, and her mother a librarian, which accounts for her literary interests. She then invokes interest in science and a desire to go into medicine when she was in college, which she did not pursue because she had started too late. The next reason for her present position is that the writer she chose for her dissertation research was a theologian with strong interests in science. Finally, she tells a story of being influenced by hearing a lecture by a well-known woman professor whose interests combined the literary and the scientific. None of these accounts would be strongly adequate alone, but taken all together, they argue that her life was clearly pointed in the direction she eventually took.

Inadequate Accounts—The Management of Discontinuity

There are many accounts which can be given that are in some way inadequate or problematic, what we may call "discoherent." These can be divided into accounts structured in terms of accident, and accounts which contain a socially recognizable discontinuity. Both of these raise the possible dangers of excessive determinism or excessive randomness, and require work on the part of the speaker, either to deny these possibilities, or to show that some appropriate adjustment has been made to them. *Accident.* In the account by the medievalist (Figure 1 and Example 2) we see a clear case of the management of accident. In the narrative, the speaker evaluates her choice of field as "more or less an accident." This evaluation raises the question of what accident could possibly mean in such a use. We are happiest analyzing some event like an avalanche or a plane crash as an accident: the prototypical accident has little or no contribution from human actors, at least not from the people who analyze it as an accident. (That is, a car crash may be seen by a passenger as an accident, and by the driver—or the driver's boss—as caused by fatigue, which itself resulted from being forced to work overtime, and so on.)

Let us examine the work that the speaker does with this analysis as accident. She follows it with an explanation which shows that the accident is not really an accident at all. In detail, she shows, that though the particular details of her professional history were an accident, the other paths that she might have taken would have led to the same place. Thus, although the route was an accident, the destination was not. This pattern of multiple routes to the same point is very common; I have found it in every account which explicitly or implicitly is presented as accidental. It has the effect of showing that apparent accident was in fact more determined than it might at first seem—a clear case of the philosophical wobble which I have claimed speakers must perform. *The Management of Discontinuity.* In presenting a life story, the speaker may frame it as discontinuous. One of the clearest coherence principles that emerges from this data is that discontinuity must be managed in some way. If a speaker presents a sequence as discontinuous, some account will always be provided for it; speakers never present a discontinuity without an evaluation or an explanation. It is impossible to list all possible strategies for the management of discontinuity since they depend on the ingenuity of the speaker. I will simply sketch the common ones present in the data:

1. *Discontinuity as Apparent Break.* Discontinuity may be managed by seeing it as only apparent, not real. A later state appears to be very different from an earlier one, but they can both be seen as having characteristics which make them continuous. An example in the data is a housing administrator who previously worked in the theater. He manages this apparent discontinuity by showing that what appealed to him in housing was what appealed to him in theater—the chance to be an administrator, since his work in theater was as a producer.

2. *Discontinuity as Temporary.* In this strategy, an apparent break is shown to be due to a temporary discontinuity; for example, an early interest was abandoned and then resumed. One example of this is given by a speaker who describes herself as having had an interest in science in college, which she abandoned because she did not have the background to do well in it. She resumed that interest by working on the literary works of a 17th century scientist for her dissertation.

3. *Discontinuity of Actor.* Speakers may handle discontinuity in their life stories by assuming a position of distance from themselves. There is an example of this strategy in which the speaker, a professor of sociology, starts by saying that her academic interests were a product of her father's and grandfather's academic interests. She then states that as a high school and college student, she worked as an actress and a folksinger. Her management of this discontinuity is to present the person who acted and sang as very different from the person telling the story. She accomplishes this by speaking of the singer/actor as an untalented adolescent with unrealistic fantasies. Of course, this shifts the discontinuity from the series of events to the person, but it allows the speaker to acknowledge the discontinuity without having to

justify it. That is, by distancing herself in this way, by indicating so clearly that she knows that these interests were discontinuous, she avoids the problem of having to reconcile an interest in folk singing with an interest in psychology.

4. *Discontinuity as Continuity.* The last of these strategies is logically the most complex. In this strategy, the speaker takes a series of events and analyses them as discontinuous in order to establish that, for the speaker, discontinuity forms a kind of continuity. Examples of this strategy include on-the-road stories, and statements like "I'm the kind of person who likes to try everything," and "I hate to be tied down to any one thing." There is an example in the data of a speaker evaluating a discontinuous series of jobs by saying "I think I could be a dilettante all my life as long as I could, could do it with some intensity." In his use of the normally pejorative word "dilettante," the speaker provides a reevaluation of a discontinuous sequence.

CONCLUSION: THE INTERNAL SENSE OF LIFE STORY

In this paper, I have proposed a new notion of the life story as one example of a temporally discontinuous discourse type. In describing its properties, I have given two different types of characteristics. One is social, or linguistic; that is, the life story consists of those stories we tell about ourselves again and again. The other type of characteristic refers to some internal notion of life story: the sense that the life story consists of "What you must know about me to know me." This internal sense of a life story can be observed only by introspection. I believe that this internal life story serves not only as a guide to the shaping of socially exchanged stories, but also as one of the means we use for understanding ourselves and our lives. I believe that the social requirements of coherence and continuity are also requirements of our own private understandings, and that the process of constructing meaning is done as much for ourselves as for others.

The internal sense of life story, its relation to the socially exchanged life story, and its role in the construction of the sense of self are issues which lie beyond the bounds of the present work. To some extent, they are discussed in Linde (forthcoming); to a greater extent, they remain open to investigation. In conclusion, though, I would suggest that if they are to be investigated at all, they will require a prior understanding of the life story as a linguistic unit.

REFERENCES

Becker, A.L. (1979). Text-building, epistemology and aesthetics in Javanese shadow theater. In A.L. Becker & A.A. Yengoyan (Eds.), *The imagination of reality: Essays in Southeast Asian coherence systems.* (pp. 211–243). Norwood, N.J.: Ablex.

Fillmore, C. (1980). *Some thoughts on boundaries and components of linguistics.* Unpublished manuscript.

Goffman, E. (1976). Replies and responses. *Language in Society, 5,* 257–313.

Goguen, J.A., Weiner, J., Linde, C. (1983). Reasoning and the natural explanation. *International Journal of Man-Machine Studies, 19,* 521–559.

Grosz, B. (1977). *The representation and use of focus in dialogue understanding* (Technical Note 151). Menlo Park, Ca.: Stanford Research Institute.

Gumperz, J.J. (1977). Sociocultural knowledge in conversational inference. In M. Saville-Troike (Ed.), *Georgetown Round Table on Languages and Linguistics 1977* (pp. 191–212). Washington, D.C.: Georgetown University Press.

Gumperz, J.J. (1980). The sociolinguistic basis of speech act theory. *Versus, 26–27,* 101–121.

Hymes, D. (1968). The ethnography of speaking. In J. Fishman (Ed.), *Readings in the sociology of language* (pp. 99–138). The Hague: Mouton.

Hymes, D. (1972). Models of the interaction of language and social life. In J.J. Gumperz & D. Hymes (Eds.), *Directions in sociolinguistics: The ethnography of communication* (pp. 35–71). New York: Holt, Rinehart & Winston.

Labov, W. (1972). The transformation of experience into narrative syntax. In *Language in the inner city* (pp. 354–396). Philadelphia: University of Pennsylvania Press.

Labov, W., & Fanshel, D. (1977). *Therapeutic discourse.* New York: Academic Press.

Labov, W., & Waletzky, J. (1967). Narrative analysis: Oral versions of personal experience. In J. Helm (Ed.), *Essays on the verbal and visual arts* (pp. 12–44). (Proceedings of the 1966 Annual Spring Meeting of the American Ethnological Society.) Seattle, London: University of Washington Press.

Linde, C. (1974). *The linguistic encoding of spatial information.* Unpublished doctoral dissertation, Columbia University, New York.

Linde, C. (in press). The organization of discourse. In T. Shopen, A. Zwicky & R. Griffen (Eds.), *The English language: English in its social and historical context.* Boston: Winthrop.

Linde, C. (forthcoming). *The creation of coherence in life stories.* Norwood, N.J.: Ablex.

Linde, C., & Goguen. J.A, (1978). Structure of planning discourse. *Journal of Social and Biological Structures, 1,* 219–252.

Linde, C., & Labov, W. (1975). Spatial networks as a site for the study of language and thought. *Language, 51,* 924–939.

Morgan, J.L. (undated). *Toward a rational model of discourse comprehension.* Unpublished manuscript.

Polanyi, L. (1978). *The American story.* Unpublished doctoral dissertation, University of Michigan, Ann Arbor.

Polanyi, L. (1979). So what's the point? *Semiotica, 25,* 207–241.

Sacks, H. (1974). An analysis of the course of a joke's telling in conversation. In R. Bauman & J. Sherzer (Eds.), *Explorations in the ethnography of speaking* (pp. 337–353) Cambridge: Cambridge University Press.

Sacks, H., Schegloff, E.A., & Jefferson, G.A. (1974). A simplest systematics for the organization of turn-taking for conversation. *Language, 50,* 696–735.

Schegloff, E., & Sacks, H. (1973). Opening up closings. *Semiotica, 8,* 289–327.

Tannen, D. (1979). *Processes and consequences of conversational style.* Ann Arbor, Mich.: University Microfilms.

Weiner, J. (1979). *The structure of natural explanation: Theory and application.* Santa Monica, Ca.: System Development Corporation.

Wolfson, N. (1976). Speech events and natural speech: Some implications for sociolinguistic methodology. *Language in Society, 5,* 189–209.

Fourth Session:
Narrative Understanding and Production

Chair: D. Tannen

CHAPTER 19

Understanding Understanding

DAVID E. RUMELHART
University of California at San Diego

What is understanding? How do we make sense out of what we read or are told? I believe that over the past several years a substantial consensus has arisen in the field of Cognitive Science about the broad outlines of this process (cf. Fillmore, 1975; Minsky, 1975; Rumelhart, 1977; Rumelhart & Ortony, 1977; Schank & Abelson, 1977). In this paper I wish to sketch the basic features of those outlines and to show how this sketch can be given some reality by a careful analysis of the interpretations people actually make of stories and story fragments. Consider the following brief fragment of a story:

> Mary heard the ice cream truck coming down the street. She remembered her birthday money and rushed into the house.

Upon hearing just these few words most readers already have a rather complete interpretation of the events in the story. Presumably Mary is a little girl who wants to buy some ice cream from the ice cream man and runs into the house to get her money. Of course, it doesn't *say* this in the story, there are other possibilities. Mary could, for example, be afraid that the ice cream man might *steal* her birthday money. Still, most readers find the first interpretation most plausible and retain it unless later information contradicts it.

Consider, in contrast, the following story fragment:

> Mary heard the bus coming down the street. She remembered her birthday money and rushed into the house.

Upon hearing a fragment such as this, most people get a rather different notion of what the story might be about. The story fragment is less coherent. For most, Mary is older. Rather than the 4 to 8 year old of the previous paragraph, Mary is now at least a teenager and possibly even an adult woman. Moreover, the quantity of money is somewhat greater. Almost surely the money is not needed to buy the passage on the bus itself—somehow bus fare is too mundane for birthday money.

Preparation of this paper was supported by NSF grant BNS-76-15024 to D. E. Rumelhart, and by the Office of Naval Research under contract N00014-79-C-0323.

Consider still another variation on the same story.

Mary heard the ice cream truck coming down the street. She remembered her gun and rushed into the house.

Here we get a rather different interpretation again. Is Mary going to rob the ice cream man? Does she fear for her life? Note how the modification of a single word or phrase signals an entirely different interpretation. What sort of process could be accounting for such radical differences? Surely, it cannot be a process which takes word meanings and parlays them into sentence meanings and then those into text meanings.

The purpose of this paper is to explore the processes involved in these preceding examples, to give a general account of these processes, and to describe some experiments I have been doing in an attempt to understand them more fully.

To begin, let me lay out a general theoretical account of the comprehension process as I understand it and then turn to some data which, I believe, help explicate this process.

A SCHEMA-THEORETIC MODEL OF UNDERSTANDING

In my attempts to account for the above phenomena I have found it useful to appeal to the notion of *schemata*. Before proceeding with a discussion of comprehension itself, it might be useful to explicate my notion of schemata.

A schema theory is basically a theory about knowledge. It is a theory about how knowledge is represented and about how that representation facilitates the use of the knowledge in particular ways. According to "schema theories" all knowledge is packaged into units. These units are the schemata. Embedded in these packets of knowledge is, in addition to the knowledge itself, information about how this knowledge is to be used.

A schema, then, is a data structure for representing the generic concepts stored in memory. There are schemata representing our knowledge about all concepts: those underlying objects, situations, events, sequences of events, actions and sequences of actions. A schema contains, as part of its specification, the network of interrelations that is believed to normally hold among the constituents of the concept in question. A schema theory embodies a *prototype* theory of meaning. That is, inasmuch as a schema underlying a concept stored in memory corresponds to the meaning of that concept, meanings are encoded in terms of the typical or normal situations or events which instantiate that concept.

Perhaps the central function of schemata is in the construction of an interpretation of an event, object or situation—that is, in the process of comprehension. In all of this, it is useful to think of a schema as a kind of informal, private, unarticulated theory about the nature of the events, objects or situations which we face. The total set of schemata we have available for interpreting our world in a sense constitutes our private theory of the nature of reality. The total set of schemata instantiated at a particular moment in time constitutes our internal model of the situation we face at that moment in time. Or, in the case of reading a text, a model of the situation depicted by the text.

Thus, just as the activity surrounding a theory is often focused on the evaluation of the theory and the comparison of the theory with observations we have made, so it is that the primary activity associated with a schema is the determination whether it gives an adequate account for some aspect of our current situation. Just as the determination that a particular theory accounts for some observed results involves the determinations of the parameters of the theory, so the determination that a particular configuration of schemata accounts for the data presently available at our senses requires the determination of the values of the variables of the schemata. If a promising schema fails to account for some aspect of a situation, one has the options of accepting the schema as adequate in spite of its flawed account or of rejecting the schema as inadequate and looking for another possibility. Therefore the fundamental processes of comprehension are taken to be analogous to hypothesis testing, evaluation of goodness of fit, and parameter estimation. Thus, a reader of a text is presumably constantly evaluating hypotheses about the most plausible interpretation of the text. Readers are said to have understood the text when they are able to find a configuration of hypotheses (schemata) which offer a coherent account for the various aspects of the text. To the degree to which a particular reader fails to find such a configuration, the text will appear disjointed and incomprehensible.

Schemata are like theories in another important respect. Theories, once they are moderately successful, become a source of predictions about unobserved events. Not all experiments are carried out. Not all possible observations are made. Instead, we use our theories to make inferences with some confidence about these unobserved events. So it is with schemata. We need not observe all aspects of a situation before we are willing to assume that some particular configuration of schemata offers a satisfactory account for that situation. Once we have accepted a configuration of schemata, the schemata themselves provide a richness which goes far beyond our observations. Upon deciding that we have seen an automobile, we assume that it has an engine, headlights, and all of the standard characteristics of an automobile. We do this without the slightest hesitation. We have complete confidence in our miniature theory. This allows our interpretations to far outstrip our observations. In fact, once we have determined that a particular schema accounts for some event we may not be able to determine which aspects of our beliefs are based on direct information and which are merely consequences of our interpretation.

ON GETTING SOME EVIDENCE

I have been investigating story comprehension for several years. I have developed a story grammar (Rumelhart, 1975) which has proven rather useful in the analysis of story comprehension and recall. More recently (Rumelhart, 1977) I have recast that original work in the general framework described above and have developed a model capable of accounting for the kinds of summaries people give to very simple stories. Although this general approach to story understanding and story memory has proven rather popular, I have been dissatisfied with the work on two counts:

1. Although much of the work (including my own) has focused on the process of story understanding, most of the experiments employed post-comprehension measures. Usually the measures have employed story recall, and occasionally they have employed summarization. I have wished increasingly for truly "on-line" measures of comprehension.

2. The story grammar approach has tended to focus on rather abstract features of story comprehension. By its nature, the story schemata I and most others have studied offer a very general account of the structure readers see in stories. This generality is a plus in the sense that the schemata are very generally used, but they are a minus in the sense that they ignore the vast amount of other information which subjects can and do bring to bear in understanding stories.

During the last couple of years I have been attempting to develop some experimental techniques which could offer on-line information about subjects' comprehension processes. In the series of studies described in this paper, I set out to study this process of hypothesis generation and evaluation *during* the process of comprehension.

Perhaps the simplest way to determine what people are thinking while they are understanding is to ask them. The basic experimental paradigm involved presenting subjects a series of stories a sentence at a time and, after each sentence, asking them WHO they thought the characters under discussion were, WHAT they felt was going on in the story, WHY the characters behaved as they did, WHEN they thought the event described took place, and WHERE they thought the story was set. A series of 10 pairs of stories and/or story fragments were prepared. Most of the stories were based on initial segments of actual short stories written by well known authors. The segments were edited slightly so that an alternate version of each story could be created through the modification of one or two words or phrases. The two story versions were designed, like the example story fragments at the beginning of this paper, so that the modification led to a rather different interpretation of the whole story. Each subject read one version of each one of the ten different stories. In order to assess the effects of the line at a time interpretation procedure on comprehension, some subjects were presented the stories two lines at a time, some four lines at a time and still others were presented the whole story at one time.

There are two results which emerged immediately from this procedure:

1. The process is very natural. Subjects report that it is very easy to describe the hypotheses that come to mind as they read. Unlike problem solving,

where the collecting of protocols seems to interfere with the process, our evidence indicates that, if anything, it actually improves comprehension.
2. Subjects show a remarkable degree of agreement. With just three or four subjects the broad outlines of the sorts of results generally obtained becomes clear.

Perhaps the best way to illustrate the procedure and the kinds of results obtained is by example. Consider the following sentence, which is the first line from one of my stories.

I was brought into a large white room and my eyes began to blink because the bright light hurt them.

Consider this sentence and what scene comes to mind. There was a good deal of agreement among my subjects. Almost without fail people believed that either this was an INTERROGATION situation in which the protagonist is being held prisoner or, it was a HOSPITAL scene in which the protagonist is a patient. It is also of some interest that when asked (after they had finished the story) why they had thought it was whatever they thought, almost all reported that it was the *bright lights* or the *large white room* which had tipped them off. In point of fact, further experimentation seems to indicate that it was the *was brought* which was the key, putting the protagonist in a passive situation. The large white room and bright lights simply further specify the basically passive situation aroused by the particular construction.

THE OIL CRISIS STORY

As a second example, consider the following brief passage used in my experiment:

Business had been slow since the oil crisis.
Nobody seemed to want anything really elegant anymore.
Suddenly the door opened and a well dressed man entered the showroom floor.
John put on his friendliest and most sincere expression and walked toward the man.

Although merely a fragment, most people generate a rather clear interpretation of this story. Apparently, John is a car salesman fallen on hard times. He probably sells rather large elegant cars—most likely Cadillacs. Suddenly a good prospect enters the showroom where John works. John wants to make a sale. To do that he must make a good impression on the man. Therefore he tries to appear friendly and sincere. He also wants to talk to the man to deliver his sales pitch. Thus, he makes his way over to the man. Presumably, had the story continued, John would have made the sales pitch and, if all went well, sold the man a car.

How do people arrive at such an interpretation? Clearly, people do not arrive at it all at once. As the sentences are read, schemata are activated, evaluated, and refined or discarded. When people are asked to describe their various hypotheses as they read through the story, a remarkably consistent pattern of hypothesis generation and evaluation emerges. The first sentence is usually interpreted to mean that business is slow because of the oil crisis. Thus, people are led to see the story as about a business which is somehow dependent on oil and suffers for it. Frequent hypotheses involve either the selling of cars, or of gasoline. A few interpret the sentence as being about the economy in general. The second sentence, about people not wanting elegant things anymore, leads people with the gas station hypothesis into a quandary. Elegance just doesn't fit with gas stations. The gas station hypothesis is weakened, but not always rejected. On the other hand, people with hypotheses about the general economy or about cars have no trouble incorporating this sentence into their emerging interpretation. In the former case they conclude it means that people don't buy luxury items and in the latter they assume it means that people don't often buy large elegant cars—Cadillac's—anymore. The third sentence clinches the car interpretation for nearly all readers. They are already looking for a business interpretation—which most probably means a SELLING interpretation—and when a *well dressed man* enters the door he is immediately labeled as someone with MONEY—a prospective BUYER. The phrase *showroom floor* clearly invalidates the gas station interpretation and strongly implicates automobiles, which are often sold from a showroom. Moreover, the occurrence of a specific event doesn't fit at all well with the view that the passage is a general discussion of the state of the economy. Finally, with the introduction of John, we have an ideal candidate for the SELLER. John's actions are clearly those stereotypic of a salesman. John wants to make a sale and his "putting on" is clearly an attempt on his part to "make a good impression." His movement toward the man fits nicely into this interpretation. If he is a salesman, he must make contact with the man and deliver the stereotypic "pitch."

Qualitatively, this account fits well with the general theoretical approach I have been outlining. The process of comprehension is very much like the process of constructing a theory, testing it against the data currently available, and as more data becomes available, specifying the theory further—that is, refining the default values (as perhaps was the case when those holding the "car hypothesis" from the beginning encountered the sentence about nobody wanting anything elegant anymore). If the account becomes sufficiently strained, it is given up and a new one constructed, or, alternatively, if a new theory presents itself which obviously gives a more cogent account, the old one can be dropped and the new one accepted.

But where do these theories come from? The theories are, of course, schemata. Presumably, through experience we have built up a vast repertoire of such schemata. We have schemata for salesmen, the kinds of motives they have, and the kinds of techniques they employ. We have schemata for automobiles, including how and where they are sold. We have built up schemata for the "oil crisis," and what kinds of effects it has on what kinds of businesses. Prime candidates for these are, of course, automobile related businesses. We have schemata about business people, the kinds of motives they have, and the kinds of responses they make to these motives. The knowledge embedded in these schemata form the framework for our theories. It is some configuration of these schemata which ultimately form the basis for our understanding.

But how does a relevant schema suggest itself? Presumably, it is the "bottom-up" observation that a certain concept has been referenced that leads to the suggestion of the initial hypotheses. The notion that business was slow, suggests schemata about business and the economy. Since the slowness was dated from the occurrence of the oil crisis, it is a natural inference that the oil crisis was the cause of the slowness. Thus, a BUSINESS schema is activated. The particular TYPE of business is presumably a variable which must be filled. The information about the oil crisis suggests that it may be an oil related business. Thus, readers are led to restrict the TYPE variable of the BUSINESS schema to oil related businesses.

At this point, after the bottom-up activation of the high level BUSINESS schema has occurred, this schema would generate a top-down activation of the various possible oil related businesses. Prime candidates for these are, of course, automobile related business. Of these, selling gasoline and automobiles are the two most salient possibilities.

When the second sentence is encountered, an attempt is made to fit it into the schemata currently considered most promising. As I discussed above, this information could serve to further restrict the TYPE variable in the automobile BUSINESS schema, but doesn't fit well with the gasoline business schema.

The BUSINESS schema presumably has, as part of its specification, a reference to the BUY or SELL schema. Once activated these schemata search for potential variable bindings. In the case of the automobile business, the MERCHANDISE variable is bound to an automobile. The second sentence suggests an elegant automobile. The reader has, when the third sentence is encountered not yet found a candidate for BUYER or SELLER. The sentence about a well-dressed man immediately suggests a potential BUYER. The phrase "showroom floor" offers additional bottom-up support for the automobile hypothesis. In fact, it is a strong enough clue itself that it can suggest automobile sales to a reader who currently considers an alternative schema more likely. We thus have a BUYER and some MERCHANDISE. The well-dressed quality of the BUYER is consistent with our view that the MERCHANDISE is elegant and therefore expensive—being well-dressed suggests MONEY. We need only a SELLER— that is, an automobile salesman. Readers probably already bring a relatively complete characterization of the "default value" for car salesman. We need but little additional information to generate a rather detailed description of his goals and motives.

In spite of the length of this example, it should be noted that I have provided only a sketch of the elaborate processing which must occur in the comprehension of even so simple and direct a story as this. The problem is indeed a complex one and no one yet has been able to construct a model capable of actually carrying out the tasks involved. It is the conviction that the concept of the *schema* is the most promising route to the solution to these problems that has led to its current popularity.

It is, in general, a difficult matter to analyze free-form responses of the sort obtained in this experiment. I have, however, devised a data representation scheme which allows the tracking of a subject's hypotheses through a story. The basic idea is illustrated in Figure 1. At any point in time a subject's hypothesis state can be characterized as a region in a multidimensional hypothesis space in

Figure 1.   A representation of a subject's shifting hypotheses while reading a story. One dimension represents the sequence of sentences in the story. The other two dimensions represent the subject's hypotheses with respect to WHO the characters are and WHERE the action is taking place. The vector passing through the space represents a possible sequence of hypotheses.

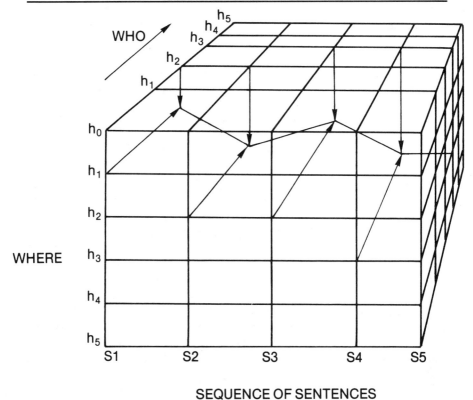

which one dimension is time (or place in the story) and the other dimensions represent the subject's momentary beliefs about WHO the characters are, WHAT is going on in the story, WHERE the story is set, and so on. Just two dimensions, WHERE and WHO, are illustrated in the figure. Each point in the space represents a possible hypothesis at some point in time. A particular subject's sequence of hypotheses can be represented as a path passing through the space. We can imagine that at particularly critical times during the reading of the story, the path will turn sharply in several dimensions. At start, we might imagine that different subjects would occupy a fairly wide region of the space. By the end, all of the paths for the different subjects should have converged on one or two points in the space. Of course, the dimensions other than the dimension of time are purely nominal, and of course, subjects often hold several hypotheses at once (that is to say, they occupy not a point, but a region of the space); nevertheless, this general representation proves useful in charting subjects' changing hypotheses.

I will illustrate the general form of analysis by looking at some of the results from the "Oil Crisis" story. In order to analyze the data, the responses for each question were categorized, and for each subject it was recorded which of the responses was given. For example, there were five different categories of answers to WHERE the story took place. The five categories were:

1. *Indefinite:* when subjects said they had no clear idea.
2. *Gas station:* when subjects believed that the action was occurring at a gas station.
3. *Showroom:* when subjects believed that the action took place in an automobile showroom.
4. *Luxury store:* when subjects believed that the action took place in a luxury store such as a jewelry store or a fancy furniture or clothing store.
5. *Nation:* when subjects believed that the story was a general statement about the national economy.

Figure 2 illustrates the patterns of responses observed from the ten subjects who read this version of the story. Each line on the graph represents a pattern of responses. The number on the lines represents the number of subjects showing that pattern. We can see that five subjects had no clear idea where the events were taking place after the first sentence. One subject thought from the start that it was in an automobile showroom. Four subjects thought, after the first sentence, that the story was taking place in a gas station. We can see that after the second sentence four people moved to the view that it was an automobile showroom, three thought it was in a luxury store, two were still indefinite, and one thought it was a general discussion of the national economy.

There is not space here to illustrate the whole pattern of results for this story, rather, I turn now to a discussion of a second story which shows a more dramatic pattern of results.

Figure 2.   Set of paths through the hypothesis space for the question of WHERE the "Oil Crisis" story was taking place.

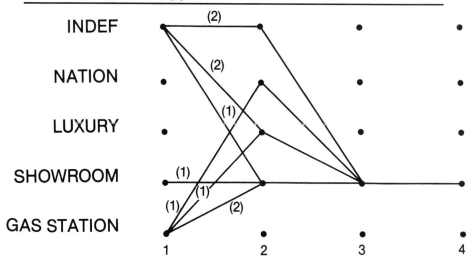

SENTENCE NUMBER

THE DEAR LITTLE THING STORY

Consider, now the following story used in my experiment:

(1)   Dear little thing.
(2)   It was nice to feel it again.
(3)   She had taken it out of its box that afternoon, given it a good brush and rubbed life back into its dim little eyes.
(4)   Little rogue! Yes, she really felt that way about it.
(5)   She put it on.
(6)   Little rogue, biting its tail just by her left ear.
(7)   When she breathed something gentle seemed to move on her bosom.
(8)   The day was cool and she was glad she had decided on her little fur.

The results for this story are particularly interesting. As people read the story they form clear impressions of certain aspects of the story, but none of them considers the possibility that the story might be about a fur until the fifth line of the story and for some, this is not clear until the last line of the story. From the beginning, however, many readers have an impression that the speaker in the story is a woman. Of the twenty people to read the first line of the story, seven mentioned that they thought that it was a woman speaking. In none of my other stories did people spontaneously assign a sex to the speaker after only reading the first sentence. Apparently a number of the readers interpret the pattern of speech here to be typically feminine. This is illustrative of the subtlety of the kinds of clues readers pick up on, and that authors count on.

Perhaps the most interesting responses were those that subjects made to the WHAT questions. Here we get the clearest picture of their overall assessment of what the story is about. There were six categories of responses given by our subjects. These were:

1. CLOTHING: they thought that the woman was talking about a hat or some jewelry.
2. FUR: They thought the woman was talking about a fur.
3. LETTER: They thought someone was writing a letter.
4. PET: They thought the story was about a pet.
5. STIMULATION: They thought the story was about sexual stimulation.
6. TOY: They thought the story was about a stuffed animal or doll.

Figure 3 shows the pattern of hypotheses held by the ten people who read this version of the story. After the opening line, "Dear little thing," people were about evenly split between the possibility that it was about a pet or letter writing. The second line, "It was nice to feel it again," discouraged all but one of the letter writing hypotheses. Some of these decided that it was a "toy" or stuffed animal that the story was about. Others assumed it was about sexual stimulation or had no clear idea. The third line moved almost everyone who didn't think it was a "pet" to the view it was a "toy." The fourth line offered no new information, and people held on to their previous hypotheses. The fifth line, "She put it on," was difficult to assimilate with any of the hypotheses and, as is evident from the figure, nearly everyone switched to the view that it was either a piece of clothing or jewelry, or to the view that it was a fur piece. The seventh line strengthened the FUR hypothesis, and the eighth line clinched it for everyone.

The figure clearly shows the critical nature of the fifth sentence. We can see subjects, on the basis of such "bottom up" information as the use of the word "dear," determine that it might be a letter or a diminutive reference to a pet. Then, once having found a satisfactory hypothesis, maintaining and refining it until disconfirming information is made available. Then, when disconfirmation occurs, searching out a new workable hypothesis.

Clearly, in such cases, my subjects are behaving according to the hypothesis evaluation mode that I have suggested. But, is this the normal way of processing? Doesn't the procedure force them to respond in this way? These are serious questions. Indeed, I do believe that there is an effect of the procedure. However, I believe that it is better categorized as making subjects read more carefully than as modifying the basic procedure. One bit of evidence for this view is that over all of the stories, subjects who interpreted the stories a line at a time more often

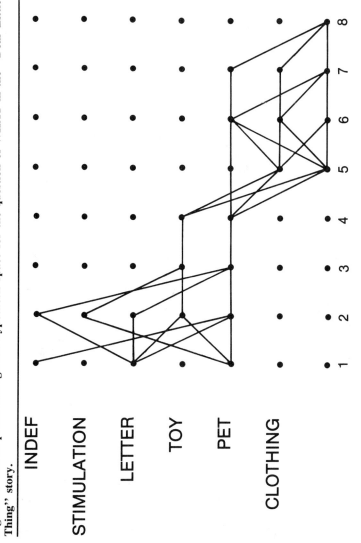

Figure 3. Set of paths through the hypothesis space for the question of WHAT in the "Dear Little Thing" story.

agreed with each other (and with the experimenters) about the interpretation of the story than subjects who gave an interpretation only after having read the whole story. In addition, a second experiment was carried out to try to get an alternative measure of ''on-line'' processing. In this experiment the subjects were not asked to make any interpretations of the story. Rather, they were presented the story one word at a time and asked to press a button after they read each word to get the next word. The time to read each word was recorded. We can then compare different versions of the same story, one in which we know from the ''interpretation'' experiments requires a rather dramatic shift in hypotheses, and another which requires no such shift, or a shift at a different place. The ''Dear Little Thing'' story offers an ideal example. The alternative version of this story differed in three words. Sentence 5 was ''She put it down'' rather then ''She put it on.'' Sentence 6 ended ''by her left ankle'' rather than ''by her left ear,'' and sentence 8 ended ''take her pet along'' rather than ''take her fur along.'' Thus, for one version, the FUR version, subjects probably had to shift hypotheses after line 5. For the other version, the PET version, subjects probably already had the correct hypothesis by line 5. Thus, the two stories were identical for the first 49 words and differed in only three of the final 38 words.

Since we know from the interpretation experiment that a good deal of re-evaluation occurs in the FUR form of the story after line 5, and that a large number of subjects have the PET hypothesis well before line 5, people should read the last 38 words of the story more slowly in the FUR version. Table 1 shows the average reading time per word for the first 49 and last 38 words for the two versions of the story. The expected difference is apparent in the table. The average reading time for the first half of the story is about the same for the two groups. Those with the FUR version were about 200 msec slower over the last half of the story. Unfortunately, the magnitudes in the table are probably somewhat misleading. There is an average difference of some 20 milliseconds between the groups for the first half of the story. In fact, this average is a mixture of some early slow responses and some later fast responses for the PET group. A better estimate for the difference between the two groups' base line reading speed is 125 milliseconds per word. Thus, the apparent 200 milliseconds per word difference evident in the table is probably actually closer to a 75 millisecond difference per word. Nevertheless, even with this conservative estimate of the difference between the base reading rate of the two groups, 75 milliseconds per

Table 1. Mean Reading Time per Word in Milliseconds

Story Version	First 49 Words	Last 38 Words
FUR	886	1011
PET	864	801

word over 38 words amounts to an average difference of almost 3 seconds longer for the FUR group. Thus, inspite of some difficulties with the data here, it would appear that we have been able to see, in slower reading times, the same hypothesis reevaluation our subjects in the interpretation experiment told us about.

A somewhat closer look at the data appears to confirm this conclusion. Much of the effect is already evident on the reading of the last word of line 5. Figure 4 shows the reading times for each word in the line. The most obvious characteristic of these curves is the increased reaction time for the last word of the sentence for both versions of the story. This upswing on the last word of a sentence is normal in all of our experiments of this sort. It appears to represent some sort of "consolidation" phase of the reading process. More important to the present discussion, however, is the difference in response time between those subjects who heard the word "on" and those who heard the word "down" as the last word of the sentence. Upon hearing the word "on", the PET or TOY hypotheses are disconfirmed, and subjects are forced to begin to reevaluate their hypotheses. This reevaluation apparently takes time. Indeed, as Figure 5 indicates, many of the subjects are apparently still formulating more hypotheses through the following sentence. Notice, for example, the time required by the subjects with the FUR version as compared with those on the PET version for the word "tail." Presumably those with the PET version have already hit upon the pet hypothesis and thus the word "tail" fits nicely into their existing interpretation. Many of those in the FUR version have probably opted for the hypothesis that the story is about a piece of clothing or jewelry and thus are not able to integrate "tail" into their existing interpretation. Similarly, for the last word of the sentence. Subjects with the PET version have little or no trouble with the pet being near the woman's ankle. The FUR subjects find it difficult to reconcile something with a tail being near the woman's ear.

Overall, in spite of the unfortunate baseline differences between the two groups, the reading time results do appear to confirm the view that a very different method of gaining access to on-line processing leads to a generally congruent pattern of results.

GENERAL COMMENTS

I have tried, in this section, to present a flavor of the results I have been collecting in the context of story comprehension. Due to limitations of space I have been unable to present a complete analysis of all of my data. Nevertheless, these examples should serve to illustrate the major points. When asked to generate interpretations of stories while reading through a story line by line, subjects generate hypotheses about the possible contents of the story and evaluate them against the sentences as they read them. If they find the new information confirmatory, they maintain and further elaborate their hypotheses. If they find the new

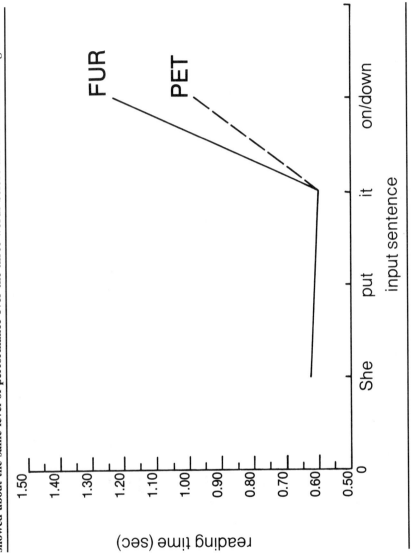

Figure 4. Adjusted word-by-word reading times for the two versions of line 5 of the "Dear Little Thing" story. Due to overall differences in the reading rates of the two groups, the times for the FUR group were adjusted downward by subtracting 125 msec for each point. This value was chosen so that the two groups showed about the same level of performance over the three words before the two stories diverge.

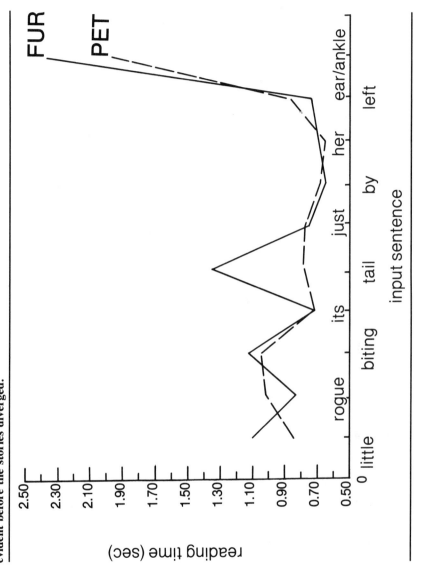

Figure 5. Adjusted word-by-word reading times for the two versions of line 6 of the "Dear Little Thing" story. Again the times for the PET data represent raw data, while the FUR curve has been adjusted downward by 125 msec to adjust for overall differences in reading time between the two groups which were evident before the stories diverged.

224

information disconfirmatory, they eliminate the hypothesis and construct another consistent with the input data. This process seems to involve both "top-down" and "bottom-up" processes. Certain words and phrases appear to "suggest" from the bottom up certain frameworks of interpretation—such as the INTER-ROGATION framework in the first example. Once a particular interpretation has received a moderate degree of support, it can come to guide the processing and interpretation of future inputs. Subjects find it relatively easy and natural to go rather substantially beyond the specifics of what the input sentences actually say. Their interpretations contain material about aspects of the situation which are totally unaddressed in the input text.

To what degree is this a natural process, as the schema theory sketched in the first section suggests, and to what degree does the procedure force the subjects to behave as the theory suggests they would? This is a difficult question for this approach. It is extraordinarily difficult to get data which bear on this issue. Three approaches have been tried:

1. I have collected word-by-word reading times for subjects not instructed to generate interpretations and have looked for correlations between points in the story where we believe subjects to be evaluating new hypotheses and those where we observe elevated response times. By and large, as the examples presented above illustrate, these two measures correlate.
2. I have collected interpretations of subjects after they read the whole story and compared them with those of subjects who read the stories a line at a time. The results showed that subjects who interpreted a line at a time nearly always generated the same interpretations as those who gave us an after-the-fact interpretation. The only discernable difference was that those who gave an interpretation only at the end showed somewhat more variability in their interpretations. It appears that this results from more careless reading on the part of the subjects offering an interpretation only at the end.
3. I have asked a few subjects immediately after the stories for retrospective analyses of the processes they went through while reading the stories. Although such subjects mention fewer hypothesis changes than those giving on-line interpretations, the overall structure of their reports seem to parallel those of the on-line subjects.

None of these methods is really totally convincing in and of itself. Nevertheless, the combination of the facts that (a) the response times seem to follow the hypothesis interpretations, (b) the interpretation paradigm doesn't seem to affect the final interpretations subjects generate, and (c) in informal observations subjects retrospective reports seem very similar to the line at a time results, points strongly to the view that the general pattern of hypothesis generation observed in our experiments is present in normal reading.

ON UNDERSTANDING AND MISUNDERSTANDING

Before concluding, it is useful to consider the application of this general theory to the notion of misunderstanding. As discussed above, the process of understanding discourse is the process of finding a configuration of schemata which offers an adequate account of the passage in question. The analysis of the "oil crisis" story given above illustrates generally how such a process is supposed to operate. Clues from the story suggest possible interpretations (instantiations of schemata) which are then evaluated against the successive sentences of the story until finally a consistent interpretation is discovered. Sometimes, a reader fails to correctly understand a passage. There are at least three reasons implicit in schema-theory as to why this might occur:

1. The reader may not have the appropriate schemata. In this case he/she simply cannot understand the concept being communicated.
2. The reader may have the appropriate schemata, but the clues provided by the author may be insufficient to suggest them. Here again the reader will not understand the text, but with appropriate additional clues, may come to understand it.
3. The reader may find a consistent interpretation of the text, but may not find the one intended by the author. In this case, the reader will "understand" the text, but will misunderstand the author.

There are numerous examples of these three phenomena in the literature. Perhaps the most interesting set of studies along these lines was carried out by Bransford and Johnson (1973). They studied the comprehension of texts in which subjects lacked the appropriate schemata, texts in which the schemata were potentially available, but there were not sufficient clues to suggest the correct ones, and texts in which subjects were led to choose a "wrong" interpretation. Consider, as an example, the following paragraph used in one of their studies.

> The procedure is actually quite simple. First you arrange things into different groups. Of course, one pile may be sufficient depending on how much there is to do. If you have to go somewhere else due to lack of facilities that is the next step, otherwise you are pretty well set. It is important not to overdo things. That is, it is better to do too few things at once than too many. In the short run this may not seem important but complications can easily arise. A mistake can be expensive as well. At first the whole procedure will seem complicated. Soon, however, it will become just another facet of life. It is difficult to foresee any end to the necessity for this task in the immediate future, but then one can never tell. After the procedure is completed one arranges the materials into different groups again. Then they can be put into their appropriate places. Eventually they will be used once more and the whole cycle will then have to be repeated. However, that is part of life. (p. 400)

Most readers find this passage extremely difficult to understand. However, once they are told that it is about washing clothes, they are able to bring their clothes washing schema to the fore and make sense out of the story. The difficulty with this passage is thus not that readers don't have the appropriate schemata, rather, it stems from the fact that the clues in the story never seem to suggest the appropriate schemata in the first place. The "bottom-up" information is inadequate to initiate the comprehension process appropriately. Once the appropriate schemata are suggested, most people have no trouble understanding the text.

Although most readers simply find the passage incomprehensible, some find alternative schemata to account for it and thus render it comprehensible. Perhaps the most interesting interpretation I have collected was from a Washington bureaucrat who had no difficulty with the passage. He was able to interpret the passage as a clear description of his job. He was, in fact, surprised to find that it was supposed to be about "washing clothes" and not about "pushing papers." Here then, we have an example of the third kind of comprehension failure, "understanding the story," but "misunderstanding the author."

CONCLUSION

At this point, it might be useful to put this comprehension theory in the context of a theory of communication. I find it useful, in this regard, to think of the general view of comprehension put forth here as suggesting that the problem facing a comprehender is analogous to the problem that a detective faces when trying to solve a crime. In both cases there is a set of clues. The listener's (or reader's) job is to find a consistent interpretation of these clues. In so doing, the listener uses prior experience and knowledge of the speaker to create a most plausible possibility. Just as the meaning of a particular clue that a detective might find cannot be determined except in relation to the way it fits into the whole situation, so too the meaning of a particular word, phrase, or even sentence cannot be interpreted except in relation to the way it fits into the whole of the story. Similarly, from the speaker's point of view. The speaker's (or writer's) problem is to leave a trail of clues which, in the opinion of the speaker, will lead the reader to make the inferences that the speaker wishes to communicate. Thus, speakers must use their knowledge of the listener or, at least, of the cultural expectations of the listener, to create the set of clues which most reliably and economically leads the listener to the desired hypotheses.

Thus, the authors of short stories need not spell out every detail. Instead, they provide the reader with subtle clues which they can expect the reader will pick up on. In the example of the INTERROGATION scene, the author, by subtle use of the passive, and the mention of bright lights and a white room, has generated in the reader a full-blown image of an entire INTERROGATION scene. The remainder of the story can then play off of these subtle clues and needn't waste time or words setting the scene. Similarly, in the "Dear Little Thing" story the author has, in a single phrase, suggested to many a woman speaking. I suspect that these stories are not at all unusual. I suspect that in general all of the inferences we wish to communicate can never be "spelled out" and that we must always depend on our ability to draw forth the appropriate schemata in the listener through a large variety of clues.

Finally, let me comment on the direction I wish to push the sort of work I have discussed here. I have, for the past several years, been attempting to create a computer simulation system capable of comprehending language according to the kinds of principles just described. I have taken as an empirical goal the creation of a program capable of mimicking the experimental results from the interpretation experiments. Obviously, a detailed account of the comprehension process requires a detailed description of the schemata readers have available, as well as an account of the conditions under which certain of these schemata are activated. There is a startling amount of knowledge brought to bear on even the simplest story comprehension task. Nevertheless, I believe that data of the sort I have described above will provide a useful data base against which to evaluate models of comprehension.

REFERENCES

Bransford, J.D., & Johnson, M.K. (1973). Considerations of some problems of comprehension. In W.G. Chase (Ed.), *Visual information processing* (pp. 383–438). New York: Academic Press.

Fillmore, C.J. (1975). An alternative to checklist theories of meaning. In C. Cogen *et al.* (Eds.), *Proceedings of the First Annual Meeting of the Berkeley Linguistics Society* (pp. 123–131). Berkeley, Ca.: Berkeley Linguistics Society.

Minsky, M. (1975). A framework for representing knowledge. In P. H. Winston (Ed.), *The psychology of computer vision* (pp. 211–277). New York: McGraw-Hill.

Rumelhart, D.E. (1975). Notes on a schema for stories. In D.G. Bobrow & A.M. Collins (Eds.), *Representation and understanding: Studies in cognitive science* (pp. 211–236). New York: Academic Press.

Rumelhart, D.E. (1977). Understanding and summarizing brief stories. In D. LaBerge & S.J. Samuels (Eds.), *Basic processes in reading: Perception and comprehension* (pp. 265–303). Hillsdale, N.J.: Lawrence Erlbaum.

Rumelhart, D.E., & Ortony, A. (1977). The representation of knowledge in memory. In R.C. Anderson, R.J. Spiro & W.E. Montague (Eds.), *Schooling and the acquisition of knowledge* (pp. 99–135). Hillsdale, N.J.: Lawrence Erlbaum.

Schank, R., & Abelson, R. (1977). *Scripts, plans, goals and understanding: An inquiry into human knowledge structures.* Hillsdale, N.J.: Lawrence Erlbaum.

CHAPTER 20

Understanding Producing

HANS W. DECHERT
Gesamthochschule Kassel

If understanding has something to do with making oneself understandable in order to be understood, and I feel it certainly has, "making sense of what we are told," to quote Rumelhart, seems only to denominate one aspect of understanding, and leaves out saying something understandable to others.

The question I would like to raise to complement Rumelhart's paper, thus, would be: "How does a speaker (or writer), in the effort to be meaningful, manage to make sense of what is told (or written) for a listener (or reader)?" Or, to put it differently, "How are the basic prototypical structures that underlie the understanding of verbal information made understandable in the act of communication in order to 'lead the listener to the desired hypotheses'?"

The answer to these questions is obviously closely connected with schema (or frame or script) theory, as outlined and specified in the preceding major address. I need not repeat here the recent discussion on schema theory; I would just like to refer to the elaborate summaries of Winograd (1977), Richard Anderson (1978) and Tannen (1979), and, especially, to Thorndyke and Yekovich's (1980) critical review of the literature; this is aside from, of course, the important contributions some of the participants of the Kassel Workshop have made to this area of research.

A topic that should be taken up, however, is the relation between schema theory and the hypothesis testing construct (Levine, 1975) that has been so strongly suggested by Rumelhart. When people listen to (or read) stories they activate and test hypotheses about schemata. Schemata are hypothetical models of understanding. Are they also models of production?

In a recent paper (Dechert, 1980a), I have tried to interpret second language speech production as a kind of hypothesis testing which depends on and leads to the creative construction of coherent episodic contexts. My hypothesis in answer to the question put forward above is therefore that: The set of schemata we have available for interpreting our world constitutes our internal model of the situation we face and provides the hypotheses to be activated, refined and tested when language dealing with this situation is produced. The particular linguistic means used to express these hypotheses as well as the hesitations, false starts, and corrections produced in the course of such a testing, evaluation, and restating

229

process provide additional evidence for the understanding of understanding and producing.

There is general agreement that schemata are to a certain extent culture specific. This means that the expectations we have upon entering a situation which is somehow different from the same situation in our own culture will collide with reality and cause problems in our understanding of what is going on and how to cope with it. There will be competition among behavioral plans (and linguistic plans); between the "old" plans guided by established schemata and "new" plans stimulated by the particular demands of the unexpected event. This also applies to cases of narrative discourse in which culture specific narrative schemata are involved (Bartlett, 1932; Chafe, 1980; Kintsch, 1977a,b; Kintsch & Greene, 1978; Kintsch & Kintsch, 1978; cf. also Goffman, 1974; Hymes, 1974). Indian stories, for instance, which do not follow the temporal-causal sequencing we are used to in understanding and telling "European" stories, are hard to understand and hard to retell. They are considered—I quote, here, from an interview I will discuss later—"strange" and "hard to memorize because of their unusual content and sequencing of events." Understanding and retelling such a story by applying a "European" schema may lead to a misunderstanding of the text's real message. The application of non-Indian schemata elicited in the production of Indian stories promises to help us understand producing, or in other words, understand the functioning of schematic hypothesis testing in speech production.

Let me give some evidence from our own data. For a number of years, using a variety of elicitation procedures, we have had students produce different kinds of texts in English and French. In the analysis of these speech samples we have concentrated on temporal variables and speech errors (Baars, 1980). In addition, we have recorded interviews with our students concerning the planning problems they had. We feel the same way Rumelhart does: one way to determine what people have been thinking during the production of speech is to ask them— although we also realize that not all of what they say after such a retrospective analysis is relevant.

The particular problems advanced second language learners have when producing speech reflect general production problems. Second language speech is an interesting data base for the assessment and modeling of psycholinguistic theories of production. "Contrastive psycholinguistics" (Dechert & Raupach, 1980) appears to us to be a promising research strategy.

A SPEECH SAMPLE

The following analysis of a speech sample, given in Appendix A, is part of a study on the application of European narrative schema by German second language learners during the reading and oral reproduction of the English translation of a Seminole story, "The Opossum Calls Her Lost Baby" (Levitas, Vivelo & Vivelo, 1974).

In order to avoid advance organizing (Mayer, 1978), both at the level of topic intrusion (Brown et al., 1977; Sulin & Dooling, 1974), as in the well-known Bransford experiments mentioned by Rumelhart (Bransford & Johnson, 1973), and at the level of paragraph organization (Kieras, 1978), a subject, a 22-year-old female student of English at Kassel University, was given an unstructured continuous text with no title (cf. Appendix A). Her reproduction of this "strange" story with its "unusual content" is admittedly the most fluent one we have so far analyzed. Since the subject had spent a year in England, she had—as she remarks in the interview—very few word-finding or phrasing problems. In spite of a number of hesitations and false starts, which do indicate planning problems, her text, due to her linguistic competence, is comparatively nativelike. She produces a highly structured story which partially resembles the story grammar of the original Indian version, but also reflects a new "processing grammar" (Glenn, 1978; Mandler, 1978; Mandler & Johnson, 1977; Rumelhart, 1975, 1977; Stein & Glenn, 1979; Thorndyke, 1977). The transcript of Dorothy's reproduction (Appendix B) discloses this grammar. It is based on an analysis of its pausal, suprasegmental, and linguistic constituents. I have shown elsewhere (Dechert, 1980a,b) how I have arrived at the concept of "episodic unit" for decoding a particular type of processing unit to be found in narrations. Episodic units may stand for an entire episode in a story or part of it. In the latter case, they primarily consist of narrative functions such as setting, exposition, complication, and goal.

ANALYSIS OF A STORY RETELLING

Since the text of the story in Appendix A had been presented to the subject mentioned earlier without title and without paragraph indentations, no extralinguistic cues were available concerning its internal structure as four events:

Event 1: Search for the baby
Event 2: Finding the baby
Event 3: Death of the baby
Event 4: Death of the opossum

Each of the four events consists of an ARRIVAL and a DEPARTURE, as the very first sentence of the story, *The opossum came . . .* , and the very last one, *They . . . sang her lonesome song,* indicate. This four-event plot reflects a well-known type of Indian prose.

The subject was not only aware of this "grammar" but made it more explicit. In this context the "lonesome-song" passages have an important structural function. After listening to the recording made of her retelling, one of the two self-corrections the subject spontaneously made was "That made three times she sang her song" (cf. Appendix B, 1. 261). This correction obviously aims not only at a linguistic improvement but at an improvement that is superior in terms of its structural function as well.

The second self-correction made after the playback expressed the subject's own surprise: "And they both died. How could I forget that! It's really a strange story!" She realizes, in other words, that she has left out the central message of Event 4, the death of the opposum, and replaces the open-ended closing marker *They both lay on the ground and sang together her lonesome song,* with it.

A considerable variety of opening/closing signals not found in the Indian version is introduced in the retelling:

(Line 121)   *Then she had met . . .*
(Line 122)   *and every time . . .*
(Line 231)   *After a while . . .*
(Line 243)   *. . . and went away*
(Line 251)   *On her way she killed . . .*
(Line 371)   *Suddenly a wolf came by . . .*
(Line 391)   *That was the fourth time . . .*

These additions considerably elaborate and emphasize the episodic structure of the production.

The subordinate clause in the sentence *Suddenly a wolf came by because he had smelt the meat* (l. 371) is the result of a particular testing and planning process, as shown by the false start "and." The connective "because" and the past perfect "had . . . smelled" clearly introduce the principle of causality. Three other cases of hypotaxis are also indications of a way of subordinate sequencing not found in the original text.

With the introduction of a consistent referential network the subject constructs a less bizarre context. In line 111 she starts out with "The opossum" (with the definite article) instead of the "she" in the Indian text; and for the rest of the production all dependent relations are made perfectly clear. The noun phrase "the baby" is without exception changed to "Her baby." The same intention is expressed by dropping "somebody" and "The person in the house" in the original, in which the referents are not clear. The subject's version, "She asked the people if they had seen her baby. The people answered yes" (lines 111–2), creates full referential coherence in spite of the fact that the phrase "She had met two people" (line 121) must remain ambiguous as to the kind and number of people involved, and as to which episode it refers to. For reasons of coherence, "The opossum" is substituted for "The mother" in the Indian version, which leaves the reader uncertain as to whether they are identical or not. The addition of "about it" (line 243) relates the opossum's state of mind "was very angry" to the cause inferred from the preceding sentence, "Someone had killed a rattlesnake and cooked it and given it to her baby." The presupposition is that either the rattlesnake should not have been killed and fed to the baby, or that the rattlesnake should not have been cooked and given to the baby, or that the baby should not have been fed with the cooked rattlesnake, all of which point back to the cause of the opossum's feeling and forward to the fatal complication of the story.

The "wolf" event (lines 371–391) in the subject's reproduction contains a number of basic changes. From the phrase in the original text where the setting for a new event is presented, "A wolf came to that place," the indefinite deictic expression "that place" is dropped, the verb is slightly modified and, as we have seen before, a temporal connective is added, "Suddenly a wolf came by" (line 371). In the following line another connective is added, "but the opossum tried to pretend" (line 372). With this addition the two sentences are connected, and the temporal order of events in the original is given up in favor of an inferred presupposition beyond the sentence level. The opossum knows that the wolf has smelled the meat of the fawn and realizes that he is after it. She anticipates that she and her baby are in great danger. This episode foreshadows the baby's death at the end of this event and her own death at the end of the story.

It is through the creative reconstruction of a suprasentential crossreferential network that the events and episodes in the subject's version are connected with each other and given a coherent semantic structure.

CONCLUDING REMARKS

The preceding analysis reveals the activation of schema hypotheses which guided the process of story restructuring. These hypotheses were that:

- the story had a suprasentential coherence;
- the story had a coherent event structure;
- the story's events had a coherent episodic structure.

In using and testing these hypotheses the subject clearly went beyond the original story. This shows that she understood the text "better" than the text suggests, although she also clearly misunderstood it. In this study the selection of schema hypotheses was influenced by a structurally similar but thematically different story in German which the subject had read and reproduced before reading and producing the Indian story (cf. Thorndyke, 1977; Thorndyke & Hayes-Roth, 1979). Linguistic changes were made by the subject on her own.

Let me raise one final issue. Narratives normally fulfill all kinds of communicative goals; some are told for the fun of it, some serve, as Linde's contribution to this volume makes quite clear, to make one's life coherent, or at least to make it appear coherent.

The number, types, and functions of narratives in natural discourse are immense. This seems to be the case because narrative schemata are more easily available than non-narrative ones. Since narrative schemata are culture rather than language specific, they are metalinguistic (Kintsch, 1977a; Glenn, 1978;

Mandler, Scribner, Cole, & Deforest, 1980). In the case of second language learners, they help the speaker (or writer) to cope with language specific, lower level processing problems such as syntactic interference, and lexical search. For primary language speakers (or writers), they are topic-independent universal devices to get at and around arguments. As the natural speech corpora we have looked at (Crystal & Davy, 1975; Fanshel & Moss, 1971; Labov, 1972; Labov & Fanshel, 1977) demonstrate over and over again, narrative components very often help speakers to overcome or to avoid planning problems on a thematic level and therefore contribute considerably to making their speech more consistent and fluent.

For the above reason, schema (or frame or script) theory is of very great interest in our efforts both to understand understanding and to understand producing. Indeed, its relevance extends far beyond the particular area of second language production and still farther beyond the immediate interest in narrative discourse of this session.

Whether the very specific role of narrative schemata in the understanding and production of speech in general is a consequence of the particular phenomenon of episodic chunking, as suggested by Tulving (1972) and Pribram (1977), or of the structure of episodes in memory as suggested by Schank (1975), remains an open question (cf. also Chafe, 1973, 1977a,b; Glenn, 1978).

APPENDIX A

She came to a house. Somebody was there and she asked if they had seen anybody going by, carrying a baby. The person in the house said "Yes." The opossum went in the direction they indicated and on the road she met two people and asked them the same question. Then she had been to two places and met two people, and sang her "lonesome song" twice. After a while she came to another place. In that place the baby had been hidden. There were four or five houses, some occupied and some empty. The opossum asked her question and somebody pointed to a house saying, "They got the baby in there." She went over, opened the door and found the baby inside. Somebody had killed a rattlesnake, cooked it, and given it to the baby to eat. The mother was angry and told them to take it away. She took the baby and started home. She killed a little fawn, ate some of the meat, and gave some to the baby. They stayed there a while. That made three times she sang the song. A wolf came to that place and smelled the meat. The opossum lied and said she had no meat, but the wolf smelled the meat. The wolf got a bow and arrow. Then the opossum was afraid she would be killed. She went up a big tree, took the baby with her and stayed up in the top of the tree. The baby died up there in the tree. That was the fourth time she sang the song. The old opossum came down and walked away. She found a skunk who was her friend and went home with the skunk. They lay down together and sang. They sang another "lonesome song" and then they both died.

Appendix B

EV	EP	EU	
1	1	1	THE OPOSSUM CAME TO A HOUSE (16) WHERE SHE ASKED THE PEOPLE IF THEY HAD SEEN (56) HER BABY (50) /
1	1	2	THE PEOPLE ANSWERED YES (10) /
1	1	3	AND the w THE OPOSSUM WALKED IN(84)TO THE: (50) DIRECTION THE PEOPLE POINTED TO (143) //
1	2	1	uhm (149) THEN SHE HAD (39) MET (122) TWO PEOPLE (11) /
1	2	2	AND EVERY TIME (70) SHE SANG HER LONESOME SONG (266) //
2	3	1	AFTER A WHILE SHE CAME TO A FEW HOUSES (24) /
2	3	2	SOME WERE EMPTY AND (69) SOME WERE OCCUPIED (90) /
2	3	3	AND: SOMEONE POINTED (28) S (132) uhm (16) TO THE HOUSE WHERE HER BABY WAS (140) //
2	4	1	she found (410) uh SHE FOUND HER BABY IN ONE HOUSE (46) /
2	4	2	SOMEONE HAD (108) KILLED A RATTLESNAKE (18) AND (68) GIVEN (30) COOKED IT AND GIVEN IT to TO HER BABY (58) /
2	4	3	THE OPOSSUM WAS ang (10) VERY ANGRY ABOUT IT (10) TOOK HER BABY AND WENT AWAY (28) (coughing) (210) //
2	5	1	ON HER WAY (176) SHE (46) KILLED A FAWN (104) HAD SOME OF THE MEAT AND GAVE SOME TO HER BABY (104) /
2	6	1	THERE WAS THE TIME (22) WHEN SHE SANG HER THIRD s(120) uh SONG (200) //
3	7	1	SUDDENLY A WOLF CAME BY and (170) BECAUSE HE HAD SMELT THE MEAT (149) /
3	7	2	BUT THE OPOSSUM (12) TRIED TO PRETEND (54) THAT SHE HADN'T ANY MEAT (110) /
3	7	3	BUT THE WOLF THREATENED HER BECAUSE HE KNEW BETTER (416) /
3	8	1	THE OPOSSUM GOT AFRAID AND (80) WENT UP A TREE AND TOOK HER BABY WITH HER (134) /
3	8	2	AND ON THAT TREE THE BABY DIED (338) //
3	9	1	THAT WAS THE FOURTH TIME (17) THE OPOSSUM SANG (80) HER LONESOME SONG (136) //
4	10	1	WHEN SHE CAME DOWN THE TREE (22) SHE MET A sSKUNK (44) AN OLD FRIEND OF HERS (260) /
4	11	1	AND THEY (116) BOTH LAY ON THE GROUND AND SANG TOGETHER (93) HER LONESOME SONG //

KEY TO SYMBOLS:

(266)	Pause (tenths of seconds) 2 7/10 sec.
uh	Filled Pause
AND:	Prolongation, Drawl
ang	False Start
/	Unit Boundary Lines:
	Rise — Fall
	Intonation Contour + Pause
	Fall — Rise
//	Falling Intonation Contour + "Long" Pause
EV	Event
EP	Episode
EU	Episodic Unit

235

REFERENCES

Anderson, R.C. (1978). Schema-directed processes in language comprehension. In A.M. Lesgold, J.W. Pellegrino, S.D. Fokkema & R. Glaser (Eds.), *Cognitive psychology and instruction* (pp. 67–82). New York, London: Plenum Press.

Baars, B. (1980). The competing plans hypothesis: An heuristic viewpoint on the cause of errors in speech. In H.W. Dechert & M. Raupach (Eds.), *Temporal variables in speech: Studies in honour of Frieda Goldman-Eisler* (pp. 39–49). The Hague: Mouton.

Bartlett, F.C. (1932). *Remembering: A study in experimental and social psychology.* Cambridge: Cambridge University Press.

Bransford, J.D., & Johnson, M. (1973). Considerations of some problems of comprehension. In W.G. Chase (Ed.), *Visual information processing* (pp. 383–438). New York: Academic Press.

Brown, A.L., Smiley, S.S., Day, J.D., Townsend, M.A.R., & Lawton, S.C. (1977). Intrusion of a thematic idea in children's comprehension and retention of stories. *Child Development, 48,* 1454–1466.

Chafe, W.L. (1973). Language and memory. *Language, 49,* 261–281.

Chafe, W.L. (1977a). Creativity in verbalization and its implications for the nature of stored knowledge. In R.O. Freedle (Ed.), *Discourse production and comprehension* (pp. 41–55). Norwood, N.J.: Ablex.

Chafe, W.L. (1977b). The recall and verbalization of past experience. In R.W. Cole (Ed.), *Current issues in linguistic theory* (pp. 215–246). Bloomington, London: Indiana University Press.

Chafe, W.L. (1980). *The pear stories: Cognitive, cultural and linguistic aspects of narrative production.* Norwood, N.J.: Ablex.

Crystal, D., & Davy, D. (1975). *Advanced conversational English.* London: Longman.

Dechert, H.W. (1980a). Contextual hypothesis-testing procedures in speech production. In H.W. Dechert & M. Raupach (Eds.), *Towards a cross-linguistic assessment of speech production* (pp. 101–121). Frankfurt, Bern, & Cirencester: Lang.

Dechert, H.W. (1980b). Pauses and intonation as indicators of verbal planning in second language speech productions: Two examples from a case study. In H.W. Dechert & M. Raupach (Eds.), *Temporal variables in speech: Studies in honour of Frieda Goldman-Eisler* (pp. 271–285). The Hague: Mouton.

Dechert, H.W., & Raupach, M. (Eds.). (1980). *Temporal variables in speech: Studies in honour of Frieda Goldman-Eisler.* The Hague: Mouton.

Fanshel, D., & Moss, F. (1971). *Playback: A marriage in jeopardy.* New York, London: Columbia University Press.

Glenn, C.G. (1978). The role of episodic structure and of story length in children's recall of simple stories. *Journal of Verbal Learning and Verbal Behavior, 17,* 229–247.

Goffman, E. (1974). *Frame analysis: An essay on the organization of experience.* New York: Harper & Row.

Hymes, D. (1974). Ways of speaking. In R. Bauman & J. Sherzer (Eds.), *Explorations in the ethnography of speaking* (pp. 433–451). London: Cambridge University Press.

Kieras, D.E. (1978). Good and bad structure in simple paragraphs: Effects on apparent theme, reading time, and recall. *Journal of Verbal Learning and Verbal Behavior, 17,* 13–28.

Kintsch, W. (1977a). *Memory and cognition.* New York, Santa Barbara, London, Sydney, & Toronto: John Wiley & Sons.

Kintsch, W. (1977b). On comprehending stories. In M.A. Just & P.A. Carpenter (Eds.), *Cognitive processes in comprehension* (pp. 33–62). Hillsdale, N.J.: Lawrence Erlbaum.

Kintsch, W., & Greene, E. (1978). The role of culture-specific schemata in the comprehension and recall of stories. *Discourse Processes, 1,* 1–13.

Kintsch, W., & Kintsch, E. (1978). The role of schemata in text comprehension. *International Journal of Psycholinguistics, 5–2*(10), 17–29.

Labov, W. (1972). *Language in the inner city: Studies in the black English vernacular.* Philadelphia: University of Pennsylvania Press.

Labov, W., & Fanshel, D. (1977). *Therapeutic discourse: Psychotherapy as conversation.* New York, San Francisco, & London: Academic Press.

Levine, M. (1975). *A cognitive theory of learning: Research on hypothesis testing.* Hillsdale, N.J.: Lawrence Erlbaum.

Levitas, G., Vivelo, F.R., & Vivelo, J.J. (Eds.). (1974). *American Indian prose and poetry. We wait in the darkness.* New York: G.P. Putnam's Sons & Capricorn Books.

Mandler, J.M. (1978). A code in the node: The use of a story schema in retrieval. *Discourse Processes, 1,* 14–35.

Mandler, J.M., & Johnson, N.S. (1977). Remembrance of things parsed: Story structure and recall. *Cognitive Psychology, 9,* 111–151.

Mandler, J.M., Scribner, S., Cole, M., & Deforest, M. (1980). Cross-cultural invariance in story recall. *Child Development, 51,* 19–26.

Mayer, R.M. (1978). Advance organizers that compensate for the organization of text. *Journal of Educational Psychology, 70,* 880–886.

Pribram, K.H. (1977). *Languages of the brain: Experimental paradoxes and principles in neuropsychology.* Monterey, Ca.: Brooks/Cole Publishing Company.

Rumelhart, D.E. (1975). Notes on a schema for stories. In D.G. Bobrow & A. Collins (Eds.), *Representation and understanding: Studies in cognitive science* (pp. 211–236). New York: Academic Press.

Rumelhart, D.E. (1977). Understanding and summarizing brief stories. In D. LaBerge & S.J. Samuels (Eds.), *Basic processes in reading: Perception and comprehension* (pp. 265–303). Hillsdale, N.J.: Lawrence Erlbaum.

Schank, R.C. (1975). The structure of episodes in memory. In D.G. Bobrow & A. Collins (Eds.), *Representation and understanding: Studies in cognitive science* (pp. 237–272). New York: Academic Press.

Stein, N.L., & Glenn, C.G. (1979). An analysis of story comprehension in elementary school children. In R.O. Freedle (Ed.), *New directions in discourse processing* (pp. 53–120). Norwood, N.J.: Ablex.

Sulin, R.A., & Dooling, D.J. (1974). Intrusion of a thematic idea in retention of prose. *Journal of Experimental Psychology, 103,* 255–262.

Tannen, D.F. (1979). What's in a frame? Surface evidence for underlying expectations. In R.O. Freedle (Ed.), *New directions in discourse processing* (pp. 137–181). Norwood, N.J.: Ablex.

Thorndyke, P.W. (1977). Cognitive structures in comprehension and memory of narrative discourse. *Cognitive Psychology, 9,* 77–110.

Thorndyke, P.W., & Hayes-Roth, B. (1979). The use of schemata in the acquisition and transfer of knowledge. *Cognitive Psychology, 11,* 82–106.

Thorndyke, P.W., & Yekovich, F.R. (1980). A critique of schemata as a theory of human story memory. *Poetics, 9,* 23–49.

Tulving, E. (1972). Episodic and semantic memory. In E. Tulving & W. Donaldson (Eds.), *Organization of memory* (pp. 381–403). New York: Academic Press.

Winograd, T. (1977). A framework for understanding discourse. In M.A. Just & P.A. Carpenter (Eds.), *Cognitive processes in comprehension* (pp. 63–88). Hillsdale, N.J.: Lawrence Erlbaum.

CHAPTER 21

Beyond Bartlett: Issues in the Study of Comprehension

JANICE M. KEENAN
University of Denver

According to Rumelhart (this volume), understanding involves utilizing existing knowledge structures or schemata to organize and interpret incoming data and to predict what future data to expect. Utilization of schemata is said to involve at least three processes: (1) activating relevant schemata; (2) evaluating how well the schemata fit the data; and (3) adjusting parameters or variables in the schemata to obtain better fits.

As Rumelhart states, this characterization is the consensus view of comprehension currently held within the field of cognitive science. What is remarkable is that this view is also, in most fundamental respects, the view offered by Bartlett back in 1932. On the face of it, this similarity seems to suggest that we have made little progress in our understanding of comprehension over the past fifty years. It might be useful, therefore, to begin this discussion by considering the ways in which our understanding of comprehension has advanced over that offered by Bartlett.

HOW HAVE WE PROGRESSED BEYOND BARTLETT?

One way that the current conception of comprehension represents a fundamental advance over Bartlett lies in the way in which it was developed. Recall that even though the current conception is identical in all fundamental respects to that of Bartlett, it is in no way directly descendant from Bartlett. Rather, it was independently discovered, or rediscovered, as the case may be, after other accounts of comprehension—stimulus-response theory and syntactic theories—were shown to be grossly inadequate both in the realm of machine comprehension and human comprehension.

The fact that the current view was formulated independent of Bartlett certainly

Preparation of this paper was supported by a grant to the author from the National Institute of Education, NIE-G-78-0173.

lends validity to the general characterization and may be viewed as a sign of progress. After all, consensus has been achieved despite large differences in the intellectual environments of the theorists. Even more important, however, is the fact that the current view was arrived at only after very careful consideration of other approaches. This indeed represents an advance over Bartlett because now the very same characterization of comprehension not only says what comprehension is, but also, by reference to its history, says what comprehension is not.

A second way in which the current view of comprehension represents an advance over Bartlett is in the characterization of knowledge structures involved in comprehension. Starting with Quillian's (1969) work on semantic memory and progressing through the propositional structures proposed by Anderson and Bower (1973), Kintsch (1974), and Norman and Rumelhart (1975), to Minsky's (1975) frames and Schank and Abelson's (1977) scripts, plans and goals, Bartlett's vague notion of "schema" has been fleshed out into a variety of formal specifications for the structuring of knowledge. The results have been remarkable. We now have machines that can understand natural language, at least in those limited domains for which they have schemata. When one considers the achievements of these machines, it is difficult to argue that our understanding of comprehension has not progressed much beyond that of Bartlett.

The fact that the only way to get a computer to comprehend language is to build into it general knowledge about the world provides very compelling support for the constructivist account of comprehension; certainly it is more compelling than any data offered by Bartlett. However, it must be remembered that as impressive as the behavior of these machines may be, we still have not advanced very far in working out the particulars of a constructivist account of comprehension. The problem is that even though each of these computer programs embodies particular formulations of knowledge structures and processes that operate on these structures, there have been few attempts to empirically test these formulations.

Artificial intelligence researchers may occasionally test their formulations by expanding the types of inputs to the program and determining whether the particular knowledge structures and processes contained in the program can accommodate these new inputs. But these tests are hardly sufficient. Within the very limited range of linguistic inputs and behaviors examined to date, it is likely that many different formulations can equally well accommodate the input. What is needed are tests that go beyond simple global input-output comparisons.

In constructing programs to comprehend language, a tremendous number of assumptions must be made concerning how schemata are to be structured, what elements control the activation of schemata, how many schemata can be activated at a given point in time, how much information within a schema can be activated, what the duration of activation is, and so on. Lacking empirical constraints on almost all of these issues, artificial intelligence researchers make decisions based either on intuition or ease of programming. Because the only tests applied to these models are tests of the whole system, it is difficult to know which, if any, of these assumptions are valid.

If we are to advance beyond the general characterization of comprehension offered by Bartlett, therefore, we need to develop a set of empirical constraints that can be used to assess the adequacy of the particular assumptions implemented in the comprehension models offered by those in artificial intelligence. These empirical constraints can only come from careful experimentation on the effects of various types of text structure manipulations on human comprehension.

Unfortunately, many of the cognitive psychologists who do this type of experimentation are unfamiliar with the kinds of questions that arise when one tries to implement a model of comprehension on a computer. Consequently, the results of their research efforts are often irrelevant to the types of questions that need to be answered. Such is not the case, however, with someone like Dave Rumelhart. He is one of the few individuals in the area of comprehension research who is simultaneously involved in developing computer models of comprehension and in testing out particular assumptions of the model by doing experiments with human subjects. This involvement in both modelling and experimentation puts him in a unique position to substantially advance our understanding of comprehension beyond that of Bartlett.

The degree to which Rumelhart's work can advance our understanding of comprehension will, of course, be constrained by the adequacy of the methods he uses to test the assumptions of his model. For the remainder of this paper, therefore, I wish to examine the adequacy of the method that Rumelhart has currently chosen to use—the method of protocol analysis.

PROTOCOL ANALYSES AND THE STUDY
OF COMPREHENSION

Rumelhart seems to say that the principal advantage of comprehension protocols is that they provide an on-line measure of comprehension processes. This point is surely debatable. Although the protocol is generated as the person is reading the text, each particular entry in the protocol is generated only after the person has comprehended the input. Thus, it is not as truly an on-line measure as comprehension latencies. Regardless of the "on-lineness" of the measure, though, it appears that the principal advantage of the protocol method is that it generates a tremendous wealth of data from which many different hypotheses can be formulated. To demonstrate, let us examine Rumelhart's explication of the *Oil Crisis* story to see how one might begin to formulate the issues involved in one of the main processes of comprehension, namely, the activation of schemata.

What activates a schema? Rumelhart states that, initially, schemata are generated in a bottom-up fashion. The question is, however, what counts as "the bottom?" From his explication of the *Oil Crisis* story, it is clear that the bottom refers to particular words in the text. But which words? Do all content words activate schemata? It appears that the answer is no. The initial phrase, "business was slow" is said to activate a BUSINESS schema, but not a schema for SLOW THINGS.

These observations suggest a number of interesting questions concerning the criteria which determine whether or not a word will activate a schema. Noting that *business* is the topic of the sentence, we can ask whether it is the case that only the topic words of sentences generate schemata? Probably not, because in the "classic" sentence, "John went to a restaurant," *restaurant* is not the topic of the sentence and yet it is said to activate the RESTAURANT script. Perhaps it is the syntactic category of the word that determines whether or not it will activate a schema. Thus, *business* activates a schema because it is a noun, while *slow* does not activate a schema because we have no schema for SLOW THINGS. Thus, even though we can classify things such as turtles and certain elevators as slow, there may be no specific knowledge structure for slow things inherent in the system.

These are just a few examples of the kinds of questions that can be generated from examining protocols. Additional questions would concern how various text structure factors influence the evaluation of which of the activated schemata best fit the data. For example, it would be interesting to know whether syntactic structures and topicalization play much of a role in this evaluation or whether the evaluation is based mainly on the semantics of the schemata.

As useful as the protocol method is in providing a rich data base from which to generate experimental questions, however, it must be recognized that it is also an extremely risky method to use. The risk stems from the fact that it is easy to forget that these introspective reports are nothing more than data which need to be accounted for. Because the protocols refer to knowledge structures that are activated and processes that are involved in understanding, it is very easy to make the mistake that these reports are direct reflections of the operations that occur during comprehension. Thus, I fear that Rumelhart may end up using these protocols not to guide experimentation, but rather to structure his simulations to operate according to the way subjects think they are operating.

There are two ways in which the use of protocols to structure one's model can be shown to be an erroneous approach. First, introspections are incapable of being verified. Therefore, they are no basis on which to build a theory. Second, introspective reports may bear little or no resemblance to the cognitive processes actually utilized by the subject. Recall Clark Hull's (1920) classic study on concept learning, in which subjects learned to consistently classify Chinese letters correctly but were totally unable to formulate their solution verbally. It may also be the case that the hypotheses actually utilized by subjects during comprehension are no more available to conscious inspection than those utilized by Hull's subjects.

Rumelhart himself seems to recognize the unreliability of subjects' verbal reports. He states that although subjects claimed that the phrases *bright light* and *large white room* were responsible for their activation of *HOSPITAL* and *INTER-ROGATION* schemata for the sentence, ''I was brought into a large white room and my eyes began to blink because the bright light hurt them,'' other measures indicated that it was actually the phrase *was brought* that was responsible for these schemata. As Nisbett and Wilson (1977) recently concluded from an extensive review of verbal report studies, it appears that there may be little or no direct access to higher-order cognitive processes. As a result, we need to be very careful about the status we accord to comprehension protocols.

Another problem is that unlike other measures such as latencies, protocols are limited in the kinds of questions they can be used to answer. An example of a question that cannot be answered using protocols is the question of which aspects of a schemata are activated. It seems unlikely that one could get a subject to unpack all the information that is currently activated, and even if one could, its reliability would be questionable. In contrast, comprehension latencies can be easily used to determine whether or not a concept is currently activated.

To summarize, although the protocol method is useful for generating experimental questions, it has a number of potential risks which, if not recognized, could result in a methodology that violates the basic tenets of the scientific method. Thus, if we hope to further advance our understanding of comprehension beyond that of Bartlett (1932), we need, at the least, to use methods of verification that are not pre-Bartlett.

REFERENCES

Anderson, J.R., & Bower, G.H. (1973). *Human associative memory.* Washington, D.C.: Winston & Sons.

Bartlett, F.C. (1932). *Remembering: A study in experimental and social psychology.* Cambridge: Cambridge University Press.

Hull, D.L. (1920). Quantitative aspects of the evolution of concepts. *Psychological Monographs, 28.*

Kintsch, W. (1974). *The representation of meaning in memory.* Hillsdale, N.J.: Lawrence Erlbaum.

Minsky, M. (1975). A framework for representing knowledge. In P.H. Winston (Ed.), *The psychology of computer vision* (pp. 211–277). New York: McGraw-Hill.

Nisbett, R.E., & Wilson, T.D. (1977). Telling more than we can know: Verbal reports on mental processes. *Psychological Review, 84,* 231–259.

Norman, D.A., & Rumelhart, D.E. (1975). *Explorations in cognition.* San Francisco: Freeman.

Quillian, M.R. (1969). The teachable language comprehender: A simulation program and theory of language. *Communications of the Association for Computing Machinery, 12,* 459–476.

Schank, R., & Abelson, R. (1977). *Scripts, plans, goals and understanding.* Hillsdale, N.J.: Lawrence Erlbaum.

CHAPTER 22

Interim Questions

ROLAND POSNER
Technische Universität Berlin

In his paper Rumelhart (this volume) sketches the outlines of the process of understanding as he has analyzed it in his approach to cognitive science. In order to account for the comprehension of stories and story fragments, he introduces the concepts of KNOWLEDGE, SCHEMA, COMPREHENSION, PROTOTYPE, VARIABLES OF SCHEMATA, DEFAULT VALUES, SCHEMA ACTIVATION, BOTTOM-UP ACTIVATION, TOP-DOWN ACTIVATION, CLUES, and INTERPRETATION AS SCHEMA INSTANTIATION. It is shown that these concepts can provide a reasonable basis for further theoretical and empirical work in understanding understanding. However, it is also obvious that they raise a host of problems that do not yet seem to have been considered with sufficient care. If current work in understanding understanding is to continue with useful results, these problems have to be addressed explicitly and kept in mind, even if they cannot be solved immediately. The following paper gives a fragmentary list of such interim questions in order to initiate discussion of the underlying problems.

How can the notion of a schema be made less ambiguous and metaphorical? If all knowledge is packaged in units and these units are schemata, what is the unifying principle that underlies knowledge units? Do all knowledge units have the same kind of structure? Can all knowledge units perform the same kinds of functions? Does not the nature of a schema vary widely depending on the circumstances? If so, how useful can such a notion be, and what are the limits of its use in the explanation of cognition?

What is the epistemological status of a schema? Are there any discovery procedures for schemata? Is a schema and its structure postulated on the basis of the cognitive scientist's introspection? Or on the basis of the lexical and syntactic structures of a given language (cf. Posner, 1980)? Or on the basis of the habits of the people in a given culture?

How does a Cognitive Scientist know whether a given piece of knowledge corresponds to one or two schemata? How does the cognitive scientist isolate one knowledge unit from another or find out which are the predicates, variables and default values of a schema? How does one know whether a given constituent of a schema is to be regarded as primitive or whether a given data structure for the representation of a schema is complete? How can two given schemata be compared as to their complexity?

Do we need the notion of a schema in cognitive science in addition to the notions of concept (philosophical tradition), presupposition (linguistic tradition), analogical or other inference (logical tradition), case frame (Fillmore), frame (Minsky), script (Schank), and implicature (Grice)?

What is the psychological status of a schema? To what extent are schemata psychologically real? On the basis of what criteria can this question be answered? What is the relationship between knowledge structure and brain structure? Is it reasonable to assume that memory and processing of a particular schema are located in a particular part of the brain different from the location of other schemata? In what sense can one say that schemata are stored in short-term memory and long-term memory? Can one find schemata in iconic memory? What forms of representation and processing do the different parts of the brain provide for a schema? Do schemata differ as to complexity? Is it reasonable to assess the number and complexity of the schemata a person can accomodate mentally in order to specify that person's intellectual capacity? How are schemata learned? In what circumstances can we assume that a particular schema of a given person has changed (has been specialized, generalized, modified, or given up)?

What is the logical status of a schema? Is a schema identical with a concept, or does it only represent a concept? In what way does a schema "correspond to the meaning of a concept"? Is a schema the sense of a linguistic expression or its reference? Is a schema the meaning of an abstract lexical item or of words-in-use? Can a schema be a proposition? Can a schema contain propositions? What is the relationship between the meaning structure of the word "story" and the structure of stories? Which of the two is specified by the story schema?

Is a schema a logical, psychological or ontological item? Can a schema be a situation, or a fact, or the structure of a situation or a fact (cf. van Dijk & Kintsch, 1983)? Is reality a configuration of schemata or can it be subsumed under a configuration of schemata?

What is the appropriate system of representation for schemata? Natural language? Intensional logic? Active Structural Networks? Semantic Operating Language? Phrase-structure-trees? How are constraints on the values that variables can take represented in a schema? How are general propositions such as "We often want what we like," "One ordinarily likes what one buys," "Many people buy ice cream" (Rumelhart & Ortony, 1977) represented in a schema?

Is it reasonable to assume the existence of a sign system representing all the schemata of a person, of a language community, of a culture, of mankind, of a particular animal species in a unified way? If not, what aspects and types of knowledge should be represented in such a way?

According to Rumelhart (1977),

"The process of COMPREHENSION *is taken to be identical to the process of selecting and verifying conceptual schemata to account for the situation (or text) to be understood."* (p. 268) . . . *"Moreover, a schema is said to account for any situation that can be considered an instance of the general concept it represents."* (p. 266)

How should we conceive of this process of selecting and verifying schemata in reading a text?

What is the basis of schema selection and verification in the text if not word meanings and sentence meanings? What bits of information in the text tend to start a schema search process and which do not? Are there general principles specifying which parts of a schema must be mentioned in a text to activate the whole schema? Under what circumstances can information that is only implied by the text activate a schema? How long can one keep a detail in mind before trying to accommodate it in a schema or forgetting it? How many unconfirmed or partly confirmed schemata can be held in mind simultaneously by the comprehender before deciding in favor of one of them?

In what way are schemata available to the comprehension process? Are schemata stored in long-term memory as fully explicit data structures that are recalled instantaneously? Are they stored in implicit form to be reconstructed upon demand? If so, which parts of a schema are immediately accessible and which must be reconstructed?—Or does this change according to the circumstances? If it does, how does schema selection differ from analogical reasoning (cf. Rumelhart & Ortony, 1977)? Are there texts consisting of linguistically well-formed sentences for which it is impossible to find a fitting configuration of schemata? If not, why? Under what circumstances does a comprehender cease to look for an appropriate schema in memory and construct a new one instead?

How does schema construction during story comprehension work? Does it take the comprehender's attention away from what is being read? To what extent does a comprehender make explicit predictions about unobserved events during story comprehension? What principles determine the assignment of a default value to a particular variable, if that value depends on the values of other variables (cf. Rumelhart & Ortony, 1977)?

What are the search strategies a comprehender applies in looking for schemata that might account for the situation depicted in the text? If the search process can be compared with theorizing in science, is it more like theory production or theory application? In what sense can schemata play the role of naive theories? What kinds of hypotheses can be derived from these schemata? In what sense are schemata supposed to be true, and how can they be verified?

If the interpretation of parts and wholes proceeds simultaneously in both bottom-up and top-down directions (Norman & Rumelhart, 1975), which structural qualities of a schema facilitate parallel processing in both directions? What principles guide the bottom-up subsumption of a given concept under a more general one? What principles guide the top-down search for a more specific concept on the basis of a more general one? How do we proceed in choosing concepts out of a virtually infinite number of possible candidates (e.g., for the preconditions or consequences of a given action concept)? If schemata are data structures representing general concepts stored in memory, how specific can a schema get?

If memory is filled with schemata, how does the comprehender find the relevant subcomponents in memory that contain those schemata that might be accurate guesses? Does the search process contain algorithmic procedures? What role does induction play in this process?

In what way do language producers' comprehension and their assumptions about an addressee's comprehension influence language production? What role do schemata play in the design of a story during story production? Does the language producer's behavior include schema selection and verification in the same sense as the addressee's? What sorts of additional apparatus are needed to put schemata to work in simulating story production? In what way do schemata guide the linguistic encoding of stories? Can "the gist of a story" be captured by the application of a schema?

REFERENCES

Norman, D.A., & Rumelhart, D.E. (1975). *Explorations in cognition.* San Francisco: Freeman.

Posner, R. (1980, February). *Wissensrahmen und Handlungsschema—Wie Kinder Filme nacherzählen.* Paper presented at the Second Annual Meeting of the Deutsche Gesellschaft für Sprachwissenschaft, Berlin.

Rumelhart, D.E. (1977). Understanding and summarizing brief stories. In D. LaBerge & S.J. Samuels (Eds.), *Basic processes in reading: Perception and comprehension* (pp. 265–303). Hillsdale, N.J.: Lawrence Erlbaum.

Rumelhart, D.E., & Ortony, A. (1977). The representation of knowledge in memory. In R.C. Anderson, R.J. Spiro & W.E. Montague (Eds.), *Schooling and the acquisition of knowledge* (pp. 99–135). Hillsdale, N.J.: Lawrence Erlbaum.

van Dijk, T.A., & Kintsch, W. (1983). *Strategies of discourse comprehension.* New York: Academic Press.

Fifth Session:
Verbal Interaction

Chair: C. Linde

CHAPTER 23

Conversational Style

DEBORAH F. TANNEN
Georgetown University

In 1927, Sapir included ''style'' as the fifth level of speech contributing to judgments of personality. Devoting only a paragraph to it, he defined style as ''an everyday facet of speech that characterizes both the social group and the individual'' (1949, p. 542). Ervin-Tripp defines style as ''the co-occurrent changes at various levels of linguistic structure within one language'' (1972, p. 235). Robin Lakoff (1979) notes that style refers to all aspects of a person's behavior that are popularly thought of as ''character'' or ''personality.''

Anything that is said or done must be said or done in some way, and that way constitutes style. If you sit in a chair, motionless, you are nonetheless sitting in a certain position, dressed in certain clothes, with a certain expression on your face. Thus you sit in the chair in your own style. You can no more talk without style than you can walk or sit or dress without style. Anything you say must be said at a certain rate, in certain words, at a certain pitch and amplitude, in certain intonation, at a certain point in interaction. All these and countless other linguistic choices determine the effect of an utterance in interaction and influence judgments that are made both of what is said and of the speaker who said it.

Style is not something extra or frivolous, added on like frosting on a cake. It is the stuff of which the cake is made. Conversational style is a semantic process; it is the way meaning is encoded in and derived from speech.

My notion of conversational style grows out of R. Lakoff's work on communicative style as well as Gumperz's on conversational inference: the function of paralinguistic and prosodic features, which he calls contextualization cues, to maintain thematic cohesion and signal how conversational contributions are intended. When a speaker says something, s/he signals what ''speech activity'' (Gumperz, 1977) or ''frame'' (Bateson, 1972) is being engaged in (joking, lecturing, arguing, etc.), that is, how the message encoded is to be taken. Ways of signaling frames or ''metamessages'' about the relationship of interlocutors

---

I shall always be indebted to Wallace Chafe, John Gumperz, and Robin Lakoff for continuing dialogue as well as specific comments on the initial study on which the present paper draws. Subsequent developments in my thinking have been immeasurably enriched by interchanges with Marilyn Merritt and Ron Scollon, as well as many of my colleagues and students at Georgetown.

251

(Bateson, 1972) seem self-evident to speakers but in fact are culturally specific and make up the speaker's style. Insofar as speakers who come from similar speech communities use contextualization cues in similar ways, style is a social phenomenon. Insofar as speakers use features in particular combinations in various settings, to that extent style is an individual phenomenon.

Interest in style is not new, but no one, to my knowledge, has tried to describe the specific linguistic features that constitute style. This is what I set as my task. Initial findings are discussed in detail in Tannen (1979a); the present paper draws upon these findings.

THEORETICAL FRAMEWORK

Style is the result of automatic linguistic and paralinguistic cues that seem self-evident and natural, based on previous interaction in a speech community (Gumperz, 1964, 1977) which has conventionalized their use. Although "style" is thus automatic, we may nonetheless seek to understand the broad strategies motivating stylistic choice. This is what I will do in the remaining pages. Toward that end, I will trace some theoretical developments in a number of related fields and then show how they contribute to a theory of conversational style which explains strategic differences found in the present data.

Much current theory in pragmatics derives from Grice's (1975) *conversational maxims,* said to govern linguistic choice in talk:

1. Quantity. Say as much as necessary and no more.
2. Quality. Tell the truth.
3. Relevance. Be relevant.
4. Manner. Be clear. Don't obfuscate.

When a speaker violates these maxims, a hearer looks for an explanation in *conversational implicature.*

R. Lakoff (1973, 1979) observes that speakers rarely opt to follow these maxims, preferring to avoid saying what they mean in the interest of social goals which they pursue by adhering to one of three *Rules of Politeness* (later renamed the *Rules of Rapport*). Each rule is associated with a communicative style growing out of habitual application of that rule:

R1. Don't impose (Distance)
R2. Give options (Deference)
R3. Be friendly (Camaraderie)

To illustrate (with my own examples), if a guest responds to an offer of something to drink by saying, "No, thank you; I'm not thirsty," s/he is applying R1. If s/he says, "Oh, I'll have whatever you're having," s/he is applying R2. If s/he marches into the kitchen, throws open the refrigerator, and says, "I'm thirsty. Got any juice?" s/he is applying R3.

Individuals differ with regard to which sense of politeness they tend to observe and how they observe them. Cultural differences are reflected in the principles favored by most members of a group under most circumstances. Lakoff suggests that Japanese speakers are more likely to opt for R1 politeness, whereas American speakers are more likely to opt for R3, giving rise to mutual stereotyping of Japanese as formal and Americans as brash (or Japanese as polite and Americans as friendly, depending upon the bias of the judges). Of course, application of one form of politeness or another is not an on/off matter but rather a range on a continuum (Lakoff, 1979).

Speakers, more often than not, prefer not to say just what they mean directly, for two reasons: *defensiveness* and *rapport*. Defensiveness is the desire to be able to renege, to say (perhaps sincerely) "I never said that," or "That's not what I meant." Rapport is the fine feeling of being "on the same wave length" that accrues when one gets what one wants without asking for it, when one feels understood without having explained oneself. Defensiveness is associated with Distance and R1 "Don't impose." Rapport is associated with Camaraderie and R3 "Be friendly."

Another quite separate yet deeply related strand of research in sociology is brilliantly elaborated by Goffman, following Durkheim. Durkheim (1965) distinguishes between negative and positive religious rites. Negative rites are religious interdictions, a "system of abstentions." However, "the negative cult is in one sense a means in view of an end: it is a condition of access to the positive cult." That is, by denying the profane, one prepares for union with the sacred. Goffman (1967) builds upon this dichotomy in his notion of *deference,* "the appreciation an individual shows of another to that other, whether through avoidance rituals or presentational rituals" (p. 77). Presentational rituals include "salutations, invitations, compliments, and minor services. Through all of these the recipient is told that he is not an island unto himself and that others are, or seek to be, involved with him and with his personal private concerns" (pp. 72–73). On the other hand, avoidance rituals are "those forms of deference which lead the actor to keep at a distance from the recipient" (p. 62) and include "rules regarding privacy and separateness" (p. 67), such as use of polite forms of address, avoidance of certain topics, and so on.

Building upon the work of Lakoff and Goffman, Brown and Levinson (1978) suggest two overriding goals of politeness in human interaction: positive and negative face. Negative face is "the want of every adult member that his actions be unimpeded by others." Positive face is "the want of every adult member that his wants be desirable to at least some others." These goals are served through positive and negative politeness.

All these schemata for organizing interaction draw upon the two basic human needs to be involved with other humans, and to be left alone: the dual human needs for community and for independence. The tension between these two conflicting needs motivates linguistic choices, just as it motivates so many (perhaps all) personal choices. Stylistic choices such as those that will be described below are conventionalized devices for honoring one or the other of these needs.

Another related strand of research is relevant as well. In much of my recent writing (Tannen, 1980b, 1980c) I have tried to glean insight from work comparing oral vs. literate tradition (Goody, 1977; Havelock, 1963; Olson, 1977; Ong, 1967). I suggest that strategies which have been associated with oral tradition grow out of an emphasis on the interpersonal dynamic of communication: involvement between communicator and audience. In contrast, strategies that have been associated with literate tradition grow out of emphasis on decontextualized content, de-emphasizing involvement between communicator and audience. Thus written fiction and letters often employ features expected of spoken language, because they depend on communicator/audience identification, which Havelock (1963) and Ong (1967) note is the basis of knowledge in bardic oral tradition.

Scollon and Scollon (1984) point out that Athabaskan oral tradition differs strikingly from the "bard and formula" notion outlined by Lord (1960) and taken as the basis for the above research on oral and literate tradition. In Athabaskan oral tradition, storytelling is a matter of joint sensemaking between speaker and audience, a process of negotiation for the point of the story. An Athabaskan speaker does not try to make singlehanded sense and impose it on a hearer. In contrast, the bard and formula approach suggests that oral presentation is a matter of draping fixed formulas on the skeleton of a familiar narrative structure. What these quite different oral traditions have in common, I suggest, is their recognition of the relationship between audience and speaker. For Athabaskans, speaker/audience independence is signalled. For westerners, shared meaning is cued by familiar formulas, signalling community. Thus involvement can be signalled by honoring positive or negative face.

I shall now present findings from an empirical study of conversational style, demonstrating the effects in interaction of sharedness and lack of sharedness of stylistic expectations. Following the presentation of these data, I shall suggest how the theoretical framework outlined above accounts for the stylistic strategies described.

THE STUDY

In order to account for the use of linguistic features by certain speakers in prolonged interaction, I taped two and a half hours of naturally occurring conversation among six participants at a Thanksgiving dinner in 1978. The dinner took place in the home of Kurt,[1] a native New Yorker living in Oakland, California,

---

[1] With the exception of my own, names of participants have been changed. I want to express here, as I have before, my gratitude to all of them for their initial permission to tape, and their patient and perceptive subsequent comments.

and the guests included his brother, Peter; his friend, David; his former wife, Sally; David's friend Chad; and his "best friend," me. Thus I was both perpetrator and object of my analysis. My role in the interaction was not so much participant-observer—typically an observer who becomes a participant for the purpose of observation—but rather a natural participant who simultaneously, or rather, subsequently, also observed. At the time of the dinner I was in the habit of taping many interactions in which I participated, and I had not yet decided to use this conversation in particular.

In carrying out the analysis, I had to confront my lack of objectivity. I suggest that while such unavoidable lack of objectivity is a danger, the danger is minimized by the process of playback (a term from Labov & Fanshel, 1977), by which all interpretations are checked with others, both participants and nonparticipants; and that it is outweighed by the advantage of insight into what was going on, which would be impossible for a nonparticipant to achieve. Moreover, only by taping an event at which one is a natural participant is it possible to gather data which are not distorted by the presence of a non-participant analyst, or an analyst whose participation would not ordinarily be a component of the event.

My initial intention in approaching this study was to analyze the features making up the styles of all participants. It soon became clear, however, that I could not do this. For one thing, three of the participants, those who were natives of New York City, had in some way "dominated," according to the perceptions of some of those present. This is not to say that there is anything inherently dominating about the styles of these three, or of New Yorkers (although this may be the case). Rather, as Sapir (1958) notes, "It is always the variation that matters, never the objective behavior as such" (p. 542). Thus the styles of the participants can only be judged as they surfaced in interaction with these other participants. As Scollon and Scollon (1984) put it. "What is critical is the difference. Where one is faster and the other is slower relative to each other, the two tend to polarize into a voluble one and a taciturn one."

A second factor which is also, in part, a function of pacing differences, was that there were numerous examples throughout the conversation of talk between two or three New Yorkers, to the exclusion of the others, while there were no examples of talk among non-New Yorkers in which the New Yorkers did not participate. Thus I had no examples of co-stylistic talk among the non-New Yorkers.

Finally, it became clear that I could not equally rely on my native speaker judgments—that basic linguistic tool—in accounting for the speech behavior of all participants. Like everyone, I am a speaker of a particular style. During playback, I found that my intuitions about the speech of the other New Yorkers were, for the most part, corroborated by them. However, understanding the speech behavior of the non-New York participants (two from Los Angeles and one from England), was at times like doing field work in an exotic language.

Their explanations and comments during playback often were revelations to me. In other words, I was able to understand intuitively the nature of many of the linguistic devices of the New Yorkers, whereas I could arrive at an understanding of many of the others' devices only by intellectual processes.

For these reasons, I decided to limit my task to an analysis of the styles of these three participants, and to consider the styles of the others as they contrasted. I would like to note here that throughout this discussion I shall talk about two styles, that of the New Yorkers and that of the non-New Yorkers, as if they were discrete entities. Of course, this is a falsification, an idealization for heuristic purposes. The longer discussion (Tannen, 1979a) makes clear that each individual had a distinctive style, made up of clusters of features. But to the extent that particular features are used more often and in similar ways by certain participants, and used not at all or in different ways by other participants, to that extent style may be said to be shared or not shared.

In the remainder of this paper I shall outline the main features of the style of the New Yorkers in the group as they surface in the interaction and demonstrate their operation in (a) talk with those who share expectations about their use, and (b) talk with those who do not share expectations about their use. Finally, I shall suggest how the theoretical framework presented above may explain the motivating principles underlying the linguistic choices which have become conventionalized in the speech of these participants.

THE NATURE OF ACCOUNTABILITY IN INTERPRETATION

Before presenting the findings, I would like to say a few words about the nature of this kind of discourse analysis. It is, in some sense, an extension of frame semantics (Chafe, 1977; Fillmore, 1976; see Tannen, 1979b, for summary and discussion of theories of frames, scripts, schemata, and so on). In order to understand any word in context, one must be familiar with a set of associations based on cultural experience. Similarly, successful participation in a conversation depends upon shared expectations about how meaning will be signaled, and what the expressive vs. conversational signals are. For example, what use of pitch is normally expected to show contrastiveness, as opposed to pitch shifts marked to show expressiveness? Agrawal (1976) and Gumperz (1978) have shown that speakers of Indian English use heightened pitch as a device for gaining the floor, but they are misunderstood as showing annoyance by speakers of British English.

Such analysis is not available simply by observing surface features of talk; it is a matter of interpretation, as Bennett (1978) has shown for analysis of overlaps. Such analysis may be congenial to anthropologists and students of literature, but less so to psychologists and linguists. Experimental psychologists are likely to look for accountability in data through control groups, statistical significance, and quantifiability. Linguists, on the other hand, are little troubled by the use of one kind of data rather than another—they have been in the habit of thinking up their data—but they expect analysis to yield predictive rules. In discourse analysis, however, as Fillmore (1974) puts it:

> The concern is neither with prediction nor with prescription but rather with norms of interpretation. Discourse grammarians are responsible, not for making probabilistic statements about what people will actually say in given situations, nor for giving advice on what people should say, but rather for characterizing the competence which reliable interpreters of a language possess which enables them to judge appropriateness of given utterances in given contexts. (p. V-7)

If an interpretation is not provable in a statistical sense, it can nonetheless be accountable—that is, demonstrable. The present analysis rests on tangible evidence of three sorts:

1. recurrence, and redundancy of channels;
2. internal and external evidence;
3. the aha factor.

I shall illustrate these with reference to the question of when an overlap is to be interpreted as an interruption (Tannen, 1983).

(1) Recurrence and redundancy. Interpretation is not based on a phenomenon that occurs once, but on recurring phenomena. Furthermore, it is not based on a single feature such as lexical choice, syntax, intonation, or the content of an utterance. Rather, it is based on mutually reinforcing features. As Labov and Fanshel (1977) note, human communication is overdetermined: messages conveyed in one channel are reinforced by messages in others, and within a channel there are multiple indicators of intent.

(2) Internal evidence of participants' interpretations of utterances is found in (a) rhythmicity, synchrony (Erickson, 1979), and other surface features of conversation flow; and (b) content of responses. Thus, if a person feels interrupted, the flow of her/his talk will be discontinuous, and s/he may say something like, "I didn't finish." External evidence is deduced from playback, in which the tape is played and responses are again taped from (a) participants and (b) other informants. Thus a participant, listening to the tape later, comments: "I never got to say what I meant," or nonparticipants, upon listening to it, may comment, "I think s/he wasn't finished."

(3) If an interpretation is correct, a majority of people, upon hearing or reading it, will exclaim, "Aha!" It will make sense, will "click," will seem to explain something they have experienced. Sapir again is our guide: "It therefore becomes the task of an intellectual analysis to justify for us on reasoned grounds what we have knowledge of in pre-scientific fashion" (1949, p. 537).

Finally, an interpretation such as is about to be presented is not intended to be the only one possible. The process demonstrated, certainly, is going on; but so are innumerable other processes. As Goffman states for his analysis, "for every event cited additional interpretations would be in order, for instance, psycho-analytical ones'' (1967, p. 48).

FEATURES OF A CONVERSATONAL STYLE

Following are the main features found in the talk of three of the six Thanksgiving celebrants. (More detailed discussion of these can be found in Tannen 1979a, 1980a, 1980b, 1983.)

1. *Topic* (a) prefer personal topics, (b) shift topics abruptly, (c) introduce topics without hesitance, (d) persistence (if a new topic is not picked up by others, reintroduce it. Data show persistence up to a maximum of seven tries).
2. *Genre* (a) tell more stories, (b) tell stories in rounds, in which (i) internal evaluation (Labov, 1972) is preferred over external (i.e., demonstrate the point of the story rather than lexicaling it), (ii) omit abstract (Labov, 1972) (i.e., plunge right in without introduction; cohesion is established by jux-taposition and theme); (c) preferred point of a story is the emotional experi-ence of the teller.
3. *Pace* (a) faster rate of speech, (b) pauses avoided (silence has a negative value; it is taken as evidence of lack of rapport—Tannen, 1984); (c) faster rate of turntaking, (d) cooperative overlap (the notion of back-channel re-sponses [Duncan 1974] is extended to include lengthy questions and echoes, resulting from a process of participatory listenership).
4. *Expressive paralinguistics* (a) expressive phonology, (b) pitch and ampli-tude shifts, (c) marked voice quality, (d) strategic pauses.

A fifth category, discussed elsewhere (Tannen, 1979a), is humor, but this ap-pears to be more individual, or perhaps sex-linked, and is therefore excluded from the present discussion.

All of these features were marshalled in service of an "enthusiasm con-straint" which has previously been found to operate for speakers of modern Greek (Tannen, 1981). That is, speakers who employ these features in linguistic devices in conversation expect a more elaborate show of enthusiasm if ex-pressions of rapport (i.e., interest, approval, understanding) are to be taken directly.

The present forum does not allow for a detailed presentation of these phe-nomena in co-stylistic interaction; therefore I shall present just two examples.

The features outlined above co-occur in the speech of the three Thanksgiving participants who are natives of New York City; the features combine in identifia-ble linguistic devices. One such device is the machine-gun question (Tannen, 1980a). In its prototypical form, this is a question uttered quickly, timed to overlap or latch (Sacks, 1970) onto another's talk, and characterized by reduced syntactic form, and marked high or low pitch. It asks for information relevant to the other's talk, often of a personal nature. Often, it comes in a series. Questions such as these are used only by the New Yorkers: Kurt, Peter, and myself. When directed at other New Yorkers, these questions do not disrupt the rhythm of conversation. They are either answered in like fashion (quickly, with marked high or low pitch); answered in the course of talk (so that the answer cannot be distinguished from the ongoing talk, since the speaker continues without a hitch in timing); or not answered at all. In the last case, there is no evidence that the one who asked the question is disconcerted that the question is ignored. In contrast, when machine-gun questions are asked of the non-New Yorkers, there is disruption in conversational rhythm; the response is asynchronous and otherwise paralinguistically different from the question; the question is never ignored; and the non-New Yorkers report having felt "caught off guard" or otherwise imposed upon.

I suggest that the form of the machine-gun question: its rapid rate of utterance and timing, reduced syntax, and marked pitch signal the metamessage that the question is not turn-claiming but rather "by-the-way." In other words, the form of the question is intended to convey, "I'm so interested that I can't wait to ask for this extra information, but of course it's still your turn; I don't want to interfere with your talk; answer quickly if you can and if you feel like it, and then go on." The testimony of participants, my own intuition, and evidence in the form of its effect on interaction all support this hypothesis. Those who are not familiar with this stylized form of questioning—are not accustomed to its formulaic nature, one might say—miss the metamessage and take the question as they would any other: a demand for immediate information. To the extent that the particular paralinguistic features are perceived, they are interpreted to show impatience, boredom, lack of interest, and so on.

I have made reference to the formulaic nature of machine-gun questions. This is an important concept. There has been much recent interest among linguists in formulaic expressions and the fixed rather than analytic nature of semantic structures in language (Bolinger, 1976; Coulmas, 1980; Fillmore, 1979; Matisoff, 1979; Tannen & Öztek, 1977). The present study represents a furthering of this approach. Conversational style reflects the tendency to use particular familiar patterns, like machine-gun questions. As Jarrett (1978) has demonstrated for blues lyrics, strings of words that have never before been uttered can nonetheless be formulaic by adhering to fixed patterns in recognizable contexts. In this sense, we are all "inevitably traditional," and our ability to send and receive meaning through language depends upon ability to manipulate and recognize these patterns.

The following examples, selected from many in the data, will illustrate the operation of a series of machine-gun questions in co-stylistic and cross-stylistic talk. In the first segment, I am asking Chad, a native of Los Angeles whom I have just met, a series of questions about himself. As seen in his hesitant responses, the rhythmic asynchrony of the interchange, and Chad's later commentary, the questions failed to "get him talking" because they made him feel "on the spot."[2] (Arrows mark machine-gun questions.) (See Appendix for explanation of markings.)

→ (1)   DT   ⌐Yoù live in LÁ?
   (2)   Ch   Yeah.
→ (3)   DT   ⌐Y'vísiting hére?
   (4)   Ch   Yeah.
→ (5)   DT   What do you ⌐dó there?
         . . . .
   (6)   Ch   uh: I work at Disney Prosuh? . . . Walt Dísney . . . .
                   ⌐ a:nd
→ (7)   DT   └ Yoù an ártist?
   (8)   Ch   N: no.
→ (9)   DT   Writer?
  (10)   Ch   Yeah:. I write . . . ádvertising copy.

In contrast, observe the following excerpt in which I ask a series of machine-gun questions of Kurt. In this segment, Kurt and Peter are operating a duet (Falk, 1979), since they are brothers and equally expert on their childhoods. The subject is the effect of television on children.

   (1)   K   I think it's basically done . . . dámage to children. . . . . That what
                                                    p   dec→
               góod it's dòne is . . . outwéighed by . . . the dàmage.⌉
→ (2)   DT   └ Did yóu
               two grow up with télevision?
   (3)   P   Véry lìttle. We hád a TV ⌐in the quonset
→ (4)   DT   └ How old were you
               when your parents got it?⌉
   (5)   K   └ We hád a TV̀ but we didn't wátch it
               all the time. . . . We were véry young. I was fóur when my
               parents got a TV.⌉
→ (6)   DT   parents got a TV.└ You were four?

---

[2] The following transcription conventions have been gleaned from a variety of sources, including Schenkein (1978), and those developed by Gumperz and his collaborators and Chafe and his collaborators at the University of California, Berkeley.

   . .   noticeable pause or break in rhythm
   . . .   half second pause, as measured by a stop watch
           an extra dot is added for each half second of pause
           marks primary stress
           marks secondary stress
           underline marks emphatic stress
           CAPS mark very emphatic stress
           high pitch on word

(7) P   I even remember that. . . . . . ⌐I don't remember / ? →
(8) K   └I remember they got a →
     P   ??   /⌐
     K   TV before we moved out of ─┘ the quonset huts.
           In níneteen fifty foùr.⌐
(9) P   │ I remember we got it
                                   └
           in the quonset huts.
→(10) DT (chuckle) ⌐You lived in qúonset huts? . . . .
           ⌐When you were hów old?

           . . . . .

(11) K   Y'know my fáther's dentist said to him whát's a quónset hut.
           . . . And he said Gód, yóu must be younger than my children.
           . . . . He wás. . . . . Yoùnger than bóth of us.

Of the four questions asked in this segment, (2) is answered immediately in (3);
(4) is answered, but only after the answer to (2) is completed in (5); (6) is not
answered at all, since it is a back-channel response; and (10) is not answered at
all, even though Kurt and Peter were not otherwise conversationally engaged at
that point (witness the second and a half pause). They simply prefer not to
answer, as Kurt offers instead a short story suggested to him by the topic (11).
(For more detailed discussion of these and similar examples see Tannen, 1979a
and 1980a.)

EXPRESSIVE RESPONSES

One additional device using features outlined above will be illustrated:
    At numerous times during Thanksgiving dinner, one or another New Yorker
responds to someone else's talk with utterances that are paralinguistically exaggerated, that is, with marked high or low pitch, increased amplitude, and any of a
range of marked voice qualities. When used with others who also use such
devices, the exaggerated responses become part of a web of increasingly paralinguistically exaggerated talk. However, when used with those who do not share
expectations about them, such responses stop conversation rather than encouraging it. One example follows.
    Chad and David (good friends, both from Los Angeles), operating as a duet,
are jointly telling about a mutual friend, Randy, who attended a meeting of
speech pathologists discussing the origin of "the gay voice." Chad, David,
Randy, and Kurt (the host) are all gay men. Therefore, the idea of heterosexual
scientists analyzing homosexual voice quality is objectionable to them—and to
the other participants, friends and relatives, who identify with them and therefore
are "wise" in Goffman's (1963) sense.

(1) Ch Yeah the ⌐gáy voìce.   She was talking about gáy voìces.
(2) Da   └The gay voice┘
(3)   And Rándy was sitting there símmering.

(4)   Ch   Right ⌜ / ? /
(5)   DT   ⌞ What was he sáying.
(6)   Ch   They were wondering whether or not it was . . . hormónal.
(7)   Da   Whether the ⌜gáy voice was hormònal.
(8)   ⌞‖ WHAT!
                        ff
(9)   Ch   Yeah. Whether the gáy voice was hormònal.
(10) DT   ⌞You're kidding!
             . . . . . .
(11) DT   Wo::w.
             . . . . . .
(12) K .   Oh God!
             p . . . .
(13) Ch   Or whether it was léarned behavior, or was w whether it was . . .
           uh *learned* behavior, o:r genetic, or hormonal or what.⌜ / ? as they
           were gonna/   ⌞ Oo: that
(14) K   *p, dec*
           makes my skín creep. . . . . e::w. .

There is evidence that something has gone awry in the long pauses between
(10), (11), (12), and (13). While such pauses would not be surprising at the end
of a speaker's narrative, Chad and David were in the middle of their story about
Randy when these occurred. In playback, both David and Chad volunteered,
each alone and independently, that they had been stopped short by my exaggerated responses (8) and (10); they wondered what was wrong and waited to be
told. Only when they got nothing but more such responses did they continue
(13). David further noted something that I would never have understood: Chad's
way of murmuring (13) signalled the same meaning as Kurt's exclaiming (12)
and (14): they both were showing scorn for the hypothesis that the gay voice may
be hormonal. However, Kurt showed it by expressive paralinguistics, while
Chad showed it by listing alternatives in a voice that trailed off.

This process spontaneously recurred during playback with Chad. He made a
comment which I found particularly surprising and insightful, and I showed my
appreciation by exclaiming, "Oh! How INTeresting!" My response was sudden,
drawn out, and uttered in a voice that showed intensity and enthusiasm through
rapidity of timing, exaggerated low pitch, and thick quality. Chad stopped talking, and there was a fleeting look of astonishment on his face. I tried to repair the
situation, instinctively, by repeating "That's interesting" in a more casual way:
faster, more clipped, with higher pitch. Suddenly I recalled the "WHAT!"
phenomenon and asked Chad if my exaggerated response had stopped him again.
He said it had. I have since received testimony from many other people of this
phenomenon operating in their conversation. For example, the daughters of a

native New Yorker who were raised in upstate New York and Vermont complained that when they tell their mother about their experiences, she sometimes responds with utterances that scare them. She thinks she is showing interest, and they look around to see what terrible thing has suddenly happened.

Finally, David, upon reading my analysis of the Thanksgiving conversation, realized that this stylistic difference is a source of difficulty between him and his friend Kurt. He explained that Kurt habitually responds to stories he tells by exclaiming, for example, "WHAT? How could they do *that*?" David interprets Kurt's disbelief as directed at David—that is, that Kurt doubts David's veracity. In fact, as Kurt avers and I instinctively know, the disbelief is directed at the story, not the teller, and its swift and paralinguistically gross character is intended to reassure David that he has told a good story. In effect, Kurt is taking David's point of view in his response.

These examples reveal a number of crucial aspects of the process of crossstylistic interaction as suggested by Gumperz (1977). First, one's interpretation of interlocutors' intentions is automatic and unequivocal. One does not think, "If I said that, I'd mean X, but you may mean something else." Second, judgments are made not about linguistic style, which is "invisible," but about intentions or personality. If one feels imposed upon, one concludes that the other is rude; if one feels embarrassed, one concludes that the other intended to embarrass, or, at the very least, was "thoughtless." Finally, reactions to utterances in communication are emotional. Analysis such as is presented here can only be post hoc. If one has had a mismatch pointed out in a certain case—for example, if one is truly convinced that the other's intention was not to embarrass or impose but rather to show rapport—one is nonetheless likely to react the same way the next time the same mismatch occurs. However, having understood the process of differing styles, speakers can catch themselves afterwards and say, "Oh, it was *that* again."

The use of linguistic features which constitute style seems a self-evident way of signaling intentions and meaning in conversation. Style provides a conventionalized means of encoding messages while honoring interpersonal needs for community and independence, or positive and negative face. In the struggle to characterize the overriding strategies motivating the devices displayed in my data, I began by calling the strategy of one group "rapport-based," because they put the signaling load (term from Gumperz) on an overt show of interpersonal involvement. The strategy seemed to be: when in doubt, talk. Ask questions. Talk fast, loud, soon. Overlap. Show enthusiasm. Prefer personal topics, and so on. In contrast, I called the other style "defensive," because it placed the signaling load on distance. The strategy was: allow longer pauses. Hesitate. Don't impose one's topics, ideas, personal information. Use moderate paralinguistic effects, and so on (Tannen, 1979a). But I was dissatisfied with the apparent bias of this terminology, for rapport is the goal of both styles. Rapport is always the happy result when style is shared, and any attempt to establish rapport can fail miserably when its intention is missed. Therefore I took to calling one style "high-involvement" and the other "high considerateness" (Tannen 1980a). Yet this terminology too seemed to ascribe to each group sole rights to properties that certainly both sought.

Considerateness and involvement can be signaled by honoring either of the two overriding, co-existent human needs for community and independence. Personal and cultural preferences for the various stylistic devices that have been discussed reflect conventionalized ways of establishing interpersonal involvement and showing considerateness (or its opposite). In interaction with others who habitually use devices based on different ways of honoring these human needs, misinterpretation of intentions is likely. Any device intended to signal involvement by honoring the need for community can be interpreted as a violation of the need for independence. Any device intended to signal involvement by honoring the need for independence can be interpreted as a violation of the need for community. "Style" is invisible when expectations about the use of linguistic devices to signal intentions and meaning are shared. Differing expectations about such devices makes the others' linguistic devices noticeable and therefore makes visible conversational style.

APPENDIX

⌐high pitch on phrase, continuing until punctuation
.   sentence-final falling intonation
?   yes/no question rising intonation
ʔ   glottal stop
:   indicates lengthening of preceding vowel sound
→   at the left draws attention to indicated line
an arrow at the right indicates speech continues →
  without break in rhythm (look for continuation)
p   piano (as in musical notation), spoken softly
pp   pianissimo, spoken very softly
f   forte, spoken loudly
ff   fortissimo, spoken very loudly
dec   spoken slowly

/ʔ/   indicates inaudible segment
/words/   in slashes indicate uncertain transcription
    ⌐Penned brackets between lines indicates overlapping speech.
    └Two people talking at once.
    Penned brackets with reversed flaps⌐
             └Second utterance latched onto
             first without pause.

REFERENCES

Agrawal, A. (1976). Who will speak next. *Papers in Linguistic Analysis, 1*, 58–71.

Bateson, G. (1972). *Steps to an ecology of mind.* New York: Ballantine.

Bennett, A. (1978). Interruptions and the interpretation of conversation. In J.J. Jaeger *et al.* (Eds.), *Proceedings of the Fourth Annual Meeting of the Berkeley Linguistics Society* (pp. 557–575). Berkeley, Ca.: University of California, Department of Linguistics.

Bolinger, D. (1976). Meaning and memory. *Forum Linguisticum, 1*, 1–14.

Brown, P., & Levinson, S. (1978). Universals in language usage: Politeness phenomena. In E.N. Goody (Ed.), *Questions and politeness: Strategies in social interaction* (pp. 56–289, 295–310). Cambridge: Cambridge University Press.

Chafe, W. (1977). Creativity in verbalization and its implications for the nature of stored knowledge. In R.O. Freedle (Ed.), *Discourse production and comprehension* (pp. 41–55). Norwood, N.J.: Ablex.

Coulmas, F. (Ed.). (1980). *Conversational routine.* The Hague: Mouton.

Duncan, S. (1974). On the structure of speaker-auditor interaction during speaking turns. *Language in Society, 2*, 161–180.

Durkheim, E. (1965). *The elementary forms of the religious life.* New York: The Free Press. (Originally published, 1915.)

Erickson, F. (1979). Talking down: Some cultural sources of miscommunication in interracial interviews. In A. Wolfgang (Ed.), *Nonverbal Behavior: Applications and cultural implications* (pp. 99–126). New York: Academic Press.

Ervin-Tripp, S. (1972). On sociolinguistic rules: Alternation and co-occurrence. In J.J. Gumperz & D. Hymes (Eds.), *Directions in sociolinguistics: The ethnography of communication* (pp. 213–250). New York: Holt, Rinehart & Winston.

Falk, J. (1980). The conversational duet. In B.R. Caron *et al.* (Eds.), *Proceedings of the Sixth Annual Meeting of the Berkeley Linguistics Society* (pp. 507–514). Berkeley, Ca.: University of California, Department of Linguistics.

Fillmore, C.J. (1974). Pragmatics and the description of discourse. In *Berkeley Studies in Syntax and Semantics* (Vol. 1, pp. V-1–V-21). Berkeley, Ca.: University of California, Department of Linguistics and Institute of Human Learning.

Fillmore, C.J. (1976). The need for a frame semantics within linguistics. In H. Karlgren (Ed.), *Statistical methods in linguistics* (pp. 5–29). Stockholm: Skriptor.

Fillmore, C.J. (1979). On fluency. In C.J. Fillmore, D. Kempler & W.S.-Y. Wang (Eds.), *Individual differences in language ability and language behavior* (pp. 85–101). New York: Academic Press.

Goffman, E. (1963). *Stigma.* Engelwood Cliffs, N.J.: Prentice-Hall.

Goffman, E. (1967). *Interaction ritual.* Garden City, N.Y.: Doubleday.

Goody, J. (1977). *The domestication of the savage mind.* Cambridge: Cambridge University Press.

Grice, H.P. (1975). Logic and conversation. In P. Cole & J. Morgan (Eds.), *Syntax and Semantics: Vol. 3. Speech Acts* (pp. 41–58). New York: Academic Press.

Gumperz, J.J. (1964). Linguistic and social interaction in two communities. In J. Gumperz & D. Hymes (Eds.), *The ethnography of communication.* (American Anthropologist, *66,*(6: pt.2), 137–153).

Gumperz, J.J. (1977). Sociocultural knowledge in conversational inference. In M. Saville-Troike (Ed.), *Georgetown Round Table on Languages and Linguistics 1977* (pp. 191–212). Washington, D.C.: Georgetown University Press.

Gumperz, J.J. (1978). The conversational analysis of interethnic communication. In E.L. Ross (Ed.), *Interethnic communication* (Southern Anthropological Society. Proceedings, No. 12, pp. 13–31.) Athens, Ga.: University of Georgia Press.

Havelock, E. (1963). *Preface to Plato*. Cambridge, Mass.: Harvard University Press.

Jarrett, D. (1978). The singer and the bluesman: Formulations of personality in the lyrics of the blues. *Southern Folklore Quarterly, 42*, 31–37.

Labov, W. (1972). *Language in the inner city: Studies in the Black English vernacular*. Philadelphia: University of Pennsylvania Press.

Labov, W., & Fanshel, D. (1977). *Therapeutic discourse: Psychotherapy as conversation*. New York: Academic Press.

Lakoff, R.T. (1973). The logic of politeness; or, minding your p's and q's. In C. Corum, T.C. Smith-Stark & A. Weiser (Eds.), *Papers from the Ninth Regional Meeting of the Chicago Linguistics Society* (pp. 292–305). Chicago, Ill.: Chicago Linguistics Society.

Lakoff, R.T. (1979). Stylistic strategies within a grammar of style. In J. Orasanu, M. Slater & L.L. Adler (Eds.), *Language, sex, and gender* (Annals of the New York Academy of Sciences, *327*, 53–78). New York: The New York Academy of Sciences.

Lord, A. (1960). *The singer of tales*. Cambridge, Mass.: Harvard University Press.

Matisoff, J. (1979). *Blessings, curses, hopes, and fears: Psycho-ostensive expressions in Yiddish*. Philadelphia: Institute for the Study of Human Issues.

Olson, D. (1977). From utterance to text: The bias of language in speech and writing. *Harvard Educational Review, 47*, 257–281.

Ong, W. (1967). *The presence of the word*. New Haven, Conn.: Yale University Press.

Sacks, H. (1970). [Unpublished lecture notes].

Sapir, E. (1949). Speech as a personality trait. In D.G. Mandelbaum (Ed.), *Selected writings of Edward Sapir in language, culture and personality* (pp. 533–543). Berkeley, Los Angeles: University of California Press. First published in *American Journal of Sociology* (1927), *32*, 892–905.

Schenkein, J. (1978). *Studies in the organization of conversational interaction*. New York: Academic Press.

Scollon, R., & Scollon, S.B.K. (1984). Cooking it up and boiling it down: Abstracts in Athabaskan children's story retellings. In D. Tannen (Ed.), *Coherence in spoken and written discourse* (pp. 173–197). Ablex.

Tannen, D. (1979a). *Processes and consequences of conversational style*. Ann Arbor, Mich.: University Microfilms.

Tannen, D. (1979b). What's in a frame? Surface evidence for underlying expectations. In R.O. Freedle (Ed.), *New directions in discourse processing* (pp. 137–181). Norwood, N.J.: Ablex.

Tannen, D. (1980a). Toward a theory of conversational style: The machine-gun question. *Working Papers in Sociolinguistics 67–73* (No. 73, pp. 1–16). Austin, Tex.: Southwest Educational Development Laboratory.

Tannen, D. (1980b). Implications of the oral/literate continuum for cross-cultural communication. In J.E. Alatis (Ed.), *Georgetown Round Table on Languages and Linguistics 1980* (pp. 326–347). Washington, D.C.: Georgetown University Press.

Tannen, D. (1980c). Spoken/written language and the oral/literate continuum. In B.R. Caron *et al.* (Eds.), *Proceedings of the Sixth Annual Meeting of the Berkeley Linguistics Society* (pp. 207–218). Berkeley, Ca.: University of California, Department of Linguistics.

Tannen, D. (1981). Indirectness in discourse: Ethnicity as conversational style. *Discourse Processes, 4*, 221–238.

Tannen, D. (1983). When is an overlap not an interruption? One component of conversational style. In R. Di Pietro, W. Frawley & A. Wedel (Eds.), *The first Delaware symposium on languages and linguistics* (pp. 119–129). Newark, Del.: University of Delaware Press.

Tannen, D. (1985). Silence: Anything but. In D. Tannen & M. Saville-Troike (Eds.), *Perspectives on silence* (pp. 93–111). Norwood, N.J.: Ablex.

Tannen, D., & Öztek, P.C. (1977). Health to our mouths. Formulaic expressions in Turkish and Greek. In K. Whistler (Ed.), *Proceedings of the Third Annual Meeting of the Berkeley Linguistics Society* (pp. 516–534). Berkeley, Ca.: University of California, Department of Linguistics. (Reprinted in F. Coulmas (Ed.), *Conversational routine* (pp. 37–54). The Hague: Mouton, 1980.)

CHAPTER 24

Verbal Routine: A Stylistic Variable

FLORIAN COULMAS
Universität Düsseldorf

Given my own line of interest, it is not surprising that I am sympathetic to Professor Tannen's arguments. Some of the problems she is dealing with have been bothering me for some time (cf. Coulmas, 1977, 1979b, 1980a), and when I first read her stimulating paper I felt that it would not be difficult to comment on many of the points she tackles. Recalling, however, what she said about the difficulties in accounting for speech behavior in her analytic work, I soon realized that it was not at all easy to state and defend comments or to advance criticism. She tells us that analyzing the conversational behavior of non-New York speakers of American English "was at times like doing field work in an exotic language." In many cases, her native New York intuition failed her in understanding non-New York speech behavior. I do not think that she emphasized this point as a precaution in order to ward off criticism, but rather because it is true. How much more must it be true for anyone who is not a native speaker of any variety of English like myself.

If non-native judgements on grammar are precarious, they are outright impossible regarding style. Stylistically adjusted speech behavior is undoubtedly the most advanced level of language performance, and requires absolutely nativelike command. We do not consciously control stylistic variation, and the factors conditioning it are still little understood. I do agree with Deborah Tannen that we cannot but rely on our own intuitions, as a heuristic tool at least, in order to make the linguistic dimension of style open to scientific treatment. Since my own intuitions about English are worthless, I have decided to refrain from any comments about "machine-gun questions" and other peculiarities of New York style.

Instead, I will confine myself to a few considerations about a feature of discourse deserving of closer attention when one tries to characterize different styles. I am in agreement with Tannen when I claim that the degree of routinization is one of the characteristics which distinguishes one style from another. It may also contribute to clarifying the very notion of style insofar as it can help to relate individual and social aspects of style.

First, let me introduce a distinction which is of major importance for my conception of *verbal routine*. The analysis of verbal routine is to be carried out on two levels: For the first, it has to account for prepatterned units of speech which are bound to recurrent communication situations. For the second, verbal routine manifests itself in the execution of standardized strategies and action patterns in speech behavior. (See Coulmas, 1980b, for a more detailed discussion of these two levels of verbal routine.) The notion of *verbal routine* allows us to put into common perspective a great variety of phenomena ranging from social conventions and their sociolinguistic implications to automatic speech in a neurolinguistic sense. Such phenomena testify to a very basic requirement, or rather, precondition, of human communication: repetitive use. Among the expressive means that satisfy this need are all kinds of fixed expressions such as routine formulae, clichés, slogans, idioms, conventional euphemisms, familiar quotations, proverbs, aphorisms, and stereotyped collocations, as well as strategic devices such as routine frames, prepatterned sequences, and gambits. For obvious reasons, I cannot go here into a lengthy discussion of all of these linguistic repetition devices. Rather what I can do is raise a couple of questions about them that seem important with respect to the concerns of this conference and of this session:

1. In what way do styles differ with regard to verbal routine?
2. How can we understand the role of verbal routine in language production?

As for the first question, there are obviously a number of routine formulae employed and expected when certain styles or registers are used. "Ladies and gentlemen," for instance is used in a formal speech. Other formulae such as, for example, "to whom it may concern" only occur in writing. "We'll now take questions from the floor" or "the paper is open for discussion" are also typically tied to formal occasions, or, to put it differently, to occasions requiring a formal style. Doctor-patient communication is characterized by different routines than juridical discourse or classroom interaction. Notice, however, that we are referring to particular settings, rather than styles existing independent of situational variables. Those of us who have a background in sociolinguistics will recall the notions of elaborated and restricted code introduced by Basil Bernstein in order to capture the relationship between linguistic and societal variables. The restricted code was allegedly characterized, among other things, by a high degree of predictability. While Bernstein's arguments were quite persuasive at first, further investigations did not substantiate the claim that there were particular codes, particular linguistic varieties, that is, used by particular social groups of speakers which were restricted and predictable. Rather, communicative settings were found to differ on a wide scale as regards restrictedness and linguistic variability.

By the same token, it is setting or situational frame, as I have called it elsewhere (Coulmas, 1979a), rather than style that demands or makes probable the use of a particular routine formula or strategy. There is, of course, a correlation between style and setting, and a large part of sociolinguistic research has been devoted to that investigation. The problem with the notions of restricted and elaborated code was that this correlation was almost completely ignored. Codes were supposed to vary with groups of speakers rather than with communicative settings and participant configurations. This mistake should not be repeated in the attempt to clarify the notion of style. While there are undoubtedly routine formulae as well as strategies which are indicative of particular styles, others do not vary with style but rather with setting. Consider, for instance, the routinized exchange

Lawyer: Objection!
Judge: Sustained!

that regulates the course of verbal interaction at particular stages in a court room. This sequence is strictly tied to this setting, and it is certainly not the only routine which is shared by those getting involved in juridical discourse in the respective roles. Yet, despite a number of common routines, there is considerable room for stylistic variation. Hence, the relationship between style and verbal routine is a complex one.

Routines are bound to characteristic settings or institutions, and they may be indicative of particular styles; but they do not define styles. The enactment of routines in many cases is an essential part of following established patterns of behavior in reacting appropriately to the ever recurrent typical situations of social life. These patterns do not, however, determine conversational interaction so narrowly as to preclude individual variation.

Ceremonial and ritual interaction is characterized by a reduction of the range of individual variation. Conversational routine, in turn, can also be seen as reducing individual variation, and in so doing it serves as a means of establishing and maintaining communication. However, individual style is of course in no sense precluded by conversational routine. Rather, the ways prepatterned linguistic units are combined with newly synthesized constructions, as well as the ways routine stategies are made use of, can be regarded as one of the dimensions of individual stylistic variation. On the other hand, the overall range of variability in this respect varies with the communicative setting. In other words, the possibility of giving expression to individual style depends to some extent on the properties of socially defined settings in which a variety of routines are obligatory, tolerable, or inadmissible.

Let me turn now briefly to the second question raised above: How can we understand the role of verbal routine in language production? The production of utterances is a creative process. The recursive nature of language enables its users to meet the demands of producing a potentially infinite variety of ever new sentences. Yet, most sentences are not new, particularly from a structural view. And while nobody denies that the generative capacity of language is one of its essential properties, warranting its universal applicability as a means of communication, a psycholinguistic model of production cannot be reduced to a model of generativity. There is need for new sentences, but there is need for repetition as well. Repetition invites conventionalization and, in some cases, routinization. Not every utterance needs to be constructed from scratch. To a greater or lesser extent speakers always make use of prepatterned units and employ routine strategies. In this regard, linguistic production is an equilibrium between the novel and the familiar. The use of routine strategies and formulaic frames enables the speaker to concentrate on the message he or she wants to convey instead of its wrapping. Formulaic frames with slots, for instance, provide a means of putting a new message into a prepatterned form. "Not that I disagree with you, but . . ." or "Much as I would like . . . (+Negation)." are linguistic devices of this sort. Rather than being put together every time they are used, they are drawn from memory and combined with a variety of newly composed phrases to form a complete message.

As for routine strategies, conventional implicature is one example. Conventional implicatures are part of social knowledge in that they constitute habitual allusions to inferences to be drawn from a given utterance and a number of presupposed principles. Some routine formulae are "dead implicatures." By this I mean that conventionalized inferences necessary for understanding an implicative utterance have ceased to be drawn consciously or even subconsciously in connection with some routinized expressions. Thus, it is conventional knowledge that "don't mention it" is an appropriate response to thanks or apologies. Yet, the actual inferences as to why this should be so are hardly ever drawn. Comprehension and production of such utterances is guided not by the principles of implicature, but by routine.

It is important to account for the discrepancy between the potentially synthesizable and the actually synthesized, which brings me to another significant point concerning the role of verbal routine in production. Routines testify to the asymmetry between production and reception/interpretation: Many routines can be broken down into smaller units if necessary, but they do not have to be synthesized every time they are produced. The structure of many formulaic utterances is transparent; and conventional as well as dead implicatures can be analyzed and reconstructed. This of course does not imply that they are utilized. Hence, interpretation may be analytic where production is holistic.

By way of conclusion, I want to mention one last, rather general point. From what I have said so far, it ought to be clear that verbal routine has to do with the division of labor between combinational manipulation and memory. To put it more accurately, verbal routine is a means of minimizing processing effort. Prepatterned units can be drawn from memory and, when used, provide time for discoursive planning.

One of the consequences of the preceding observations is that a psychologically real model of production will have to incorporate a highly redundant lexicon containing many complex wholes, in addition to entries for their constituent parts. In general, routines appear to point towards a model where storage space is large and easily available, but computation expensive.

REFERENCES

Coulmas, F. (1977). *Rezeptives Sprachverhalten: Eine theoretische Studie über Faktoren sprachlichen Verstehens.* Hamburg: Buske.

Coulmas, F. (1979a). On the sociolinguistic relevance of routine formulae. *Journal of Pragmatics, 3,* 39–66.

Coulmas, F. (1979b). Sprache und Kultur. In D. Hymes, *Soziolinguistik: Zur Ethnographie der Kommunikation* (F. Coulmas, ed., pp. 7–25). Frankfurt: Suhrkamp.

Coulmas, F. (1980a). "Poison to your soul": Thanks and apologies contrastively viewed. In F. Coulmas (Ed.), *Conversational routine: Explorations in standardized communication situations and prepatterned speech* (pp. 69–91). The Hague: Mouton.

Coulmas, F. (1980b). Introduction: Conversational routine. In F. Coulmas (Ed.), *Conversational routine: Explorations in standardized communication situations and prepatterned speech* (pp. 1–17). The Hague: Mouton.

CHAPTER 25

Elements of Style or Strategy in Interaction

STARKEY DUNCAN, JR.

University of Chicago

Professor Tannen's topic—conversational style—is an ambitious one. Her use of the term "style" appears to coincide broadly with what I and other investigators have referred to as "strategy." The issues involved here are particularly fascinating to me because Donald Fiske and I have been engaged for over two years now in analyses of interaction strategy. In order to clarify the perspective from which I view Professor Tannen's paper, let me describe as basically and briefly as possible what I mean by strategy. I wish to consider strategy here strictly in terms of patterns of action observable within an interaction; I do not refer to plans of action or intentions that lie behind those patterns. (Professor Tannen uses the term "strategy" in the sense of broad motivations.)

I shall define interaction style or strategy as the product of choice in the face of alternatives, where the alternatives are framed by conventions. I believe there are two broad areas of choice that are exercised by a participant in an interaction: (a) choice of conventions to be used, and (b) choice of actions in performing those conventions.

I take it that, in approaching an occasion of interaction, a participant must define the situation in terms of applicable social categories. I have already touched on this process in my discussion of Professor Sajavaara's paper. Once the situation is defined, the participant must choose conventions to perform that are appropriate to that definition; there is also the choice of whether or not to ratify conventions that are chosen by the partner. This is the first broad area of strategic choice. Investigators of forms of personal address and authors such as Goffman have clearly indicated the significance and subtlety involved in the choice and ratification of conventional forms.

Let us assume for the moment that participants have chosen and agreed upon a set of conventions to be used in an interaction. The second major area of strategy then becomes available: the choice of actions in performing the conventions. To describe this area, I must first outline certain basic characteristics of interaction structure.

I suggest that a description of interaction structure must involve at a minimum a two-part interaction sequence *A-B,* where *A* is an action by a participant, and *B* is a subsequent action by the partner. I suggest that there are only two basic types of rules that apply to the occurrence of *A* and *B:* rules specifying obligatory action, and rules specifying optional action.

In obligatory sequences, once the participant has performed action *A,* the partner definitely "should" perform action *B.* An example would be the rule that, under specified circumstances, an offer to shake hands (*A*) should be followed by an acceptance of that offer (*B*). An example from our work on turn-taking phenomena is the rule that, when the speaker is gesticulating, the auditor must not take the turn. (Of course, obligatory rules may also describe actions that must not be taken.)

In optional sequences, the partner may appropriately do *B* only after the occurrence of *A;* but, upon the occurrence of *A,* the partner has the legitimate choice of doing *B* or not doing *B.* An example from the turn-taking results would be the hypothesized turn signal. The rule attaching to this signal is that the auditor may appropriately act to take the turn only after display of the signal; but, upon display of the signal, the auditor chooses whether or not to take the turn. That is, display of the signal by the speaker indicates points at which the auditor may appropriately exercise the option of taking the turn.

Given this perspective on interaction structure, it follows that there are two major types of choice available to participants: (a) the choice to violate the rules, and (b) the choice to exercise legitimate alternative actions. It is always possible to violate the rules. One may fail to perform obligatory actions at the appropriate points. For example, an auditor may attempt to take the speaking turn while the gesticulation signal is displayed. When a rule specifying legitimate alternatives is operative, one may take the specified actions at inappropriate points in the stream of interaction. For example, the auditor may attempt to take the speaking turn when the turn signal is not displayed. Thus, it is always possible to violate the conventional rules prevailing in an interaction. Each choice by a participant to violate or not to violate specific rules in an interaction would be an element of that participant's strategy or style.

When rules specifying legitimate alternatives are operating, participants must choose at each option-point which of the available alternatives to exercise. For example, the speaker chooses the frequency with which the turn signal is displayed. Correspondingly, upon each display of the turn signal, the auditor must choose whether or not to take the turn. Each choice of signal display and each choice of legitimate alternatives is an element of a participant's strategy.

If my presentation has not been concise to the point of being cryptic, it will be apparent that, within this framework, convention and strategy are inextricably related. One simply cannot engage in convention-based action without concomitantly engaging in two aspects of strategy: the choice and ratification of the conventions being used, and the choice of actions in performing the conventions, including both legitimate actions and actions in violation of the convention. In this sense I believe Professor Tannen is quite correct in stating that "style is not something extra or frivolous, added on like frosting on a cake. It is the stuff of which the cake is made." What we see in interaction—the observable actions—is strategy. But strategy cannot be interpreted apart from convention; strategy cannot be analyzed in and of itself. The description and interpretation of strategy is strictly limited by the accuracy and completeness of the description of the underlying conventions. In pursuing questions of strategy, the investigator cannot proceed in a straight line but rather must detour by way of convention. From the raw observations of stylistic material the investigator must infer the underlying conventions, generating hypotheses as detailed as possible. This, of course, is the everyday work of linguists, as well as of investigators of interaction structure. When attempts are made to describe style relatively directly without going by way of convention, then the relevant conventions are merely assumed and left implicit, to be inferred by the reader. This makes the evaluation of results more difficult.

I believe that Professor Tannen is premature in reaching the conclusion that "style is the result of automatic linguistic and paralinguistic cues that seem self-evident and natural, based on previous interaction in a speech community . . . which has conventionalized their use." It may be that, when interaction situations are recurrent and familiar, strategy in the sense of choice of convention becomes a relatively routine affair. Nevertheless, even when this is the case, our studies suggest that strategy in the sense of patterns of action within the constraints of conventions is a highly flexible, adaptable process, subject to many sources of influence. Patterns of action choice by a participant may often vary markedly in the course of a single interaction, as well as between two interactions. For this reason, it seems useful to distinguish carefully between the different aspects of interaction strategy.

In discussing style in a six-person conversation, Professor Tannen chooses to focus primarily on that aspect of strategy stemming from the choice of conventions, as opposed to the choice of actions within conventions. The problems of disruption and misinterpretation that she considers apparently stem, not from a conflict over choice or ratification of conventions to be used, but rather from the fact that the two groups of participants come from different subcultures; certain conventions routinely chosen by one group simply are not familiar to members of the other group, and vice versa. One cannot conduct oneself appropriately within the framework of unfamiliar conventions, much less correctly interpret the actions of the person who is using them. In this sense, a major topic of Professor Tannen's paper concerns the dynamics of cross-subcultural interaction.

In gathering the materials to be analyzed, Professor Tannen apparently made a tape recording of the interaction which is the topic of her paper. This is a straightforward and fairly common decision, influenced no doubt by many pragmatic factors. After all, in no study are all the observable actions analyzed. Her data include paralanguage and careful tracking of interaction sequences. I am hesitant, however, to accept her higher level rationale for her selection of data, namely, that messages in speech are merely reinforced by actions in body motion. It would seem that she is claiming that nonlinguistic aspects of interaction function mainly in the service of redundancy. This position seems to be even more language-centered than the standard linguistic position of thirty years ago that language is the central core of interaction, and that paralanguage and body motion serve only as weak modification or elaboration. Even weak modification or elaboration seems a more significant function than redundancy. Current studies of interaction are predicated on the notion that the interrelation of language and nonlinguistic actions in the process of interaction is an empirical issue, not decidable a priori. Even when speech and body motion are entirely congruent—that is, non-contradictory—our studies of turn-related phenomena in two-person conversations suggest that there is useful information in nonlinguistic actions that is not recoverable from the analysis of speech alone.

Finally, I cannot forbear noting, if only in passing, an interesting relationship between what Professor Tannen describes as her own personal style—a description in the paper exemplified mainly by "machine-gun questions"—and the achievement, through stylistic means, of rapport, community, and the sacred. In contrast, the more laid-back, "defensive," "high-considerate" style of her California friends represents only a preliminary stage in the achievement of these ultimate goals. I do not believe that I am in a position to evaluate the validity of this judgment, but I can, at least, be amazed at the scope of the conceptual leap.

CHAPTER 26

Aspects of Style

JOCHEN REHBEIN
Ruhr-Universität Bochum

"Style" is a form of speaking which covers more than a single event of speech production. If one tries to single out elements of what style is one has to go into social determinants of the psycholinguistic object "speech production." This is what D. Tannen (this volume) did in her paper. In oral communication, participants proceed according to forms which are mutual to all of them in order that communication be successful and free of misunderstandings. One of these mutual forms is "style." Some of Tannen's observations on it are the subject of the following not very systematic remarks.

"RAPPORTS SOCIAUX"

One of the basic concepts under which some definitions of style come together is, according to Tannen, the notion of "rapport." This term has its own tradition, in which it is used—especially in the Durkheimian notion of "rapports sociaux"—to define social groups through a medium of common ideas. If one thinks of "rapports" as mechanisms of social expressions, one can make fruitful use of the notion in clarifying the role of style. "Style," in this sense, refers to systems of common understandings, of common interpretations of actions, events, signs, and so on—and of forms of speaking. It is not "conversational knowledge" alone, and is related to inexplicit, mutual ways of thinking and conceiving, to latent systems of acting (Ehlich & Rehbein, 1972). In this way, style functions as a "membership categorization device" (Sacks, 1972) which checks the "appartenance au groupe."

Another characteristics of style is the capability of producing speech formulas of mutual meaning. This is so because style offers forms for preverbal experiences, because it corresponds to repetitive situations and helps the members of a system of action to get through. So, style expresses collective images and evaluations within particular settings, and is, in turn, produced by them.

Systems of acting and speaking can produce "speech cultures," to use Neustupný's (1978) term. Speech cultures create complex forms of social life such as ensembles of jokes, stories, puns—in short, an oral tradition—and ways of processing these forms. Style seems to be one element of the reproduction of a speech culture. Willis (1977) has pointed out that speech cultures within the institution of the school establish anti-cultures which function to prepare students for the world of labor and its "pseudo-culture." Style can be used for different "cultural" goals.

Speech culture affects distinctive styles in gatherings, courts, hospitals, churches, and a number of other institutions (cf. Firth, 1957; Ehlich & Rehbein, 1980), and styles in which ideological systems of the collectivity are reflected.

The point here is that style is bound to common forms of social life which are prefabricated; the individual communicator only makes use of them. All these various forms offer plans—prefabricated plans—which the individual speaker adopts in verbalizing. In general, one has to differentiate an interactive "processing" function and a "discourse-transfer" function of style. I shall explain them both by starting with examples given by Tannen.

MACHINE-GUN QUESTIONS REVISITED

Tannen says that "machine-gun questions," as an example of conversational style, reflect "the tendency to use particular familiar patterns." Let me add some remarks in going over two of her examples, one concerning Chad, the other Kurt and Peter.

In the case of Chad, speech is initiated by DT, the questioner. But this does not meet the conversational requirement for machine-gun questions because they are to be slotted into the speaker's turn without being interruptions. Admittedly DT opens this segment of the conversation with a machine-gun question in order to turn the initiative over to her interlocutor, Chad; nevertheless, Chad interprets her questions as deriving from some other type of discourse, such as a hearing, an examination, or interview, embedded within a Thanksgiving conversation which is itself a special type of discourse. He may take her questions as forming a "question sequence" (cf. Rehbein, 1980). On this interpretation, Chad reinterprets the type of discourse, thereby producing a misunderstanding and a discourse discordance (see below).

In the second example, when Kurt or Peter are speaking, DT comes in with questions which occur immediately before the relevant turn-taking points. DT interrupts without any intention of claiming a turn—and the New Yorkers know this. Their knowledge is specific to their speech culture. Within this speech culture, DT's questions:

1. demonstrate the hearer's interest in what is said;
2. request further elaboration, clarification, explanation, and so on, of what was said by the speaker;
3. are attached to certain propositional aspects of Kurt's and Peter's utterances; questions like these never bring a new theme into the conversation, they only thematize aspects of foregoing utterances;

4. have the property of repair-initiating utterances which occur several times, making the conversation as a whole appear to be a "cascade"; and, because the repair mechanism is applied several times, the thematic progression itself develops fragmentized character.

Let me form two hypotheses from the above observations. First, machine-gun questions, as fired by the hearer, DT, work conversationally by guiding the speaker's thematic organization of speech; they belong to a *communicative apparatus* which guides both the speaker and hearer (cf. Rehbein, 1979). Second, machine-gun questions, as misinterpreted by Chad, are functionally used in a specific type of discourse which is accessible through the medium of a wider range of culture. Because Chad does not participate in this culture, he attributes machine-gun style to a different type of discourse which he is familiar with.

Thus, "style" turns out to be both a speech production phenomenon, in the first case, and a speech comprehension phenomenon in the second case.

COMMUNICATIVE APPARATUS AS PRODUCING CONVERSATIONAL STYLE

Machine-gun questions, taken in their functional sense, belong to the apparatus of speaker-hearer guidance. This apparatus is not culture specific in principal matters. If we look upon the conversational work of this apparatus, we can explore a large number of stylistic phenomena, such as the different uses of "tag questions," in different social groups, within different patterns of action, and within cross-cultural communication.

A specific phenomenon belonging to this type of discursive element can be found in an interview in French with an Algerian immigrant: he uses French cajolers like "hein," "voyez," "bon," "alors," "ah," and "oh" several times within a single utterance. These formulas function as substitutes for propositional content. The immigrant wants to counterbalance the circumstances of the interview by implying a large share of common knowledge with the interviewer. The interviewer himself regards this procedure as a "bad use" of his native language, as bad style. But the communicative apparatus supported, through its tendency toward "formulaic fall-out," the interviewee's strategy of avoiding concrete answers. Thus, the interviewee ended up guiding the interviewer (in this specific case of intercultural communication).

TRANSFER OF DISCOURSE TYPE

Stylistic phenomena, it was said above, can be taken as indicators of common interpretations of a context by participants who are operating within a common form of speaking and acting, that is, within a common speech pattern. In pointing to "genre" as an important characteristics of style Tannen aims, I think, in a similar direction.

For example, a person wanting the help of a friend to operate a gas stove will use short sentences, many repetitions, slow pronunciation, and so on; there will be a use of hyper-instructive discourse within the form of a request for help. If one person describes an other by imitating the other's monotone voice, a sort of *mimetic discourse* arises within a description. When information is given to a person asking directions, the speaker may suddenly remember the route as a familiar one and transfer a type of discourse of remembrance into the informational discourse.

It often happens that speakers follow more than one pattern of speech at a time; they may have complex goals, may have to satisfy different needs simultanously, or may have to adapt a particular pattern to the situation they are in. These demands, at the crossroads of which speakers act, lead to specific procedures for harmonizing conflicting tendencies by transferring to one discourse type while using another. Thus, stylistic phenomena occur when participants pass through patterns of speaking within specific settings of social action.

CONCLUDING REMARKS

At the moment, I do not see any possibility of binding all stylistic phenomena into a unified analysis. Some of them can be classified as phenomena of "rapport" as Tannen puts it, but others can not. Many of them come together in that they are culturally specific enrichments of discourse. But "culture" itself is not at all a homogeneous concept—there are minority group "cultures," there is the "culture" produced by different institutions, and there is the "culture" which reflects different social organizations and societies. The same is true of "style."

REFERENCES

Ehlich, K., & Rehbein, J. (1972). Erwarten. In D. Wunderlich (Ed.), *Linguistische Pragmatik* (pp. 99–114). Frankfurt: Athenäum.

Ehlich, K., & Rehbein, J. (1980). Sprache in Institutionen. In H.P. Althaus, H. Henne & H. Wiegand (Eds.), *Lexikon der Germanistischen Linguistik* (2nd ed., Vol. 2. pp. 338–345). Tübingen: Niemeyer.

Firth, J.R. (1957). The technique of semantics. In J.R. Firth, *Papers in linguistics 1934–1951* (pp. 7–33). London: Oxford University Press.

Neustupný, J.V. (1978). The concept of language treatment. In J.V. Neustupný (Ed.), *Post-structural approaches to language: Language theory in a Japanese context*. Tokyo: University Press.

Rehbein, J. (1979). Sprechhandlungsaugmente. Zur Organisation der Hörersteuerung. In H. Weydt (Ed.), *Die Partikeln der deutschen Sprache* (pp. 58–74). Berlin: de Gruyter.

Rehbein, J. (1980). *Frage-Sequenzen*. Unpublished manuscript.

Sacks, H. (1972). On the analyzability of stories by children. In J.J. Gumperz & D. Hymes (Eds.), *Directions in sociolinguistics: The ethnography of communication* (pp. 325–345). New York: Holt, Rinehart & Winston.

Willis, P. (1977). *Learning to labour: How working class kids get working class jobs.* Hampshire: Saxon House.

Final Discussion

Chair: J. Meisel

CHAPTER 27

Psycholinguistic Model Construction: Some Current and Future Issues

Meisel: I would like to suggest that we briefly go through the reports of the chairpersons of the different sessions, trying to concentrate on some topics, issues and concerns which came up repeatedly. In addition to that, we should also discuss what you might have expected to happen here and what did not happen. For there are certain things which apparently did not come up during this meeting and which might have been dealt with.

Keenan: I am taking Walter Kintsch's place. These are what Walter Kintsch considered to be the main issues and themes of the first session. One concerns the changes that are taking place in the conception of language, moving from an associationistic S-R approach to an information-theoretic approach, to computational linguistics, computational psycholinguistics. I think the question here is exactly: what are we gaining by shifting approaches?

Another thing concerned the issue of the boundary between language and cognition. It is clear that in talking about language we need to talk about cognition; but it is not so clear where to draw the line. Related to this point is the issue of what is a sentence. Is it an instruction or a set of clues to the listener from which he has to infer what the speaker meant, or is it an independent meaningful linguistic entity in and of itself?

Similarly, should the coherence of a message be defined in terms of the text plus the context, in other words, text plus the shared knowledge structures between the speaker and the listener, or should coherence be defined purely at the linguistic level?

Another issue concerns the nature of models. Should we try to account for all important aspects in one complex, highly interactive system, or should we try to decompose these more global processes of production and comprehension into modular models and then try to investigate more simplified sub-models?

The final issue that Walter has down here is, what is the relation between production and comprehension?

Posner: In the session on a cognitive-based model of production, starting from the remarks of the main speakers, Kenneth Ruder, and Amy Finch, that comprehension and production must be viewed as separate but related processes, the discussants advocated differentiation of different kinds of production (Coulmas) and different kinds of comprehension (Keenan). The differences among the concepts of comprehension, perception, reception, input and understanding were discussed (Rieber).

Ruder and Finch's crucial experiment for the separation of production and comprehension skills in children was criticized with the argument that the experimental tasks compared involve different levels of abstraction. The discussion then centered around the question of how the separate cognitive underpinnings of comprehension and production in children become one unified component in adults.

This was discussed especially with regard to the nature of self-monitoring involved in the speaker's production behavior. All discussants agreed that we need a more refined conceptual framework in which to formulate more specific hypotheses about the interrelation of comprehension and production.

Ruder: Two major themes emerged from the session on second language learning. . . One, what constitutes fluency in speech production in second language learners, and two, how is that fluency achieved?

Sajavaara pays least attention to form in his major presentation, a great deal of emphasis is placed on the mechanism wherein speech fluency is achieved. In his presentation Sajavaara stressed that fluency is not generally achieved in the second language simply by classroom teaching. What is required to achieve fluency in second language learners is a dynamic approach in which context and communication interaction are basic. Central to this theme is the notion that language is learned only in a functional context. The more functional and natural the context, the more fluent is the resulting speech. Meisel and Rehbein generally concurred with the emphasis on learning languages in interactive settings. Meisel made the point that interaction should be the starting point for the study of language production, and Rehbein concurred.

Sajavaara also stressed the importance of acquiring strategies and tactics in achieving fluent second language production. Raupach enlarged on this notion, to discuss at length the definition of "strategy" and how the second language learner goes about the task of discovering these strategies. He differentiated between strategies for learning language and strategies for discourse, emphasizing that acquiring the appropriate strategies was the key to production learning in second language acquisition. Sajavaara basically concurred, but would not specify where or how these strategies were acquired, only that he would not attempt to teach them.

Two other discussion papers, those by Clahsen and Duncan, respectively, focused on issues not dealt with in detail in the major address by Sajavaara. Clahsen proposes a developmental model of second language learning. The basis for this claim stems from data gathered in a naturalistic second language learning situation. These data showed, contrary to Sajavaara's assumption, that second language learners in unguided types of language development environments did acquire an automatic linguistic knowledge about German word order, and that during the course of acquisition, the second language learners made frequent use of strategies of simplification.

Duncan focused his comments on the non-verbal aspects of the message and its relationship to linguistic aspects of speech production process. Language and non-verbal communication are joined by what Duncan refers to as "indexicality." Linguistics proper deals largely with the referential aspect of language; paralinguistic communication—non-verbal, intonation, voice quality, etc.—indexes its referential aspect. This indexicality should be a strong determinant of fluency in a target second language and should be considered basic to a model of second language production. Finally, there was general agreement that fluency in second language learning was a desirable goal. Disagreement and uncertainty arose when attempts were made to define fluent speech production. Fluency at one point was described in general terms as a reduction in hesitations and speech errors, but data presented by Rehbein indicated that such a definition was oversimplified, and his subjects showed an individual variability: where one subject achieved a sense of fluency by using pauses to plan for speech units to be produced in the ensuing speech event, another used speech errors to avoid pausing and, hence, also achieved a sense of fluency. In the ensuing discussion it was generally agreed that context plays an integral role in what one perceives as being fluent.

Finally, some discussion centered on the content or a lack thereof of the "yellow boxes" which replaced "black boxes" in Sajavaara's model of speech production. There was some concern for the lack of input and output specification in the model presented. The bidirectional flow of input and output from one component of the model to another seemed to weaken the predictive value and explanatory adequacy of the model, while at the same time indicating that perception and production of language were simply directional differences of an identical process. While there was a general dissatisfaction with the model of language production presented, there were no alternatives presented in the ensuing discussion.

Sajavaara: In the second part of the third session, Walter Kintsch, in his model of psychological processes in speech production, concentrated on how ideas are generated in the writing process. The most important part of his model was the retrieval of information from the knowledge base, which he described as a major element in long-term memory. This retrieval was, we were told, taking place under the constraints of topic, type of text and intended reader. He also drew attention to the importance of various classical rhetorical structures.

In her comments, Dorothea Engel-Ortlieb asked to what extent list-learning paradigms were relevant for discourse. She also brought up the integration of rhetorical descriptions into list-learning paradigms. She further asked whether Kintsch's model was actually production specific.

Susan Kemper brought up the following points. She wanted to extend the constraints to a fourth type of constraint, and that was the writer's goals and motives. Then she took up the possibility of using speech act theory for the description of the goals of the writer. She finally asked whether literary criticism and analysis could also be used as sources for additional indicators of various levels of the writing process.

During the general discussion the following topics, among others, came up. First the nature of LTM: whether LTM was to be described as a kind of storehouse or whether it was a creative process, and I got the impression that the idea of a LTM being a creative process and not a storehouse was more popular among the audience. Then we discussed the nature of propositions and the interrelationship between linguistic and non-linguistic representation. My impression was that the non-linguistic nature of various things in the human mind was more popular. Then there was the question of the dependence of the organization of knowledge on language, whether we organize our knowledge on the basis of language or something else. I think this relates to the previous question of what is the nature of propositions and how propositions interrelate to non-linguistic representations.

Then, taking up a point discussed before, the question was raised of how Kintsch's model, and models in general, could be tested. Here again the directionality of the model came up in connection with my, or our, "yellow boxes." And it was asked whether there was any distinction in the model between structural elements and processes, something which we didn't discuss the previous day, but was represented in the "yellow boxes." Finally, the question was asked, how the various processes in the model were controlled.

Tannen: In the fourth session, "Understanding understanding," or "Comprehending comprehending," Rumelhart began with an overview of his theory of schema and a representation of his notion of the communicative system to give what he called his "orienting attitude" towards schema theory. That system involved both speaker and hearer, having goals, methods and knowledge, all of which could be interrelated with the other in any order. He went on to develop what he called his "metatheoretical concept." He presented a story fragment and talked about the fact that most people seem to achieve a pretty high degree of agreement about the interpretation of that story, and that schema theory might explain the fact that there was this kind of agreement. He suggested that a schema theory embodies a "prototype" theory of meaning and said that in his notion of schema, a schema is a data structure for representing the generic concepts stored in memory. Rumelhart then said he was dissatisfied with how far he had gotten with his story grammar for two reasons. First of all, the measures that had been employed to judge comprehension in this model were based on having subjects recall or give some reason for what they had read, and he wanted something that was more of an on-line measure of comprehension. Furthermore, he said that the story-grammar approach focused on very abstract features of comprehension, so that, for example, it could not account for the difference between "Mary had a gun" and "Mary went in to get her money." So he developed a new experimental design in which subjects gave an on-line account of their comprehension. They were given a story line by line and were asked, following each line, to give an account of what they made of the story thus far. He found two major results: first of all, subjects not only were easily able to do this line report of comprehension, but furthermore it seemed not only not to interfere with, but, if anything, to improve their comprehension. And again, there was a remarkable degree of agreement. He was able to map out their shifting hypotheses and pinpoint the critical times in the story when their interpretations tended to converge.

I am going to lump together the issues that were raised in discussion. First of all, there was a discussion of the problem of accepting subjects' self-reports of their comprehension, of the question of whether this kind of self-report was taken as simply further data to be analyzed in various ways, or whether it was to be accepted as a fact. There seemed to be consensus both among the discussants and the original presenter that it was the first—that these reports are not to be accepted at face value.

Then the question was raised of how new all this was, how far we have come since Bartlett, and to what extent were these theories representing any further development of schema theory. And the question of how schema theory is to be implemented in the specific application to texts. As a response to this, Rumelhart stated his assertion that in fact he was not developing a new schema theory but presenting synthetic work in the interest of developing what he called a "coherent meta-theory." There was further discussion of the problem with the computer model. The concern was expressed by some people that there was some danger involved in accepting the computer model. The response to this seemed to be "You can use the computer without having the computer use you"—you don't have to accept the computer model as the metaphor for the human mind, you can simply use it for whatever it is worth in manipulating data. And finally some discussion on formalization. And the suggestion seemed to be: whenever you formalize you lose something, but perhaps it is worth it because you gain something at the same time.

Kemper: The discussion of Charlotte Linde's paper seemed to focus on issues external to her paper. Her paper examined the strategies speakers use to produce coherent life-stories, and the organization of various components of life-stories. The discussion focused on two issues: the methodological issues concerned with the analysis of oral discourse and functional considerations.

The discussion that focused on methodological issues was concerned with whether one can trust either the internal or external validity of these life-stories, whether the use of an elicitation technique might distort the object of inquiry, and how one goes from a collection of life-stories to the identification of units and relationships between the units. That part of the discussion that focused on functional considerations seemed to be concerned with why we might study stories that people tell during the course of their lives, why people might tell stories, what do these stories create or maintain in the way of social relationships. I did not feel that the discussion really concerned the content of Charlotte's lecture in terms of the analysis of the life-stories themselves.

Linde: The last session, on Verbal Interaction, was Deborah Tannen's paper on conversational style which was a description of certain features which, taken together, comprise a particular conversational style. In this paper, style is a description of a process of signaling metamessages, messages about the relationship between the interlocutors, the nature of interaction, etc. The features used to describe this particular style were, in the oral version of the paper, pace and expressive paralinguistics; there were others, such as type and use of stories, mentioned in the written version. Here the focus was on pace and expressive paralinguistic cues and their combination, particularly their combination into the machine-gun question, as one characteristic of the style,—one characteristic of the style of certain, but not all of the speakers in this data. A number of issues which arose out of this were first of all that by style Tannen does not mean stylistic level or register, which is one way that style has been investigated in the past. For her, a person's style is present in interactions of whatever register, so the personal conversational style is identifiable with cross-registers. Other issues which arose in the discussion were first of all the question of how one associates a cluster of stylistic devices with any given characterization of their user; that is, one might associate this cluster of expressive paralinguistic 'pace', use of narratives, etc., with a person who is of a given ethnic background or of a given geographic background, or a member of a certain subculture, or perhaps of a given personality type. The question then is, What warrant does one have for saying that some particular identification is the relevant identification?

In the discussion, Florian Coulmas brought up the issue of routines, frozen forms, etc. He made the point that in describing differences between registers one can make use of the notion of degree of routinization. He raised the question of to what extent this question of routinization can be transferred to style in the sense that Tannen is working with it.

An issue which I think was present for all of the discussants, and for a number of the questioners from the audience as well, was the question of to what extent such stylistic factors are automatic, and to what extent they are the product of choice. Duncan, particularly, suggested that there is a higher degree of choice present in these than Tannen appeared to suggest. Finally, the session ended with the discussion on comparison of stylistic mismatch across subcultures with a stylistic mismatch across languages. It was suggested that, again, to some extent clear indications of being a foreigner make the situation easier rather than more difficult, that if one is identifiable as a foreigner the same kinds of misunderstandings may not arise.

Meisel: I think the main interest of the final discussion could be to raise the issue of what we now understand better, what should be done, and what has been left out here. We also might come back to the methodological question, if you want.

Sajavaara: I have several questions to ask. Do we know of production, today, more than we knew on Sunday? The reason why I ask this is that I have the feeling that, yesterday, we did not really say a word about production. Gradually, the whole production business faded away and we started dealing with something else. All these things relate to production, but we should come back to the major problem.

Linde: I am pleased to disagree. I think in fact that the discussions yesterday focused on an issue which I think has been running all through this conference, and that is, exploring the question of what is it that is produced. I think that previously general production models in fact focused on information very often; that information is some sort of package which I have and you want, and I somehow wrap it up in the way that I can send it to you, and then I send it to you and you have gotten it, and that's communication; and I think that in many different ways during this conference people have been trying to suggest that it isn't like that. I suppose Deborah's paper was certainly a very powerful argument against models of communication as in Rumelhart's paper, Kintsch's paper, and against a number of things that came up during discussions. So I think that what we may have done is to step back from the question of production and say, well, what is it that's produced. Maybe we are not so sure as we were of what it is that's produced, and that would mean to look at that question again, rather than assuming that we know what it is that's produced.

Kemper: Let me underscore what I think Charlotte is saying. One of the things that has come to my mind as a result of this workshop has been to realize that those of us who would be trying to develop a model of production from our own perspective would be quite limited. I think one of the results of the workshop has been, making us all aware of concerns and problems and research interests of others, in related but slightly different disciplines. I think the psychologist and the psycholinguist have now become aware that there is interesting work going on in sociolinguistics that we should include in our models. Those who are working in applied linguistics in second language acquisition have perhaps seen some phenomena that should be of relevance to their work, and those of theoretical linguistics have also discovered some phenomena that should be included in that sort of model of speech production. Though we may not be able to form an ideal model based upon all these different perspectives, perhaps it will be the case that we will be able to build a better model as a result of this, each within our own perspectives or our tradition.

Posner: I think we all have become a bit less optimistic about model building in language production, and this is maybe also a good result of the conference.

This became very clear in Sajavaara's contribution: as soon as one starts to relax the structures which linguists, for instance, have tried to find in language production, and one really analyzes what goes on, then the model seems to disappear, and what we are left with is some kind of "geography of the area of language production." We can find a number of catch words in order to situate a number of problems. And concerning those problems, I was most interested in how language production begins and how language production stops.

For the first question I did not get much of an answer. Rumelhart told me a bit; . . . one of the models he is thinking of is like that: language production in the beginning normally starts with some kind of goal which is a very vibrating overall goal and is then implemented by a number of subgoals until we get to some kind of formulation. This is one possibility.

The other end of the production process, I think, is also very important for beginning research in language production. What I mean is that once we have gotten away from that information package model, we can more easily analyze the ways in which people are influenced by what we do when we formulate something. In that respect, I missed some of the results of linguistic pragmatics here. I think there has already been done much more than came to the floor, not only concerning what some people called "the indirect speech" act problem, but also all kinds of non-literal interpretation, of context-dependent non-literal interpretation or literal formulations.

Tannen: What I want to say is related to a lot of the comments that have been made: what really is the relationship between an understanding of production and a model of production? Do you need to have a model in order to have understanding? It seems to me that that is a basic assumption of the psycholinguist, that if you don't have a model that you can present well, then you really haven't been saying anything well. And it seems to me that an assumption of the sociolinguist is that if you have a model and you've left out so much of what's important, then you really have nothing, and so you really don't want a model at all. And it shows up, I think, in the kind of data that we look at. For example, the schema theory; if you look at the story that was presented in the schema theory approach, which was basically two lines and probably not the sort of story anyone would ever tell at a Thanksgiving dinner. You now look at the kinds of stories that Charlotte and I were talking about; how would you reconcile these two approaches? It comes down, I guess, to the question that came up after Rumelhart's paper, about formalization: how much do you need of formalization in order to say that you really have a scientific investigation? And I say this really quite sincerely; I worry about this a lot, because I, myself, after listening to sociolinguists' talk, often think, oh, all they did was give me a series of insights, you know, I might as well have been sitting around having a chat, and yet, is there a way in which a series of insights is really how you build up an understanding of something?

Sajavaara: I don't really disagree with the people who said that we have been dealing with production all the time. I threw the argument in, in case we would not have had a discussion. But since we were told that people generally disagreed with the model with "yellow and green boxes": perhaps it is wrong to call it a model; perhaps a model, for other people, means something else than it means for us. . . But it is not supposed to represent something that goes on in my mind at this moment. We want it to be a representation of the kind of problems which there are; we want to have some kind of representation of the kinds of things that are relevant for message reception and message production. So that if we write "in" and "out" this does not mean that something goes in here and then goes around all these boxes and circles and then comes out again. . . I am quite sure that as a model of that kind of flow it is totally wrong. So it is a collection of hypotheses and a kind of geography as you said.

Meisel: I think you were right with your first statement, that we were repeatedly shifting away from the topic of "production." I don't say that we didn't talk about production, but there was a certain tendency to talk about other things, like comprehension; I think, at the moment, there is more to say about comprehension, for instance, than about production. And I might add that although the nonlinguistic part and the context are important, I would have liked to see more of the more strictly linguistic part, that is, also more of what is in those boxes, for instance.

Ruder: This point interested me somewhat, too. I got the feeling throughout several occasions at least that, I am paraphrasing this now, Chomskyan Linguistics, if not Chomsky himself, was dead, and you'd be surprised to hear that. I was also disappointed by the fact that we seemed to be ignoring some of the basic units of production, and they still boil down to the fact that there is a syntax, at least from my standpoint, the linguistic standpoint, that has to be considered even within the larger context, and phonological units were not discussed at all, and those are very important, I think, for the production process.

Lehtonen: For me the role of psycholinguistics would be to find out what is the problem of the linguistic structures and the linguistic entities in language processing. What do these rules of syntax and morphology and so on do in the actual processing, in the mental process of speech production or the neurological process and the like? I agree with my colleague Kari that we did not emphasize strongly enough the fact that those boxes in our model were not at all meant to be boxes in the traditional sense of the word. They should have been very fuzzy in character. They were only colored illustrations of the factors which enter into the processing of speech. I also agree with Kari on what he said on the focus of interest during our discussions. It is my impression, too, that we have discussed the speech product and the properties of the produced speech, and a little of what is the function of the text, but not very much what the processes are which led to the product of speech. And saying this, I have the paper of Prof. Dechert in mind and his concept of "Contrastive Psycholinguistics." I am a little disappointed that this area wasn't discussed more in this workshop, because "Contrastive Psycholinguistics" could be a means to find out something about the actual process of speech production by comparing the production in different languages and the production of students of foreign languages on different levels; a method which might also have something to give to the science of foreign language didactics.

Rieber: It has bothered me for a long time, and still does, not as a product of this conference, I assure you, but as a product of thinking: What in the world holds all those things together? And if we ask questions like, What should be the model of production?, What should be the model of understanding?, there must be something that enables these concepts to function together and to be a part of a whole for us to explain. And that leads me to the point. The point is: what are the basic assumptions that we have about language and mind? Separately or together? And unless these basic assumptions—that's a theory—are explicitly communicated to ourselves and to others, then we struggle with the inadequacies of this model, that model, this concept, that concept, because we don't have a basic frame of reference to put the pieces together with. That seems to me to be a perennial problem in every conference I've ever been to. This is no exception, and I wonder why it is that we can't get down to business in these conferences.

Sajavaara: May I take up the problem of there not being enough discussion of grammar here. We behave somewhat strangely: we bring in a number of boxes and then say there are no boxes, and our model is not really a model. And then I say there had not been enough talk on production, and then I agree with people who disagree with me. So, in our paper I seem to deny the problems of grammar, but actually I agree with you that grammar is very important. And denying the importance of grammar to me meant, at least in this particular paper, just trying to point out that none of the existing grammars is sufficient for the purposes of a psycholinguistic description of speech production. . . . So, Chomsky is still there, is a very important man still for many people and is very important in the history of linguistics, and his grammar is, I think, as good as any other of the existing grammars, but to me it is not any better either. I think that the kind of descriptions we need would resemble some sort of a valency grammar or a certain type of dependency grammar.

Rieber: Let me ask a question. Suppose we had this conference, by some miracle, six years ago? Do you think we would talk the same way that we are talking now, six years ago? And I have in mind Chomsky, of course. We wouldn't talk the same way. Now, what happened in six years to make us now ignore Noam Chomsky? Something very important must have happened within six years, yet somehow or other we go ahead and do whatever we do without, I think, even being aware what actually happened in six years to make a profound change in the way we talk about the subject matter that we talked a lot about six years ago in a much different way. That, I think, is a terribly important thing to become conscious of, if we are going to make some progress in the next six years.

Sajavaara: So, six years ago, we would have talked about transformations and the psycholinguistic reality of TG grammar, but if I dare make a prediction, a prognosis for the future, I think within six years from now we will be back to discussing grammar, and perhaps we can have another conference on psycholinguistic models then.

Rieber: I only can understand your prediction if you tell me whence it comes, in other words, that prediction, which interests me, that you say that, must come from an understanding of what has happened and why we are now doing what we are doing. If there is the swing of the pendulum then the only way we can predict the pendulum is going to go back is because you know why it went this way.

Posner: But I think part of the answer to your remark, why we are talking not Chomsky but psycholinguistics today, is that the attention has shifted from an analysis of the sign matter of the objects which we, as Charlotte said, transport from one to the other, or seem to transport, to the processes which are not really transport but different processes, processes of stimulating other processes in the listener. So I think there is a kind of change in the ontological entities which we prefer to see as the main entities in speech production/comprehension. What we have seen here is that with this change in the fundamental terminology, a new kind of uncertainty has come, because we don't have a formal apparatus yet to describe those processes. There are a number of mathematical models, some of the concepts from them have been used in quite a metaphorical way, like the concept of strategy for instance, or tactics, but it doesn't seem that those concepts have been implemented with empirically gained knowledge about speech production and comprehension, yet. The real thing I wanted to say, however, was something which might sound orthodox now, after I have said something about processes versus products. I think we have not yet used every piece of possible insight from analyses of products. It was only in the talk of Prof. Slama-Cazacu that semiotic tools were mentioned, and I think we would also gain more insight into the processes and their differences if we were able to analyze in a more detailed way the differences between unintentional signals of body posture, paralinguistic features and so on, versus intentional conventional signs which are mainly given by means of grammar and lexicon, versus indexical information on the speaker's attitudes, plans, goals, versus iconic information which was mentioned by Charlotte Linde. I think that these different types of information, given in these different ways, have very different importance for how the speaker expresses himself. For instance, I think that iconic procedures seem to be much deeper with respect to what the speaker wants to communicate than conventional means.

Keenan: I was going to respond to the pendulum swinging from grammar to sociolinguistics, and a lot of non-grammatical things. I think what has happened over the six years has been that, well, first of all the experiments were done to test the psychological validity of transformational grammar and it was shown that it is not really a very adequate account. A number of phenomena demonstrated that we need to take into account other factors, pragmatics, put a greater emphasis on semantics in order to be able to account for language behavior. And then, also, what happened was that there were just repeated failures in trying to get machines to comprehend language using, say, purely syntactic kinds of accounts. It was very clear from that, I should say, that you needed to build into the system knowledge about the world, knowledge about interactions and that kind of stuff. So, now people are trying to find out what are all these other factors that feed into grammar; they are leaving the grammar over here and going and searching for all these other factors that need to be taken into account, and then what's going to happen, I would predict, in six years from now would be, I think you are right, we'll be back to talking about grammar. But the grammars are going to look very different in that they are going to have all these somewhat non-linguistic, pragmatic kinds of factors that play a role.

Rieber: And then we go round and round and round again. . .

Meisel: I don't think we are going round, Bob; you know, some years ago, there was an overemphasis on transformations, and some of that was just too naive, and then there was more emphasis on other factors which have been discussed during this conference, but by then we had forgotten or neglected some aspects of grammar, and we will come back to it, and it's not going in circles I think, if the grammars will look different. There are also very interesting developments in linguistics, I would say, even at M.I.T., things which have to be taken into account.

There is of course another aspect of this pendulum swing which is not a scientific one, one which might be labeled as the social-psychology of scientists. You know you can get more attention if you contradict certain things than by just elaborating them.

Rieber: What I was really objecting to was that we specify in our concerns a particular subject matter, like grammar of pragmatics. And we say, now "This is the thing when we will catch the consciousness of the king," this is the thing that everybody should concentrate on and study, and this is the thing we should have a conference on and this is the thing we should write books about and when we find out that this is not the thing, then we go on to the next thing. And that's the next decade, and then the next decade. That's, I think, a fruitless effort to look at science that way, because then you keep going around and around, and the pendulum keeps going back. You say, well, but we added a little bit more to that thing. Wouldn't it be better to consider not one thing at the expense of another, but to look at the broad base from which all of these things come, and to try to see how they fit together? For instance, you mentioned that the sociolinguists would not look at a model with great excitement and enthusiasm, because that hampers their style, and their style is to look at a broad loose social network that they can involve themselves with and observe and study and do their thing. That certainly is not the style of Kintsch or someone else who wants to do a model, research laboratory study of something, or of Chomsky. For good reasons, because they had different premises and different values about what they want to discover. What happens is that we have become overenthusiastic, almost evangelic, about a particular idea and a particular person if he happens to be powerful enough and charismatic enough, and this carries us away into areas that do not produce the kind of progress that we should make.

Coulmas: I don't think that going round and round necessarily means going round in a circle, we might as well go round in a spiral and advance the level of our knowledge very well. To my mind it is absolutely not surprising that we have not been discussing Chomsky very much in this conference, simply because he has nothing to say about production, and he would not claim that he had anything to say about it, I think. On the other hand, people who take a psycholinguistic approach or a psychological approach have absolutely no idea how grammar fits into a psychological model. On the other hand, Chomsky and people who do formal grammar have every reason to do that, because there is ample evidence that grammar, to some extent, is a self-contained system. There is, on the other hand, no doubt that there is great need to add many of the factors; but I would think that grammars, as you said, will look very, very different within six years from now as regards the inclusion of the other factors, they just get too complex. I think one has to look for possibilities to interconnect other things; but I really don't think that the development of grammar will be severely affected by things like that which have been brought up at this conference.

Posner: I'd like to disagree with the last part of what you just said. I think if in six years we have the same grammars as we are having now, it would be a pity. Not because of possible additional things we could put into our present grammars, but because of the very format of present-day grammars. I think we really need a rewriting of the grammars, and this may even be important if we don't acquire new grammatical knowledge. It would be important if we were able to make grammatical knowledge available to the psycholinguists and psychologists in such a way that they can include it in their flow models of language production. Presently, all we have in grammatical description, at least in linguistic grammatical description, does not fit into a flow model.

Keenan: As a psychologist I have always thought that the linguist's goals are simply to describe the structure of language, and there is no reason to believe that the kind of structural models that they develop would have anything to do with how people actually use language, just like no psychologist would think that Russell and Whitehead's *Principia Mathematica* should have anything to do with how a child learns to do arithmetic. But nonetheless, psychologists or psycholinguists, in saying how people produce language, how people understand language, do need to have some sort of procedures or processes to explain how sentences get structured in certain ways and how people judge that this is a well-formed sentence and this is not. So we need some kind of grammar, and it seems like now there are some psycholinguists—I am just thinking of like Elizabeth Bates and Brian MacWhinney—who are developing sort of psychologically based grammar. So that is why we are talking about subjects and objects, or Noun Phrases and Verb Phrases, or talking about the functions that particular concepts have, the psychological functions, talking about dimensions like perceptual salience and all that to determine word order and things. I don't know if these kinds of grammars will be of any use to the linguist, but I certainly think that there will be differences in grammars, whether the linguist's grammars or the psycholinguist's grammars, in the next six years.

Tannen: I think nevertheless it is true that there is less interest now in developing grammars than there was. If you look at the major grammars that were around six years ago, they are not around anymore. People have abandoned the search for formalizations and for grammar, kind of throwing up their hands and saying, well, there is too much more going on, so we are going to go on and see if we can capture the bigger things that are going on.

Meisel: I am not sure whether it is very useful to discuss this in these terms, to say the least. I think one good reason to believe that things are coming back is that, at least in Germany, I have never heard as often as during the last 15 months that Chomsky is dead. When for some years Chomsky was not mentioned anymore, and now people keep repeating that he is dead, that is a good sign that he is very much alive.

Linde: This discussion that Bob started has focused for me on what has been a subtext of this conference, which is really: is there progress?

I have heard many people during the course of this conference say, well, in a way it is really all in Bartlett, or in Wundt, or in Hegel, or in Condillac or in St. Augustine, we have gone fairly far back. This is something embarrassing, that we are just saying it again and again, and I think all of this discussion right now is predicated on the notion that progress is possible. And I wonder if that's true, I wonder if that's what we are really doing, I wonder if another possibility, and I don't see this, is the case: it just is a wonder that in each intellectual generation we try to find some way of saying what we understand in a way as to make it understandable to as wide an audience as possible. So, I think that one thing that is very striking about Chomsky is that he made questions about language accessible to a wider intellectual audience. Now, here I am speaking about the situation in the United States, but the American Structuralist School were very insightfully talking to themselves for 30 years about language, and somehow that was not in any way important or relevant for anyone outside that very small group of people, and that somehow one thing that Chomsky did was open up a number of issues in language to people outside of the community of linguists, and that perhaps is his achievement, and that was the progress. And now we are starting to be interested in other kinds of things and the question is: who can we make that relevant to?, rather than: do we progress?

Sajavaara: If I may now answer Bob's question concerning my theory, my comment on progress in our kind of science. I think that earlier grammars were based on kinds of natural language data which were derived from literary material, written texts, but when structuralism turned into TG grammar, a kind of idealized sentence in competence was the basis of description which did not really exist in natural language data. Now we have reentered the era of studying natural language, but now the main emphasis in most cases seems to be on spoken language, the way people use language in everyday conversation. We don't have grammars for describing conversation, so I believe that in six years time we may have a better kind of grammar, where we pay attention to the fact that actually incomplete sentences are the natural way of speaking in natural conversation, and not complete full sentences which are based on some people's constructs. To me this means progress, and we don't go back to the same place where we started. . . .

Rieber: A revolution has taken place, and the revolution is over.

Sajavaara: What revolution?

Rieber: Chomsky started a revolution.

Sajavaara: In the United States.

Rieber: In the United States, right. The revolution only started in one place. The repercussions eventually get all over the place, if you give it enough time. But a revolution really took place. In my mind a very serious political revolution took place, science is not free from politics. And the politics of science, in this sense, are relevant to what science does, whether science likes it or not. The political aspects that Chomsky was concerned about in his revolution was a kind of empiricism which offended his sense of what he felt was right. A kind of rationalism which he wanted to put in its place, just like any revolution sees a particular dogma or a particular point of view that it must get rid of to put something in its place. And that's what he did. He put something in its place and he gathered converts and supporters and he produced a new way of looking at things. Now people are searching for something different to latch themselves on to and certain basic political problems that still are hanging, which are really not resolved. For instance, if you call yourself a sociolinguist, or a straight linguist, or a psycholinguist, in fact, there are certain political implications about calling oneself those terms, whether you are conscious of them or not, they are there, and they work their way into what you do, and what your profession does. We are talking about several disciplines attempting to work together here, and every once in a while we say: but you know the linguists will never buy that, or: the sociolinguists will never buy this, and: the psycholinguists, well, you better put it this way, so that they will receive it. These are negotiations, agendas in order to communicate with one another in order to achieve something. Yet, we rarely take seriously the problems that are inherent in this political negotiation process to achieve knowledge, which is our goal. There are serious problems, because I think a very important historical event took place when Chomsky made this revolution, and the repercussions of that revolution are bound to affect us in what we do for several decades to come, and if we are not to continue to make mistakes—well, we will always make them, but not continue to make too many of them so that we completely fool ourselves—then we have to get in touch with the dynamic forces that are bringing about what we do.

Posner: I would agree in a very partial point to what you just said, namely concerning the general outlook: empiricism versus rationality and so on. That will stay around a long time, and I hope it will stay around a long time; but that was tied to formalism, for instance, which, seen from that perspective, was entirely accidental. I think what we need is a different formalism which will lead to a kind of linguistics that will not close itself in as much as it has been in the last 15 years. I think the task we have to do is something for a new generation, maybe a generation that even doesn't come from the linguistic side. As for me, the reason to come here was that I wanted to see what people outside of linguistics could contribute to linguistics, with that other goal. So I think within linguistics it might be the functional tradition, functional linguistics. Outside of linguistics it might be artificial intelligence, which, I still think, is a possible background for this new model we are looking for, game theory, theory of rational behavior, outside of linguistic rationalism. I think we cannot yet predict where it will come from, but we can already see a number of possible approaches.

Ruder: I just wanted to put Chomsky in a somewhat different perspective than what he has been put in, in the last several comments here. Granted, there is great political orientation to Chomsky and his contribution, however, I think it is more than simply a revolution, if you look beneath activity that went on. One way of looking at what Chomsky did, at least for the field of psycholinguistics, is that he not only drew little boxes, but he had content in there that led to a number of hypotheses that completely revolutionized the way we looked at child language acquisition, and from that point the language intervention literature. Along the same line, we have been talking a lot this last week about black boxes and yellow boxes and green boxes, and I don't think we should apologize for drawing boxes. It is what is in those boxes that is going to be the fruit for further research.

Slama-Cazacu: . . . I have lived with this revolution from the beginning, since in '58 Roman Jakobson came to Bucharest immediately when the first book of Chomsky had appeared; and in a conference he showed it to us: this book will mark a revolution in linguistics; and he was true, because Roman Jakobson is a very brilliant and a very intelligent linguist, and he knows very much about all the history of linguistics. From the beginning I criticized Chomsky from a scientific point of view. What I am saying now is not because of an opportunism, that now I begin to be an anti-Chomskian; and I continued to criticize him. However, I respected him as a scientific person and as a man. And I don't understand why it is always said: Chomsky is dead, Chomskianism is dead, and so on. If one would make a frequency count of the names which were mentioned in this discussion, the name of Chomsky is among the most frequent. What I want to say is that you are obsessed, especially in the American context, by the name of Chomsky, and by the concepts of competence and performance, and so on. In spite of the subjects that are of interest in our concrete situation, you cannot help coming back to Chomsky, who has nothing to do—or very little— with our problems of production and so on. This has very much to do with the fact that he stimulated criticism, seeing what is negative and what should be done further on. But I think that now it would be very useful if one could come back to these problems, what should be done for the future, instead of discussing Chomsky, as we have done for the last fifteen minutes or so.

Rieber: I want to underline in reference to your comment, it is a difference that makes the difference to say that it is the revolution that's dead, not Chomsky. And you get this too confused. There is a kind of distortion that Chomsky was the revolution and therefore Chomsky is dead. That's not at all the case. It's the revolution that's dead, Chomsky still lives on.

Meisel: I think it would be a pity if you thought that we were not discussing production for the last half hour or so. I think we have been. At least that's how I view it. And if we named Chomsky repeatedly, we didn't really discuss Chomsky: You mention the name, and you mean a certain kind of approach. I think we have been discussing the importance of this kind of approach—which has not been dealt with during the last days—and this is one of the questions I was interested in: should we use that kind of approach? So, I think this discussion was to the point, although superficially we were discussing a person.

Author Index

Subject Index